# Improving College Management

Thomas E. Tellefsen

# Improving
# College
# Management

## An Integrated
## Systems Approach

A Publication of
the United Negro College Fund

 Jossey-Bass Publishers
San Francisco   •   Oxford   •   1990

IMPROVING COLLEGE MANAGEMENT
*An Integrated Systems Approach*
by Thomas E. Tellefsen

Copyright © 1990 by: Jossey-Bass Inc., Publishers
350 Sansome Street
San Francisco, California 94104
&
Jossey-Bass Limited
Headington Hill Hall
Oxford OX3 0BW

**Library of Congress Cataloging-in-Publication Data**

Tellefsen, Thomas E.
  Improving college management : an integrated systems approach /
Thomas E. Tellefsen.
    p.  cm. — (The Jossey-Bass higher education series)
  "A publication of the United Negro College Fund."
  Includes bibliographical references.
  ISBN 1-55542-182-2
  1. Universities and colleges — Administration.  I. United Negro
College Fund.  II. Title.  III. Series.
LB2341.T37  1990
378.1 — dc20                                                    89-45604
                                                                    CIP

Manufactured in the United States of America

The paper in this book meets the guidelines for
permanence and durability of the Committee on
Production Guidelines for Book Longevity of
the Council on Library Resources.

JACKET DESIGN BY WILLI BAUM

FIRST EDITION

*Code 9005*

The Jossey-Bass
Higher Education Series

# Contents

ix

# Decision Matrices

xi

# *Preface*

Over the past decade managers in higher education have been grappling with major challenges to the stability and survival of their institutions: rising operating and capital costs, increasing legal confrontations, declining enrollments, shifting emphases in study fields, an uncertain job market, increased competition for public and private funds, and growing public dissatisfaction with the entire higher education enterprise, to name a few. To prosper in the face of such challenges, many institutions have had to make major adjustments in all areas of their operations and rethink their overall management strategies in the light of new realities. In many instances, colleges have borrowed promising and highly publicized management techniques — such as management information systems (MIS) and management by objectives (MBO) — from the corporate sector, in the hope that these techniques would improve efficiency and effectiveness in academic environments as well. Yet the results of these efforts are mixed: some institutions have used these techniques and begun to prosper; others have been able only to maintain the status quo; still others have lost ground and are threatened.

Barring blatant evidence of mismanagement, what factors really make the difference between a successfully managed college or university and one that is poorly or merely adequately managed? This book posits that successful management begins with a clear understanding of institutional purposes and soundly developed policies and procedures for carrying out those purposes. If a college's or university's fundamental structures and procedures are flawed, no management style or approach will work, and efforts to achieve institutional goals are doomed to fail.

This book offers higher education administrators guidance for ensuring the kind of management structure needed to undergird all institutional operations and activities. It presents an approach to developing, monitoring, and improving administrative functions so that they efficiently and effectively support the needs, goals, and values of colleges and universities at individual, departmental, divisional, and institutional levels.

In writing this book, I have drawn on my experience as a consultant to two small private colleges that were in extremely precarious financial condition. In each case, I worked successfully with the institution's management team to identify problems causing the financial difficulty, revise existing operations to correct those problems, and train administrative staff in new procedures aimed at avoiding those problems in the future.

I attribute the success of those efforts to my use of strategies that encompassed areas of management activities rather than isolated functions within the organization. Like all organizations, colleges and universities are composed of many interconnected subsystems functioning simultaneously, and sometimes even in unison, in support of a broad set of goals and purposes. A problem that seems localized in one subsystem directly or indirectly affects the functioning of others; indeed, the cause of that problem may actually lie elsewhere in the organization. Effectively managing a college and solving problems within it therefore require a broad understanding of how the entire system works and how its various parts are related. They also require integration of efforts and a clear flow of information across all operational areas or subsystems. This approach to college and university management is called the *integrated systems* approach, and it provides the foundation on which this book rests.

To illustrate the integrated nature of administrative functions, this book focuses on the matrix as a primary tool. In describing, for example, the complexities of institutional fund raising, a single matrix can display all the major tasks involved in that process, indicate essential divisions of authority and responsibility, and show where and how fund-raising operations affect or require support and approval from others (such as trustees, the president, or the alumni director). The matrix therefore offers a shorthand method of organizing a complex array of tasks, responsibilities, concepts, and effects into a clear and useful whole. It is also an important component of this book.

### Overview of the Contents

A brief introductory chapter explains the underlying rationale for the integrated systems approach to improving management (ISATIM) and describes how the book should be used and how it can be applied to diverse institutional needs. The remainder of the book consists entirely of the ISATIM standards and matrices, organized into five sections representing the chief domains of managerial activity: overall management, governance, and leadership; academic affairs; student affairs; development; and business and fiscal affairs. Chapters grouped under each of these headings set out the essential standards for good management in each area and present one or more matrices depicting the procedures and interactions necessary to ensure good standards of practice. Explanatory notes accompany each matrix.

Part One covers governance, leadership, and overall management in two chapters focusing on trustees (or regents) and the president and two chapters on the institution-wide processes of multi-year planning and budgeting.

Part Two covers academic affairs in three chapters on academic administration, registration and academic records, and grant and contract administration. Matrices in these chapters cover virtually every facet of academic policy, including curricular concerns, faculty affairs, research, and academic reporting and record keeping.

Part Three covers student affairs in three chapters on student activities and services, recruiting and admissions, and financial aid. On some campuses today, recruitment and admissions are managed as part of the institutional development function; however, I believe these activities are better coordinated with financial aid offices and are subject to stronger checks and balances when they are part of the student affairs unit.

Part Four covers institutional advancement or development in a single chapter with four matrices.

Part Five divides the complex area of business and fiscal management into five chapters on business management, personnel administration, plant operation and management, auxiliary enterprises, and fiscal management.

Seventy-nine matrices, each with explanatory material, support these chapters and clearly reveal the links among them.

A glossary lists and defines the various position titles and management functions used in the book. Since positions and titles differ from institution to institution, I opted to use either generically descriptive titles or those titles most commonly in use; I hope they will be understood by readers whose institutions use somewhat different ones. To minimize language complexities, male and female pronouns are used interchangeably throughout the book, since I believe that gender is irrelevent to effective performance in any position and at any organizational level.

## Audience

The ISATIM sponsors and I offer the standards of good practice contained in this book not as the only way to manage a college or university, and certainly not as a substitute for an institution's own documented set of operating procedures, but rather as guidelines. The introductory chapter acknowledges some of the limitations of this book and suggests instances where the standards may not fully apply. But the ISATIM standards nevertheless represent basic management tenets that many institutions have used successfully, and the project sponsors and I feel confident that they can provide a solid foundation for effective management in most colleges and universities.

This book is therefore recommended to administrators in all areas and at all levels of college and university management.

New administrators can use it as a learning resource, seasoned administrators as a guide to increasing the efficiency of their own areas and their effectiveness in interacting with others. For trustees, students, and scholars of higher education, this book offers a much-needed reference to the fundamental structure and workings of the academic organization; and for presidents and executive officers, it provides a means of surveying the entire academic enterprise.

## Acknowledgments

I wish to express my deep appreciation to all the authors who contributed papers to the ISATIM project: James E. Benken, Purdue University; Albert E. Berrian, Institute for Services to Education; Steve Collins, Boston College; William B. Cutler, retired; Arthur Danner, University of the District of Columbia; Robert G. Foreman, University of Michigan; Norman H. Gross, University of California; Jessie Hailey, Institute for Services to Education; Richard T. Ingram, Association of Governing Boards; John E. Lewis, Loyola Marymount University; David R. Meabon, Wichita State University; R. Keith Moore, Carnegie-Mellon University; Edward W. Morris, Kentucky State University; Nelso Parkhurst, Purdue University, retired; Joyce P. Peoples, Institute for Services to Education; David W. Phipps, University of Alabama; Irma R. Rabbino, Mount Holyoke College; James J. Rhatigan, Wichita State University; Arthur Sandeen, University of Florida; Robert S. Sorenson, Purdue University; George O. Weber, independent management consultant; Ronald G. Weber, president emeritus, Mount Union College; and Marwin O. Wrolstad, Lawrence University.

Special thanks are also extended to the members of the ISATIM project steering committee: Christopher F. Edley and Leonard Dawson, representing UNCF; D. Frances Finn and Caspa L. Harris, Jr., representing NACUBO; Robert L. Gale and David F. Johnson, representing AGB; Jerry W. Miller and James R. Jordan, representing ACE; and Willa B. Player and John F. Potts, representing the public.

Further assistance in identifying potential authors of the

papers and in advising me throughout this project was provided by Alfred Berrian, Institute for Services to Education; J. Douglas Connor, American Association of Collegiate Registrars and Admissions Officers; James L. Fisher, Council for Advancement and Support of Education; Alan Kirschner and Haywood Strickland, United Negro College Fund; Paul T. Knapp, Association of Physical Plant Administration for Colleges and Universities; Dallas Martin, National Association of Student Financial Aid Administrators; Steven Miller, College and University Personnel Association; Mable Phifer, Moton Institute; and Richard F. Stevens, National Association of Student Personnel Administrators. A special acknowledgment is given to Arlon Elser, program officer of the W. K. Kellogg Foundation, for the funding and other support that made the ISATIM project a reality.

Finally, I am deeply grateful to the late James R. Jordan, without whose assistance in bringing the ISATIM project to fruition this book would never have been written.

*Woodinville, Washington*                              Thomas E. Tellefsen
*November 1989*

# The Author

Thomas E. Tellefsen majored in accounting at Pierce College in Philadelphia. After serving in the Navy during World War II, Tellefsen served for seventeen years with the board of trustees of the American University of Beirut, first as assistant treasurer and then as executive secretary. His accomplishments there included the physical reconstruction of the campus to foster the expansion of graduate instruction and research programs, the negotiation of over $100 million in contracts and grants with the U.S. government, the complete revision of the accounting system and pension program, and the introduction of data-processing systems.

Tellefsen later became an educational consultant with Peat, Marwick, Mitchell and Company and served as the national director of educational consulting services with Coopers & Lybrand. During this period he also developed the planning, budgeting, and accounting manual and the student records manual for the National Association of College and University Business Officers and assessed the financial status of private New York colleges and universities for the New York State Governor's Select Committee.

Tellefsen retired from Coopers & Lybrand in 1978 but has continued to provide consulting services to the Ford Foundation and was lead consultant to the United Negro College Fund's program (1983–1987) to assist its member institutions in improving their management capabilities. Tellefsen and his wife Jean have two children and live in Woodinville, Washington.

# Improving
# College
# Management

# Introduction:
## Interactive Decision Making and Communication in the Successfully Managed College

All colleges and universities are complex organizations managed by a board of trustees or board of regents, a president, and other administrators. Institutions of higher education also share an organizational structure that encompasses a number of academic and nonacademic departments grouped into four general areas: academic affairs, student affairs, advancement or development, and business and financial affairs. Each of these areas contributes to the institution's societal purposes of accumulating, storing, and disseminating knowledge. A smoothly functioning organization is basic to an institution's ability to fulfill these purposes. An effective organizational structure is one that is clearly defined, understood, and accepted by all institutional participants and constituencies and managed by knowledgeable, competent personnel.

Efficient and effective administrative management can exist only if those involved have a clear understanding of how authority and responsibility are distributed and where they overlap. In a very small institution, much of the management and decision-making authority may rest with the president and a relatively small group of senior administrators, but in larger or more complex institutions, authority may be delegated either directly to those who perform tasks or to a small group of people who supervise others in carrying out assigned tasks.

1

In an environment as diverse as that of an academic institution, however, management and leadership are not a straightforward process of top-down decision making. In all areas related to the functions of accumulating and transmitting knowledge, for example, the faculty has considerable authority in determining the policies and procedures that guide it in carrying out the institution's educational mission. This authority is appropriately executed through the faculty's recognized, organized internal structures, such as academic departments or the faculty senate, which are an integral dimension of overall institutional administration. And since decisions related to the curriculum frequently bear on the needs and interests of student affairs, finance, and other operational areas, they cannot be made without the involvement and support of the administrators of those areas.

Hence, successfully managing an academic organization requires cooperation and collaboration across operational divisions. The four-part structure of academic affairs, student affairs, development, and business affairs serves as a general framework for assigning administrative authority and responsibility, but the lines dividing these areas are often blurred. Administrative overlap is a fact of academic life and is actually desirable for institutional purposes because it necessitates ongoing coordination and interaction among administrators in all four areas. Such coordination and interaction are essential to the setting of clear, thoughtful institutional and educational goals, the capacity for effective strategic planning, and the efficient use of human, financial, and technological resources.

Those who manage academic institutions thus need not only special expertise for their immediate administrative roles but also broad understanding of other operational areas; perhaps even more important is their ability to interact across administrative areas and levels. Yet few administrators can meet these criteria, for the increasingly specialized nature of many administrative roles is producing larger numbers of managers who may be well equipped to handle a narrow range of tasks but who are surprisingly ignorant of how other parts of their institutions function or how other areas intersect with their own. For example, business officers may revise a departmental budget with-

out consulting the department chair and inadvertently under-
fund a scheduled program. An academic dean developing a
freshman seminar may not think to consult with student affairs
professionals. Facilities managers may reassign classroom space
without adequately considering instructors' needs. A student
affairs administrator may implement a program without discuss-
ing it with legal counsel. And so on.

Trustees, too, are likely to lack specific knowledge of institutional functioning. Their experience typically lies in nonacademic organizations; further, they spend little time on the
campuses they serve. Though trustees have the ultimate responsibility for the activities of the institutions they govern, their
involvement in day-to-day operations typically is restricted to
matters brought to their attention by the president. Given these
circumstances, operational decision making and problem solving at the trustee level can be ineffective and often are costly. The
problems themselves, as well as their effects on institutional functioning, are likely to have worsened by the time they reach the
trustees for resolution, and the trustees' solutions may not fit
the special needs of the academic environment. Hence, it is in
every institution's best interest to foster skillful decision making, collaboration, and communication across all its administrative functions and at all levels.

## Background of the Book

In 1982 the concept of integrated management attracted
the attention of Christopher F. Edley, president and chief executive officer of the United Negro College Fund (UNCF), and
James R. Jordan, at the time on loan from the Ford Foundation to the American Council on Education (ACE) to assist in
strengthening ACE's programs of service to minority institutions.
Edley and Jordan believed that the integrated systems approach
could be useful to any institution that wanted to improve its
operations, and through their efforts a project was initiated in
1983 to test and refine the approach in the UNCF member institutions. These institutions were deemed especially appropriate
for the project because as a group of small private institutions

they could act cooperatively as a controlled, easily monitored test group. In addition, these institutions had already recognized the desirability of improving their management effectiveness and efficiency and were seeking a means of accomplishing improvements.

The objective of the project was to develop for each area of institutional operations a set of basic standards for good management that could be implemented without a significant increase in resources. These standards would reflect the principles of the integrated systems approach and also would make use of the matrix concept as a resource for administrators and trustees in understanding and applying the approach. The standards themselves would include sound policies and procedures within the immediate responsibilities of each area, and they would also emphasize the full scope of interactions with other areas that are essential to the effective functioning of the area itself and of the institution as a whole.

UNCF collaborated with ACE to develop a program called the Integrated Systems Approach to Improving Management (ISATIM), along with supporting materials to be used in campus assessments and field tests. UNCF is indebted to the W. K. Kellogg Foundation and the Pew Memorial Trust for financial support for the project. The W. K. Kellogg Foundation awarded grants totaling $5.8 million to support a six-year effort to strengthen the management capabilities of the UNCF colleges. Pew provided over $700,000 in additional support. Of special assistance to the ISATIM efforts was Arlon Elser, program officer of the W. K. Kellogg Foundation, who dedicated considerable time and effort to ensuring ISATIM's success. Additional advisory expertise was recruited from the Association of Governing Boards (AGB), the National Association of College and University Business Officers (NACUBO), and several other professional organizations and agencies, thus ensuring that the project had expert advice in all the major management dimensions.

The first step in the ISATIM project was the generation of a set of papers, written by carefully chosen experts, to provide a knowledge base of essential standards for effective management in key operational areas. The authors were asked to address this question: When you, as an expert in your field of institutional operations, are asked to evaluate that area of operations at another institution, what do you consider essential to find in the way of policies, practices, and interactions to assure management that the operation is being carried out as effectively as possible, given the resource limitations normally inherent in a small private college or university?

I synthesized these papers into a comprehensive list of management standards and practices, which in turn was reviewed and further refined by the sponsors of and advisers to the ISATIM project. The results were incorporated into a set of matrices that have since been field-tested and are contained in this book.

The standards and matrices underwent rigorous field testing to see if they indeed could improve management effectiveness. Teams of evaluators and technical advisers visited participating campuses to assess how existing policies and operations measured up to the ISATIM standards. Written reports based on these assessments were sent to institutional leaders; these reports described what the institutions were already doing well, areas in which changes in policies or procedures could improve operations, the extent to which such changes required better interaction across administrative levels, and which of the proposed changes could be handled by institutions with their own resources and which would require outside support. For those institutions that agreed to make the suggested changes, financial and technical support was obtained to ensure that changes could be implemented exactly as the standards required. Periodic on-campus visits were conducted to verify that changes were being implemented as recommended.

It is clear that ISATIM had a significant effect on the participating institutions. The strength of ISATIM was that it allowed each institution to make changes at its own rate according to its available internal resources, supplemented by those provided by ISATIM. Thus, the essential standards were flexible rather than rigidly imposed. Two presidents new to their institutions in 1981 — Cordell Wynn of Stillman College and Benjamin Payton of Tuskegee Institute—used the ISATIM assessments as blue-prints for change. Both reported that the documents provided them with instant knowledge of the problems, promise, and potential of their institutions; comprehensive long-range plans up to the year 2000 resulted from the initial assessments. Both presidents highlighted computerized planning and management as indispensable ingredients of future development and success. ISATIM funds provided both hardware and software to facilitate these efforts.

Spelman College realized a rare opportunity to lay the groundwork for a total information plan for the institution. Representatives of the college invited Peat, Marwick, Mitchell and Company to develop a set of MIS flowcharts, or schematics, depicting the overall flow of information within and among the administrative offices that were participating in MIS. This set of schematics was designed to allow the college officers and deci-sion makers the opportunity to acquire a better understanding not only of information processes within their individual offices and departments but also of the way their MIS operations affected other offices and vice versa. ISATIM provided the funds for this effort, as well as support for the office of institutional research, which monitored and evaluated the process.

Johnson C. Smith University used ISATIM funds to develop a comprehensive computer system and computerized record keeping. The university acquired an IBM System 38 and implemented the Colgate Software Package for administration, registration, alumni affairs, and development. Administrators, through participation in multi-year planning workshops, focused on identifying and solving problems and designing ways of im-plementing a total integrated systems approach to management and decision making. Johnson C. Smith University continues to use ISATIM as its management guide.

Benedict College saw several important outcomes of the ISATIM process, among them data processing and computer services. More than ten discrete administrative office operations using a total of forty terminals were brought on-line. One notable result was that the time required to complete the development office reporting process was reduced from three months to one month. In the area of business affairs and fiscal management, an effective on-line accounting system was established. The business office staff was reduced by two persons as a result of the implementation of viable computerized accounting and financial information systems. Funds were also used to develop a personnel administration office and a plant operations and facilities plan.

Though much remains to be done, enough has been learned to verify that the ISATIM standards hold up as guidelines for effective management and that their implementation improves the management capabilities of institutions that abide by them. They are presented here in the hope that other institutions will find them equally beneficial in developing or improving administrative systems and procedures, fostering greater understanding of individual operational areas as well as the links among operational areas, and facilitating an increased flow of communication, information, and expertise across administrative levels.

## Purpose, Organization, and Scope of This Book

This book has been written to help institutions overcome impediments to effective functioning. The chapters and matrices were designed specifically to encourage communication and shared expertise across all areas of academic administration and to provide a basis for informed decision making and action. While other publications on college and university management tend to focus on individual management areas and problems, this book stresses the integration of management efforts and the interaction necessary among all operational systems and levels.

The book is organized into five parts: The first provides a general overview of institutional governance, leadership, and management; the remaining four offer a more detailed analysis of the major operational units of academic affairs, student affairs, development, and business and financial affairs. Individual chapters focus on key domains of institutional operations. The full range of responsibilities is described for each domain, along with the activities initiated by or within that domain, and essential

standards for good management are set forth. Administrators
will find these standards unusually comprehensive. They cover
topics as diverse as division of authority; decision processes;
routine tasks and procedures; planning and budgeting; space
and resource use; personnel management; data collection, record
keeping, and documentation; accounting and accountability;
legal and ethical guidelines; service organization and delivery;
guiding concepts and principles; and timetable of events.

Following the standards of good management are one or
more decision matrices that not only provide a visual analysis
of tasks and responsibilities but also show where and how these
tasks and responsibilities require interaction with other administrative areas. (See Table 1, which provides an index of the
decision matrices and shows which administrators should be involved in each type of decision.) For example, a student affairs
administrator charged with developing a new code of student
conduct will find in Chapter Eight the key steps and considera-
tions for this task. Using Decision Matrix 36, the practitioner
will also see when and to what extent he or she needs to involve
trustees, legal counsel, the chief academic officer, and others
in the process. Through the use of this single matrix, the student affairs administrator can understand who has the authority
to act, recommend action, and approve actions at specific stages
and who should be called on for support and advice. The very
sensitive task of developing a student code of conduct is therefore
explained as an institutional activity rather than as the work
of a single beleaguered individual. By organizing and carrying
out this task according to the matrix, both the student affairs
administrator and institutional leaders can be sure that the final
product meets the needs of the college or university as a whole.

Each matrix is followed by an explanation in which the
diverse roles and levels of participation are elaborated and additional responsibilities and exceptions to normal procedures are
noted.

This approach to organizing the book was chosen because
the sponsoring organizations and I believe that managing an
institution of higher education is a team responsibility. Although
administrators who use this book will naturally want to turn

first to the chapter or chapters covering their particular areas of responsibility, the ISATIM project sponsors and I emphasize the importance of reading the whole book to achieve a complete understanding of their roles and responsibilities in academic management. Though matrices in each chapter show the links among administrative areas, full details of these links and the rationales underlying them can only be gained from a careful reading of all the chapters. The comprehensive goals and purposes of an entire college or university may not be evident in the operations of just one of its subsystems; they must be understood and evaluated on the basis of all institutional activities. By the same token, readers can maximize their effectiveness as administrators only by mastering the knowledge contained in all the chapters, for it is all this information taken together that constitutes the total operation of an academic institution. Table 1 summarizes the integrated management system and will help readers identify the chapters and matrices of greatest interest to them.

## Faculty and Student Roles in Institutional Decision Making

Though this book was designed primarily with administrators and trustees in mind, it does not overlook the important roles that faculty members and students play in key decision processes. Accordingly, chapters and matrices also explain how these groups, through their formally chosen representatives, should participate in an effectively managed organization. This book does not, however, dwell on these groups as separate organizational entities within a college or university, so a few words on this topic should be said here.

In most institutional management structures faculty members are represented as a body through their own organizations, each of which has its own leadership and is recognized by the board of trustees. For these organizations to function effectively, a faculty should have its own operational guide in the form of a clearly written handbook. Today the faculty handbook is widely recognized as a legal document, so its content should be devel-

Table 1. Index of Decision Matrices and Administrators.

| Decision Matrix | Chapter | Board of Trustees | President | Planning Director | Grant and Contract Administration Director | Chief Academic Officer | Academic Department Heads | Chief Development Officer | Alumni Relations Director | Public Relations Director | Publications Director | Chief Student Affairs Officer | Health Services Director | Financial Aid Director | Recruiting and Admissions Director | Registrar | Chief Fiscal Officer | Personnel Director | Physical Plant Director | Student Housing Director | Food Service Director | Bookstore Manager | Student Union Director | Intercollegiate Athletics Director |
|---|---|---|---|---|---|---|---|---|---|---|---|---|---|---|---|---|---|---|---|---|---|---|---|---|
| 1. Presidential Search and Selection | 1 | x | | | | | | | | | | | | | | | | | | | | | | |
| 2. Selection of Trustees, Officers, Committee Chairpersons, and Committee Members | 1 | x | x | | | | | | | | | | | | | | | | | | | | | |
| 3. Presidential Assessment | 1 | x | x | | | | | | | | | | | | | | | | | | | | | |
| 4. Board Self-Study | 1 | x | x | | | | | | | | | | | | | | | | | | | | | |
| 5. New Trustee Orientation | 1 | x | x | | | x | | x | | | | x | | | | | x | | | | | | | |
| 6. Developing Planning Guidelines | 3 | x | x | x | x | x | x | x | x | x | x | x | x | x | x | x | x | x | x | x | x | x | x | x |
| 7. Developing Academic Program Plans | 3 | | x | x | x | x | x | | | | | | | | | x | | | | | | | | |
| 8. Developing Support Service Program Plans | 3 | | x | x | x | | | x | x | x | x | x | x | x | x | x | x | x | x | x | x | x | x | x |
| 9. Final Review and Approval | 3 | x | x | x | x | x | | x | x | x | x | x | x | x | x | x | x | x | x | x | x | x | x | x |
| 10. Development and Delegated Revisions of Annual Operating Budget | 4 | x | x | x | x | x | | x | x | x | x | x | x | x | x | x | x | x | x | x | x | x | x | x |
| 11. Annual Operating Budget—Board-Authorized Revisions | 4 | x | x | x | x | x | | x | x | x | x | x | x | x | x | x | x | x | x | x | x | x | x | x |

| | |
|---|---|
| 12. | Capital Projects |
| 13. | Formulation of Academic Policies and Procedures — 5 |
| 14. | Curriculum and Academic Program Revision — 5 |
| 15. | Promotion and Appointment to Tenure Status — 5 |
| 16. | Processing Requests for Sabbaticals and Leaves of Absence — 5 |
| 17. | Faculty Performance Evaluation — 5 |
| 18. | Faculty Retention — 5 |
| 19. | Faculty Recruitment and Appointment — 5 |
| 20. | Comprehensive Career Development Program — 5 |
| 21. | Registration — 6 |
| 22. | Change in Enrollment Status — 6 |
| 23. | Grade Reporting — 6 |
| 24. | Encumbrance of Academic Records and Transcripts — 6 |
| 25. | Commencement — 6 |
| 26. | Attrition Analysis — 6 |
| 27. | Revision of Academic Calendar — 6 |
| 28. | Receipt of New Sponsored Agreement — 7 |
| 29. | Time and Effort Reporting — 7 |
| 30. | Hiring Consultants — 7 |
| 31. | Sponsored Agreement Budget Reallocation — 7 |
| 32. | Reallocation of Incurred Costs on Sponsored Agreements — 7 |
| 33. | Equipment Procurement for Sponsored Agreements — 7 |
| 34. | Travel and Supply Procurement for Sponsored Agreements — 7 |
| 35. | Close-Out of Sponsored Agreements — 7 |
| 36. | Developing Student Code of Conduct — 8 |
| 37. | Administration of Student Discipline — 8 |

Table 1. Index of Decision Matrices and Administrators, Cont'd.

| Decision Matrix | Chapter | Board of Trustees | President | Planning Director | Grant and Contract Administration Director | Chief Academic Officer | Academic Department Heads | Chief Development Officer | Alumni Relations Director | Public Relations Director | Publications Director | Chief Student Affairs Officer | Health Services Director | Financial Aid Director | Recruiting and Admissions Director | Registrar | Chief Fiscal Officer | Personnel Director | Physical Plant Director | Student Housing Director | Food Service Director | Bookstore Manager | Student Union Director | Intercollegiate Athletics Director |
|---|---|---|---|---|---|---|---|---|---|---|---|---|---|---|---|---|---|---|---|---|---|---|---|---|
| 38. Revising Health Care Program | 8 | | x | | | x | x | x | | | | x | x | | | | x | | | | | | | x |
| 39. Establishing Nonacademic Counseling Program | 8 | x | x | | | x | x | x | | | | x | | | | | | | | | | | | |
| 40. Student Activities and Government | 8 | x | x | | | x | | x | | | | x | | | | | x | | | x | x | x | x | x |
| 41. New Student Orientation Program | 8 | | x | | | x | | x | | | | x | | | | | x | | | x | x | x | x | |
| 42. Conducting Recruiting and Admissions Operations | 9 | x | x | | | x | | x | | x | | x | x | x | x | x | x | | | x | | | | |
| 43. Developing and Implementing Financial Aid Plan | 10 | x | x | x | | x | | | | x | x | x | | x | x | x | x | | | | | | | |
| 44. Initial Financial Aid Award Process | 10 | x | x | | | x | | | | | x | x | | x | x | x | x | | | | | | | |
| 45. Conditional Financial Aid Award Process | 10 | x | x | | | x | | | | | | x | | x | x | x | x | | | | | | | |
| 46. Revision of Financial Aid Awards | 10 | | | | | | | | | | | | | x | x | x | x | x | | | | | | |
| 47. Student Employment | 10 | | x | | | x | | x | | | | x | | x | x | x | x | x | | | | | | |

48. Fund-Raising Projections for Multi-Year Planning — 11
49. Application for Restricted Grants or Contracts — 11
50. Nonprogram Fund Raising and Gift and Grant Processing — 11
51. Publications — 11
52. Purchasing and Accounts Payable Activities — 11
53. Central Stores Operation — 12
54. Cash Management of Operating Funds — 12
55. Endowment Fund Investment Management — 12
56. National Direct Student Loan Management — 12
57. Formulating Nonacademic Personnel Policies and Procedures — 12
58. Employment of Nonacademic Staff — 13
59. Change in Status of Nonacademic Employee — 13
60. Employee Discipline and Termination — 13
61. Basic Nonacademic Wage and Salary Administration Program — 13
62. Affirmative Action Compliance — Nonacademic Staff — 13
63. Performance Evaluation of Nonacademic Employees — 13
64. Maintenance Services — 14
65. Campus Security and Safety — 14
66. Energy Conservation — 14
67. Custodial Services — 14
68. Grounds Care Services — 14
69. Delivery of Special Services by Auxiliary Enterprise Units — 15
70. Bookstore or Student Store Operations — 15
71. Food Service Operations — 15
72. Student Housing Operations — 15
73. Faculty and Staff Housing — 15

# Table 1. Index of Decision Matrices and Administrators, Cont'd.

| Decision Matrix | Chapter | Board of Trustees | President | Planning Director | Grant and Contract Administration Director | Chief Academic Officer | Academic Department Heads | Chief Development Officer | Alumni Relations Director | Public Relations Director | Publications Director | Chief Student Affairs Officer | Health Services Director | Financial Aid Director | Recruiting and Admissions Director | Registrar | Chief Fiscal Officer | Personnel Director | Physical Plant Director | Student Housing Director | Food Service Director | Bookstore Manager | Student Union Director | Intercollegiate Athletics Director |
|---|---|---|---|---|---|---|---|---|---|---|---|---|---|---|---|---|---|---|---|---|---|---|---|---|
| 74. Student Union Operations | 15 | x | x |  |  | x |  | x |  |  |  | x |  |  |  |  | x |  | x |  |  |  | x |  |
| 75. Campus Parking Operations | 15 | x | x |  |  | x |  | x |  |  |  | x |  |  |  |  | x |  |  |  |  |  |  |  |
| 76. Formulating Intercollegiate Athletics Policies and Procedures | 15 | x | x |  |  | x | x | x |  |  |  | x | x | x | x | x | x |  |  |  |  |  |  | x |
| 77. Implementing Intercollegiate Athletic Program | 15 | x | x |  |  | x |  | x |  | x |  | x | x | x |  |  | x |  | x |  |  |  |  | x |
| 78. Processing Cash Receipts and Disbursements | 16 |  |  |  |  |  |  | x |  |  |  |  |  |  |  |  | x |  |  | x | x | x | x | x |
| 79. Payroll Disbursement — Regular Employees | 16 | x | x | x | x | x | x | x | x | x | x | x | x | x | x | x | x | x | x | x | x | x | x | x |

oped with great care. The handbook should specify, among other things, the structure, purposes, membership, responsibilities, and limits of authority of each faculty organization; to whom each organization is responsible; how membership is to be determined; the number and schedule of meetings; requirements for meeting minutes and other forms of record keeping and reporting; and procedures for changing the constitution and by-laws.

Obviously, no institution should undertake to change its faculty organizations without the consent and active involvement of the faculty members themselves. By the same token, no institution should bypass its faculty in considering or instituting changes in academic programs, curriculum or instructional methods, faculty personnel policies, admissions or academic requirements, grading policies, or other areas that bear on the work or the professional welfare of the faculty. The matrices in this book show clearly where faculty interests are important and should be formally represented in institutional decisions.

However, there are areas of institutional decision making in which the faculty does not have a formal role. These include the review and approval of the annual operating budget, the establishment of internal fiscal control procedures, the determination of faculty salaries, the management of cash or endowment funds, the planning and management of fund-raising programs, physical plant operation and management, the awarding of student financial aid, and student government and other student activities. Since faculty perspectives and advice can be useful in many of these activities, however, I suggest appointing a faculty member to the president's advisory committee, which will deal with key issues in most of these areas.

Students also can contribute to the formulation of sound management decisions, and their participation should also be encouraged wherever it may be appropriate. Their participation can, for example, contribute to the acceptance and support of policies that affect the student body, improve campus morale, increase students' understanding of overall institutional operations, and perhaps help prevent hostility and disruption when volatile issues surface. Like faculty members, students should participate in institutional management processes through their own formally recognized student organizations or by appointment to recognized faculty organizations or committees established by the president. In all instances the students' role should be defined clearly, and their authority to vote, advise, or merely observe should be understood by all participants.

The organizations through which students' activities are carried out, the guidelines, policies, and procedures under which they function, and the campus rules, regulations, and requirements affecting student life should be spelled out in a student handbook. This handbook, like its faculty counterpart, is considered a legal document, and its periodic review and revision should be a priority across all areas of institutional operation.

Like faculty members, students should have no decision-making roles in certain areas. These include all matters relating to the employment and compensation of faculty and staff, budgetary review and approval, the setting of academic requirements and grades, accounting and fiscal control policies and procedures, grant and contract policies and procedures, the awarding of financial aid, and the setting of tuition and room and board charges.

### Limitations and Uses of ISATIM Standards

The standards of good management and the decision matrices presented here are intended as a guide to effective institutional management. They have been carefully reviewed by ISATIM sponsors, project advisers, and participants and field-tested by members of the ISATIM teams, who confirmed their value in actual practice. Hence, readers who choose to adapt or deviate from the ISATIM standards should do so with caution.

Nevertheless, these standards are not set in stone, and they have some limitations that should be mentioned. First, they were developed for small private colleges and universities, and while most of them are transferable to other kinds of institutions, they may not fully encompass the administrative complexities characteristic of large, multicampus, or public institutions.

Second, the processes elaborated in the matrices and explanatory notes are not as complete or as comprehensive as an institution's *own* procedural documents need to be. Administrators may wish to expand the matrices to reflect the special circumstances of their institutions, perhaps by adding steps or data required for their own decision processes. Further, the matrices have been prepared on the assumption that each time a decision is required, that decision will be affirmative. Common sense says that this happy state of affairs is unlikely to occur very often in the early stages of a task or activity. Therefore, institutions will need to incorporate into their own procedures the necessary loops to be followed whenever negative decisions are reached. For example, if the student affairs administrator encounters resistance to the proposed code of student conduct from any of the groups whose support and approval are essential, he or she will have to repeat steps in the process or create new steps until the impasse has been cleared.

Third, the president of each institution has the ultimate power to decide how much authority and responsibility to delegate to others and how to delegate that authority and responsibility. This book reflects divisions of responsibility and distributions of authority that are fairly representative of the smaller institutions for which it was designed, but its recommendations may not fit the needs of an institution managed in a significantly different way.

Fourth, the book does not take into account political and motivational aspects of institutional management and change. The matrices depict the procedures, events, and linkages that should exist for specific tasks and activities, but they cannot anticipate and accommodate political and emotional reactions to each management step (such as turf battles and resistance to change). Many other publications offer help in coping with such problems, and administrators are advised to read widely in the literature on organizational psychology and change.

With these limitations understood, how can this book support and enhance the management of colleges and universities? I suggest the following as just a few of the many possible applications.

*Formulating Operating Procedures.* Each institution should have its own documented operating policies and procedures that should guide both the conduct and the evaluation of institutional operations. The ISATIM standards can serve as the basis for carefully crafted policies and procedures tailored to institutional needs.

*Increasing Personal Administrative Expertise.* Administrators at all levels can use this book as an ongoing reference for improving their day-to-day performance and strengthening their interactions with other departments. The standards help administrators become more aware of how they should represent their interests to other units, what information and data other administrators may need from them in the way of support, and how they themselves can support the work of their colleagues.

*Training and Orienting New Staff and Trustees.* Because they provide a comprehensive view of institutional operations, the ISATIM standards can serve as a valuable resource for training new administrators and support staff. Trustees will find this book helpful in understanding the structure, organization, and interdependence of college and university functions.

*Developing and Improving Systems, Policies, Programs, and Services.* The ISATIM standards facilitate the planning, evaluation, implementation, and changing of systems, policies, programs, and services by clearly identifying key components, tasks, participants, and essential supporters of these efforts. The resulting changes are more durable because important constituencies and issues were not overlooked along the way.

*Monitoring and Strengthening Key Operational Areas.* Institutional leaders can measure their own operational systems against the standards set out in this book, identify weaknesses, and take corrective action.

*Clarifying Administrative Roles and Developing Job Descriptions.* Tasks and responsibilities are clearly defined and described in this book and can help administrative leaders in designing staff positions, selecting properly qualified administrators to fill these positions, and assigning responsibility.

*Conducting Institutional Self-Studies.* This book offers an ideal starting point for examining institutional performance against proven standards of effective management practice and in the light of stated missions and goals.

The ISATIM sponsors and I hope this book will lead to improved understanding of managerial roles, organizational purposes, and overall institutional functioning at all kinds of colleges and universities. We believe this book can make the academic administrator's life easier while at the same time enhancing his or her effectiveness. Administrators who understand how their roles fit into a larger organizational whole will be able to carry out their immediate responsibilities with increased efficiency, work more purposefully toward larger institutional goals, and respond successfully to new challenges in the interests of institutional progress and well-being.

# Part One:
# Executive Roles
# and Activities

This part contains chapters related to the operation of the board of trustees, the president, and multi-year planning and budgeting. The board of trustees is ultimately responsible for the overall operation of the institution it governs. The president, as the institution's chief executive officer, is responsible to the board of trustees for seeing that the activities that the board has authorized are carried out efficiently under the policies adopted by the board. Multi-year planning and budgeting are activities for which the president is responsible and that require the participation of all segments of institutional operations.

Trustees and presidents who read this book should be aware that the material in Part One is limited to the activities that each is directly responsible for initiating. Thus, to understand fully the scope of their responsibilities, they should read all parts. For example, the president is responsible for, among other things, formulating policy recommendations suitable to the institution's mission and needs for submission to the board of trustees for adoption. The president is also responsible for seeing that appropriate reports are prepared by each segment of institutional operations to keep the president and the board informed regarding the status of those operations. The extent and nature of these policies and reports are set forth in the narrative portion of each of the chapters that describe the activities of the administrator whose area of responsibility is most directly involved in the day-to-day administration of the policies and operations. The extent and nature of involvement by other administrators in the formulation of policies and the provision of data for reports are set forth in the decision matrices that appear in each chapter.

# Governing Boards

The board of trustees is one of the key elements of an institution's management team. Acting as a body, trustees are charged by the institution's charter with the responsibility of operating the institution they manage. These responsibilities involve selecting the president to manage the day-to-day affairs of the institution; establishing the institution's mission, goals, and objectives; establishing the policies under which the institution is to be operated; monitoring the institution's operation to verify that the policies established are being adhered to; approving the institution's annual operating and capital budgets; and preserving the institution's assets. How the board of trustees carries out these responsibilities directly affects the ability of the institution's administration to administer its operations effectively and efficiently. Trustees may be held collectively and individually liable for failure to act prudently in carrying out their responsibilities. The board, therefore, should seek to ensure that its members have the requisite skills to carry out its responsibilities.

To facilitate good institutional management, the board of trustees should adhere to the following essential standards of good management:

★ The board should schedule its meetings to coincide with the institution's need for decisions regarding matters that are

23

properly the responsibility of the board. As Chapter Three shows, all institutions operate in accordance with cycles that are beyond their control. For example, the timetable for recruiting new students is dictated by the calendars of the secondary schools and community colleges from which such students will be sought. Thus, colleges and universities concentrate their main recruiting efforts between November and April of the school year prior to the academic year for which the students are being recruited. Decisions regarding changes in academic programs, tuition and fees, and other matters that may affect a prospective student's decision to matriculate should be made sufficiently in advance of November to permit authorized changes to be included in recruiting material. This means that a board meeting should be scheduled for October to approve the institution's multi-year plan, which should be submitted for board approval at that time. (See Chapter Three for further clarification.) At this meeting the board should also review the actual enrollment for the current academic year and determine whether any modifications to the year's operating budget are required as a result of variances between actual and projected enrollment. Additional meetings should be scheduled for January or early February, April or May, and July or August.

★   An agenda for each meeting, together with supporting material, should be developed jointly by the chairperson of the board and the president and sent to each member with the notice of the call for the meeting, at least ten days in advance of the scheduled meeting date. The circulation of such material in advance of the meeting will provide the members with time to consider the matters to be acted on at the meeting and should make discussion of such matters more meaningful.

★   The board should have an executive committee empowered to act on its behalf between regularly scheduled meetings to deal with matters where required board of trustee action cannot wait until the next regular meeting. Care, however, should be taken to ensure that the executive committee does not become a vehicle for circumventing full board consideration of matters that can and should wait for action until the next regular meeting. Further, all actions taken by the executive committee should be ratified at the next regular meeting of the full board. To ensure the broadest possible consideration of matters presented to the executive committee for action, its members should include the chairperson of the board and the chairpersons of each standing committee of the board.

★  In addition to an executive committee, the board should have a number of standing committees related to various aspects of institutional operations. At a minimum, such committees should include a committee on trustees or nominating committee, a finance committee, an academic and faculty affairs committee, a student affairs committee, a development or institutional advancement committee, and a building and grounds committee. Unlike the executive committee, the standing committees, with the exception of the finance committee, should not be empowered to act on behalf of the full board of trustees. The authority of the finance committee to act on behalf of the full board should be limited to decisions regarding the management of endowment fund investments or short-term investments. Rather, these committees should be responsible for keeping the board informed regarding activities that fall within their sphere of operation. Standing committees should meet at least once a year, on campus, with such members of the faculty, staff, or study body as the committee deems appropriate, to assess what is happening in the areas of its responsibility and to consider how its activities could be made more effective or efficient. In so doing, committee members must exercise caution to avoid getting involved in institutional operations or decisions and refrain from making commitments that could be construed as binding on the board of trustees.

★  Minutes of each meeting of the board or any of its committees should be prepared promptly after each meeting. Such minutes should be circulated to all members of the board of trustees and approved or accepted at the next meeting of the board. For standing committees, such minutes are not required if the committee's meeting immediately precedes a full board meeting at which its activities are reported and covered by the regular board meeting minutes.

★ The operations of the board of trustees should be conducted in accordance with a set of published bylaws that should not be inconsistent with any limitations set forth in the charter. At a minimum, the bylaws should cover the responsibilities and powers of the board; board membership, including the number of members authorized, terms of office, number of classes, and mandatory retirement; the officers of the board and such officers of the institution as are deemed appropriate, including the terms and duties of each officer; the time and place of regularly scheduled meetings of the board, including the identification of the meeting that is considered the annual meeting of the board; the committees of the board, their composition and responsibilities; the indemnification of members, officers, and administrators; and the process required to amend the bylaws. In addition, the bylaws should clearly define the major responsibilities of the board of trustees. These responsibilities should include, at a minimum, the selection of a president; the selection of trustees to fill vacancies; the selection of external auditors and legal counsel; the determination and systematic review of the institution's mission through adoption of long-range plans, annual operating budgets, and institutional activities designed to carry out that mission; the adoption of policies under which the institution is to be operated; the acquisition, disposal, improvement, or renovation of land and physical facilities; the investment of endowment funds or short-term excess operating funds; the acceptance of restricted gifts, the maintenance of the institution's fiscal viability, and the addition or deletion of academic programs; the granting of tenure for faculty members; and the awarding of all degrees, including honorary degrees. Decision Matrices 1 and 2 present the steps involved in the selection of a president and the selection of trustees to fill vacancies.

★ The president should be an ex officio, nonvoting member of the board of trustees. The president should attend all meetings of the board or its executive committee and should also have the right to attend any meeting of the board's standing committees. As the chief executive officer selected by the board to operate the institution it governs, the president will be presenting recommendations for action on which he has already taken a position. He therefore should not be in a position to vote on his own recommendations. He should, however, have the right to present such recommendations, to discuss with the board his reasons for making them, and to hear the board's discussion regarding their acceptability. In addition, he should be relied on by the board to present to it the current status of operations, problems, and opportunities from his perspective.

★ The board should be responsible for the establishment of the policies under which it wishes the institution to be operated. While it should monitor the efficiency and effectiveness of institutional operations, it should avoid interference in administrative matters. The type and nature of policies that should exist are set forth in this and ensuing chapters, as are procedures showing how such policies should emerge as recommendations from the institution's administration. The board's monitoring activities should result primarily from reviewing the various reports covering institutional operations, which should come to it regularly. The types of report it should receive are also identified in the ensuing chapters. A review of Table 1 in the introduction will identify the chapters in which trustee action on policy and review of operational reports are contained.

★ The board should have a policy statement on conflicts of interest that applies to its members, its officers, and institutional administrators. I do not wish to impugn in any way the integrity of board members, officers, or other administrators. Rather, conflicts of interest should be avoided for both their benefit and the institution's benefit. For example, if a board member is an insurance broker, it is prudent management to seek his advice regarding the nature and extent of risk that should be covered by insurance and the adequacy of existing or proposed policies. However, he should not be the broker through which such policies are placed.

★  The board should periodically conduct a self-study assessment of its own organization and performance. As a self-perpetuating body, the board should regularly evaluate whether changes in institutional operations, its need for advice and guidance, or existing members' ability to meet that need dictate a change in the board's organizational structure or membership (see Decision Matrix 4). For its members, the Association of Governing Boards (AGB), One Dupont Circle, Washington, D.C. 20036, offers a program that assists boards of trustees in conducting self-studies of their effectiveness and operations. AGB also provides a form entitled "Self-Study Criteria for Governing Boards of Private Colleges and Universities" to assist boards of trustees in conducting evaluations of their organization and performance.

★  A profile of board membership should be prepared annually to guide the committee on trustees or a nominating committee in its development of recommendations for election or reelection of trustees. The AGB can also provide a sample profile form for use by member institutions.

★  An orientation program should be conducted for all new board members giving adequate attention to the responsibilities of trusteeship and the characteristics of the institution (see Decision Matrix 5).

★  The board should meet independently with its appointed external auditors to review the results of the annual audit of institutional operations as well as the findings included in the auditors' management letter to the president. Particular attention should be paid to any findings regarding deficiencies in fiscal management or internal control that were included in the auditors' previous management letters and have not yet been corrected by the administration.

★ The board should conduct a formal assessment of the president's performance on a periodic basis consistent with the term of appointment, if term appointments are used (see Decision Matrix 3).

While not deemed essential, it is considered desirable that the following additional standards be adhered to in board operations:

★ Each standing committee of the board should be provided with staff support selected by the president from among key administrators in the committee's area of operation.

★ The number of standing committees established to be essential should be expanded by providing separate committees on academic affairs and faculty affairs and committees on investment and audit that are separate from the finance committee.

The board of trustees has a great responsibility in institutional management. In carrying out its responsibilities, it should work very closely with the president, to whom it has delegated the responsibility for management of the day-to-day operation of the institution and implementation of plans and policies it has authorized. For those readers desiring a deeper understanding of the responsibilities and operation of governing bodies, the *Handbook of College and University Trusteeship,* by Richard T. Ingram and Associates (Jossey-Bass, 1980), is recommended.

# Decision Matrix 1. Presidential Search and Selection.

Legend of decision-making roles

1 – Authorizes action
2 – Action responsibility
3 – Approves recommendation
4 – Recommends action
5 – Provides input

| Procedural Steps | Participants in Decision-Making Processes | | | | | | | |
|---|---|---|---|---|---|---|---|---|
| | Board of Trustees | Board Chairperson | Search Committee | Faculty | Students | Alumni | Applicants | Others |
| 1. Authorize search for new president | 2 | | | | | | | |
| 2. Formulate search procedures and search committee composition | 2 | | 5 | 5 | 5 | | | |
| 3. Appoint members of search committee: | | | | | | | | |
| (a) board members | 1 | 2 | | | | | | |
| (b) non-board members | 1 | 2 | | | | | | |
| 4. Advise committee members of desired characteristics of new president | | 2 | | 5 | | 5 | | |
| 5. Maintain records of search activities | | | 2 | | | | | |
| 6. Formulate specific search criteria and procedures | | | 2 | 5 | 5 | 5 | | |
| 7. Develop pool of candidates | | | 2 | 5 | 5 | 5 | | |
| 8. Screen candidates, formulate a ranked slate of candidates to be recommended to the board for consideration, and inform candidates of their status | 5 | | 2 | | | | 5 | 5 |
| 9. Review slate of candidates, rank order negotiation, and authorize negotiation for appointment | 2 | | 4 | | | | | |
| 10. Negotiate terms of appointment with candidates | 2 | 2 | | | | | 5 | |
| 11. Select and appoint new president | 2 | 4 | | | | | | |
| 12. Announce appointment | 1 | 2 | | | | | | 5 |
| 13. Submit report of search and selection activities | | | 2 | | | | | |
| 14. Determine desirable changes for next search | 2 | | 4 | | | | | |

*Explanation of Decision Matrix 1.*

| Step | Action Responsibility | Action |
|------|----------------------|--------|
| 1. | Board of Trustees | Determines characteristics desired in new president and authorizes search. |
| 2. | Board of Trustees | Determines the type of search committee required and search procedures to be followed after obtaining input from faculty, students, and alumni. |
| 3 & 4. | Board Chairperson | Appoints board and non-board members to the search committee, designates a chairperson, and advises the committee of characteristics desired in new president and search procedures to be followed. |
| 5. | Search Committee | Designates one of its members to act as secretary to the committee and maintain a complete record of the entire search and selection process. |
| 6. | Search Committee | Develops specific criteria by which the new president will be chosen in line with characteristics identified by the board in Step 1 and additional input obtained from faculty, students, and alumni. |

*Explanation of Decision Matrix 1, Cont'd.*

| Step | Action Responsibility | Action |
|---|---|---|
| 7. | Search Committee | Develops pool of candidates from applications received or recommendations made by committee members, other board members, faculty, students, alumni, or others. |
| 8. | Search Committee | Screens candidates, determines interview procedure to be used, conducts interviews, determines a ranked slate of candidates to be recommended to the board, and informs candidates of their status. |
| 9. | Board of Trustees | Reviews committee's slate of recommended candidates and determines ranked slate of candidates with whom negotiations should be conducted, establishes contractual terms that may be offered, and authorizes the chairperson to conduct negotiations. |
| 10. | Board chairperson | Conducts, in ranked order, such negotiations as are necessary to determine final candidate to be recommended to board for appointment as president. |
| 11. | Board of Trustees | Reviews and approves chairperson's recommendation and terms of appointment. |

*Explanation of Decision Matrix 1, Cont'd.*

| Step | Action Responsibility | Action |
|------|----------------------|--------|
| 12. | Board chairperson | Announces appointment of new president in accordance with board authorization. |
| 13. | Search Committee | Submits report covering all search activities to board. |
| 14. | Board of Trustees | Reviews committee report, identifies ways in which it may be improved upon in the next presidential search, and discharges the committee. |

**Decision Matrix 2. Selection of Trustees, Officers, Committee Chairpersons, and Committee Members.**

Legend of decision-making roles:
1 – Authorizes action
2 – Action responsibility
3 – Approves recommendation
4 – Recommends action
5 – Provides input

| Procedural Steps | Board of Trustees | Nominating Committee | Board Chairperson | President | Standing Committee Chairpersons | Standing Committee Staff | Faculty | Students | Alumni | Community and Church leaders |
|---|---|---|---|---|---|---|---|---|---|---|
| *Participants in Decision-Making Processes* | | | | | | | | | | |
| 1. Conduct assessment of board needs and prepare profile of board members | 1 | 2 | 5 | 5 | | | | | | |
| 2. Formulate a statement of trustee responsibility | | 2 | 5 | 5 | | | | | | |
| 3. Evaluate trustees whose terms are expiring and formulate recommendations for reelection | | 2 | 5 | 5 | 5 | 5 | | | | |
| 4. Review committee's assessment of board needs, statement of trustee responsibility, evaluation of trustees whose terms are expiring, and recommendations for reelection; determine the number of vacancies, by class, to be filled by election of new trustees | 2 | 4 | | | | | | | | |

| | | | | | | | | | |
|---|---|---|---|---|---|---|---|---|---|
| 5. Identify candidates for election to board of trustees | 5 | 2 | 5 | 5 | 5 | 5 | 5 | 5 | 5 |
| 6. Determine nominees to be screened | | 2 | | | | | | | |
| 7. Screen candidates and formulate slate of candidates | | 2 | | | | | | | |
| 8. Elect candidates to be invited to join the board | 2 | 4 | | | | | | | |
| 9. Extend formal invitation to join the board | | | 2 | | | | | | |
| 10. Review performance of standing committees and formulate recommendations for changes in committee position or chairpersons | | 2 | 5 | 5 | 5 | | | | |
| 11. Review performance of officers of the board | | 2 | 5 | | | | | | |
| 12. Elect officers and approve standing committee appointments and chairpersonships | 2 | 4 | 4 | | | | | | |

*Explanation of Decision Matrix 2.*

| Step | Action Responsibility | Action |
|------|----------------------|--------|
| 1. | Nominating Committee | Conducts an assessment of the type of members the board needs to strengthen its operation and prepares a profile of existing board members with input from the president and the chairperson of the board. |
| 2. | Nominating Committee | Formulates a statement of trustee responsibility with input from the president and the chairperson of the board. |
| 3. | Nominating Committee | Evaluates the performance of trustees whose terms are expiring and formulates recommendations for reelection to the board with input from the president, the chairperson of the board, and the standing committee chairpersons and staff. |
| 4. | Board of Trustees | Reviews and approves nominating committee's recommended statement of trustee responsibility, evaluation of existing trustees, and recommendations for reelection of |

*Explanation of Decision Matrix 2, Cont'd.*

| Step | Action Responsibility | Action |
|------|----------------------|--------|
| | | existing trustees whose terms are expiring; determines the number of vacancies, by class, to be filled by the election of new trustees. |
| 5. | Nominating Committee | Identifies candidates for election to the board with input from the president, chairperson of the board, standing committee chairpersons and staff, other trustees, faculty, students, alumni, and community and church leaders. |
| 6 & 7. | Nominating Committee | Evaluates candidates against board needs, formulates list of candidates to be screened, screens candidates, and formulates a slate of candidates to be nominated for election to the board. |
| 10. | Nominating Committee | Reviews the performance of standing committees and formulates recommendations for changes in committee membership and chairpersons with input from the president, chairperson of |

*Explanation of Decision Matrix 2, Cont'd.*

| Step | Action Responsibility | Action |
|------|----------------------|--------|
|      |                      | the board, and chairpersons and staff of standing committees. |
| 11.  | Board Chairperson    | Reviews performance of officers of the board and formulates recommendations for change or reappointment. |
| 12.  | Board of Trustees    | Reviews nominating committee's recommendations for standing committee appointments and chairpersonships and board chairperson's recommendations for election of board officers; elects officers and approves standing committee's appointments and chairpersonships. |

**Decision Matrix 3. Presidential Assessment.**

Legend of decision-making roles
1 – Authorizes action
2 – Action responsibility
3 – Approves recommendation
4 – Recommends action
5 – Provides input

| Procedural Steps | Participants in Decision-Making Processes | | | |
|---|---|---|---|---|
| | Board of Trustees | Board Chairperson | Assessment Committee | President |
| 1. Establish presidential assessment criteria and appoint ad hoc assessment commitee | 2 | 4 | | 5 |
| 2. Develop assessment procedures, including self-assessment requirements, and establish assessment timetables | | | 2 | 5 |
| 3. Review and approve procedures and timetable | 2 | | 4 | 2 |
| 4. Complete self-assessment | | | | 2 |
| 5. Carry out assessment procedures, review president's self-assessment report, and formulate assessment report | 5 | | 2 | |
| 6. Review assessment committee's findings and report with president | | 2 | 5 | |
| 7. Review assessment committee's report and determine whether any action is required | 2 | 5 | 4 | 5 |
| 8. Review assessment program and determine whether changes are desirable for next assessment | 5 | 5 | 2 | 5 |

*Explanation of Decision Matrix 3.*

| Step | Action Responsibility | Action |
|------|----------------------|--------|
| 1. | Board Chairperson | Recommends, with advice from the president, the development of presidential assessment criteria and the composition of ad hoc assessment committee to the board of trustees. |
| | Board of Trustees | Establishes assessment criteria and authorizes appointment of members of the ad hoc assessment committee. |
| 2. | Assessment Committee | Designs, with assistance from the president, assessment procedures, guidelines, timetable, questionnaires, and president's self-assessment instrument and presents plan to the board. |
| 3. | Board of Trustees | Reviews and approves the assessment committee's plan for assessment and authorizes its implementation. |
| 4. | President | Completes self-assessment. |
| 5. | Assessment Committee | Administers assessment program, collects the president's self-assessment, and reviews the results with the participation and assistance of the board of trustees; formulates assessment report. |

*Explanation of Decision Matrix 3, Cont'd.*

| Step | Action Responsibility | Action |
|------|----------------------|--------|
| 6. | Board Chairperson | Reviews the results of assessment with the president with assistance from representatives of the assessment committee. |
| 7. | Board of Trustees | Reviews the assessment committee's report and determines whether any action is required. |
| 8. | Assessment Committee | Consults with the board, its chairperson, and the president, reviews the assessment program, and determines desirable changes for future assessment programs. |

## Decision Matrix 4. Board Self-Study.

Legend of decision-making roles

1 – Authorizes action
2 – Action responsibility
3 – Approves recommendation
4 – Recommends action
5 – Provides input

| Procedural Steps | Participants in Decision-Making Processes | | | | | |
| --- | --- | --- | --- | --- | --- | --- |
| | Board of Trustees | Board Chairperson | Nominating Committee | President | Professional Assistance | Board Secretary |
| 1. Authorize establishment of board self-study program | 2 | 5 | 4 | 5 | | |
| 2. Establish self-study procedures, criteria, and timetable | 2 | 5 | 3 | 5 | 4 | |
| 3. Implement self-study | 1 | | 2 | 2 | | |
| 4. Complete self-study questionnaire | 2 | | 5 | 5 | | |
| 5. Tabulate and summarize self-study results | | | 5 | 4 | | 2 |
| 6. Review results and authorize their use | | 3 | 5 | | 5 | |
| 7. Discuss and interpret self-study results in a workshop or retreat | 5 | 5 | | 5 | 2 | |
| 8. Determine which recommended changes should be implemented and rank those changes | 2 | 5 | | 5 | 4 | |
| 9. Evaluate self-study program and recommend ways in which it can be improved in the future | | 3 | 4 | 5 | | |

*Explanation of Decision Matrix 4.*

| Step | Action Responsibility | Action |
|------|----------------------|--------|
| 1. | Nominating Committee | Consults with the board chairperson and the president and presents recommendations to the board regarding the establishment of a self-study program and the need for professional assistance from a qualified third party (such as the Association of Governing Boards) in carrying out the program. |
| | Board of Trustees | Authorizes the self-study program and the selection of professional assistance. |
| 2 & 3. | Professional Assistance | Consults with the board chairperson and president and presents recommendations on self-study procedures, criteria, and timetable to the nominating committee. |
| | Nominating Committee | Approves recommendations of professional assistance and recommends approval by the board. |
| | Board of Trustees | Authorizes the nominating committee to implement the self-study plan. |

*Explanation of Decision Matrix 4, Cont'd.*

| *Step* | *Action Responsibility* | *Action* |
|---|---|---|
| 4. | Board of Trustees and President | Members of the board and the president complete the self-study questionnaire with assistance from the nominating committee. |
| 5. | Board Secretary | Tabulates and summarizes the results of the self-study with assistance from the nominating committee and the president. |
| 6. | President | Consults with the nominating committee and recommends action to be taken on the use of the self-study results to the board chairperson. |
|  | Board Chairperson | Approves president's recommendation. |
| 7. | Professional Assistance | Analyzes the results of the self-study and discusses the analysis with the board in a workshop or retreat attended by members of the board and the president. |
| 8. | Professional Assistance | Presents recommendations for changes in board organization and operations, based on results of self-study, to the board of trustees. |

*Explanation of Decision Matrix 4, Cont'd.*

| Step | Action Responsibility | Action |
|------|----------------------|--------|
| | Board of Trustees | Decides which recommended changes to accept and establishes priorities for implementing them. |
| 9. | Nominating Committee | Evaluates self-study program with assistance from the president and recommends to the board chairperson ways in which the next evaluation can be improved. |
| | Board Chairperson | Approves the nominating committee's recommendations for changes in the self-study program. |

## Decision Matrix 5. New Trustee Orientation.

Legend of decision-making roles
1 – Authorizes action
2 – Action responsibility
3 – Approves recommendation
4 – Recommends action
5 – Provides input

*Participants in Decision-Making Processes*

| Procedural Steps | Board of Trustees | Board Chairperson | Nominating Committee | Standing Committees | President | Senior Administrators | New Trustees |
|---|---|---|---|---|---|---|---|
| 1. Authorize establishment or revision of new trustee orientation program | 2 | | 4 | | | | |
| 2. Formulate plans and timetable for conducting new trustee orientation program and determine who should participate | | | 2 | | 5 | 5 | |
| 3. Review and approve plan and timetable | 2 | | 4 | 5 | | | |
| 4. Assemble resource materials for new trustee packet | | | 5 | | 2 | 5 | |
| 5. Conduct the portion of the program devoted to institutional operations | | | | | 2 | 5 | |
| 6. Conduct the portion of the program devoted to board operations and responsibilities of trusteeship | | 5 | 2 | 5 | | | |
| 7. Evaluate program and recommend desirable changes | 5 | 5 | 2 | 5 | 5 | 5 | 5 |

*Explanation of Decision Matrix 5.*

| Step | Action Responsibility | Action |
|------|----------------------|--------|
| 1. | Nominating Committee | Presents recommendations regarding the establishment or revision of a new trustee orientation program to the board of trustees. |
| | Board of Trustees | Authorizes the implementation of an orientation program. |
| 2. | Nominating Committee | Consults with the president and senior administrators and formulates a recommendation for a new trustee orientation program. |
| 3. | Board of Trustees | Reviews and approves the plan of action recommended by the nominating committee. |
| 4. | President | Assembles materials describing institutional and board operations to be included in a packet for new trustees with input from senior administrators, standing committees, and the nominating committee. |
| 5. | President | Conducts the part of the new trustee orientation program that is devoted to |

*Explanation of Decision Matrix 5, Cont'd.*

| Step | Action Responsibility | Action |
| --- | --- | --- |
| | | institutional operations with assistance from senior administrators. |
| 6. | Nominating Committee | Conducts the part of the new trustee orientation program that is devoted to explanation of the trustee's responsibilities with assistance from the board chairperson, the president, and standing committees. |
| 7. | Nominating Committee | Presents to the board of trustees its recommendations for revising the new trustee orientation program based on its evaluation of the program and inputs obtained from the president, the board chairperson, standing committees, senior administrators, and new trustees who have participated in the program. |

# 2

## The President

The president is responsible to the board of trustees for the overall management of the institution and for directing its activities to achieve its planned, board-approved mission, goals, and objectives in accordance with the policies adopted by the board. He is also responsible for seeing that the board of trustees is kept informed regarding the results of institutional operations and changes in approved policy and authorized levels of activity that have been required in order to keep the institution fiscally solvent and enhance its ability to accomplish its mission, goals, and objectives. Further, he is responsible for presenting the institution to its various constituencies in the best light and for helping obtain from them the maximum possible financial support.

In carrying out his responsibilities, the president must rely on his senior administrators for assistance in the day-to-day management of institutional operations. He therefore must determine the nature of the organizational structure he needs to balance his own strengths and weaknesses and his desire to concentrate his involvement in particular areas of institutional operations. Once he has determined the organizational structure he needs, he must determine and communicate to his senior administrators the responsibilities assigned to them, the procedures they are to follow in carrying out their responsibilities, the degree of authority delegated to them, and the extent and

**49**

nature of the management reports he requires to keep himself and the board of trustees informed about their activities. These senior administrators in turn need to make similar decisions and communicate them to their subordinate department heads, on whom they must rely in carrying out the day-to-day management of the activities assigned to them.

The following essential standards should be adhered to in determining the organizational structure of an institution, regardless of the particular structure deemed most appropriate to a given institution.

⋆ The authority to determine how best to structure and staff the administrative organization of an institution should be delegated by the board of trustees to the president. The board of trustees' only involvement in the selection of senior administrators should be to advise and consent on personnel appointed by the president. The president, however, should keep the board of trustees informed regarding changes he plans to make in the institution's organizational structure or in personnel assignments to fill senior administrative positions.

⋆ The organizational structure developed by the president should be set forth in a series of tables of organization. The tables should show who is responsible for administering each activity and to whom each administrator reports in the administrative hierarchy. The tables of organization should include for each position the position title and the name of the person appointed to fill it. The president, however, should not finalize the suborganizational structure of the four major organizational units without consulting with appointed senior administrators; their concurrence is needed when responsibility for activities is realigned, along with their recommendations when personnel are to be appointed to administer the activities of the suborganizational units.

⋆ The president's selection of personnel to fill senior administrative positions should take into consideration his own strengths and weaknesses, his operating style and the type of people he is most comfortable working with, their strengths and weaknesses, their workload responsibilities and span of control capabilities, desired checks and balances, and interpersonal relationships that can affect communications and the efficiency or effectiveness of institutional operations. It is the hope of all presidents to fill all positions with the most qualified personnel that can be found. Unfortunately, a lack of resources or other factors can make that ideal virtually unattainable for smaller, resource-constrained institutions. Therefore, it is my hope that this book, when used with the more technical, task-oriented publications available through the professional associations, will contribute to the growth and effectiveness of all administrators.

★   A position description should exist for each administrative position shown on the tables of organization. Position descriptions should set forth the position title, to whom the position reports, other positions reporting to it, assigned responsibilities, delegated authority, qualification requirements, and salary range.

★   The president should make sure that all administrators know who, in the absence of a given administrator, is responsible for carrying out the tasks assigned to that administrator's position.

★   The president should protect subordinates by ensuring that all instructions directing their activities are conveyed to them by or through the administrator to whom they report or the administrator's delegated replacement.

It is particularly important that the president avoid giving operating instructions to a subordinate who reports to an employee or department head who in turn reports to one of the senior administrators. It is also important that, when a president deems it necessary to reverse a decision made by one of his subordinates, he inform the responsible administrator of his decision and his reasons for it. He should then work out with the administrator the best way of handling the situation so as to not undermine the administrator's ability to function effectively as a manager.

## 3

# Multi-Year Planning

---

Multi-year planning is an ongoing part of fiscal control and management. Other parts are budgeting, implementation of operations, and evaluation of the results of operations. In this chapter, aspects of planning and the cycles of operation related to it are dealt with in detail, including the role of planning in the management process, the planning timetable, essential standards that should be adhered to and desirable procedures to be followed in developing a multi-year plan, participation in each step of such procedures, and the operating cycles that affect and should govern the planning timetable.

### Aspects of the Planning Process

Multi-year planning is one of the most important elements in the effective management of any enterprise. Planning is the process by which an enterprise defines, in relationship to its own mission,

- what it wishes or needs to accomplish during a given period in order to move forward in carrying out that mission;
- where it is now in relation to its objectives;
- what factors will affect its ability to move forward;

52

- what resources it believes will be available to support its endeavors; and
- what programs or levels of activity need to be carried out, and in what sequence, by each functional component of its operation to permit it to attain its objectives with the available resources.

The development of a plan forces management to identify the data it needs about each aspect of its operation in order to determine where it is at any given moment and what progress is being made toward its objectives. In arriving at these determinations, management also can identify the data sources that will usually provide the most accurate information. Thus, the planning process results in the definition of important elements of management information systems.

The following essential standards should be adhered to in the formulation of a multi-year plan:

★ The president should be held responsible for seeing that a plan exists covering three to five years of operation and that this plan is updated annually. He should be supported in this effort by a director of planning, who should report directly to him. Because it takes a long time to bring about change in an institution of higher education, the period covered by its multi-year plan needs to be longer than for other types of enterprises, which are able to react more rapidly to changes. The existing literature on planning for colleges and universities advocates either a three-year or a five-year period. One theory holds that planning beyond the third year becomes so nebulous as to be virtually meaningless. The other theory holds that, although longer plans may be nebulous, the planning should nevertheless project the effects of changes throughout the period of enrollment of students who matriculate during the first year of the plan. This is particularly true where changes in academic program are proposed. Under such circumstances, the impact of changes on students enrolled in the first year of a plan should be considered for at least the next four years. I recommend that planning cover a five-year period; a three-year period, however, is acceptable.

★ The plan should cover all aspects of institutional operations. Therefore, it should involve the formulation of a planning committee composed of representatives of the various segments of institutional operations. If possible, a representative of the board of trustees should participate. The selection of a trustee representative should be worked out between the president and the chairperson of the board. The president's recommendation of an appropriate trustee representative should take into consideration the recommendations of his senior administrators. The final decision regarding selection, however, should be made by the chairperson of the board or the board acting as a body, depending on how the chairperson wishes to deal with the matter.

The appointed trustee representative, in all likelihood, will not be able to be as involved in the planning process as other members of the planning committee. Nevertheless, she should be kept informed of committee deliberations and actions through copies of committee meeting minutes, study materials, and the like prepared by the director of planning, acting as secretary to the committee.

The addition of a trustee member to the institutional planning team is desirable because she can present the board of trustees' perspective regarding proposed changes in institutional mission, environmental assumptions, proposed changes in institutional policy, projections of revenue from non-operationally generated sources, proposed facility construction or renovation projects, proposed changes in levels of compensation or fringe benefits, and proposed changes in academic programs. These are only some of the benefits that can be derived from trustee participation in the planning process. They indicate the desirability of selecting for participation a trustee who has been a board member long enough to have a good idea of what the board's attitude toward such matters is likely to be.

★ The chief fiscal officer should be held responsible for assuring the president and the board of trustees that the revenue and expense projections in the plan are reasonable and mathematically accurate. (Decision Matrix 13, in Chapter Five, shows the processes that should be followed in providing the chief fiscal officer with projections of income to be obtained from fund raising.)

★   The preparation of the plan should follow this sequence: the establishment of planning guidelines, the development of academic program plans, the development of support service program plans, review by an analytical studies group, and final approval by the board of trustees. Decision Matrices 6, 7, 8, and 9 show the procedures involved in each step. For detailed information about the steps in the formulation of a multi-year plan and the nature and format of data applicable to each step, the reader is encouraged to obtain *A Planning Manual for Colleges* from the National Association of College and University Business Officers, One Dupont Circle, Washington, D.C. 20036.

★   The timetable for the preparation of the plan should permit board-authorized changes in academic program or operating policies or procedures that affect students, faculty, or staff to be included in revisions of recruiting materials, the catalogue, and student, faculty, and staff handbooks. In addition, the timetable should permit the board of trustees' approval of the full plan to be obtained at least six and one-half months prior to the beginning of the first fiscal year of the plan. Actions that affect the direction an institution plans to take or the policies it plans to follow should be authorized by the governing body before implementation. The timetable for multi-year planning, therefore, is dictated by the cycles of operation that affect it and by the timing of related actions that should take place prior to the beginning of the first fiscal year covered by the plan. These actions include notification to faculty of retention, change in status, or dismissal that results from planned changes in academic programs, academic organization, or curriculum and notification to existing and prospective students, through the catalogue, student handbook, or recruiting material, of planned changes in academic programs, student life programs and policies, fee structure, payment policies, and the like, all of which may affect their matriculation decisions.

In these days of consumer activism, the timely performance of the latter actions becomes increasingly important. In
addition, it is important that recruiters be informed of such
changes before recruiting efforts are undertaken, so as to avoid
misunderstandings in the recruitment process or the establishment of commitments inconsistent with planned programs or
policies. Further, if the plan contemplates a change in the size
or mix of the student body, recruiting efforts must be tailored
to achieve new enrollment objectives. For example, if the objective of increasing the percentage of students enrolled in the
upper divisions has been defined, recruitment efforts must be
targeted toward bringing in more junior college graduates or
transfer students.

Inasmuch as recruiting efforts usually begin in about
November and intensify through the spring term, plans and
policies affecting the recruitment of students must be approved
by the governing body some six and one-half months before
the beginning of the first fiscal year covered by the plan if the
institution is to adhere to the management philosophy set forth
above. Likewise, even though current American Association
of University Professors (AAUP) guidelines permit notification of faculty retention, promotion, or dismissal to be delayed
until February or March, earlier notification promotes good
employer-employee relations. However, academic planning
must be in place before the institution can consider its faculty
staffing needs and make appropriate retention and promotion
decisions. Thus, to make early notification possible, the timetable should schedule the approval of planned academic programs and staffing requirements in the same six-and-one-half-
month period.

In order to permit timely governing-body approval of institutional plans, the planning process itself must begin early.
The time at which planning efforts must commence can be determined by working backward through the steps of the planning
process:

• Support service program plans should not be developed until
  academic program plans have been agreed upon.

- Academic program plans should not be developed until guidelines based on assumed environmental factors, enrollment projections, and resource availability have been agreed on.
- Academic program plans should be completed before the end of the spring term to avoid the problems that would be caused by the absence of faculty during the summer term.
- Thus, the planning process should start early enough to permit academic planning guidelines to be developed and approved at least two months before the expiration of the spring term.

Table 2 presents a timetable for developing a plan for the period beginning July 1, 1990. This timetable is recommended for an institution whose fiscal year begins on July 1, whose academic calendar comprises two semesters plus a summer program, and whose management processes do not include multi-year planning.

Table 2. Recommended Timetable for Developing a Plan for the Fiscal Year Beginning July 1, 1990.

| Task | Timetable |
|---|---|
| 1. Develop planning assumptions, policy revisions, enrollment projections, resource projections, and academic planning guidelines and obtain governing board approval for these items. | 2/15/89–3/31/89 |
| 2. Develop academic plans and obtain institutional approval for them. | 4/1/89–5/31/89 |
| 3. Develop support service plans and obtain institutional approval for them. | 6/1/89–8/31/89 |
| 4. Consolidate academic and support service plans, complete analytical study group review, and finalize planning document for submission to governing board. | 9/1/89–10/31/89 |
| 5. Obtain governing board approval of the plan. | 11/1/89–12/15/89 |

★   Once approved by the board of trustees, the plan should
be binding on the institution. A plan developed and approved
by an institution's board of trustees or governing body represents
an agreement between the administration and its governing
board as to where the institution is going and what programs
and levels of activity it will use to get there. That is not to say
that a plan, once adopted, becomes cast in concrete, but rather
that the approval of the governing board is required for a change
in a planned program or activity. This does not apply to minor
changes in programs or activities; such management decisions
are expected to be made by the president. It does, however,
preclude the administration from deviating from an approved
course of action without authorization, even when additional
resources are available to do so. For example, should the institution be offered funding to establish a center for international
studies, it should obtain board approval before accepting the
funds if the establishment of such a center is not contemplated
in its plan. On the other hand, if the establishment of such a
center is contemplated in the plan but at a later time, the administration should be able to accept the gift and undertake the
establishment of the center, but it should promptly advise the
board of its actions.

Similarly, the plan, once developed and approved, constitutes an agreement between the president and the senior administrators who are responsible for managing the functional
units of the institution's operations. No plan, regardless of the
extent of participation in its development, will satisfy everyone
who must be involved in its implementation. Nevertheless, it
is imperative that each administrator involved in its implementation adhere to the precepts on which it is based. Differences
of opinion regarding courses of action will exist and administrators will argue for the courses of action they believe most
desirable. Once a decision has been made, embodied in the plan,
and approved by the board, however, administrators must either
adhere to the decision or resign. Likewise, the president must
also adhere to the decision. If he begins a process of rule by
exception, the willingness of other administrators to adhere to
the plan will be undermined and ultimately destroyed.

This is not to say that no deviation from the precepts on which the plan is based can or will take place. In fact, it should be expected that deviations will become necessary or desirable. When such occasions arises, however, the need for or desirability of change should be reviewed with all administrators who will be involved in the implementation of the change or whose operations will be affected by it. In this manner, the change becomes a revision of the planned course of action rather than an exception to it. The occasion for a change of plan can arise during any phase of institutional operation as the result of changes in the environment, changes in resource availability, changes in federal or state regulations, the development of new or more accurate data, and the like.

### Cycles of Operation That Affect Planning

Colleges and universities, like other enterprises, are subject to operating cycles beyond their control. Therefore, institutions must either anticipate these cycles in their planning or react to the cycles as their effects reach them. Obviously, it is to the institution's advantage to plan for such effects rather than to react to them extemporaneously.

Two types of cycles exist — namely, predictable and unpredictable. Predictable cycles have emerged over time in relation to academic timetables and include the academic calendar, the related fiscal calendar, and governmental operations in support of education. Unpredictable cycles are those related to economics, technology, and changes in demand for and supply of trained workers. In this book, we are primarily concerned with the predictable cycles, since these are the ones for which plans can be established to maximize opportunities and minimize negative impacts.

*Academic Calendar Cycles.* The academic calendar has its roots in our agrarian heritage, which required our youth to be available for work on the farm during the growing and harvesting seasons. This heritage still influences the traditional academic calendar, in which fall, winter, and spring are the primary period of academic operations.

The establishment of this academic calendar cycle has resulted in other predictable cycles. Students in the main desire to make decisions about continuing their education before the summer, and colleges and universities need long lead times to prepare to serve students' educational needs. Therefore, a student recruitment cycle from early winter to late spring has become the norm. Because all institutions are competing for students from the same pool at the same time, the institution that shows the students that it can best meet their learning needs in an attractive environment stands the best chance of meeting its enrollment objectives. This in turn dictates that the institution's academic program plans, student services and activity plans, and financial aid plans be clearly articulated in published recruiting material and communicated by its recruiters. Thus, the multi-year planning process must be completed before the recruiting cycle commences.

Both the academic calendar and the student recruitment cycles in turn affect the cycle of faculty recruitment. The results of failure to consider the cyclical nature of this aspect of institutional operation and its impact on individual faculty members have led, over time, to the formulation of a generally accepted schedule for notifying faculty of institutional decisions regarding continued employment and promotion. The need to ensure adequate staffing for academic plans, coupled with the need of departing faculty to find new positions, has caused faculty recruitment to be concentrated between late winter and late spring. Thus, the academic program plans of an institution need to be established before faculty recruiting commences.

Obviously, the impact of anticipated changes in an institution's environment must also be taken into consideration in planning for its future operations. These factors are among the environmental assumption factors related to long-range planning, which is covered later in this chapter.

*Governmental Operations Cycles.* While governmental programs that support higher education are designed to take into consideration the cyclical nature of institutional operations, they also have their own cycles. These cycles are related to the legislative and administrative activities that are tied to their authorization, funding, and implementation; these activities in turn are influenced by factors unrelated to education support needs or the desire to meet those needs.

The cycles of the governmental programs that provide funding for various aspects of institutional operations should be monitored, understood, and taken into consideration in planning. This is particularly true in the case of an institution that plans to serve significant numbers of economically and educationally disadvantaged students or that participates in the federal government's Title III (Developing Institution) program. Care should be taken by the grant and contract administrator and the chief development officer to maintain due-date records for new and renewal grant and contract applications (see Chapters Seven and Eleven for processes that ensure that application deadlines are met). Such institutions' heavy dependence on governmental funding limits their flexibility because all such funds may be used only for specifically designated elements of institutional operations. Such institutions, therefore, must plan carefully in order to maximize the usefulness of these funds in achieving institutional objectives and to avoid seeking funding from programs that lead them away from their objectives.

Heavy dependence on governmental funding also carries with it the need to have systems in place that ensure timely and accurate reporting and accounting. The governmental agencies that administer these programs consider their primary responsibility to be protecting the government and the public from misuse of appropriated and awarded funds. The institution that makes the lives of these agencies' administrators as easy as possible will have its problems and needs more favorably considered than the institution that does not.

The reader should consider how the operations of the institution he or she is concerned about are geared to these cycles. Many chapters in this book — such as Chapter Four, which discusses budgeting — identify timetables of one sort or another that set forth the timing and types of decisions that are related to these cycles. These timetables are important for good management because the failure to make conscious decisions at the right time means that the wrong decision may be arrived at by default.

**Decision Matrix 6. Developing Planning Guidelines.**

Legend of decision-making roles
1 – Authorizes action
2 – Action responsibility
3 – Approves recommendation
4 – Recommends action
5 – Provides input

*Participants in Decision-Making Processes*

| *Procedural Steps* | Board of Trustees | President | Advisory Committee | Planning Committee | Director of Planning | Senior Administrators | Other Administrators | Faculty | Students | Supporting Constituencies | Chief Academic Officer | Chief Student Affairs Officer | Registrar | Recruiting and Admissions Director | Financial Aid Director | Chief Fiscal Officer | Chief Development Officer | Grant and Contract Administration Director |
|---|---|---|---|---|---|---|---|---|---|---|---|---|---|---|---|---|---|---|
| 1. Appoint institutional members of planning committee | 2 | 2 | 4 | | | | | | | | | | | | | | | |
| 2. Select trustee member of planning committee | | 4 | 4 | | | | | | | | | | | | | | | |
| 3. Review existing multi-year plan | 2 | 2 | 5 | 2 | 2 | | | | | | | | | | | | | |
| 4. Revise external environmental assumptions | 5 | 5 | | | 2 | 5 | 5 | 5 | 5 | 5 | | | | | | | | |
| 5. Approve proposed revisions of external environmental assumptions | | 3 | | 4 | 4 | | | | | | | | | | | | | |
| 6. Revise internal environmental assumptions | | 3 | | | 3 | 5 | 5 | 5 | 5 | 5 | | | | | | | | |

| Step | C1 | C2 | C3 | C4 | C5 | C6 | C7 | C8 | C9 | C10 |
|---|---|---|---|---|---|---|---|---|---|---|
| 7. Approve proposed revisions of internal environmental assumptions | 3 | 4 | 5 | | | | | | | |
| 8. Revise mission statement | 5 | | | 5 | 5 | 5 | | | | |
| 9. Revise goals and objectives statement | 5 | | 5 | 5 | 5 | 5 | 2 | 5 | | |
| 10. Approve revised mission and goals and objectives statements | 3 | 4 | | | | 5 | 2 | | | |
| 11. Revise statement of institutional policies | 3 | 2 | 5 | 5 | | | | | | |
| 12. Approve revised statement of institutional policies | 3 | 4 | 5 | 5 | 5 | | | | | |
| 13. Adopt revisions proposed as a result of steps 4 through 12 | 2 | 4 | 5 | | | | 5 | | | |
| 14. Prepare enrollment projection | | | 2 | | | | | 5 | 5 | 5 |
| 15. Approve enrollment projection | 3 | 4 | 5 | | | | | | 5 | 5 |
| 16. Prepare preliminary fiscal projections | | | 5 | | | | | | 5 | 2 |
| 17. Approve preliminary fiscal projections | 3 | 4 | | | | | | | | 5 |
| 18. Appoint analytical studies team | 2 | 4 | | | | | | | | |
| 19. Prepare planning guidelines and request for academic program plans | 1 | 2 | | | | | | | | |
| 20. Issue planning guidelines and request for academic program plans | | 2 | | | | | | | | |

*Explanation of Decision Matrix 6.*

| Step | Action Responsibility | Action |
|---|---|---|
| 1 & 2. | President | Appoints institutional members and recommends appointment of trustee member of planning team on the basis of recommendations from the advisory committee. |
| | Board of Trustees | Appoints trustee member of planning team. |
| 3. | President and Planning Committee | Review existing multi-year plan. |
| 4. | Director of Planning | Formulates recommendations for a statement of external environmental assumptions, to be used in developing a new multi-year plan, on the basis of input from trustees, the president, the advisory committee, supporting constituencies (such as alumni, churches, and community leaders), senior administrators, faculty and student organizations, and other administrators. |

*Explanation of Decision Matrix 6, Cont'd.*

| Step | Action Responsibility | Action |
|------|----------------------|--------|
| 5. | Planning Committee | Reviews the recommended statement of external environmental assumptions submitted by the director of planning for adequacy and acceptability; recommends presidential approval. |
| | President | Approves the statement of external environmental assumptions. |
| 6. | Director of Planning | Formulates recommendations for a statement of internal environmental assumptions, to be used in developing a new multi-year plan, on the basis of input from senior administrators, faculty and student organizations, and other administrators. |
| 7. | Planning Committee | Reviews the recommended statement of internal environmental assumptions and supporting data submitted by the director of plan- |

*Explanation of Decision Matrix 6, Cont'd.*

| *Step* | *Action Responsibility* | *Action* |
|---|---|---|
| | | ning for reasonableness and acceptability; recommends presidential approval. |
| | President | Approves the statement of internal environmental assumptions. |
| 8. | Chief Academic Officer | Reviews the statements of external and internal environmental assumptions and the current mission statement. Formulates recommendations for changes, if any, in mission statement on the basis of input from trustees, supporting constituencies, the chief student affairs officer, and faculty organizations. |
| 9. | Chief Academic Officer | Formulates recommendations for changes in the statements of goals and objectives on the basis of the statements of external and internal environmental assumptions, recommended revisions of |

*Explanation of Decision Matrix 6, Cont'd.*

| Step | Action Responsibility | Action |
|------|----------------------|--------|
| | | the mission statement, and input from trustees, other senior administrators, faculty and student organizations, supporting constituencies, and other administrators. |
| 10. | Planning Committee | Reviews recommended changes to the statements of mission, goals, and objectives submitted by the chief academic officer for appropriateness and acceptability; recommends presidential approval. |
| | President | Approves recommended revisions of the statements of mission, goals, and objectives. |
| 11. | Director of Planning | Reviews the statements of internal and external environmental assumptions, the statement of changes in mission, goals, and objectives, and current policy statements. Formulates recommended |

*Explanation of Decision Matrix 6, Cont'd.*

| *Step* | *Action Responsibility* | *Action* |
|--------|------------------------|----------|
| | | changes in policies on the basis of these statements and input from faculty, students, and administrators whose operations or activities would be affected by the recommended policy changes. |
| 12. | Planning Committee | Reviews recommended changes in policy submitted by the director of planning for appropriateness, acceptability, and effects on institutional operations; recommends presidential approval. |
| | President | Approves recommended policy changes. |
| 13. | President | Submits statements of external and internal environmental assumptions and proposed changes in mission, goals, objectives, and policies to the board of trustees with a recommendation that they be approved. |
| | Board of Trustees | Reviews planning guidelines, obtaining clarification from the president, the chief academic officer, and the |

*Explanation of Decision Matrix 6, Cont'd.*

| Step | Action Responsibility | Action |
|------|----------------------|--------|
| | | director of planning; approves the guidelines and authorizes the president to complete the multi-year planning process based on them. |
| 14. | Director of Planning | Prepares enrollment projections on the basis of input from the registrar, the director of recruiting and admissions, the director of financial aid, and the chief fiscal officer (about the number of currently enrolled students likely to be denied readmission for financial reasons). |
| 15. | Planning Committee | Reviews enrollment projections submitted by the director of planning for reasonableness and acceptability; recommends presidential approval. |
| | President | Approves enrollment projections. |
| 16. | Chief Fiscal Officer | Prepares preliminary resource availability and allocation projections on the basis of the approved enrollment projection and |

*Explanation of Decision Matrix 6, Cont'd.*

| *Step* | *Action Responsibility* | *Action* |
|---|---|---|
| | | input from senior administrators, the chief development officer, the director of grant and contract administration, and the director of financial aid. |
| 17. | Planning Committee | Reviews preliminary resource availability and allocation projections submitted by the chief fiscal officer for completeness and reasonability; recommends presidential approval. |
| | President | Approves preliminary resource availability and allocation projections. |
| 18. | President | Appoints members of the analytical studies team on the basis of recommendations made by the advisory committee. |
| 19 & 20. | Director of Planning | When authorized by the president, prepares and issues letter requesting that academic departments prepare their academic program plans and transmitting for their guidance the planning guidelines developed as a result of steps 1 through 17. |

Decision Matrix 7. Developing Academic Program Plans.

| Legend of decision-making roles | | | | | | | | |
|---|---|---|---|---|---|---|---|---|
| 1 – Authorizes action | | | | | | | | |
| 2 – Action responsibility | | | | | | | | |
| 3 – Approves recommendation | | | | | | | | |
| 4 – Recommends action | | | | | | | | |
| 5 – Provides input | | | | | | | | |

| Procedural Steps | Participants in Decision-Making Processes | | | | | | | |
|---|---|---|---|---|---|---|---|---|
| | President | Planning Committee | Director of Planning | Chief Academic Officer | Department Heads | Department Faculty | Faculty Committee | Registrar |
| 1. Establish academic planning parameters | | | 5 | 2 | 4 | | | 5 |
| 2. Develop departmental program plans | | | | | 2 | 5 | | |
| 3. Review departmental program plans | | | | 2 | 4 | | | |
| 4. Synthesize departmental program plans | 5 | | | 2 | | | 4 | |
| 5. Summarize academic program plans | | | 2 | 1 | | | | |
| 6. Review academic program plans | 3 | 4 | 5 | 5 | | | | |
| 7. Prepare request for support service departmental program plans | | | 2 | | | | | |
| 8. Issue request for support service departmental program plans | 1 | | 2 | | | | | |

*Explanation of Decision Matrix 7.*

| Step | Action Responsibility | Action |
|------|----------------------|--------|
| 1. | Chief Academic Officer | Obtains from the registrar historical data regarding student demand for instruction, course and section offerings, faculty staffing, and faculty loads for each academic area. Meets with department heads and, with assistance from the director of planning, reviews approved planning guidelines and documentation requirements and establishes a timetable for the completion of academic planning. |
| 2. | Department Heads | Meet with departmental faculty to review planning guidelines, documentation requirements, and planning timetable. Obtain faculty recommendations for changes in departmental operations and complete planning documents for departments. |
| 3 & 4. | Chief Academic Officer | Reviews the departmental plans submitted by each department head for acceptability and con- |

*Explanation of Decision Matrix 7, Cont'd.*

| Step | Action Responsibility | Action |
|------|----------------------|--------|
| | | sistency with planning guidelines. Reviews composite plans for all departments to ensure that planned departmental programs are properly integrated and that gaps and overlaps are eliminated. Reviews composite plan with appropriate faculty committees and obtains their recommendations. Reviews composite plan and faculty committee recommendations with president. Notifies faculty committees of decisions reached regarding their recommendations. |
| 5. | Director of Planning | Prepares summary of academic program plans when authorized to do so by the chief academic officer. |
| 6. | Planning Committee | Reviews the academic program plan summary submitted by the director of planning, obtaining clarification from the chief academic officer; recommends presidential approval. |

*Explanation of Decision Matrix 7, Cont'd.*

| Step | Action Responsibility | Action |
|------|----------------------|--------|
|      | President | Approves academic program plan summary. |
| 7. | Director of Planning | Prepares letter for the president's signature requesting that senior administrators of support service activity areas prepare their program plans and transmitting to them planning guidelines, academic program plan summaries, and forms to be used. |
| 8. | Director of Planning | Obtains the president's signature and authorization to issue a letter requesting the preparation of support program plans; issues the letter. |

## Decision Matrix 8. Developing Support Service Program Plans.

Legend of decision-making roles

1 – Authorizes action
2 – Action responsibility
3 – Approves recommendation
4 – Recommends action
5 – Provides input

*Participants in Decision-Making Processes*

| Procedural Steps | President | Planning Committee | Director of Planning | Senior Administrators | Department Heads | Departmental Staff |
|---|---|---|---|---|---|---|
| 1. Establish support service planning parameters | | | | 2 | 4 | |
| 2. Develop support service departmental program plans | | | | | 2 | 4 |
| 3. Review support service departmental program plans of each department | | | | 2 | 4 | |
| 4. Synthesize support service departmental program plans of each department | | | | 2 | | |
| 5. Synthesize all support service program plans | 5 | | 2 | 5 | | |
| 6. Summarize support service program plans | 1 | | 2 | 5 | | |
| 7. Review support service program plans | 3 | 4 | 5 | 5 | | |
| 8. Prepare request for analytical studies team's evaluation of academic and support service program plans | 1 | | 2 | | | |

*Explanation of Decision Matrix 8.*

| *Step* | *Action Responsibility* | *Action* |
|--------|------------------------|----------|
| 1. | Senior Administrators | Each senior administrator, including the chief academic officer, meets with his support service department heads to review approved planning guidelines, planning forms, and documentation requirements and to establish a timetable for completion of support service planning. |
| 2. | Department Heads | Meet with departmental staff to review planning guidelines, documentation requirements, and timetable. Obtain staff recommendations for changes in departmental operation and complete planning forms and documentation for the department. |
| 3 & 4. | Senior Administrators | Each senior administrator reviews plans submitted by each department head for acceptability and consistency with planning guidelines. Reviews composite plans for all departments reporting to him to be sure that departmental |

*Explanation of Decision Matrix 8, Cont'd.*

| *Step* | *Action Responsibility* | *Action* |
|------|-----|-----|
| | | plans are integrated and that gaps and overlaps are eliminated. |
| 5. | Director of Planning | Receives departmental plans from all senior administrators. Reviews plans to ensure that all required support service activities are provided for and properly integrated and that no overlaps exist. Meets with president and senior administrators to discuss the results of this review and obtain their concurrence for any changes identified. |
| 6. | Director of Planning | When authorized by the president, prepares support service program plan summaries for all areas of activity and reviews summaries with senior administrators. |
| 7. | Planning Committee | Reviews support service plan summaries submitted by the director of planning, obtaining clarification from senior administrators. |

*Explanation of Decision Matrix 8, Cont'd.*

| *Step* | *Action Responsibility* | *Action* |
|--------|------------------------|----------|
|        | President               | Approves support service program plans. |
| 8.     | Director of Planning    | When authorized, prepares a letter for the president's signature requesting that the analytical studies team review all academic and support service plans and transmitting such plans and planning guideline documentation. |

**Decision Matrix 9. Final Review and Approval.**

Legend of decision-making roles
1 – Authorizes action
2 – Action responsibility
3 – Approves recommendation
4 – Recommends action
5 – Provides input

Participants in Decision-Making Processes

| Procedural Steps | Board of Trustees | President | Planning Committee | Director of Planning | Chief Fiscal Officer | Analytical Studies Team | Senior Administrators | Department Heads | Faculty | Staff |
|---|---|---|---|---|---|---|---|---|---|---|
| 1. Prepare revised revenue and expense projections | | | | | 2 | | | | | |
| 2. Issue request for analytical studies team's evaluation of plan | | | | 2 | | | | | | |
| 3. Evaluate plan | | | | | | 2 | 5 | 5 | 5 | 5 |
| 4. Review analytical studies team's evaluation | | 3 | 4 | | | 5 | 5 | 5 | 5 | |
| 5. Revise plan to reflect approved changes that result from analytical studies team's evaluation | | 1 | | 2 | 5 | | | | | |
| 6. Authorize implementation of plan | 1 | 4 | | 5 | | | 5 | | | |
| 7. Distribute approved plan and request preparation of annual operating budget and, where appropriate, revisions of catalogue, student, faculty, and staff handbooks, recruiting materials, and financial aid material | | 1 | | 2 | | | | | | |

*Explanation of Decision Matrix 9.*

| Step | Action Responsibility | Action |
|------|----------------------|--------|
| 1. | Chief Fiscal Officer | Prepares revised revenue and expenditure projections on the basis of approved academic and support service plans. |
| 2. | Director of Planning | Receives revised revenue and expenditure projections from the chief fiscal officer. Obtains the president's signature on a letter requesting the analytical studies team's review of the multi-year plan. Transmits the request and multi-year plan documents to the analytical studies team. |
| 3. | Analytical Studies Team | Reviews multi-year plan documents for proper integration of activities, completeness of coverage, consistency with planning guidelines, and assurance that it represents the most effective and efficient way of accomplishing planned goals and objectives. Obtains input and clarification from administrators, faculty, and staff. Recommends changes it considers desirable. |
| 4. | Planning Committee | Reviews planning change recommendations submitted |

*Explanation of Decision Matrix 9, Cont'd.*

| *Step* | *Action Responsibility* | *Action* |
|--------|------------------------|----------|
| | | by the analytical studies team, obtaining clarification from the team's chairperson. Determines which changes are desirable and recommends that they be approved by the president. |
| | President | Approves planning committee's recommendations. |
| 5. | Director of Planning | When authorized by the president, obtains revised revenue and expenditure projections from the chief fiscal officer and revises the multi-year plan to incorporate approved changes resulting from the analytical studies team's review. |
| 6. | President | Submits multi-year plan to the board of trustees with his recommendation for its approval. |
| | Board of Trustees | Reviews multi-year plan, obtaining clarification from the president, the director of planning, and senior administrators. Authorizes implementation of plan. |

*Explanation of Decision Matrix 9, Cont'd.*

| Step | Action Responsibility | Action |
|------|----------------------|--------|
| 7. | Director of Planning | When authorized by the president, prepares a letter for the president's signature requesting that administrators begin preparation of the annual operating budget; distributes the letter, along with copies of the approved plan, to the administrators. Also requests appropriate administrators to institute procedures as necessary to revise publications to reflect changes in program, policy, fee structure, and the like embodied in the approved plan. |

# The Budget Process

Although the preparation of the annual operating and capital project budgets is separate from the preparation of the multi-year plan, the two processes are linked. The annual operating budget should be a more detailed, refined version of the first year of the plan. While it is expressed in dollars and cents, the annual operating budget represents the identification of the types and extent of personnel, equipment, and other resources deemed necessary to carry out the academic programs or other activities authorized by the plan and a projection of where the funds to support these resources are expected to come from. The annual capital project budget, which must meet different standards and is prepared through different processes, should be a separate document from the annual operating budget.

## The Annual Operating Budget

The essential standards of good management in the preparation of the annual operating budget and its use as a management evaluation and control tool are set forth below.

★ Significant deviations in program or level of activity between the budget and the first year of the multi-year plan approved by the board of trustees should be limited to those resulting from significant, unanticipated changes in circumstances. The nature of these changes in circumstances and their impact on planned institutional operations should be documented and identified in the budget document submitted to the board of trustees for adoption.

★   Separate expenditure budgets should be prepared for each operating unit that, as determined by the administration, is to be separately controlled and reported on. Such operating units essentially should follow the organizational structure determined to be appropriate for the institution. Thus, the administrator of each operational unit should be involved in the preparation of an expenditure budget showing the resources required to carry out the programs or level of activity authorized in the first year of the multi-year plan for his unit. Subsequently, each administrator should be held responsible for the management of allocated resources and for seeing to it that all agreed-on programs and activities are carried out. These operational unit budgets are hereinafter referred to as departmental budgets.

★   Departmental budgets should cover all operations of the institution, including those covered by restricted funds, and should identify the portion of each category of expense that is covered by restricted gifts, grants, or contracts.

★   All department heads who are required to prepare a budget request should be provided with data on the current year's budget and projected operating costs. Those data, coupled with the approved multi-year plan data, will help them ensure that they make budgetary provision for all types of expenses that will be charged to their budgets and that such budgetary provisions are adequate to cover the level of activity for which they are responsible.

★   Revenue projections should be classified in accordance with those established by the American Institution of Certified Public Accountants (AICPA) in their *AICPA Audit Guide for Colleges and Universities* and the National Association of College and

University Business Officers' publication *CUBA-74, 1982 Edition*. Revenue from restricted gifts, grants, and contracts should not exceed the combined total of restricted expenditures included in departmental budgets plus related indirect costs or overhead recovery.

★ The categories of expenses identified in each departmental budget should be uniform for all budgets and should be consistent with the level of detail determined by the institution to be required for effective budgetary control. However, under no circumstances should the level of detail considered necessary for budgetary control exceed the level of detail of the classifications of expenses being maintained in the accounting system. This standard is designed to facilitate the use of budgetary reporting as a management tool for evaluation and control of operations. The standardization of categories of expenses in departmental budgets facilitates the consolidation of budgets for those administrators who manage the affairs of a number of operating departments. Limiting the categories of expenses to those deemed necessary for effective evaluation and control minimizes the concern with overspending and underspending where they are not really important. The limitation of detail to the level maintained in the accounting system permits the preparation of reports comparing actual expenses to budgeted expenses without requiring manual analyses of actual expenses. For example, it is normally considered desirable to establish separate budgets for in-state and out-of-state travel. However, if all travel expenses are classified as one category of expense in the institution's accounting system, such a budgetary separation would be undesirable because it would require manual analyses of all travel expense transactions to produce a report comparing actual to budgeted expense.

In determining the level of detail at which budgetary control categories should be established, the implications associated with each major category of expense should be considered. Expense budgets should be divided into at least three major categories: personnel services, equipment and books, and other costs of operation. Personnel services represent a staffing commitment extending into the future. Equipment and books represent investments that have a useful life of more than one year; there need not be a recurring expense for the same items every year. Other costs of operation represent either fixed annual commitments for debt service or variable costs (supplies, travel, postage) that can fluctuate from year to year depending on the availability of funds or circumstances beyond institutional control. These three major categories of expenses, however, are too broad to permit effective control or management evaluation. Therefore, each major category should be divided, at the very minimum, into the following budgetary control subcategories. The cost of personnel services should be divided into the subcategories of salaries and wages, student employment, and fringe benefits; equipment and books into the subcategories of equipment and library acquisitions; and other costs of operation into the subcategories of travel, supplies, utilities, telephone, debt service, mandatory transfers, goods purchased for resale, publications and printing, financial aid awards, postage, and miscellaneous. Obviously, better evaluation and control will be achieved by increasing the number of subcategories. But how far an institution can or should go depends on the extent of control and flexibility it wishes in the operations of its administrators and the limitations of its accounting system.

★   When an employee provides services to more than one department, each department's budget should bear its pro rata share of the cost of compensation, both salary or wages and benefits. Further, the projected cost of other types of expense that are incurred for the benefit of more than one department should be provided for equitably among the benefiting departmental budgets if the accounting system is capable of allocating costs equitably among the departments. This permits the budget, to the extent that it is practical, to reveal the full cost of the operations of each departmental unit. Examples of the types of expense to be considered for allocation are insurance, utilities, telephone, postage, and debt service.

★   Each administrator who is responsible for supervising the activities of more than one department for which a budget has been prepared should be provided with a consolidated budget of all departments under his jurisdiction. Consolidated budgets should be at the same level of detail as the departmental budgets. They should also be consistent with the management hierarchy established in the institution's tables of organization.

★ A separate budget should be prepared to cover costs associated with the academic portion of summer school operations; the projected revenue generated by these operations should be separately identified. The revenues and costs of summer school operations should include only those that would not be received or incurred unless a summer school program was conducted. All other departmental revenues and costs should be included in the regular departmental budgets. The projected revenues and costs of summer school operations should be a part of the budget for the fiscal year in which the majority of summer program activities are carried out. For example, if an institution's fiscal year runs from July 1 to June 30 and its summer program runs from June 15 to August 15, all revenues and costs should be contained in the budget for the fiscal year beginning July 1.

★ Planned voluntary transfers of current operating funds to cover the cost of capital projects or for investment in endowment funds should be reflected in the annual operating budget. Transfers to cover the cost of capital projects would then appear as a source of revenue in the annual capital project budget.

★ A statement of budgetary philosophy and policy should be published. The statement should cover the following points:

1. The adoption of a budget by the board of trustees constitutes its authorization to the administration to carry out the programs and levels of activity that underlie the expenditure levels contained therein, provided the revenues projected in the budget are in fact realized. The president is authorized to reduce planned programs, levels of activity, and expenditures where changes in revenue realization expectations so warrant. The president, however, may not expand pro-

grams, institute unauthorized programs, or increase levels of activity or the overall expenditure levels without board authorization, even if additional or unanticipated revenues have become available.

2.  Budgetary savings that do not curtail authorized activities (such as those resulting from unfilled positions, employee turnover, or gifts in kind of equipment, materials, or services covered by the budget) should revert to the board's control. They should be used for current operations only upon the board's specific authorization through its adoption of a revised budget. All unexpended funds at the end of the fiscal year should revert to the board's control.

3.  The level at which administrators are authorized to transfer funds between categories of expense in departmental budgets—as well as to whom such authority is delegated and which, if any, transfers should be reported to the board of trustees—should be established. The president and the board must be informed in advance of any proposed transfer of funds that would impose a commitment on future budgets and operations. The following delegation of authority has worked successfully at some institutions: department heads may transfer funds between subcategories of expense within each major category of expense; senior administrators may authorize department heads to transfer funds between major categories of expense within their own budgets and may authorize the transfer of funds between departmental budgets (provided no ongoing commitment is involved in such transfers); and the president may authorize transfers between the four major functional areas of operation.

4.  The president's contingency fund contained in the budget should be used only to cover unanticipated increases in the cost of carrying out approved programs or levels of activity (unless other purposes are identified in the budget). Should the board of trustees desire to provide the president with discretionary funds to permit him to pursue opportunities that may arise during the year, such funds should be budgeted separately from the president's contingency fund.

★   Procedures should exist for the preparation and revision of the budget. The procedures should identify the following: the timetable to be followed and forms to be used; the budget requests to be initiated by each department head; the support justification detail required for budget requests for equipment purchases, travel, alterations and improvements, major renovation and repair projects, printing and publications, and contracted services; the support justification detail required for budget requests that deviate significantly from the approved multi-year plan; and budget screening and approval processes.

★   The budget for each fiscal year should be adopted by the board of trustees at least two months prior to the beginning of that fiscal year.

★   The budget should be reviewed and revised as necessary to reflect changes in revenue projections and expenses at least once each semester. Revised budgets should also be submitted to the board of trustees for approval.

Procedures for the development and revision of the annual operating budget are shown in Decision Matrices 10 and 11.

### The Annual Capital Project Budget

A capital project expenditure budget should be prepared and submitted to the board of trustees for approval in each year in which expenditures are anticipated for the acquisition of land, the improvement of land, the construction or major renovation of buildings, or the creation of a master plan for the development of the campus. The budget should identify the projected sources of revenue and types of expenses for the project during the ensuing fiscal year as well as the estimated time for completion of each project, the estimated costs or revisions of existing cost estimates, and anticipated sources of revenue to meet estimated costs. Board approval of a capital project involves a multi-year commitment, unlike the limited, one-year authorization for annual operating expenditures.

The following essential standards should be applied to the preparation and revision of capital project budgets:

★   A separate capital budget should be prepared and board approval should be obtained for each capital project before it is begun. A revised capital budget should be submitted and approved for continued authorization to incur costs at the completion of each phase of a capital project, or prior to completion if the cost to be incurred exceeds the authorized amount. Specifically, board authorization to incur costs for a capital project should be obtained for expenditures related to construction project feasibility studies or land acquisition negotiations if they cannot be carried out by existing personnel with resources made available by the annual operating budget; the actual closing for the acquisition of land; and construction or major renovation projects at the time of the appointment of architects, the approval of architectural design, the preparation of bid documents, the approval of bid documents, the solicitation of bids, the awarding of construction contracts, and the approval of major changes in project scope or design during construction.

★   Each capital budget or revision related to the construction or major renovation of facilities should identify the cost of each major component of the project. Major components include construction; site improvement (utility hookups, walks, landscaping, parking); architectural services for project design, preparation of bid documents, and construction supervision; furniture and movable equipment; construction supervision beyond that provided by the architect; and contingency funds.

★   The chief fiscal officer should be responsible for assuring the president and the board of trustees that provisions have been included in each capital project budget to cover the costs of all aspects of the project.

★   The president and the board of trustees should be aware of the following principles related to the execution of authorized capital projects, even though they are not directly related to the preparation of capital project budgets, because they can affect the cost of construction.

★ When authorizing the execution of a project from the selection of architects to the project's completion, the board of trustees should designate one person to act as the owner's representative, identifying the level of authority delegated to him and to whom he reports. Preferably, this person should be an engineer and should not be an employee of the architectural firm selected for the project.

★ From this point on, the owner's representative should be responsible for the preparation of all capital project budget revisions.

★ The clearance of legal counsel should be required for all aspects of the project that involve specifications or contracts. Legal counsel should be held responsible for ensuring that the institution's rights are protected by such documents.

★ Bid documents should include specifications that cover defined limits of the construction site and the contractor's access to the site; the contractor's requirements for the security and safety of the site; title to material and supplies covered by partial payments; insurance and bonding coverage the contractor is required to maintain; sample and test material the contractor is required to furnish and acceptance procedures for it; the contractor's requirements to provide as-built drawings, operating and maintenance manuals for systems installed, and training for institutional maintenance staff in required operating and maintenance procedures; and pricing procedures for change orders and extras.

★ The director of physical plant should be involved in the review and approval of project design and specifications to the degree necessary to identify their effects on future custodial, operational, and maintenance service requirements.

★ Space allocations and relationships, the provision of special services or equipment, traffic flow requirements, and the like should be determined by the administration on the basis of input from the occupants and the recommendation of their senior administrators.

Procedures covering the development and revision of capital budgets are set forth in Decision Matrix 12.

*Explanation of Decision Matrix 10.*

| Step | Action Responsibility | Action |
|------|----------------------|--------|
| 1. | Chief Fiscal Officer | Formulates recommended annual operating budget policies and procedures on the basis of input from senior administrators, other department heads, and student organizations. |
| 2. | Advisory Committee | Reviews recommended policies and procedures submitted by the chief fiscal officer for appropriateness and effect on operations; recommends presidential approval. |
| | President | Approves recommended policies and procedures. |
| 3. | Board of Trustees | Reviews recommended policies, obtaining clarification from the president and the chief fiscal officer; adopts policies. |
| 4 & 5. | Chief Fiscal Officer | Receives the president's authorization to implement approved policies and procedures and distributes them to administrators who are required to prepare budgets, together with a request for the preparation of budget requests, current expenditure level data, and forms to be used. |

**Decision Matrix 10. Development and Delegated Revisions of Annual Operating Budget.**

Legend of decision-making roles
1 – Authorizes action
2 – Action responsibility
3 – Approves recommendation
4 – Recommends action
5 – Provides input

*Participants in Decision-Making Processes*

| Procedural Steps | Board of Trustees | President | Advisory Committee | Chief Academic Officer | Chief Student Affairs Officer | Chief Fiscal Officer | Chief Development Officer | Director of Planning | Department Heads | Departmental Faculty and Staff | Student Organizations | Budget Control | Recruiting and Admissions Director | Financial Aid Director | Registrar | Grant and Contract Administration Director | Managers of Auxiliary Enterprises |
|---|---|---|---|---|---|---|---|---|---|---|---|---|---|---|---|---|---|
| 1. Develop annual operating budget policies and procedures | | 3 | | 5 | 5 | 4 | 5 | | 5 | 5 | | | | | | | |
| 2. Review and approve recommended policies and procedures | | 4 | 4 | | | | | | | | | | | | | | |
| 3. Adopt annual operating budget policies | 2 | | | | | 5 | | | | | | | | | | | |
| 4. Authorize implementation of policies and procedures | | 1 | | | | 5 | | | | | | | | | | | |
| 5. Issue budget preparation request | | | | | | 2 | | | | 5 | | | | | | | |
| 6. Prepare annual operating budget requests | | 2 | | 2 | 2 | 2 | 2 | 2 | 2 | 2 | | | | | | | 2 |

7. Screen and recommend approval of departmental budget requests for

| | | | | | | | | | | |
|---|---|---|---|---|---|---|---|---|---|---|
| (a) academic activities | | 4 | | | 5 | | | | | |
| (b) student affairs and student government activities | | | 4 | 4 | 5 | 5 | | 5 | 5 | 5 | 5 |
| (c) student union and student housing activities | | | 4 | 3 | 5 | | | | | |
| (d) business and fiscal and other auxiliary enterprise activities | | | | 4 | 5 | | | | | |
| (e) development activities | | | | 4 | 5 | | | | | |
| 8. Receive, analyze, and consolidate budget requests | 5 | 5 | 5 | 2 | 2 | | 5 | 5 | 5 | 5 |
| 9. Prepare revenue projections | | | 2 | 5 | | | | | |
| 10. Review and approve recommended consolidated budget | 3 | 4 | | | | | | | |
| 11. Adopt annual operating budget | 2 | 4 | 5 | 5 | 5 | | 5 | | | |
| 12. Implement authorized budget activities | | 1 | 2 | 2 | 2 | 2 | 2 | | | |
| 13. Issue delegated authorization to transfer budgeted funds | | | | | | | | | | |
| (a) between subcategories within major categories of expense | | | | | | 2 | | 2 | 5 |
| (b) between major categories of expense within departments | | | 2 | 2 | 2 | 4 | | 2 | 5 |
| (c) between departments | | | 2 | 2 | 2 | 4 | | 2 | 5 |
| (d) between functional operating areas | | 2 | 4 | 4 | 4 | 1 | 2 | 2 | 5 |
| 14. Revise budgets | | | | | | | | 2 | |

*Explanation of Decision Matrix 10, Cont'd.*

| Step | Action Responsibility | Action |
|------|----------------------|--------|
| 6. | Senior Administrators | Review approved multi-year plan and prepare annual operating budget requests on the basis of input from faculty and staff. |
| 7. | Senior Administrators | Screen and recommend approval of budget requests submitted by the heads of departments or organizations for which they are administratively responsible. |
| 8 & 9. | Chief Fiscal Officer | Receives recommended budget requests submitted by senior administrators. Reviews them for reasonableness, consistency with the multi-year plan, and mathematical accuracy. Prepares consolidated budgets related to hierarchical organizational structure, summary budgets for submission to the board of trustees, and final revenue projections based on input from the chief development officer, the director of recruiting and admissions, the registrar, the director of financial aid, the director of grant and contract administration, and |

*Explanation of Decision Matrix 10, Cont'd.*

| *Step* | *Action Responsibility* | *Action* |
|--------|------------------------|----------|
| | | managers of auxiliary enterprise units. |
| 10. | Advisory Committee | Reviews the recommended consolidated budget submitted by the chief fiscal officer for reasonableness and consistency with the approved multiyear plan; recommends presidential approval. |
| | President | Approves recommended budget. |
| 11. | President | Submits summarized recommended budget to the board of trustees with a recommendation for its adoption. |
| | Board of Trustees | Reviews budget request, obtaining clarification from the president and senior administrators; adopts recommended budget. |
| 12. | Chief Fiscal Officer and Auxiliary Enterprises Managers | Receive the president's authorization to implement the |

*Explanation of Decision Matrix 10, Cont'd.*

| Step | Action Responsibility | Action |
|------|----------------------|--------|
| | | approved budget and enter budget data into the general ledger accounting system. Distribute approved budgets to senior administrators, department heads, and student organizations. |
| | Senior Administrators, Department Heads, and Student Organizations | Carry out activities and programs authorized by the approved budget. |
| 13 & 14. | Chief Fiscal Officer | Receives notification of the desire to transfer budget funds and verifies that the funds requested are available for transfer. Also verifies that the notification contains the necessary authorizations delegated by the board of trustees or required by sponsored agreements: that transfers between line items within a departmental budget are authorized by the |

*Explanation of Decision Matrix 10, Cont'd.*

| *Step* | *Action Responsibility* | *Action* |
|--------|------------------------|----------|
| | | department head; that transfers between major categories of expense within a departmental budget have been authorized by the department heads and approved by their senior administrator; that transfers between departments under the supervision of a single senior administrator have been authorized by both department heads and approved by the senior administrator; that transfers between functional areas have been approved by both senior administrators and approved by the president; and that all transfers that involve sponsored agreement funds have been approved by the director of grant and contract administration. |
| | Budget Control | Records budgetary transfers when authorized to do so by the chief fiscal officer. |

# Decision Matrix 11. Annual Operating Budget—Board-Authorized Revisions.

Legend of decision-making roles

1 – Authorizes action
2 – Action responsibility
3 – Approves recommendation
4 – Recommends action
5 – Provides input

*Participants in Decision-Making Processes*

| Procedural Steps | Board of Trustees | President | Advisory Committee | Chief Academic Officer | Chief Student Affairs Officer | Chief Fiscal Officer | Chief Development Officer | Director of Planning | Department Heads | Departmental Faculty and Staff | Budget Control | Grant and Contract Administration Director | Managers of Auxiliary Enterprises |
|---|---|---|---|---|---|---|---|---|---|---|---|---|---|
| 1. Identify budget savings that do not curtail authorized programs or levels of activity | | | | | | 2 | | | | | 5 | | |
| 2. Delete savings from authorized budgets | | | | | | 1 | | | | | 2 | | |
| 3. Identify increases in resource availability over that projected in budget resulting from increases in earned income or gift, grant, or contract income | | | | | | 2 | 5 | | | | | 5 | 5 |
| 4. Identify opportunities to strengthen or expand existing programs and activities or to accelerate planned implementation of new programs and activities or strengthening and expansion of existing programs | | | | 3 | | 3 | 5 | 5 | 4 | 5 | | | |

|  | | | | | | | |
|---|---|---|---|---|---|---|---|
| 5. Review opportunities and new fund availability and recommend submission of a revised budget to the board | 3 | 4 | 5 | 5 | 5 | 5 | 5 |
| 6. Prepare revised budget | 1 | | 5 | 5 | 2 | 5 | |
| 7. Review and approve revised budget | 3 | 4 | | | 5 | | |
| 8. Obtain board of trustees' approval for revised budget | | | | | | | |
| budget | 2 | 4 | | | 5 | | |
| 9. Authorize implementation of revised budget | 1 | | | | 2 | | |
| 10. Distribute revised budget | | | | | 2 | | |

*Explanation of Decision Matrix 11.*

| Step | Action Responsibility | Action |
|------|----------------------|--------|
| 1. | Chief Fiscal Officer | Receives input from budget control regarding departmental budgets where planned expenditure levels are not required owing to salary savings resulting from turnover or unfulfilled positions or to gifts in kind. |
| 2. | Budget Control | Deletes from departmental budget, when authorized to do so by the chief fiscal officer, the budgetary savings identified in step 1. |
| 3. | Chief Fiscal Officer | Identifies increases in resource availability, in excess of that projected in the budget, resulting from new grants or contracts, unrestricted gifts in excess of revenue projections, and auxiliary enterprise revenue in excess of revenue projections. |
| 4. | Senior Administrators | Formulate recommendations regarding opportunities to expand authorized programs or activity levels, or accelerate the implemen- |

*Explanation of Decision Matrix 11, Cont'd.*

| Step | Action Responsibility | Action |
|------|----------------------|--------|
| | | tation of such expansion or planned new programs, obtaining input from faculty and staff and recommendations from department heads. |
| 5. | Advisory Committee | Reviews recommendations submitted by senior administrators as a result of step 4 and additional resource availability resulting from steps 1 and 3. Determines whether and how additional resources should be used to take advantage of recommended opportunities and recommends that the president authorize the submission of a revised budget to the board of trustees. |
| | President | Approves advisory committee's recommendation. |
| 6. | Chief Fiscal Officer | Prepares, when authorized by the president, a revised budget for submission to the board of trustees. |
| 7. | Advisory Committee | Reviews revised budget submitted by the chief fiscal officer for consis- |

*Explanation of Decision Matrix 11, Cont'd.*

| Step | Action Responsibility | Action |
|------|----------------------|--------|
| | | tency with its recommendations and recommends presidential approval. |
| | President | Approves revised budget. |
| 8. | President | Submits revised budget to the board of trustees with a recommendation for its adoption. |
| | Board of Trustees | Reviews revised budget, obtaining clarification from the president and the chief fiscal officer; adopts revised budget. |
| 9 & 10. | Chief Fiscal Officer | Receives the president's authorization to implement the revised budget adopted by the board of trustees and distributes revised budgets to affected administrators and budget control. |

## Decision Matrix 12. Capital Projects.

Legend of decision-making roles:
1 – Authorizes action
2 – Action responsibility
3 – Approves recommendation
4 – Recommends action
5 – Provides input

Participants in Decision-Making Processes

| Procedural Steps | Board of Trustees | Legal Counsel | Architect | Owner's Representative | Bidders or Contractor | President | Advisory Committee | Chief Fiscal Officer | Chief Development Officer | Chief Academic Officer | Chief Student Affairs Officer | Director of Planning | Building Occupants | Director of Physical Plant |
|---|---|---|---|---|---|---|---|---|---|---|---|---|---|---|
| 1. Identify capital project need | | | | | | | | | | | | | | |
| 2. Review and approve submission of recommendation for a capital project to the board of trustees | 2 | | | | | 3 | 4 | 2 | 2 | 2 | 2 | 2 | | 2 |
| 3. Approve conduct of a feasibility study | | | | | | 4 | | 5 | 5 | 5 | 5 | 5 | | 5 |
| 4. Determine feasibility of project | | | | | | 3 | | 4 | | 5 | 5 | 5 | | 5 |
| 5. Authorize proceeding with project | 2 | | | | | 4 | | 5 | 5 | | | | | |
| 6. Appoint owner's representative | 2 | | | | | 4 | | | | | | | | |
| 7. Recommend architectural contract award | | 5 | | 4 | | 3 | | 5 | | | | | | |
| 8. Authorize award of architectural contract | 2 | 5 | | 5 | | 4 | | 5 | | | | | | |
| 9. Execute architectural contract | | | 2 | | | 1 | | 2 | | | | | | |
| 10. Develop conceptual design documents | | | 2 | 4 | | 3 | | 5 | | | | | 5 | 5 |
| 11. Approve conceptual design and authorize preparation of bid documents | 2 | 5 | 5 | 5 | | 4 | | | | | | | | |
| 12. Develop bid documents | | | 2 | 4 | | 3 | | | | | | | 5 | 5 |
| 13. Approve bid documents and authorize solicitation of bids | 2 | 5 | 5 | 4 | | 4 | | 5 | | | | | | |
| 14. Obtain bids and recommend award of contract | | 5 | 5 | 4 | 5 | 3 | | 5 | | | | | | |
| 15. Authorize award of contract | 2 | 5 | 5 | 5 | 5 | 4 | | 5 | | | | | | |
| 16. Execute contract | | 5 | 5 | 5 | 2 | 1 | | 2 | | | | | | |

*Explanation of Decision Matrix 12.*

| Step | Action Responsibility | Action |
|------|----------------------|--------|
| 1. | Senior Administrators | Identify the desirability of and recommend acquiring land; installing fences, walks, roads, landscaping, utility distribution systems, or other improvements to camus land; or constructing or carrying out major renovation of buildings. |
| 2. | Advisory Committee | Reviews recommendations for capital project expenditures submitted by senior administrators or the director of physical plant for acceptability and feasibility. Identifies those projects that it recommends the president approve. |
| | President | Approves advisory committee's recommendations. |
| 3. | President | Submits capital project request to the board or trustees with the recommendation that he be authorized to proceed with a feasibility study to determine the project's scope and funding possibility. |
| | Board of Trustees | Reviews project concept and authorizes preparation of a feasibility study. |

*Explanation of Decision Matrix 12, Cont'd.*

| Step | Action Responsibility | Action |
|------|----------------------|--------|
| 4. | President | Assesses the feasibility of the project on the basis of the recommendation of the chief fiscal officer, which is in turn based on input from the proposed occupants regarding space and facility requirements, if the project involves the construction or renovation of a building, from the director of physical plant regarding the costs involved, and from the director of development regarding funding. |
| 5 & 6. | President | Submits the results of the feasibility study and requests authorization to employ an architect to do the required project design work; also requests the appointment of an owner's representative to assist the institution in the execution of the project. |
| | Board of Trustees | Reviews the feasibility study; authorizes the president to select and recommend an architect; and appoints an owner's representative. |

*Explanation of Decision Matrix 12, Cont'd.*

| *Step* | *Action Responsibility* | *Action* |
|---|---|---|
| 7. | President | Identifies the architects he recommends for the project on the basis of input from the owner's representative, who evaluates each architect's experience, ability (demonstrated in facilities the architect has designed), and current workload and staff, and from the chief fiscal officer and legal counsel regarding the terms and conditions of the proposed contract. |
| 8. | President | Recommends employment of the selected architect. |
|  | Board of Trustees | Reviews recommendation, obtaining clarification from the president, the owner's representative, legal counsel, and the chief fiscal officer; authorizes employment of an architect. |
| 9. | Chief Fiscal Officer | Executes a contract with the architect when authorized to do so by the president. |
| 10. | Architect | Prepares conceptual design drawings and the initial project budget on the basis |

*Explanation of Decision Matrix 12, Cont'd.*

| Step | Action Responsibility | Action |
|------|----------------------|--------|
|      |                      | of input from the occupants, regarding space and facility needs and traffic flow; the director of physical plant, regarding utility hookups, parking needs, walks, security requirements, and custodial and maintenance needs; the owner's representative, regarding quality standards to be adhered to as well as her recommendations regarding the input from occupants and the director of physical plant; the chief fiscal officer, regarding the adequacy and reasonableness of the project budget; and the president, who approves the conceptual design and the recommendations of the owner's representative. |
| 11.  | President            | Submits conceptual design and space allocation drawings with a revised project budget to the board of trustees with the recommendation that they be approved and that authorization to prepare bid documents be granted. |

*Explanation of Decision Matrix 12, Cont'd.*

| Step | Action Responsibility | Action |
|------|----------------------|--------|
|  | Board of Trustees | Reviews conceptual design, space allocation drawings, and project budget, obtaining clarification from the president, architect, owner's representative, and chief fiscal officer; authorizes preparation of bid documents. |
| 12. | Architect | Prepares working drawings, bid documents, and a revised project budget, obtaining more detailed input of the type provided for in step 10; also obtains input from legal counsel regarding specific terms bidders must agree to adhere to in preparing and submitting their bids and in executing the contract. |
| 13. | President | Submits bid documents — including working drawings, if the board of trustees so desires — and the revised project budget to the board of trustees with the recommendation that they be approved and that authorization to solicit bids be granted. |

*Explanation of Decision Matrix 12, Cont'd.*

| *Step* | *Action Responsibility* | *Action* |
|---|---|---|
| | Board of Trustees | Reviews bid documents and authorizes solicitation of bids. |
| 14. | Owner's Representative | Solicits bids, when authorized to do so by the president, from a panel of bidders identified as a result of input from the architect. Receives sealed bids. Opens and reviews bids in the presence of the president, the architect, legal counsel, and the chief fiscal officer, all of whom should participate in the process of selecting the successful bidder. |
| | President | Approves the selection of the contractor recommended by the bid review panel. |
| 15. | President | Submits the review of bidding results to the board of trustees and requests authorization to award a contract to the recommended bidder. |
| | Board of Trustees | Reviews bid results, obtaining clarification from the president, the archi- |

*Explanation of Decision Matrix 12, Cont'd.*

| Step | Action Responsibility | Action |
|------|----------------------|--------|
| | | tect, the owner's representative, legal counsel, and the chief fiscal officer. Authorizes the award of a contract to the recommended bidder. |
| 16. | Chief Fiscal Officer | When authorized to do so by the president, conducts final negotiations with the successful bidder with input from the architect, the owner's representative, and legal counsel. Executes a contract with the successful bidder. |

# Part Two:
# Academic Affairs
# Administration

Part Two covers the management of academic affairs, registration and academic records, and grant and contract administration. Grant and contract administration is included in this part for two reasons. First, experience shows that the majority of the grants and contracts received by smaller colleges and universities are related to some aspect of the academic program, thus requiring the director of grant and contract administration to interact regularly with the principal researchers and program directors in charge of implementing the grants and contracts. Second, the administration of grants and contracts should be separated from and serve as a check to the accounting for grant and contract funds.

Faculty members perform their role in the management of academic affairs either as members of an academic department or as members of a recognized academic committee. The committees identified in the chapter on academic administration are the minimum required to ensure that the faculty plays its proper role in the management of academic affairs. It is assumed that no faculty senate exists. Should an institution have either a faculty senate or faculty committees other than those identified, their roles in the management processes must be defined and considered in adapting the material contained in this book. The reader should also bear in mind that while this material is designed to show that the faculty should play its role in the institution's management processes by acting as a body, it is not intended to deter the president or other administrators from using individual faculty members as sounding boards or seeking their advice and counsel regarding matters related to institutional operations. Rather, where the faculty is assigned a definite role in making formal recommendations about courses of action the institution should follow, that role should be carried out by one or more of the recognized faculty organizations.

Each faculty organization recognized by the board should be identified in a faculty handbook. The faculty handbook should also identify each organization's composition, how its membership is to be determined—through election by the faculty or presidential appointment (if membership is to be determined by faculty election, the qualifications for voting should also be specified), to whom the organization is responsible, its areas of responsibility and the limits of its authority, whether the president and the chief academic officer are to be ex officio members, qualifications for membership, the number and timing of meetings, who is authorized to call a meeting, meeting notification requirements, what constitutes a quorum, minute keeping and distribution requirements, and procedures for changing the organization's constitution or bylaws.

Changes in a faculty organization, its scope of responsibility, or its constitution and bylaws should not be made until the organization has had an opportunity to consider the changes and offer recommendations. Particular care should be taken in considering or instituting changes in academic programs, curriculum or methods of instruction, faculty welfare policies or programs, admission or academic requirements, and grading policies.

The role the faculty should play in various decision-making processes is set forth in the decision matrices in the following chapters. Recognized faculty organizations should not be involved in the review and approval of the overall annual operating budget, the establishment of appropriate internal and fiscal control procedures, the determination of actual compensation to be paid to faculty members, the management of cash or endowment funds, the determination of what fund-raising programs are to be carried out, the administration of the operation and maintenance of physical plant, the awarding of financial aid, or the operation of student government or student activities. Consideration should be given, however, to appointing a faculty member to serve on the president's advisory committee, which deals with many of these matters.

# The Management
# of Academic Affairs
# and Personnel

An institution's decision about what it wishes to be academically is the most important decision it can make. Further, the management of academic affairs can be the most important factor affecting its fiscal health. What an institution desires to be academically affects its allocation of resources not only to its academic programs but also to all the services that support academic activities. In addition, once the resources have been allocated, the success of the entire endeavor depends on how well the academic community meets the commitments it has made in the formulation of the plans and budgets on which such resource allocations are based. When one considers that the budget for academic affairs is usually the largest single expenditure component — usually consuming 40 to 50 percent of the total budget — the importance of good management in this area becomes obvious.

The academic operations of an institution are usually organized into divisions or departments. In larger institutions, both divisional and departmental structures may exist. Each division or department is headed by a chairperson who is responsible for administering its affairs. For smaller institutions, a divisional structure without a departmental substructure offers greater flexibility in faculty staffing and lower administrative overhead. However, for simplicity's sake, the assumption is made here that the institution has a departmental structure, each

117

department of which is administered by a department head, and that all department heads have similar authority and responsibilities.

It is also assumed that the faculty is organized into committees through which it provides input into decisions and that the number of committees is limited to those identified below as the minimum that should exist. The author also recognizes that certain faculty inputs into decisions are departmental in nature. These are identified in the decision matrices as the action responsibility of faculty, as opposed to the action responsibility of a committee. Many institutions are expanding the activities and responsibilities of the placement office. In the past, the placement office's activities have usually been limited to assisting students in finding employment while they are enrolled or when they graduate. However, many institutions have recognized that what is learned by those carrying out placement activities can be applied to other activities that are important to the institution's strength and growth. In institutional organizational structure, the placement office has usually been a department reporting to the chief student affairs officer. However, the expanded activity of the placement office — hereinafter referred to as the career development program — should be carried out under the supervision of the chief academic officer. I assume that the institution has already accepted the expanded role of the placement office and has a career development program in place, and that the administrative supervision of that program is a part of the responsibilities of the chief academic officer. If there is no career development program, the establishment of one should be explored (see Decision Matrix 24 for processes that should be followed in establishing a career development program).

The quality of an institution's academic program depends on the quality of its faculty. Institutions should seek to retain maximum flexibility in their appointment of tenured, tenure-track, and non-tenure-track faculty; the ability to bring the ideas and experiences of new faculty members into academic programs ensures the continuous revitalization of such programs. Therefore, each institution should grant tenure only to those faculty members who have demonstrated outstanding performance; it should not grant tenure to faculty members simply because nothing negative can be said about their performance. This type of tenure policy can be made easier to administer if those faculty members whose performance does not merit tenure but whose services it is considered desirable to retain are offered the opportunity to continue teaching as non-tenure-track members of the faculty on term appointment. Should such a faculty member's performance later warrant a recommendation for tenure, the fact that the faculty member has been retained on a non-tenure-track basis should not negatively influence such a recommendation. To further enhance flexibility, about 10 percent of the total number of authorized faculty positions should be filled by temporary appointments — visiting professors, lecturers, adjunct faculty, and the like. This will not only contribute to the ongoing revitalization of academic programs but will also provide flexibility in responding to fluctuations in student demand for instruction.

The essential standards for good management in the area of academic administration are set forth below.

★   Program goals and objectives and plans for achieving them should be developed and documented for each area of academic concentration. They should be consistent with the institution's mission statement, academic goals and objectives, enrollment projections, and fiscal constraints set forth in the multi-year plan. Further, they should set forth yardsticks against which the institution's academic accomplishments and faculty performance can be measured.

★   The procedures to be followed in recruiting and appointing faculty should be documented and communicated to all who may become involved in these processes. At a minimum, such procedures should identify who has the authority to invite candidates to visit the campus for an interview, what recruiting travel costs will be borne by the institution, who has the authority to commit the institution in the appointment of faculty, and what relocation costs will be borne by the institution. The authority to commit the institution on the appointment of faculty should be delegated to the president unless the appointments involve the granting of tenure, in which case the authority should be retained by the board of trustees. In exercising this authority, however, under no circumstances should the president commit the institution to the appointment of a faculty member who is unacceptable to the chief academic officer or the department head of the organizational unit to which the faculty member will be assigned (see Decision Matrices 18 and 19).

* Departmental faculty should be involved in recruiting new faculty for their department, screening and interviewing candidates, and recommending appointments. Faculty should make sure, however, that their department heads and, through them, the chief academic officer are kept fully informed of their activities; they should also make sure that candidates clearly understand that they do not have the authority to commit the institution. This latter point is very important. In a number of instances faculty members, after appointment, have won lawsuits against the institutions by which they were employed for failure to honor commitments made by other faculty members during the recruiting process regarding released time, teaching loads, time requirements for promotion or tenure appointment, and the like. In these cases, the judges have ruled that the faculty member has the right to rely on communications written on official institutional letterhead or orally expressed in the absence of any specific notification that the person initiating the communication does not have the authority to commit the institution. It is also recommended that each institution consider establishing a search committee to assist in the recruitment, screening, and appointment of tenure-track faculty and key academic administrators.

* All faculty appointments, whether initial or renewal, and regardless of the faculty classification or rank of the appointee, should be covered by a letter of appointment or employment contract. At a minimum, such contracts or letters of appointment should specify the period covered by the appointment; the

annual salary and how it is payable; the fringe benefits to which the appointee is entitled, particularly if they differ from the standard entitlement under institutional policy; the faculty rank or classification assigned; the appointee's entitlement to engage in private practice if such entitlement is at variance with institutional norms; and the teaching, research, and administrative responsibilities assigned and the institution's right to change such assignments.

The period covered by an academic appointment can vary from a semester or quarter to as much as five years; in some cases, it may be tied to the availability of funding from a specific program or research grant or contract. If a faculty member's appointment covers an academic year — that is, two semesters — and the institution and the faculty member agree that he or she will be employed to teach during the institution's summer school program, such employment should be covered by a separate contract or letter of appointment. This contract or letter of appointment should specify whether or not the compensation earned during this period affects the faculty member's fringe benefit entitlement — for example, whether it will be considered in calculating institutional contributions toward the faculty member's pension.

An example of a fringe benefit entitlement that is outside the standard institutional policy is the case where institutional policy stipulates that new faculty members must be employed for a specific period of time before the institution contributes toward their retirement fund. Many new faculty members have been employed by other institutions whose pension coverage is insured through the Teachers Insurance and Annuity Association (TIAA) and its companion organization, the College Retirement Equity Fund (CREF). Most institutions, under these circumstances, will waive the waiting period for entitlement to institutional contribution toward the faculty member's retirement fund. If the institution has its own retirement plan covered by a different insurer, it may agree to make its retirement contribution to TIAA/CREF in lieu of the payment it would normally make to its own insurer. These variances from the institution's standard policy should be set forth in the faculty member's contract or letter of appointment. A final point to be kept in mind when considering faculty contract terms is the way faculty members are to be paid their annual salaries. Some faculty on nine-month appointment wish to have their salary paid over nine months, some over ten months, and others over eleven months. Every effort should be made to standardize faculty salary payments to ease the process of payroll preparation and to facilitate the chief fiscal officer's work in preparing expenditure projections for the balance of the fiscal year. It should be borne in mind that paying faculty salaries over eleven months will ease the institution's cash flow problems.

★   Minimum and maximum salary ranges should be established for each faculty rank and for nonranked categories of instructional personnel. These salary ranges should be published or otherwise made known to interested personnel. Further, they should be broad enough to permit the institution to pay what is necessary to attract the faculty it needs, at the rank it desires, to fill vacancies in disciplines (such as physics) that command a higher level of compensation than other disciplines (such as history or English).

★   Institutional policies regarding faculty welfare matters should be published. Such matters include tenure, including any limitations regarding the percentage or number that may hold tenure appointments; promotion, including any limitations on percentage or number by rank; released time for nonteaching assignments or private practice; requirements related to meeting class assignments and availability on campus during nonteaching hours; sabbaticals; leaves of absence, with or without pay; notification of retention and nonretention; academic freedom; the minimum size of sections that can be offered; what constitutes a full-time teaching load; and grievance procedures (see Decision Matrices 13, 14, 15, and 16).

★   The authority, responsibilities, and operating requirements of authorized faculty committees should be documented and published. Authorized faculty committees should include, at the least, committees on curriculum, student academic requirements, student and faculty conduct, promotion and tenure, faculty welfare, and the library. Documentation for each committee should specify its composition and how it is selected (by election or appointment), how the chairperson is to be selected, the frequency of its meetings, what constitutes a quorum, requirements regarding the keeping and distribution of minutes, and its responsibilities and its authority.

★   The total number of courses and sections offered during an academic term should not exceed the number necessary to meet student demand for instruction, projected enrollment, and the standard for average section size established by the institution, unless the institution has sufficient restricted or unrestricted funds to warrant an ongoing investment in elective or program enrichment courses.

The following hypothetical example demonstrates the use of this standard. It is assumed that an institution requires 120 credit hours for a degree, operates on a two-semester academic year, and has established an optimum average size of twenty students per class or section for the lower division and fifteen students for the upper division. Further, this institution has projected that its enrollment will encompass 600 full-time equivalent lower-division students and 400 full-time equivalent upper-division students, and the courses it offers average three credits each. Under these assumptions, each student will create a demand for fifteen credit hours of instruction or five courses per semester. Thus, 600 lower-division students will generate a demand for 3,000 course or section spaces, which, when divided by a desired average class size of 20, means that the optimum number of courses and sections to be offered is 150. The 400 upper-division students will generate a demand for 2,000 course or section spaces, which, when divided by a desired average class size of 15, means that the optimum number of courses and sections to be offered is 134. Thus, the combined optimum number of courses to be offered is 284. Recognizing that it is impossible to predict enrollment and student demand for instruction exactly, one should add to this total a variable factor of about 10 to 15 percent. Using a variable factor of 12 percent would increase the total number of offerings to about 320.

I have visited a large number of smaller colleges and universities and compared their offerings with the result of calculations based on the application of this standard. I have found that the average institution offers from 30 to 40 percent more courses and sections than student demand for instruction (calculated using a 12 percent variable) would justify. Further, statistics provided by the registrars show that some 20 percent of the courses offered at these institutions have enrollments of five or fewer and some 30 percent have enrollments of ten or fewer. When one considers that the cost the institution bears for such excessive offerings involves not only the cost of faculty that must be retained to teach such courses and sections but also the cost of bookstore operations, library holdings, registrar record keeping, space utilization, and so on, one can easily see why academic planning and control of academic programs and curriculum are the most important ingredients in controlling institutional operating costs.

★ The number of faculty authorized should be limited to that required to teach the courses and sections offered and to provide the released time necessary for sponsored research or sponsored program activities or for carrying out other assigned administrative or nonacademic responsibilities. Institutions are encouraged to provide released time for faculty members whom it desires to become involved in the preparation of applications for program grants or contracts.

★ The chief academic officer should maintain all faculty personnel records other than those related to compensation and fringe benefits. Records related to compensation and fringe benefits should be maintained by the director of personnel; standards for the maintenance of such records are set forth in Chapter Thirteen. The records to be maintained by the chief academic officer include those related to disciplinary action and individual performance and to recruitments and appointments that are required to ensure compliance with affirmative action regulations or to provide the affirmative action officer with information needed to meet periodic reporting requirements.

★   An evaluation of each faculty member's performance should be conducted annually in accordance with published criteria and procedures. The results of this evaluation should be documented and reviewed with the faculty member and should become a part of the faculty member's personnel file (see Decision Matrix 17).

★   Library operations and the adequacy of library holdings should be evaluated annually. One of the results of this evaluation should be the submission of a written report that makes recommendations regarding the library's acquisition program for the ensuing year to strengthen areas of weakness, the disposal of holdings and discontinuance of subscriptions to periodicals no longer considered relevant to the academic program, and changes in library operations that will enhance its usefulness. Library staff should maintain records of library utilization by both faculty and students; these records should be used in the evaluation of ways to improve library operations and utilization.

★   The chief academic officer should be responsible for seeing to it that each student is assigned a faculty adviser. She should involve department heads and faculty in determining which faculty members should be assigned to which students. She should also make sure that all faculty advisers are familiar with the institution's academic program plans, course offering schedules, degree requirements, and required course sequences. The faculty advisers should be held responsible for seeing to it that each student is able to complete the requirements for the degree selected with the minimum of disruption in the shortest possible time; that the number of courses required by only a small number of students to complete their degree requirements is held to a minimum; and that special assistance is provided through tutorial programs or other methods to help students overcome basic skill or learning deficiencies so as to reduce student attrition. The foregoing standard should be applicable to all students, whether they are enrolled in regular programs, evening or weekend college programs, or other alternative education programs offered by the institution.

★   The chief academic officer should be held responsible for arranging for the management of the storage, maintenance, inventory control, and scheduled use of all equipment and materials that can serve more than one academic department or an academic department and another activity so as to reduce the institution's cost of providing them. Equipment and materials covered by this standard include musical instruments, scores, and so on that may be used in teaching music or by the band; audiovisual equipment, slide programs, film strips, and tape recordings; athletic equipment used in teaching physical education, in student activities, or in intramural athletic programs, including equipment earmarked for use in intercollegiate athletic programs; closed-circuit televised instructional programs or computer instruction programs; and movable scientific equipment that can serve more than one laboratory or discipline.

★   The chief academic officer should be held responsible for assuring the administration that all applications for sponsored research or academically related program grants or contracts are consistent with the institution's academic mission, goals, and objectives and that they can be carried out within the terms and conditions stipulated in the applications before such applications are submitted to the grant and contract review committee for approval. Part Four describes the role of the grant and contract review committee in reviewing and approving applications for submission to a prospective agency.

★   The chief academic officer, acting through appropriate department heads, should be held responsible for seeing to it that commitments to carry out sponsored research or funded program grant or contract activities are accomplished within the applicable terms and conditions and that required reports, other than fiscal reports, related to such activities are prepared in an accurate and timely manner. The preparation of fiscal reports related to such activities is the responsibility of the chief fiscal officer. Further, coordinating the preparation of program and fiscal reports and reconciling any inconsistencies that may be contained in such reports is the responsibility of the director of grant and contract administration.

★   The chief academic officer, acting through department heads, should be held responsible for seeing to it that resources allocated through the approved budget are used wisely and in accordance with institutional policies and procedures. It is recommended that budgetary provision for faculty travel to professional meetings be centralized in the budget provided to cover the cost of operating the office of the chief academic officer.

I assume that the institutions whose operations this book addresses have already established a career development program. Such a program should be headed by a director, who will hereinafter be referred to as the director of career development. The director of career development should report to the chief academic officer and should be given academic rank but should not be given tenure in the administrative position. Also, the director should be made an ex officio member of the faculty curriculum and academic requirements committee. The career development program, in addition to providing career planning, experiential education, and placement assistance services to students and alumni, also should be considered a means of assisting in the recruitment of faculty and nonacademic employees and the improvement of academic performance. The information that becomes available to the director from administering program activities regarding job market conditions, students' career decision problems, employers' attitudes, and the like, coupled with the services provided to alumni and the facilities available to the program, can be of incalculable assistance in facilitating recruitment, strengthening academic programs, reducing attrition, and strengthening alumni ties to the institution.

The essential standards of good management of a career development program are set forth below.

★   The scope of services offered by the program should be related to the students' need for assistance in their career development. Services should assist students in self-assessment, obtaining occupational and career information, matching their skills, interests, education, and abilities to job market requirements, choosing appropriate majors, exploring careers through work experience (such as cooperative education, internships, and summer employment), obtaining job acquisition skills, adapting to the requirements of the working world, and obtaining employment. The latter should also include assistance to alumni.

★   The director should maintain records to keep other administrators who may be affected informed about the results of the program's activities. The director should be held responsible for providing information to the alumni director regarding the placement of former students; to the registrar, director of financial aid, department heads and their faculty, academic advisers, and the chief fiscal officer regarding students undertaking experiential education (work experience) for credit, providing data on credits earned, grades, employer feedback, financial arrangements, rotating schedules, and fee assessments; to the directors of housing and food services (if the student resides on campus) regarding special requirements related to the student's rotating schedule; to the director of recruiting and admissions, director of public relations, and chief development officer regarding data that can be useful in recruiting, public relations, and fund raising; and to the chief academic officer, department heads and their faculty, and academic advisers regarding what has been learned from recruiters about changing conditions in the marketplace, particular skills they are looking for in students, and the caliber of performance they have received from students previously employed.

See Decision Matrix 20 for processes to be followed in the formulation and operation of a career development program.

**Decision Matrix 13. Formulation of Academic Policies and Procedures.**

Legend of decision-making roles
1 – Authorizes action
2 – Action responsibility
3 – Approves recommendation
4 – Recommends action
5 – Provides input

| Procedural Steps | Board of Trustees | President | Advisory Committee | Chief Academic Officer | Department Heads | Faculty | Promotion and Tenure Committee | Academic Requirements Committee | Faculty Welfare Committee | Recruiting and Admissions Director | Registrar |
|---|---|---|---|---|---|---|---|---|---|---|---|
| 1. Formulate policy and procedures recommendations covering | | | | | | | | | | | |
| (a) promotion and tenure appointments | | | | 3 | 5 | 5 | 4 | | | | |
| (b) released time, faculty responsibilities, full-time loads, sabbaticals, leaves of absence, notification of retention or nonretention, compensation ranges, academic freedom, and grievances | | | | 3 | 5 | 5 | | | 4 | | |
| (c) admission requirements, degree requirements, minimum section sizes, and grading policies | | | | 3 | 5 | 5 | | 4 | | 5 | 5 |
| 2. Review and approve recommended policies and procedures | | 3 | 4 | 5 | | | | | | | |
| 3. Approve recommended policies | 2 | 4 | | 5 | | | | | | | |
| 4. Implement policies and procedures | | 1 | | 2 | | | | | | 2 | 2 |

*Participants in Decision-Making Processes*

*Explanation of Decision Matrix 13.*

| Step | Action Responsibility | Action |
|------|----------------------|--------|
| 1a. | Promotion and Tenure Committee | Formulates, on the basis of input from faculty and department heads, recommended policies and procedures covering promotion and appointment to tenure for faculty members. |
| | Chief Academic Officer | Reviews and approves the promotion and tenure committee's recommendations. |
| 1b. | Faculty Welfare Committee | Formulates, on the basis of input from faculty and department heads, recommended policies and procedures covering teaching loads and released time, faculty responsibilities, sabbaticals, leaves of absence, notification of retention and nonretention, academic freedom, compensation ranges, and faculty grievance procedures. |
| | Chief Academic Officer | Reviews and approves the faculty welfare committee's recommendations. |
| 1c. | Academic Requirements Committee | Formulates, on the basis of input from faculty, department heads, the director of recruiting and admissions, and the registrar, policies related to admissions requirements, degree |

*Explanation of Decision Matrix 13, Cont'd.*

| Step | Action Responsibility | Action |
|------|----------------------|--------|
| | | requirements, minimum section sizes, and grading. |
| | Chief Academic Officer | Reviews and approves the academic requirements committee's recommendations. |
| 2. | Advisory Committee | Reviews the recommended policies and procedures formulated in step 1 and submitted by the chief academic officer for acceptability and effect on operations; recommends presidential approval. |
| | President | Approves recommended policies and procedures. |
| 3. | President | Submits recommended policies to the board of trustees with the recommendation that they be adopted. |
| | Board of Trustees | Reviews recommended policies, obtaining clarification from the president and the chief academic officer; adopts recommended policies. |
| 4. | President | Authorizes the chief academic officer, the director of recruiting and admissions, and the registrar to implement the approved policies and procedures. |

# Decision Matrix 14. Curriculum and Academic Program Revision.

Legend of decision-making roles:

1 – Authorizes action
2 – Action responsibility
3 – Approves recommendation
4 – Recommends action
5 – Provides input

Participants in Decision-Making Processes

| Procedural Steps | Board of Trustees | President | Advisory Committee | Chief Academic Officer | Department Heads | Faculty | Curriculum Committee | Academic Requirements Committee | Recruiting and Admissions Director | Counselors | Registrar | Career Development Director | Publications Director |
|---|---|---|---|---|---|---|---|---|---|---|---|---|---|
| 1. Review multi-year planning guidelines, enrollment projections, section size objectives, and input from director of career development; determine extent of curriculum or program changes required and prepare summary course outlines covering proposed changes | | | | 3 | 4 | 5 | | | | | | 5 | |
| 2. Formulate recommendations for changes in program or curriculum on the basis of summary course outlines | | | 4 | 5 | | 5 | | | | | | | |
| 3. Review and approve recommended changes | 2 | 3 | | 3 | 5 | 5 | 4 | | 5 | 5 | | | |
| 4. Obtain board authorization for proposed changes | 2 | 4 | | | | | | | | | | | |
| 5. Authorize finalization of recommended changes | | 1 | | 2 | | | | | | | | | |
| 6. Develop syllabus for each new or revised course to be offered and, if applicable, revise sequencing and scheduling of course offerings | | 3 | | 3 | 5 | 4 | | | | | | | |

| | | | | | |
|---|---|---|---|---|---|
| 7. Develop, if applicable, new or revised admission and degree completion requirements | 3 | 5 | 5 | 4 | |
| 8. Authorize implementation of new or revised program or curriculum | 1 | | | | |
| 9. Receive and plan implementation of actions required by program or curriculum changes, course sequencing or scheduling changes, and changes in degree completion requirements or admission requirements | 5 | 2 | | | |
| 10. Revise catalogue to reflect changes | 1 | 2 | 2 | 2 | 2 |

*Explanation of Decision Matrix 14.*

| Step | Action Responsibility | Action |
|------|----------------------|--------|
| 1. | Chief Academic Officer | Reviews approved multi-year planning guidelines, including enrollment projections and section size objectives, and input from the director of career development regarding changes in employment market opportunities and conditions. With recommendations from academic department heads, determines the extent and nature of changes required in curriculum and program offerings. |
| 2. | Curriculum Committee | Reviews curriculum and program change proposals and summary course outlines submitted by academic department heads and departmental faculty. Formulates recommendations for changes in curriculum and program offerings on the basis of its review and additional input from department heads, faculty, and academic counselors. |
| | Chief Academic Officer | Reviews and approves changes recommended by the curriculum committee. |
| 3. | Advisory Committee | Reviews recommended changes in curriculum or program submitted by the chief |

*Explanation of Decision Matrix 14, Cont'd.*

| Step | Action Responsibility | Action |
|------|----------------------|--------|
| | | academic officer, obtaining from the director of recruiting and admissions her assessment of the potential effect of the proposed changes on enrollment projections; recommends presidential approval of the proposed changes. |
| | President | Approves recommended curriculum and program changes. |
| 4. | President | Submits proposed changes in program offerings to the board of trustees with the recommendation that they be approved. |
| | Board of Trustees | Reviews recommended changes in program offerings, obtaining clarification from the president and chief academic officer; approves recommended changes. |
| 5. | President | Authorizes the chief academic officer to finalize approved revisions to curriculum and program offerings. |
| 6. | Curriculum Committee | Reviews syllabus for each new or revised course and course sequencing and scheduling recommendations developed by department heads and |

*Explanation of Decision Matrix 14, Cont'd.*

| Step | Action Responsibility | Action |
|------|----------------------|--------|
|      |                      | their departmental faculty; recommends that they be approved by the chief academic officer. |
|      | Chief Academic Officer | Reviews and approves the curriculum committee's recommendations. |
| 7.   | Academic Requirements Committee | Reviews approved curriculum and program changes and recommendations for changes in admission or degree completion requirements submitted by department heads and departmental faculty; recommends that proposed changes in admission or degree completion requirements be approved. |
|      | Chief Academic Officer | Reviews and approves the academic requirements committee's recommendations. |
| 8 & 9. | Chief Academic Officer | Issues notification of authorization to implement new or revised curriculum and program offerings and changes in degree completion requirements to department heads, academic counselors, and the registrar. Notifies the director of admissions to implement new or revised admission requirements. |

*Explanation of Decision Matrix 14, Cont'd.*

| Step | Action Responsibility | Action |
|------|----------------------|--------|
| 10. | Director of Publications | Revises the catalogue to incorporate approved changes when authorized to do so by the chief academic officer. |

# Decision Matrix 15. Promotion and Appointment to Tenure Status.

| Legend of decision-making roles |
| --- |
| 1 – Authorizes action |
| 2 – Action responsibility |
| 3 – Approves recommendation |
| 4 – Recommends action |
| 5 – Provides input |

| Procedural Steps | Board of Trustees | Trustees' Academic Committee | President | Chief Academic Officer | Department Heads | Faculty | Promotion and Tenure Committee | Personnel Director | Payroll |
|---|---|---|---|---|---|---|---|---|---|
| 1. Identify candidates to be recommended for promotion or appointment to tenure status | | | | | 4 | 5 | | | |
| 2. Review qualifications of candidates recommended for promotion or tenure and determine which recommendations should be approved | | | | | 5 | | 2 | | |
| 3. Review and approve promotion and tenure committee's recommendations | | | | 3 | | | 4 | | |
| 4. Review and approve chief academic officer's recommendations | | | 3 | 4 | | | | | |
| 5. Authorize tenure appointment | 2 | 4 | 5 | 5 | | | | | |
| 6. Authorize change in status (promotion or appointment to tenure status) | | | 1 | 2 | 2 | | 2 | | |
| 7. Receive notification of change in status | | | | 5 | | | | | |
| 8. Receive notification of change in status and related compensation adjustments | | | | 5 | | | | 2 | |
| 9. Enter changes in compensation data into payroll records | | | | | | | | 5 | 2 |

*Participants in Decision-Making Processes*

*Explanation of Decision Matrix 15.*

| Step | Action Responsibility | Action |
|------|----------------------|--------|
| 1. | Department Heads | Identify, on the basis of input from departmental faculty, faculty members to be recommended for promotion or tenure appointment. To support recommendations, prepare the following documentation: evaluation of teaching capability by faculty and students; extent and nature of professional activities, including attendance of and participation in activities of professional societies, research and publication activities, and contributions to institutional and departmental growth and development; and career experience at this institution and other institutions. |
| 2. | Promotion and Tenure Committee | Reviews departmental recommendations for promotion and tenure and documentation submitted to support those recommendations. Recommends that promotion and tenure appointments be approved by chief academic officer. |
| 3. | Chief Academic Officer | Reviews the documentation supporting the recommendations for promotion and |

*Explanation of Decision Matrix 15, Cont'd.*

| *Step* | *Action Responsibility* | *Action* |
|--------|-------------------------|----------|
| | | tenure made by the promotion and tenure committee and approves the recommendations. |
| 4. | President | Reviews the documentation supporting the recommendations for promotion and tenure made by the chief academic officer and, in consultation with her, approves her recommendations. |
| 5. | Trustees' Academic Committee | Reviews the president's and chief academic officer's recommendations for tenure appointments and the supporting documentation; recommends tenure appointments for recommended faculty. |
| | Board of Trustees | Authorizes appointment to tenure status for recommended faculty members. |
| 6, 7, & 8. | Chief Academic Officer | Upon receipt of the president's authorization, notifies department heads, the personnel director, and the promotion and tenure committee of approved promotions and tenure appointments, including in the notification to personnel the authorized |

*Explanation of Decision Matrix 15, Cont'd.*

| Step | Action Responsibility | Action |
|------|----------------------|--------|
| | | changes in compensation related to changes in status. |
| 9. | Payroll | Updates payroll records with authorized changes in compensation and employee classification on the basis of input from the personnel director. |

# Decision Matrix 16. Processing Requests for Sabbaticals and Leaves of Absence.

Legend of decision-making roles
1 – Authorizes action
2 – Action responsibility
3 – Approves recommendation
4 – Recommends action
5 – Provides input

*Participants in Decision-Making Processes*

| Procedural Steps | President | Chief Academic Officer | Department Heads | Faculty | Faculty Welfare Committee | Personnel Director | Payroll |
|---|---|---|---|---|---|---|---|
| 1. Review and determine whether to recommend approval of applications for sabbaticals and leaves of absence | | | 2 | 5 | | | |
| 2. Review applications and department heads' recommendations for adherence to policy and determine whether to endorse recommendations | | | 4 | | 2 | | |
| 3. Review applications and recommendations of department heads and faculty welfare committee and determine whether to endorse their recommendations | | 2 | | | 4 | | |
| 4. Review and approve chief academic officer's recommendations | 3 | 4 | | | | | |
| 5. Authorize sabbaticals and leaves of absence | 1 | 2 | | | | | |
| 6. Receive notification of authorized sabbaticals and leaves of absence | | 5 | 2 | 2 | 2 | | |
| 7. Receive notification of changes in compensation related to authorized sabbaticals and leaves of absence | | 5 | | | | 2 | |
| 8. Enter changes in compensation data into payroll records | | | | | | 5 | 2 |

*Explanation of Decision Matrix 16.*

| Step | Action Responsibility | Action |
|------|----------------------|--------|
| 1. | Department Heads | Recommend approval of faculty members' requests for sabbaticals or leaves of absence. |
| 2. | Faculty Welfare Committee | Reviews each faculty member's application and proposed program to be carried out during the sabbatical or leave of absence; recommends approval of the request. |
| 3. | Chief Academic Officer | Reviews the faculty welfare committee's recommendation, the faculty member's proposed activity program, and the effect on departmental staffing; recommends presidential approval. |
| 4. | President | Approves the chief academic officer's recommendation. |
| 5, 6, & 7. | Chief Academic Officer | When authorized by the president, notifies the department head, the faculty member, and the faculty welfare committee that the requested sabbatical or leave of absence has been granted; notifies the personnel director regarding any change in the level of compensation related to the sabbatical or leave of absence. |
| 8. | Payroll | Enters changes in compensation data into payroll system on the basis of input from the personnel director. |

**Decision Matrix 17. Faculty Performance Evaluation.**

Legend of decision-making roles
- 1 – Authorizes action
- 2 – Action responsibility
- 3 – Approves recommendation
- 4 – Recommends action
- 5 – Provides input

| Procedural Steps | Board of Trustees | President | Chief Academic Officer | Department Heads | Faculty | Faculty Welfare Committee | Students |
|---|---|---|---|---|---|---|---|
| 1. Authorize establishment or revision of annual performance evaluation plan for faculty | | 1 | 2 | | | | |
| 2. Formulate evaluation plan, timetable, criteria to be applied, and forms to be used | | | 2 | 5 | 5 | 4 | 5 |
| 3. Review and approve recommended evaluation program | | 3 | 4 | | | | |
| 4. Authorize implementation of program | | 1 | 2 | 5 | | | |
| 5. Conduct orientation workshop | | | 2 | 2 | 5 | | |
| 6. Review program with faculty | | | | 5 | | | |
| 7. Observe faculty performance | | | | 2 | | | 5 |
| 8. Obtain student evaluations | | | | 2 | | | 5 |

|  | | | | |
|---|---|---|---|---|
| 9. Complete evaluation forms | 2 | | | |
| 10. Review evaluation results with faculty and obtain faculty member's signature to show that review has taken place | 2 | 5 | | |
| 11. Review department head and student evaluations | 2 | 2 | 5 | |
| 12. Update faculty personnel files | 2 | 2 | 5 | |
| 13. Conduct workshop to analyze program | 2 | 5 | 5 | 5 |
| 14. Prepare summary report of evaluation program and results | 2 | 5 | | |
| 15. Review summary report | 2 | 5 | | |
| 16. Review results of evaluation | 2 | 5 | | |

*Explanation of Decision Matrix 17.*

| Step | Action Responsibility | Action |
|------|----------------------|--------|
| 1. | President | Instructs the chief academic officer to establish or revise an annual faculty performance evaluation program. |
| 2. | Chief Academic Officer | Formulates recommended evaluation plan, criteria to be applied, and forms to be used on the basis of input from department heads, faculty, and students. Obtains a review of the recommended evaluation plan by the faculty welfare committee and the committee's approval for the plan. |
| 3 & 4. | President | Reviews the recommended evaluation plan and authorizes the chief academic officer to implement it. |
| 5. | Chief Academic Officer | Conducts an orientation workshop to familiarize department heads with the evaluation plan's timetable, criteria, and requirements. |
| 6 & 7. | Department Heads | Review the evaluation criteria and plan with their faculty and observe their performance during the year. |
|  | Students | Observe faculty performance during the year. |

*Explanation of Decision Matrix 17, Cont'd.*

| Step | Action Responsibility | Action |
|------|----------------------|--------|
| 8 & 9. | Department Heads | Review evaluation criteria with selected students and obtain their written evaluations of each faculty member's performance. Complete their own written evaluation of faculty member's performance. |
| 10. | Department Heads | Review evaluation results with each faculty member and obtain the faculty member's comments and signature to show that the review has been conducted. |
| 11 & 12. | Chief Academic Officer | Reviews evaluation results with department heads and files evaluation documents in the faculty member's personnel file. |
| 13. | Chief Academic Officer | Conducts a workshop with department heads, faculty representatives, and the chairperson of the faculty welfare committee to review and develop recommendations for improving the faculty performance evaluation program. |
| 14. | Chief Academic Officer | Prepares a summary report describing the evaluation |

*Explanation of Decision Matrix 17, Cont'd.*

*Step   Action Responsibility   Action*

procedures followed and the
results of the evaluation
program.

15.   President            Reviews and approves the chief
                           academic officer's summary
                           report.

16.   Board of Trustees    Receives and accepts the presi-
                           dent's report on the processes
                           that were followed in evaluating
                           faculty and the summary report
                           of the results of the evaluations,
                           obtaining clarification from the
                           chief academic officer.

*Explanation of Decision Matrix 18.*

| Step | Action Responsibility | Action |
|---|---|---|
| 1 & 2. | Department Heads | Review faculty performance evaluations and appointment terms of all faculty and recommend reappointment or release. |
| | Chief Academic Officer | Reviews and approves department heads' recommendations and recommends presidential approval. |
| | President | Reviews and approves recommended reappointment or release. |
| 3. | Chief Academic Officer | Issues, when authorized to do so by the president, reappointment contracts or notifications of nonrenewal of contract to faculty members. |
| 4. | Chief Academic Officer | Receives, from reappointed faculty, signed and accepted reappointment contracts and, from released faculty, requests for appeal hearing by the faculty welfare committee. |
| 5. | Chief Academic Officer | Notifies the chairperson of the faculty welfare committee of the request for an appeal hearing and obtains schedule for hearing. Notifies the faculty member of the date, time, and place of the hearing. |

## Decision Matrix 18. Faculty Retention.

Legend of decision-making roles
1 – Authorizes action
2 – Action responsibility
3 – Approves recommendation
4 – Recommends action
5 – Provides input

| Procedural Steps | Board of Trustees | Legal Counsel | President | Chief Academic Officer | Department Heads | Faculty | Faculty Welfare Committee | Personnel Director | Payroll |
|---|---|---|---|---|---|---|---|---|---|
| 1. Review existing faculty contracts and performance evaluations; determine faculty to be released or reappointed | | | 3 | 3 | 4 | | | | |
| 2. Review recommendations of chief academic officer and department heads | | | 3 | 4 | 5 | | | | |
| 3. Issue notification of appointment renewal or nonrenewal | | | 1 | 2 | | | | | |
| 4. Receive faculty member's notification of | | | | | | | | | |
| (a) acceptance of reappointment | | | | 2 | | 5 | | | |
| (b) decision to appeal nonrenewal of appointment | | | | 2 | | 5 | | | |
| 5. Advise faculty welfare committee of appeal and schedule hearing | | | | 2 | 5 | 5 | 2 | | |
| 6. Conduct hearing | | | | 5 | 5 | 2 | 2 | | |
| 7. Receive notification of committee's decision | | | | 2 | 2 | 2 | 5 | | |

| | | | | | | | | |
|---|---|---|---|---|---|---|---|---|
| 8. Receive faculty member's notification of appeal of committee's decision to board of trustees | | | | | | | | |
| 9. Advise board of appeal and schedule hearing | 2 | | 2 | | | | | |
| 10. Conduct hearing | 2 | 5 | 5 | 5 | 5 | 5 | 5 | |
| 11. Receive notification of board's decision | 5 | | 2 | 2 | 2 | 2 | 2 | |
| 12. Receive president's notification of release and terms of reappointment for existing faculty | | | 5 | | | | | 2 |
| 13. Complete employee benefit program actions for released faculty | | | | | 5 | | | 2 |
| 14. Update payroll records to reflect terminations and new terms of reappointment | | | | | | | 5 | 2 |

*Explanation of Decision Matrix 18, Cont'd.*

| Step | Action Responsibility | Action |
|------|----------------------|--------|
| 6 & 7. | Faculty Welfare Committee | Conducts appeal hearing with input from the faculty member, department head, and chief academic officer; notifies each of its decision. |
| 8 & 9. | President | Receives the faculty member's request for an appeal hearing by the board of trustees. Advises the board chairperson and schedules the hearing. Notifies the faculty member of the date, time, and place of the hearing. |
| 10 & 11. | Board of Trustees | Reviews the faculty welfare committee's summary report of its deliberations on the case, obtaining input from the faculty member, the chairperson of the faculty welfare committee, the department head, the chief academic officer, legal counsel, and the president. Reaches its decision and advises all interested parties of that decision. |
| 12 & 13. | Director of Personnel | Receives the president's notification of terms of reappointment for retained faculty and release of other faculty. Completes, with |

*Explanation of Decision Matrix 18, Cont'd.*

| Step | Action Responsibility | Action |
|------|----------------------|--------|
| | | insurers and faculty members, adjustments to benefit programs related to terms of reappointment and releases and updates personnel files. |
| 14. | Payroll | Enters new data regarding reappointed and released faculty into the payroll system on the basis of input from the personnel director. |

## Decision Matrix 19. Faculty Recruitment and Appointment.

Legend of decision-making roles
1 – Authorizes action
2 – Action responsibility
3 – Approves recommendation
4 – Recommends action
5 – Provides input

Participants in Decision-Making Processes

| Procedural Steps | President | Chief Academic Officer | Department Heads | Faculty | Candidates | Budget Control | Personnel Director | Payroll | Grant and Contract Administration Director |
|---|---|---|---|---|---|---|---|---|---|
| 1. Identify total number of faculty required to meet teaching, sponsored research or program, and administrative needs | | 2 | 5 | | | | | | |
| 2. Determine number of faculty gains and losses from sabbaticals or leaves of absence granted, release of existing faculty, and faculty returning from sabbaticals or leaves of absence | | 2 | 5 | | | | | | |
| 3. Identify changes in rank resulting from promotions | | 2 | 5 | | | | | | |
| 4. Determine from previous steps the number of vacancies, by rank and category, to be filled by regular or interim appointments | | 2 | 5 | | | | | | |
| 5. Make provisions in annual operating budget for funds required to meet faculty staffing needs | | 3 | 4 | | | | | | |
| 6. Receive notification of approval of budget requests | 5 | 2 | | | | | | | |

|  |  | | | | | | | | |
|---|------|---|---|---|---|---|---|---|---|
| 7. | Receive authorization to recruit new faculty | 5 | 2 | | | | | | |
| 8. | Identify candidates | 3 | 4 | 5 | | | | | |
| 9. | Obtain applications from approved candidates | | 2 | | 5 | | | | |
| 10. | Screen applications and recommend issuance of invitations for personal interviews | 3 | 4 | 5 | | | | | |
| 11. | Issue invitations | 2 | | | | | | | |
| 12. | Receive acceptance of invitations and schedule interviews | 2 | | | | | | | |
| 13. | Conduct interviews | 2 | 2 | 2 | 5 | | | | |
| 14. | Conduct reference checks | 2 | 2 | | 5 | | | | |
| 15. | Recommend appointment | 3 | 4 | 5 | | | | | |
| 16. | Prepare offer of appointment letter | 1 | 2 | | | 2 | | | |
| 17. | Encumber budgetary funds for position | 5 | 5 | | | 2 | | | |
| 18. | Issue offer of appointment | 5 | | 5 | | | | | |
| 19. | Receive acceptance of offer of appointment | 2 | 2 | | 5 | | | | |
| 20. | Receive notification of acceptance | 5 | 2 | | | | 2 | 2 | |
| 21. | Receive notification of employment | 5 | | | | | | | |
| 22. | Obtain payroll calculation and fringe benefit election data from new appointees | | | 5 | | | 2 | 2 | 2 |
| 23. | Enter data into payroll system | | | | | | 2 | 5 | 2 |

*Explanation of Decision Matrix 19.*

| Step | Action Responsibility | Action |
|------|----------------------|--------|
| 1, 2, 3, & 4. | Chief Academic Officer | Determines, on the basis of input from her department heads, the number of faculty required by the multi-year plan; the number of faculty lost to sabbaticals, leaves of absence, and nonreappointment; the number of faculty returning from sabbaticals and leaves of absence; changes in mix by rank resulting from promotions; and the number of new faculty required as regular appointees and as interim appointees. |
| 5 & 6. | Chief Academic Officer | Enters the results of steps 1 through 4 into the annual operating budget and receives notification of authorized budget from the president. |
| 7 & 8. | Department Heads | Receive the chief academic officer's authorization to recruit agreed-on new faculty and identify a slate of candidates, using input from their counterparts at other institutions, professional societies, and departmental faculty. |
|  | Chief Academic Officer | Reviews the slate of candidates with department |

*Explanation of Decision Matrix 19, Cont'd.*

| Step | Action Responsibility | Action |
|------|----------------------|--------|
| | | heads and authorizes them to seek applications from candidates. |
| 9, 10, & 11. | Department Heads | Receives applications and screens them, obtaining input from departmental faculty, and recommends applicants to be invited to the campus for personal interviews. |
| | Chief Academic Officer | Reviews department heads' recommendations and issues invitations to agreed-on applicants. |
| 12. | Chief Academic Officer | Receives applicants' notification of acceptance of invitation to visit campus and schedules interviews. |
| 13. | President, Chief Academic Officer, Department Heads, and Faculty | Conduct interviews with applicants, document results, and rank selection recommendations. |
| 14 & 15. | Chief Academic Officer | Conducts reference checks on candidates and, on the basis of input from faculty members and the department heads' recommendations, recommends making an offer of appointment to selected candidates and |

*Explanation of Decision Matrix 19, Cont'd.*

*Step*          *Action Responsibility*   *Action*

|  |  |  |
|--|--|--|
|  |  | recommends terms of appointment. |
| 16. | President | Approves the chief academic officer's recommendations and authorizes the preparation of appointment contracts. |
| 17 & 18. | Chief Academic Officer | Prepares the appointment contracts. Obtains concurrence of terms from the director of grant and contract administration if any portion of the appointees' efforts are to be devoted to sponsored agreements. Obtains budgetary encumbrance from budget control. Obtains the president's signature on the appointment contracts and sends them to the candidates. |
| 19 & 20. | President | Receives acceptances of appointment contracts from the candidates and notifies the chief academic officer and appropriate department heads of their receipt. |
| 21 & 22. | Director of Personnel | Receives notification of appointments from the chief academic officer. Obtains data required for payroll |

*Explanation of Decision Matrix 19, Cont'd.*

| Step | Action Responsibility | Action |
|------|----------------------|--------|
| | | calculation and fringe benefit coverage from the appointees. |
| 23. | Payroll | Enters data on new appointees, received from the director of personnel, into the payroll system. |

## Decision Matrix 20. Comprehensive Career Development Program.

Legend of decision-making roles
1 – Authorizes action
2 – Action responsibility
3 – Approves recommendation
4 – Recommends action
5 – Provides input

*Participants in Decision-Making Processes*

| Procedural Steps | President | Advisory Committee | Chief Academic Officer | Curriculum Committee | Faculty | Academic Advisers | Nonacademic Counselors | Career Development Director | Chief Fiscal Officer | Chief Student Affairs Officer | Alumni Relations Director | Chief Development Officer | Students | Employers |
|---|---|---|---|---|---|---|---|---|---|---|---|---|---|---|
| 1. Define scope of development program | | | 3 | 5 | | 5 | 5 | 4 | | 5 | | | | |
| 2. Define organizational structure of career development program | | | 3 | | | 5 | 5 | 4 | | | | | | |
| 3. Define program's operational relationship with nonacademic counseling programs | | | 3 | | | 5 | 5 | 4 | | 5 | | | | |
| 4. Approve scope, organization, and relationship | 3 | 4 | 5 | 5 | 5 | 5 | 5 | 5 | | | | | | |
| 5. Authorize implementation of program | 1 | | 2 | | | | | 2 | | | | | | |
| 6. Carry out program | | | 5 | 5 | 5 | 5 | 5 | 2 | 5 | 5 | | | 5 | 5 |
| 7. Conduct ongoing assessment of program through in-house and external evaluation of program | | | 5 | 5 | 5 | 5 | 5 | 2 | 5 | 5 | | | 5 | 5 |
| 8. Recommend changes in scope, organization, and relationship | | | 3 | | | | | 4 | | | | | | |
| 9. Advise affected administrators of changes necessary | | | 1 | | | | | 2 | | | | | | |
| 10. Receive program director's report of results of program operations | 2 | | 2 | 2 | | 2 | 2 | 5 | | 2 | 2 | 2 | | |

*Explanation of Decision Matrix 20.*

| Step | Action Responsibility | Action |
|------|----------------------|--------|
| 1, 2, & 3. | Director of Career Development | Formulates recommended definition of the scope of the career development program, its organizational structure and its relationship to the other academic and non-academic counseling programs on the basis of input from the chief student affairs officer and other academic and nonacademic counselors. |
| | Chief Academic Officer | Approves the program's recommended scope, organizational structure, and relationship and obtains the curriculum committee's recommendations regarding the portion of the career development program that covers experiential learning for academic credit. |
| 4. | Advisory Committee | Reviews the scope, organization, relationship, and programs of the career development program recommended by the chief academic officer, obtaining clarification from the director of career development; recommends presidential approval. |
| | President | Approves the career development program as recommended. |

*Explanation of Decision Matrix 20, Cont'd.*

| Step | Action Responsibility | Action |
|------|----------------------|--------|
| 5 & 6. | Director of Career Development | Carries out career development program, when authorized to do so by the president, working closely with other segments of campus. |
| 7 & 8. | Director of Career Development | Monitors programs, maintains records of their effectiveness, and formulates recommendations for changes in their implementation on the basis of input from employers, students, faculty, academic advisers, nonacademic counselors, the chief student affairs officer, and the curriculum committee (if changes are proposed in experiential learning for credit programs). |
|  | Chief Academic Officer | Reviews and approves recommended changes in the implementation of career development program activities. |
| 9. | Director of Career Development | Advises affected administrators and faculty of changes in implementation when authorized to do so by the chief academic officer. |
| 10. | Director of Career Development | Reports the results of the career development program to appropriate administrators. |

# Registration
# and Academic Records

The functions of registration and the maintenance of academic records, performed by the registrar, are among the most important carried out by colleges and universities. The registrar, in addition to maintaining the students' academic records, is responsible for analyzing them to determine the results of academic operations and for reporting the results of these analyses to the chief academic officer and other administrators. Therefore, the registrar should be qualified to hold and should be given academic rank. As an administrator, however, he should not be given tenure.

The following essential standards of good management are considered appropriate to the registrar's function.

★ The registrar should be responsible for developing an operating calendar that identifies the dates on which activities related to registering students or recording the results of academic operations will take place. The registrar's operating calendar must of course be related to the institution's academic calendar. Should the institution consider changing its academic calendar, he should be responsible also for the coordination of all activities related thereto (see Decision Matrix 27).

★ The registrar should be responsible for developing the plan and procedures to be followed in conducting registration.

In formulating the registration plan and procedures, he should obtain input from students, academic counselors, instructional department heads, the directors of financial aid, housing, health services, and recruiting and admission, and the chief fiscal officer. The plan and procedures should permit students to complete their registration as quickly as possible while repeating as few steps as possible.

The plan and procedures should include the following requirements. Each student should hold a permit to register showing that the student has been properly admitted, has not been dropped, and is not encumbered for financial or disciplinary reasons. Academic counselors should advise students so that the courses that are required for their degrees are taken in the proper sequence and should assist them in working out a conflict-free schedule. A course card should be issued to each student for each course to ensure a space in the class for the student and to provide the instructor with a validated "permit to enter." Before reaching the registration desk, the student should have completed and be able to present a class schedule, a course card for each course, verification of financial aid eligibility, and appropriate personal information forms. Before sending the student to the cashier's desk, the registrar should verify that all forms are properly completed and record the assessment of fees payable by the student on forms that have been designed by the registrar and the chief fiscal officer. The cashier should collect the net fees payable — that is, assessed charges less prepayments made and financial aid awarded — or obtain the chief fiscal officer's approval for a deferred payment plan before validating the student's registration document. The cashier should be responsible for seeing to it that copies of registration documents required by the fiscal officer are retained, that students receive their copies, and that the balance are returned to the registrar for his use or distribution.

In summary, the registration process should provide the student with a workable academic schedule, the fiscal office with a record of funds collected or to be collected and the type and amount of financial aid awarded each student, and the registrar with data required to produce preliminary class rosters, lists of registered students for various administrative offices, and updated personal information for each student. Where the record-keeping processes of the registrar, the financial aid office, and student accounts receivable are automated, a linkage should be established between these computer files to permit the financial aid office and student accounts receivable to obtain the personal information they need regarding students from the registrar's records. This linkage will not only eliminate the need to maintain duplicate personal information on students but should also enhance the accuracy and uniformity of such data (see Decision Matrix 21).

★    The registrar should formulate procedures covering schedule revision (add/drops) by students after registration. These procedures should be formulated in the same way and provide for the same results as those formulated for registration. With regard to the registrar's recording of add/drops, it is extremely important that the records of original registration not be erased or destroyed, because such initial registration records may be required to support financial aid awards made to the student. At many institutions, original registration records have been erased or destroyed as a result of recording subsequent add/drop transactions initiated by students after the expiration of the institution's refund policy. In several cases, this has resulted in the federal government and state governments demanding refunds from the institutions for invalid financial aid awards of hundreds of thousands of dollars. The amount of financial aid a student is entitled to under federal and state regulations depends on a number of factors. One of these factors is the student's registered status as either a full-time, three-quarter-time, or half-time student. When registration records for dropped courses are erased, the full-time student may appear to be registered only on a part-time basis. Federal and state auditors believe they should be able to rely on the registrar's records to support the enrollment status on which the students' financial aid awards were based. In auditing financial aid awards (frequently several years after the awards were made), if they find that a financial aid award was based on a student's full-time status but the registrar's records show the student enrolled only for enough credits to earn three-quarter or half-time status, they demand a refund (see Decision Matrix 22).

★ The only circumstance under which a student's registration records should be cancelled is if the student withdraws from the institution prior to the beginning of classes for a session. Under these circumstances, the student should be given a refund for any payments made for charges other than the application and registration processing fee. The student, however, should not be refunded any payments or credits to his account that were not made by him. When the student's registration is cancelled, the registrar must notify each instructor concerned (see Decision Matrix 27).

★ When a student withdraws after classes for the session have begun, the registrar should make sure that the student has obtained required clearances. Such clearances should include the library, the housing department (for a residential student), the academic adviser, the chief student affairs officer, and the chief fiscal officer.

★ Following each registration period, prior to the preparation of enrollment reports, the registrar should make sure that the admissions office, financial aid office, and students' accounts office have appropriate information about registered students and arrange for the correction of any discrepancies among their records.

★ The registrar should issue enrollment reports that are required for both current and multi-year planning. The number and types of reports to be made routinely for each session should be planned for well in advance. The general format of such reports will rarely require changes once they are determined to be adequate to meet internal needs and to comply with the external reporting requirements of state and federal agencies. Such reports should include, at the least, head counts of students by class and sex for each curriculum, with subtotals and grand totals; by age; by credit hour load; by residence classification; by ethnic group; and by housing unit. They should also include head counts of first-time admits according to whether they are beginners, transfer students, or reentries; of course enrollment by subject; and of candidates for degrees.

★   Grade reporting procedures should be developed by the registrar. Once adopted, the institution's grading policies must be adhered to strictly by all instructors. The registrar should provide the forms to be used in grade reporting and verify that grade reports for each student enrolled in each course or section are submitted when due. Grades should be recorded promptly and reported to each student as quickly as possible, with a copy of the student's grade report being made available to the adviser. Grade reports should provide not only the grades earned but also session and cumulative indices and notification of status (for example, honors, placed on probation, continued on probation, or dropped) (see Decision Matrix 23).

★   Immediately following the issuance of grade reports, the registrar should issue summary reports of student status and appropriate listings of students in each status being reported. Except for the listing of students who have achieved academic honors, these reports and listings should be for internal use only. These summary reports and listings should include, at the least, academic status by major, class, and sex; dropped students by major, class, and sex; students placed on probation by major, class, and sex; students continued on probation by major, class, and sex; honor students by major, class, and sex; and an alphabetical listing of all students showing their status. One copy of the alphabetical listing report must be submitted to the director of financial aid for use in determining future eligibility for financial aid assistance. The registrar should also provide the chief academic officer with a grade distribution report for use in evaluating faculty grading practices. This report should show the number of students receiving each grade for each section course, totals for each course, totals for all courses in the department, and grand totals for each grade. The registrar also should prepare, at the end of each session, a summary report showing the session and cumulative grade indices. This report should show the number of students by index level (from 4.0 to 0.0 with as many intervening gradations as are desired), the number of students, by sex, in each class with each index, and the percentile rank of students with each index.

★   The period of time allowed for students to have incomplete grades removed from academic records should be published and strictly adhered to.

★   Incomplete grades should not enter into the calculation of grade point averages. Including them in such calculations could lower the grade point average below that required to maintain eligibility for financial aid under state and federal programs.

★   The academic record maintained for each student should present sufficient personal data to identify the student and should be a complete and accurate record of all transfer or experiential learning credits, credits granted by departments, and credits earned at the institution. Transcripts submitted by students applying for transfer admission should be evaluated by the registrar for acceptability within established policy for general education credits. The acceptability of transfer credits for the specific requirements of the student's major should be obtained by the registrar from the appropriate departmental faculty. The registrar should then submit a written report to the director of admissions showing total transferable credits, credits applicable toward general education requirements, and credits applicable toward the degree requirements of the major to which the student is admitted. Transferable credits should not be entered on the student's academic record until the student has registered and the session is under way. Regulations and policies regarding the granting of credit by an academic department — such as advance credits, credits earned by examination, or credits earned for experiential learning — should be adhered to. The registrar should be responsible for verifying that all institutional regulations and policies have been adhered to before entering departmental credits into the student's academic record. Earned credits should be reported by instructors at the close of each session with grades. The amount of credit for each course should be fixed and not be increased or decreased by the instructor.

★ Procedures to be followed in updating a student's academic record, correcting errors in grades or personal data, recording completion of a course for which an incomplete grade was originally assigned, and recording dates of withdrawal, graduation dates, and degrees awarded should be documented. Such procedures should be designed to ensure the accuracy of all data in the student's record; the registrar should be held responsible for seeing to it that all prescribed procedures are adhered to.

★ The registrar is responsible for seeing to it that student records are protected from theft, fire, vandalism, tampering, and other catastrophes.

★ The registrar should be thoroughly knowledgeable about the Family Rights and Privacy Act of 1974, as amended, and should be responsible for informing other administrative and instructional personnel about the provisions of that law.

★ Certification of a student's status should be made only by the registrar. Only data needed to meet the certification requirements of outside agencies (classified as "directory information") or by the director of financial aid to determine eligibility for financial assistance should be released.

★ In preparation for commencement, the registrar should be responsible for arranging with each department head to have each candidate's academic record audited, arranging for diplomas, and assisting others in the printing of programs and details of the commencement exercise. Approximately thirty days after the end of each session, whether or not a commencement exercise is held, the registrar should issue a report of degrees granted showing the number and types of degrees (associate, baccalaureate, and so on) awarded to men and women for each major. Another report in the same format, required by the United States Department of Education's National Center for Education Statistics, should be prepared for each ethnic group (see Decision Matrix 25).

    ★   Transcript procedures should be developed by the registrar and documented. These procedures should be designed to ensure that transcripts are issued only upon the written request of the student concerned; that payment for such transcripts, if a fee is assessed, is received; and that no transcripts are issued to students who have a financial encumbrance on their records.

    ★   The registrar should maintain a system of recording encumbrances of academic records based on institutional regulations. This system should provide for the recording of financial encumbrances that prevent students from enrolling for another session, receiving an official transcript of their academic records, or receiving their degrees or diplomas; disciplinary encumbrances that prevent a student from registering for one or more sessions or from ever returning as a student (disciplinary encumbrances should not, however, prevent students from having transcripts issued); and academic encumbrances that prevent a student from registering again unless the student is readmitted. The encumbrance system should also provide for the removal of encumbrances. Periodically, the registrar should prepare a report identifying students with encumbrances and the reasons for them. These reports should be reviewed by the appropriate administrators to make sure that no student's records remain encumbered when the reason for the encumbrance no longer exists (see Decision Matrix 24).

    ★   At least once a year, after registration for the first session of the academic year, the registrar should provide the administration with a report that identifies attrition losses by class and type of student. All institutions will suffer some attrition losses. However, when an institution, having reviewed the registrar's report on such losses, deems them to be excessive, the president should appoint an institutional task force to identify the causes and the corrective actions that should be taken to reduce such losses to an acceptable level (see Decision Matrix 26).

★ The registrar should have a record retention policy that specifies the period for which each document in his office must be retained. Any document to be destroyed that identifies a student by name should be shredded or burned.

★ Every procedure involved in registration and the maintenance of academic records should be reviewed periodically. The purpose of such review is to identify changes that would increase accuracy or efficiency, reduce costs, enhance student relationships, or provide lead time for revising forms and for planning, developing, and testing new procedures.

Readers who desire more information about the activities related to registration and academic records should contact the American Association of Collegiate Registrars and Admission Officers (AACRAO), One Dupont Circle, Washington, D.C. 20036.

## Decision Matrix 21. Registration.

Legend of decision-making roles
1 – Authorizes action
2 – Action responsibility
3 – Approves recommendation
4 – Recommends action
5 – Provides input

*Participants in Decision-Making Processes*

| Procedural Steps | Board of Trustees | President | Advisory Committee | Chief Fiscal Officer | Academic Department Heads | Academic Advisers | Financial Aid Director | Student Housing Director | Health Services Director | Admissions Director | Chief Academic Officer | Registrar | Physical Plant Director | Students |
|---|---|---|---|---|---|---|---|---|---|---|---|---|---|---|
| 1. Formulate recommended registration plan and procedures | | 2 | 3 | 5 | 5 | 5 | 5 | 5 | 5 | 5 | 5 | 2 | 5 | 5 |
| 2. Approve registration plan and procedures | | 1 | | | | | | | | | | 4 | 1 | |
| 3. Authorize implementation | | | | | | | | | | | | 2 | | |
| 4. Make space and facility arrangements for registration | | | | | | | | | | | | | 2 | |
| 5. Provide required registration forms | | | | 2 | | | | | | | | 2 | | |
| 6. Conduct registration: | | | | | | | | | | | | | | |
| (a) verify authorization to register | | | | | | | 2 | 2 | 2 | | | 2 | | |
| (b) admit matriculants to scheduled courses and sections | | | | | 4 | 5 | | | | 2 | | 2 | | 5 |
| (c) open additional sections if required | | | | | 2 | 5 | | 2 | | | 3 | 2 | | 5 |
| (d) issue housing assignments | | | | | | | | 2 | | | | | | 5 |
| (e) provide health clearance | | | | | | | | | 2 | | | | | 5 |
| (f) verify documentation completeness and assess fees | | | | | | | | | | | | 2 | | |
| (g) determine financial aid status | | | | | | | 2 | | | | | | | 5 |
| (h) audit fee assessment, make financial arrangements, issue class admit, housing, and meal ticket authorizations | | | | 2 | | | | | | | | 2 | | 5 |

|  | | | | | | | | |
|---|---|---|---|---|---|---|---|---|
| 7. Receive copies of registration documentation and update student records | 5 | | | | | | | 2 |
| 8. Review preliminary enrollment report | 2 | 2 | 2 | 2 | | | 2 | 5 |
| 9. Receive enrollment reports | 2 | 2 | 2 | 2 | 2 | | 2 | 5 |
| 10. Receive president's report on enrollment | | | | | | 2 | | 5 |
| 11. Issue certification reports | 5 | 5 | 5 | 5 | | 5 | 2 | |
| 12. Evaluate registration process | 5 | 5 | 5 | 5 | 5 | 5 | 4 | 5 |

*Explanation of Decision Matrix 21.*

| *Step* | *Action Responsibility* | *Action* |
|---|---|---|
| 1. | Registrar | Formulates, after obtaining input from students, recommended plan and procedures for the conduct of registration, in conjunction with the chief academic officer, academic advisers, academic department heads, the chief fiscal officer, the director of financial aid, the director of admissions, the director of student housing, the director of health services, and the director of the physical plant. |
| 2 & 3. | Advisory Committee | Reviews recommended registration plan and procedures and recommends presidential approval. |
| | President | Approves registration plan and procedures and authorizes their implementation. |
| 4 & 5. | Director of Physical Plant | Sets up facilities to be used for registration when authorized to do so by the registrar. |
| | Registrar, Chief Fiscal Officer, Directors of Financial Aid, Health Services, and Student Housing | Prepare and provide all forms required for use in the registration process. |

*Explanation of Decision Matrix 21, Cont'd.*

| Step | Action Responsibility | Action |
|------|----------------------|--------|
| 6a. | Registrar | Determines that all new students wishing to enroll have been accepted for admission and are authorized to matriculate. Determines for all returning or continuing students that no encumbrance, academic or fiscal, prohibits their matriculation. |
| | Director of Admissions | Reviews each case where a new student wishing to enroll has not been accepted for admission and determines whether to authorize matriculation. |
| 6b. | Academic Advisers | Review the academic history of the matriculants and their selected courses of study; assist the matriculants in revising their academic programs and schedules when it is deemed appropriate to do so in light of their academic abilities or career objectives; sign students' academic schedules and issue, for each course or section in which they are enrolled, class admit cards for ultimate validation by the chief fiscal officer. |
| 6c. | Registrar | Is advised by academic advisers of demand for |

| Step | Action Responsibility | Action |
|------|----------------------|--------|
| | | courses where all sections are filled. Obtains authorization from the chief academic officer, with the concurrence of the appropriate academic department head, to open new sections. Advises academic advisers of new sections opened and issues class admit cards for those sections. |
| 6d. | Director of Student Housing | Issues student housing assignment authorization form, for ultimate validation by the chief fiscal officer, to students desiring to live or required to live in campus housing. |
| 6e. | Director of Health Services | Verifies that physical examination data have been submitted or schedules required physical examinations. Issues health clearance to students. |
| 6f. | Registrar | Verifies that students have met registration requirements and that their registration documentation is complete. Computes tuition and fee charges to be assessed and completes and signs the tuition and fee assessment portion of the student financial status form. |

*Explanation of Decision Matrix 21, Cont'd.*

| Step | Action Responsibility | Action |
|------|----------------------|--------|
| 6g. | Director of Financial Aid | Determines whether all documentation required to award financial aid has been received. If so, determines the amount and packaging of the award, completes an award letter, and obtains the student's signature accepting the award. Completes and signs the financial aid portion of the student financial status form. If not, assists the student in making arrangements to obtain the required documentation. Obtains data from students regarding their or their parents' financial condition; calculates a tentative award entitlement amount; completes, signs, and provides the student with a copy of a tentative financial aid entitlement calculation form. |
| 6h. | Chief Fiscal Officer | Audits tuition and fee charges assessed by the registrar; reviews final or tentative financial aid awards; determines whether the student has made any prepaid deposits and, if so, enters the amount of deposit on the financial status form; determines, for a returning student, whether any unpaid balance from |

*Explanation of Decision Matrix 21, Cont'd.*

*Step        Action Responsibility    Action*

|  |  | previous years exists; receives and receipts the student's payment and determines whether the student requires a deferred payment plan; if so, has the student sign a deferred payment plan agreement and counsels the student regarding payment obligations and penalties; and validates the student's schedule, class admit cards, housing authorization, and meal tickets, providing the student with a copy of each. |

| 7. | Registrar | Receives copies of validated registration records from the chief fiscal officer, updates student records, and prepares preliminary student enrollment status listing report. |

| 8 & 9. | Chief Fiscal Officer, Director of Student Housing, and Chief Academic Officer | Compare preliminary student enrollment status listing report with their records and reconcile discrepancies. |

|  | Registrar | Corrects discrepancies in student records and issues enrollment status reports to the president, the chief academic officer, academic advisers and |

*Explanation of Decision Matrix 21, Cont'd.*

| Step | Action Responsibility | Action |
|------|----------------------|--------|
| | | department heads, the chief fiscal officer, and the directors of admissions, financial aid, student housing, and health services. |
| 10. | Board of Trustees | Receives and accepts the president's report on enrollment status. |
| 11. | Registrar | Prepares and issues certified enrollment status reports required by financial aid funding agencies. |
| 12. | Registrar | Evaluates the registration process and formulates recommendations for improvement after obtaining input from the chief academic officer, academic advisers and department heads, students, the chief fiscal officer, and the directors of admissions, financial aid, student housing, and health services. |

## Decision Matrix 22. Change in Enrollment Status.

Legend of decision-making roles

1 – Authorizes action
2 – Action responsibility
3 – Approves recommendation
4 – Recommends action
5 – Provides input

| Procedural Steps | Participants in Decision-Making Processes | | | | | | | | | | |
|---|---|---|---|---|---|---|---|---|---|---|---|
| | Chief Student Affairs Officer | Chief Fiscal Officer | Academic Advisers | Faculty | Financial Aid Director | Student Housing Director | Librarian | Health Services Director | Chief Academic Officer | Registrar | Students |
| 1. (a) Obtain authorization to add or drop courses | | | 5 | 5 | | | | | | | 2 |
| (b) Obtain authorization to change residential status | | | | | | 5 | | | | | 2 |
| (c) Obtain authorization to withdraw from institution | 5 | | 5 | | | 5 | 5 | | 5 | | 2 |
| (d) Cancel registration | | | | | | | | | | | 2 |
| 2. Verify that student has obtained all required clearances for desired change in enrollment status and calculate fee adjustment related to changes | | | | | | | | | | 2 | 5 |
| 3. Require student to obtain financial aid and fiscal office clearances for changes in status related to 1-c | | 5 | | | 5 | | | | | | 2 |
| 4. Receive registrar's notification of cancellation of registration and update their records | 2 | 2 | 2 | 2 | 2 | 2 | 2 | 2 | | 5 | |
| 5. Receive required financial aid and fiscal office clearances obtained by student | | | | | 2 | 2 | 2 | | | 2 | 5 |
| 6. Update student's record | | | | | | | | | | 2 | |
| 7. Revise enrollment status reports | | | | | | | | | | 2 | |

*Explanation of Decision Matrix 22.*

| Step | Action Responsibility | Action |
|------|----------------------|--------|
| 1a. | Students | Obtain authorization to add or drop courses from their academic advisers and from faculty members teaching the courses to be dropped or added. |
| 1b. | Students | Obtain authorization to change their residential status from the director of student housing. |
| 1c. | Students | Obtain authorization to withdraw from the institution from their academic advisers, the chief academic officer, the chief student affairs officer, the librarian, and the director of student housing. |
| 1d. | Students | Decide to cancel registration before attending classes. |
| 2. | Registrar | Receives students' notification of their intent to change course selection or enrollment status; verifies that students have obtained all required authorizations to do so; and calculates tuition or fee charge adjustments that are associated with the changes the students are making. Notifies students that they must obtain clearances from |

*Explanation of Decision Matrix 22, Cont'd.*

| Step | Action Responsibility | Action |
|------|----------------------|--------|
|      |                      | the director of financial aid and the chief fiscal officer if the change is other than registration cancellation and involves a change from full-time to part-time enrollment status (or the reverse) or a change in assessed charges. |
| 3.   | Director of Financial Aid | Reviews with students any change in financial aid award entitlement resulting from the change in enrollment status; prepares and has students sign revised award letters; provides students with copies of the revised award letters; notifies the chief fiscal officer of revised awards; and signs clearances for change in enrollment status. |
|      | Chief Fiscal Officer | Reviews with students the effects of changes in assessed charges and financial aid awards on their financial obligation to the institution; prepares and has students sign revised deferred payment plan agreements or issues refund authorizations, as appropriate; provides students with copies of revised deferred payment agreements or refund authorizations; and |

*Explanation of Decision Matrix 22, Cont'd.*

| *Step* | *Action Responsibility* | *Action* |
|--------|-------------------------|----------|
| | | signs clearances for change in enrollment status. |
| 4. | Registrar | Notifies all affected parties of students' cancellation of registration. |
| 5, 6, & 7. | Registrar | Receives financial aid and chief fiscal officer's clearances obtained by the students, enters change in enrollment status data into the students' records, and revises enrollment status reports. |

**Decision Matrix 23. Grade Reporting.**

Legend of decision-making roles:
1 – Authorizes action
2 – Action responsibility
3 – Approves recommendation
4 – Recommends action
5 – Provides input

*Participants in Decision-Making Processes*

| Procedural Steps | Chief Academic Officer | Department Heads | Faculty | Academic Advisers | Financial Aid Director | Registrar | Students |
|---|---|---|---|---|---|---|---|
| 1. Formulate recommended grade reporting forms, procedures, and calendar | | | | | | 2 | |
| 2. Review and approve recommended forms, procedures, and calendar | 3 | | | | | 4 | |
| 3. Receive grade reporting forms for each student enrolled in courses they teach | | | 2 | | | 5 | |
| 4. Determine grades | | | 2 | | | | |
| 5. Receive grade reports and verify that all reports due have been submitted | | | 5 | | | | |
| 6. Update student records | | | | | | 2 | |
| 7. Receive grade reports | | | | 2 | | 2 | |
| 8. Prepare summary grade reports and alphabetical student status report | | | | | | 5 | 2 |
| 9. Receive alphabetical student status report | | | | | 2 | 2 | |
| 10. Receive summary grading reports | 2 | 2 | 2 | | | 5 | |
| 11. Evaluate grading practices | 2 | 2 | | | | 5 | |

*Explanation of Decision Matrix 23.*

| Step | Action Responsibility | Action |
|------|----------------------|--------|
| 1. | Registrar | Formulates recommended forms, procedures, and calendar for grade reporting. |
| 2. | Chief Academic Officer | Reviews and approves the registrar's recommendations. |
| 3. | Faculty | Receive from the registrar grade reporting forms for each student registered in each course they are teaching. |
| 4. | Faculty | Conduct examinations, determine and record students' grades on forms provided by the registrar, sign grade reporting forms, and transmit them to the registrar. |
| 5. | Registrar | Verifies that grade reporting forms have been submitted by faculty for all students registered in each course they teach and that forms have not been submitted for students not registered in such courses. Follows up with faculty to obtain missing grade reports and notifies faculty that grades will not be entered for students not registered for their courses. |
| 6. | Registrar | Enters grades into the students' records and advises |

| *Step* | *Action Responsibility* | *Action* |
|--------|------------------------|----------|
| | | students and their academic advisers of grades received. |
| 7, 8, 9, & 10. | Registrar | Analyzes grades awarded, prepares summary grade reports and alphabetical listings of students' current and cumulative grade point averages. Issues summary grade reports to the chief academic officer, academic department heads, and faculty. Issues an alphabetical listing of students' current and cumulative grade point averages to the director of financial aid for use in determining continued eligibility to receive financial aid awards. |
| 11. | Chief Academic Officer | Evaluates departmental and faculty grading practices and determines their acceptability. |

**Decision Matrix 24. Encumbrance of Academic Records and Transcripts.**

Legend of decision-making roles
1 – Authorizes action
2 – Action responsibility
3 – Approves recommendation
4 – Recommends action
5 – Provides input

| Procedural Steps | Participants in Decision-Making Processes | | | | | |
|---|---|---|---|---|---|---|
| | Chief Academic Officer | Chief Student Affairs Officer | Chief Fiscal Officer | Cashier | Registrar | Students or Alumni |
| 1. Receive notifications of encumbrance and update student records for | | | | | | |
| (a) disciplinary or academic reasons | 5 | 5 | | | 2 | |
| (b) financial reasons | | | 5 | | 2 | |
| 2. Receive notification of release of encumbrance and update student records for | | | | | | |
| (a) disciplinary or academic reasons | 5 | 5 | | | 2 | |
| (b) financial reasons | | | 5 | | 2 | |
| 3. Receive request for transcript | | | | | 2 | 5 |
| 4. Verify that no encumbrances are in force | | | | | 2 | |
| 5. Receive transcript fee and issue receipt | | | | 2 | 5 | |
| 6. Issue transcript and fee receipt | | | | | 2 | |

*Explanation of Decision Matrix 24.*

| Step | Action Responsibility | Action |
|---|---|---|
| 1 & 2. | Registrar | Records encumbrances or release of encumbrances of a student's record when instructed to do so by the chief academic officer, for academic reasons; the chief student affairs officer, for disciplinary reasons; or the chief fiscal officer, for financial reasons. |
| 3. | Registrar | Receives request and payment for transcripts from students or alumni. |
| 4. | Registrar | Verifies that no encumbrance is in force against the student's academic records. If there is, notifies the student of inability to comply with the request and returns transcript payment received. |
| 5. | Registrar | Turns payment over to cashier and obtains his receipt for it. |
| 6. | Registrar | Issues requested transcripts and sends student receipt of payment. |

*Explanation of Decision Matrix 25.*

| *Step* | *Action Responsibility* | *Action* |
|---|---|---|
| 1. | Department Heads | Receive and audit the listing of candidates for degrees and their academic records provided by the registrar. |
| 2 & 3. | Registrar | Receives returned list of candidates audited by the department heads and orders diplomas and diploma covers. |
| 4. | Registrar | Receives and audits printed diplomas, places them in labeled diploma covers, and arranges covers in alphabetical order. |
| 5 & 6. | Registrar | Receives final grades and determines whether candidates have completed all requirements. Determines, in consultation with the chief fiscal officer, whether existing encumbrances for financial reasons will be removed or new encumbrances added. |
| 7. | Registrar | Obtains from the president notification of whether students whose records are encumbered or who failed to complete academic requirements will be permitted to participate in commencement. |

**Decision Matrix 25. Commencement.**

Legend of decision-making roles
1 – Authorizes action
2 – Action responsibility
3 – Approves recommendation
4 – Recommends action
5 – Provides input

| Procedural Steps | Board of Trustees | President | Academic Department Heads | Chief Fiscal Officer | Registrar |
|---|---|---|---|---|---|
| | | | *Participants in Decision-Making Processes* | | |
| 1. Receive and audit listing of candidates for degrees and copies of their academic records | | | 2 | | 5 |
| 2. Receive audited records from department heads | | | 5 | | 2 |
| 3. Order diplomas and diploma covers | | | | | 2 |
| 4. Audit diplomas, place them in labeled covers, and arrange covers in alphabetical order | | | | | 2 |
| 5. Verify that candidates have completed final requirements | | | | | 2 |
| 6. Determine whether candidates' records are encumbered for financial reasons | | | | 5 | 2 |
| 7. Determine whether candidates who have not completed academic requirements or who have financial encumbrances will be allowed to participate in commencement exercises | | 2 | | | 5 |

| | | |
|---|---|---|
| 8. Remove diplomas and covers of students who will not be allowed to participate | | 2 |
| 9. Replace diplomas in covers of students who will be allowed to participate with letter advising them that encumbrance must be removed to obtain their diploma | | |
| 10. Obtain trustee approval to award degrees | 1 | 2 |
| 11. Receive diplomas for presentation at commencement | 2 | 5 |
| 12. Prepare report of degrees granted | 2 | 2 |

*Explanation of Decision Matrix 25, Cont'd.*

| *Step* | *Action Responsibility* | *Action* |
|---|---|---|
| 8 & 9. | Registrar | Removes diploma covers from alphabetical sorting for students who will not be permitted to participate in commencement. Removes diplomas from covers of students whose records are encumbered and replaces diplomas with letters advising students why their diplomas are withheld. |
| 10. | President | Presents the slate of candidates for degrees to the board of trustees and obtains its authorization to award degrees. |
|  | Board of Trustees | Authorizes the awarding of degrees. |
| 11. | President | Receives from the registrar diploma covers to be presented at commencement. |
| 12. | Registrar | Prepares report of degrees granted. |

# Decision Matrix 26. Attrition Analysis.

Legend of decision-making roles
1 – Authorizes action
2 – Action responsibility
3 – Approves recommendation
4 – Recommends action
5 – Provides input

Participants in Decision-Making Processes

| Procedural Steps | Board of Trustees | President | Advisory Committee | Chief Academic Officer | Chief Student Affairs Officer | Chief Fiscal Officer | Faculty | Academic Requirements Committee | Curriculum Committee | Career Development Director | Counselors | Recruiting and Admissions Director | Students | Attrition Task Force | Registrar |
|---|---|---|---|---|---|---|---|---|---|---|---|---|---|---|---|
| 1. Prepare attrition analysis report | | 2 | | 2 | 2 | 2 | | | | 2 | | 2 | | | 2 |
| 2. Receive attrition analysis report | | 2 | | | | | | | | | | | | | 5 |
| 3. Appoint attrition task force | | 2 | 4 | | | | | | | | | | | | 5 |
| 4. Receive president's report on attrition analysis and notification of his or her decision to appoint a task force to reduce attrition | 2 | 5 | | | | | | | | | | | | | |
| 5. Determine causes of attrition | | 1 | | 5 | 5 | 5 | 5 | | | 5 | 5 | 5 | 5 | 2 | 5 |
| 6. Develop recommendations for changes in policy or procedures to reduce attrition | | | | 5 | 5 | 5 | 5 | | | 5 | 5 | 5 | 5 | 2 | |
| 7. Obtain academic administration's approval if | | | | | | | | | | | | | | | |
| (a) changes in academic requirements are involved | | | | 2 | | | | 4 | | | | | | | |
| (b) changes in program or curriculum are involved | | | | 2 | | | | | 4 | | | | | 5 | |
| 8. Review and approve task force recommendations | | 3 | | | | | | | | | | 5 | 5 | 5 | |
| 9. Obtain trustee approval if policy changes are involved | 2 | 4 | 4 | 2 | 2 | 2 | | | | 2 | | 5 | | 5 | |
| 10. Implement revised policies and procedures | 2 | 1 | | 2 | 2 | | | | | 2 | 2 | | | 2 | |

*Explanation of Decision Matrix 26.*

| *Step* | *Action Responsibility* | *Action* |
|--------|------------------------|----------|
| 1 & 2. | Registrar | Prepares, immediately after final enrollment data for the fall term have been entered into the registration system, an attrition analysis report that identifies the percentage of students enrolled the prior term who did not return by class and category (U.S., foreign, residential, commuting, in-state, out-of-state, ethnicity). Provides copies of the attrition analysis report to the president, the chief academic, student affairs, and fiscal officers, and the directors of recruiting and admissions and career development. |
| 3. | Advisory Committee | Reviews the attrition analysis report prepared by the registrar and, if it determines that attrition is too high, recommends that the president appoint a special task force to determine the causes of high attrition and to formulate recommendations for corrective action to reduce attrition losses. |
| | President | Concurs with the advisory committee's recommendation and determines the composition of the task force with |

*Explanation of Decision Matrix 26, Cont'd.*

| Step | Action Responsibility | Action |
|------|----------------------|--------|
| | | input from the advisory committee. |
| 4. | Board of Trustees | Receives the president's report of the results of the attrition analysis performed by the registrar and his decision to appoint an attrition task force. |
| 5. | Attrition Task Force | When instructed to do so by the president, conducts surveys and interviews to ascertain the causes of high attrition, obtaining inputs from students, academic and nonacademic counselors, the directors of recruiting and admissions and career development, faculty, and the chief academic, student affairs, and fiscal officers. |
| 6. | Attrition Task Force | Analyzes its data; identifies the causes of attrition that are correctable by change in institutional policy, practices, or procedures; and formulates recommendations to implement such changes, after reviewing its recommendations with and obtaining input from the chief academic, student affairs, and fiscal officers and the directors of career development and recruiting and admissions. |

*Explanation of Decision Matrix 26, Cont'd.*

| *Step* | *Action Responsibility* | *Action* |
|---|---|---|
| 7. | Chief Academic Officer | Determines whether the changes recommended by the attrition task force involve changes in curriculum or academic requirements. If so, submits the task force's recommendations to the faculty's academic requirements committee or the curriculum committee, as appropriate, and obtains their recommendations regarding the proposed changes. |
| 8. | Advisory Committee | Reviews the recommendations of the attrition task force with its chairperson, obtaining input from the chief academic officer regarding the recommendations of the appropriate faculty committee where changes in academic requirements or curriculum are involved. Recommends that the president approve the task force's recommendations and take steps to implement them. |
|  | President | Approves the advisory committee's recommendations. |
| 9. | President | Reviews the changes in institutional policy recommended by the attrition task force with the board of trustees and |

*Explanation of Decision Matrix 26, Cont'd.*

| Step | Action Responsibility | Action |
|------|----------------------|--------|
| | | recommends adoption of the proposed changes. |
| | Board of Trustees | Reviews proposed policy changes, obtaining clarification from the attrition task force chairperson, and authorizes their implementation. |
| 10. | President | Notifies appropriate administrators of approved changes in policy, procedures, and practices resulting from the work of the attrition task force and authorizes their implementation. |

## Decision Matrix 27. Revision of Academic Calendar.

Legend of decision-making roles
1 – Authorizes action
2 – Action responsibility
3 – Approves recommendation
4 – Recommends action
5 – Provides input

*Participants in Decision-Making Processes*

| Procedural Steps | President | Planning Committee | Chief Academic Officer | Chief Development Officer | Chief Student Affairs Officer | Chief Fiscal Officer | Academic Requirements Committee | Curriculum Committee | Faculty Welfare Committee | Academic Department Heads | Administrative Department Heads | Physical Plant Director | Financial Aid Director | Recruiting and Admissions Director | Personnel Director | Registrar | Students |
|---|---|---|---|---|---|---|---|---|---|---|---|---|---|---|---|---|---|
| 1. Determine during the multi-year planning process that the feasibility of revising the academic calendar should be explored | 3 | 4 | | | | | | | | | | | | | | | |
| 2. Instruct registrar to explore feasibility of revising the academic calendar | 1 | | | | | | | | | | | | | | | 2 | |
| 3. Obtain input regarding effect of proposed change on | | | | | | | | | | | | | | | | | |
| (a) curriculum | | | 4 | | | | 5 | 5 | | | | | | | | 2 | |
| (b) academic requirements | | | 4 | | | | 5 | | | | | | | | | 2 | |
| (c) faculty welfare | | | 4 | | | | | | 5 | 5 | | | | | | 2 | |
| (d) student recruitment and retention | | | | | 4 | | | | | | | | | 5 | | 2 | 5 |
| (e) financial aid operations | | | | | 4 | | | | | | | | 5 | | | 2 | |
| (f) energy utilization | | | | | | 4 | | | | | | 5 | | | | | |
| (g) nonacademic employee relations | | | 4 | | 4 | 4 | | | | | 5 | | | | 5 | 2 | |
| (h) tuition, fee, and auxiliary enterprise revenue | | | 4 | | 5 | 4 | | | | | 5 | | | | | 2 | |

| | | | |
|---|---|---|---|
| 4. Evaluate input and formulate recommendation for revising the academic calendar | | | 2 |
| 5. Review and approve recommended change in academic calendar for inclusion in multi-year planning guidelines | 3 | 4 | 5 |

*Note:* See Decision Matrices 6, 7, and 8 for multi-year planning processes related to planning the implementation of a change in academic calendar and trustee approval to do so.

*Explanation of Decision Matrix 27.*

| Step | Action Responsibility | Action |
|------|----------------------|--------|
| 1. | Planning Committee | During the process of formulating multi-year planning guidelines, recommends that the feasibility be explored of improving operating efficiency and effectiveness by changing the institution's academic calendar. |
| | President | Concurs with planning committee's recommendation. |
| 2. | President | Instructs registrar to obtain necessary input and formulate a recommendation for changing the academic calendar. |
| 3. | Registrar | Through the chief academic officer, obtains the curriculum committee's evaluation of the effect of various possible changes on curriculum syllabi and course sequencing and scheduling. Through the chief academic officer, obtains the academic requirements committee's evaluation of their effect on admission and degree requirements. Through the chief academic officer, obtains the faculty welfare committee's and academic department heads' evaluation of their effect on faculty loads, compensation, attraction, and retention. Through the chief |

*Explanation of Decision Matrix 27, Cont'd.*

*Step*     *Action Responsibility*     *Action*

student affairs officer, obtains the director of recruiting and admissions' and students' evaluation of their effect on the ability to attract and retain students. Through the chief student affairs officer, obtains the director of financial aid's evaluation of their effect on the operation of the financial aid office and the adequacy of financial aid funding. Through the chief fiscal officer, obtains the director of physical plant's evaluation of their effect on energy utilization, campus safety and security, and custodial and maintenance operation. Through senior administrators, obtains their administrative department heads' and personnel's evaluation of their effect on support service operations, nonacademic employee relationships, compensation, attraction, and retention. Through the chief fiscal officer, obtains the chief student affairs officer's and administrative department heads' evaluation of their effect on revenue from student tuition, fees, and room and board charges.

*Explanation of Decision Matrix 27, Cont'd.*

| *Step* | *Action Responsibility* | *Action* |
|--------|------------------------|----------|
| 4. | Registrar | Evaluates the input obtained in step 3 and formulates a recommendation regarding the desirability of changing the academic calendar and, if appropriate, the most desirable alternative calendar. |
| 5. | Planning Committee | Reviews the registrar's recommendation and recommends its inclusion among the planning guidelines to be submitted to the board of trustees. |
| | President | Approves the planning committee's recommendation. |

# Grant and Contract Administration

The function of grant and contract administration is to verify, before an expenditure or commitment is made, that the expenditure will ultimately be acceptable as a project or program cost by the sponsoring agency under the terms and conditions of the award agreement or its underlying regulations. This is applicable to sponsored agreements funded by private sponsors as well as to those funded by federal or state agencies, except for those providing funding for student financial aid programs. Thus, the director of grant and contract administration must be thoroughly familiar with the regulations of each agency from which the institution receives restricted grants and contracts. The director of grant and contract administration is not responsible for determining how a sponsored program or project is to be carried out. That responsibility belongs to the principal researcher or program director of the project. The director of grant and contract administration, however, should have the authority to prevent the principal researcher or program director from incurring costs that violate the terms and conditions of the sponsored agreement or the regulations of the funding agency, unless the agency has provided the institution with written authorization to incur such costs. When it becomes necessary to secure such an authorization from the funding agency, the director should do everything in his power to assist the principal investigator or program director in obtaining it. The director is essentially responsible for a pre-audit of expenditure authorization. Because, in a system of checks and balances, the authorization to spend should be separated from the disbursement of funds, it is recommended that the director report to an administrator other than the chief fiscal officer, unless the institution has a controller as well as a chief fiscal officer. Inasmuch as the majority of sponsored agreements are related to academic programs, it is recommended that the director's responsibilities be subsumed under academic administration.

The essential standards of good management applicable to grant and contract administration include the following.

★   The director of grant and contract administration should be responsible for informing the principal investigators and program directors and their supervisors of any special terms, conditions, or agency regulations that they should adhere to in carrying out their activities under each sponsored agreement. Therefore, the director should be sent all sponsored agreement award documents immediately upon their receipt by the institution for review and retention. He should provide working copies of the award document to all parties who are responsible for executing the research or program activities covered by the award and their superiors (see Decision Matrix 28).

★   The director should be responsible for seeing that all accounts necessary for sponsored agreement expenditures and matching expenditures, if applicable, are opened in the institution's accounting records. He should make sure that all parties who will be involved in authorizing sponsored agreement expenditures are provided with appropriate account numbers, account titles, and explanations of the type of expenditure to be charged to each account.

★   Where a sponsored agreement requires the expenditure of matching funds, the appropriate matching share should be applied to each sponsored agreement expenditure to which the matching fund expenditure requirement is applicable. Under college and university accounting practice, funds made available to an institution from a sponsored agreement are carried as a liability in the restricted operating fund section of the balance sheet. Expenditures for sponsored agreement purposes are made from the unrestricted operating fund, the institution periodically reimbursing the unrestricted operating fund by a cash transfer from the restricted operating fund for the portion of the sponsored agreement expenditures that has been earned. Thus, if matching expenditure agreements are not properly recorded, the institution might reimburse itself for sponsored agreement expenditures that have not yet been earned.

★ The director of grant and contract administration should maintain records that provide him with reminders of due dates, as stipulated in sponsored agreements, for interim and final fiscal and operational reports, and, if applicable, for submission of applications for renewal. Further, he should be responsible for seeing to it that required reports and renewal applications are prepared and submitted on a timely basis and that the contents of the fiscal and operational reports are consistent.

★ Personnel devoting effort for which compensation is to be provided from a sponsored agreement cannot be paid supplemental or increased compensation for such effort even though the rate of compensation stipulated in the sponsored agreement budget is sufficient to cover the cost of such compensation. Auditors who find that increased or supplemental compensation has been paid will simply disallow the payments as a sponsored agreement cost and demand a refund of the excess payments charged to the agreement.

★ The director of grant and contract administration should be responsible for verifying the reasonableness and appropriateness of the workload assignments of all personnel devoting efforts to sponsored agreements. He should review workload assignments to ensure that 100 percent of each person's effort is accounted for; that the percentage of effort allocated to the sponsored agreement is reasonable in relation to other assigned responsibilities; and that the appropriate provision for allocation of a portion of each person's efforts to matching costs has been made where such cost sharing is required.

⋆   The director of grant and contract administration should be responsible for seeing to it that the required periodic certification of employee effort devoted to sponsored agreements is received from either assigned personnel or an official having firsthand knowledge of the activities of such personnel. Such certification must state that the allocation of compensation received by each person is appropriate to the activities performed and the effort expended. Further, the certification must account for 100 percent, and not more than 100 percent, of each person's efforts. Many institutions have found themselves in difficulty with sponsoring agencies for failure either to require such certifications or to adhere to the 100 percent requirement. For example, an institution has defined its full-time teaching load as consisting of five course sections per semester with the proviso that released time equal to one course section will be provided to faculty members who have more than one committee assignment. A faculty member at this institution, carrying a full load and one committee assignment, is subsequently required to devote 50 percent of her effort to a sponsored agreement and is released from teaching two course sections. This faculty member cannot certify having devoted more than 40 percent of her effort to the sponsored agreement because the three course sections she teaches are equal to 60 percent of a full load. The argument that she met the 50 percent effort requirement for the sponsored agreement by working extra hours will not be accepted because, regardless of how many hours she spent on all assigned activities, the total number of hours still constitutes 100 percent of her effort.

The director should also be responsible for maintaining certification of effort on file for the record retention periods required by the regulations of the sponsoring agencies. Further, the director should be responsible for seeing that the allocation of compensation charges in the institution's accounting records is adjusted where the certifications show that the actual effort devoted to activity assignments is different from the budgeting basis on which a person's compensation has been allocated among activities (see Decision Matrix 29).

★   When consultants are used under a sponsored agreement, the director of grant and contract administration should be responsible for seeing that sponsoring agency regulations are adhered to in their employment. These regulations may include the following requirements. First, prior authorization by the sponsoring agency must be obtained. Second, if internal faculty or staff are to be used to provide services, they may be compensated from sponsored agreement funds only if their supervisors or senior administrators have certified that they could not be relieved of regular assigned responsibilities to provide such services. Third, if external consultants are to be used, documented evidence must be on file stipulating that the services to be provided are essential and cannot be provided by personnel assigned to the project, the person or firm selected is the most qualified available, the selection of the person or firm has been properly approved and the services to be provided have been specified in a written agreement, and the rate of compensation is appropriate and does not exceed the person's or firm's normal rates. Finally, payments made must be in accordance with the written agreement and cover required services that have been rendered (see Decision Matrix 30).

★   If a budgetary transfer of funds needs to be made within a sponsored agreement or between sponsored agreements, the director of grant and contract administration should be responsible for obtaining, if required, the sponsoring agency's authorization for the transfer or for authorizing the transfer himself if agency authorization is not required. In either case, the director should maintain documentation supporting or justifying such transfers (see Decision Matrix 31).

★   The director of grant and contract administration should be responsible for authorizing any transfer or reallocation of costs incurred among sponsored agreements. Again, the director should maintain documentation that justifies or supports such transactions (see Decision Matrix 32).

★   When equipment is to be procured under a sponsored agreement, the director of grant and contract administration should be responsible for seeing to it that the sponsoring agency's regulations regarding the procurement, use, control, and disposition of equipment are adhered to. Such regulations may require obtaining the agency's prior authorization to procure equipment, verification that the procurement will be timely enough to benefit the project or program, verification that similar equipment that could be used is not already available, the existence of adequate movable equipment inventory control procedures and records, and particular procedures for the disposition of the equipment at the expiration of the project or program (see Decision Matrix 33).

★   The director of grant and contract administration should be responsible for approving requisitions covering the procurement of supplies, material, or travel to be paid for from sponsored agreement funds. The director's approval is limited to verifying the acceptability of the charges related to such procurement under the terms of the agreement and underlying regulations (see Decision Matrix 34).

★   The director of grant and contract administration should receive a copy of the monthly budget status report issued by the chief fiscal officer for each sponsored agreement in force at the institution. These reports should be used to monitor expenditures to avoid cost overruns and to determine whether budgetary underexpenditures reflect undue delays or failures to carry out the project or program as expected by the sponsoring agency. He also should review these reports to determine whether errors in expenditure account coding or other accounting errors may have occurred and should see that such errors are corrected.

★   The director of grant and contract administration should be responsible for coordinating the close-out efforts of sponsored agreements and for the submission of the final fiscal report for the agreement, prepared by the chief fiscal officer, to the sponsoring agency (see Decision Matrix 35).

The director of grant and contract administration should be a member of the grant and contract review committee and should be involved in reviewing applications for or negotiations related to the award of sponsored agreements. His participation in these activities should minimize problems that might arise during the conduct of activities under such agreements. The director also should keep the chief development officer informed of progress being made by the institution in carrying out sponsored agreements.

Readers who wish more detailed information about grant and contract administration should contact the National Association of College and University Business Officers (NACUBO), One Dupont Circle, Washington, D.C. 20036.

# Decision Matrix 28. Receipt of New Sponsored Agreement.

Legend of decision-making roles:
1 – Authorizes action
2 – Action responsibility
3 – Approves recommendation
4 – Recommends action
5 – Provides input

*Participants in Decision-Making Processes*

| Procedural Steps | President | Senior Administrators | Department Heads | Project or Program Director | Grant and Contract Administration Director | Chief Fiscal Officer | Grant and Contract Accountant | Public Relations Director | Chief Development Officer |
|---|---|---|---|---|---|---|---|---|---|
| 1. Receive notification of award of new sponsored agreement | 5 | | | 5 | 2 | | | | 5 |
| 2. Receive notification of awards not initially received by the development office | | | | | 5 | | | | 2 |
| 3. Prepare written notification of special terms or underlying regulations that must be understood and adhered to | | | | | 2 | | | | |
| 4. Obtain account numbers and titles to be used in accounting for sponsored agreement expenditures | | | | | 2 | 5 | | | |
| 5. Establish "tickler" file reminder record of report and renewal application date requirements | | | | | 2 | | | | |
| 6. Obtain required signatures accepting sponsored agreement | 5 | | | | 2 | 5 | | | |

| | | | | | | | |
|---|---|---|---|---|---|---|---|
| 7. Transmit executed sponsored agreement to sponsoring agency | | | | 5 | | | 2 |
| 8. Prepare required copies of sponsored agreement, notification of special terms and underlying regulations, and account number and titles | | | 2 | 2 | | | |
| | | | | 5 | | | |
| 9. Receive sponsored agreement documentation | 2 | 2 | 2 | | 2 | | |
| 10. Open required new accounts | | | | | 1 | | |
| 11. Receive notification of new sponsored agreement awards received | | | | | | 2 | 2 |
| awards received | | | | | | | 5 |

*Explanation of Decision Matrix 28.*

| Step | Action Responsibility | Action |
|------|----------------------|--------|
| 1. | Director of Grant and Contract Administration | Receives documents notifying the institution of a new sponsored agreement award from the president, the project director, or the chief development officer. |
| 2. | Chief Development Officer | Receives notification from the director of grant and contract administration of sponsored agreement award notification that was received by offices other than the development office. |
| 3, 4, & 5. | Director of Grant and Contract Administration | Reviews the sponsored agreement and the underlying regulations of the sponsoring agency. Prepares memorandum identifying special terms and conditions that must be understood and adhered to; determines fiscal control and reporting requirements and obtains from the chief fiscal officer the title and number of accounts that are needed to meet those requirements; and identifies program and fiscal reporting dates and, if applicable, the date by which application for renewal is required. Sets up a "tickler" file for reminding himself to follow up to be sure that |

*Explanation of Decision Matrix 28, Cont'd.*

| Step | Action Responsibility | Action |
|------|----------------------|--------|
| | | required reports are submitted when due. |
| 6 & 7. | Director of Grant and Contract Administration | Obtains signatures of people required by the sponsoring agency to indicate acceptance of the sponsored agreement. Transmits the properly executed agreement to the chief development officer for her transmission to the sponsoring agency. |
| 8 & 9. | Director of Grant and Contract Administration | Obtains the required number of copies of the sponsored agreement document and transmits a copy, with the memorandum of special requirements and names and numbers of accounts established for fiscal control and reporting requirements, to the project director, the project director's department head and senior administrator, and the chief fiscal officer. |
| 10. | Chief Fiscal Officer | Sees that the accounts required by sponsored agreements are opened in the general ledger or subsidiary ledger accounting system. |
| 11. | Director of Public Relations | Is informed of new sponsored agreement awards received. |

# Decision Matrix 29. Time and Effort Reporting.

Legend of decision-making roles
1 – Authorizes action
2 – Action responsibility
3 – Approves recommendation
4 – Recommends action
5 – Provides input

| Procedural Steps | Senior Administrator | Department Heads | Project or Program Director | Project or Program Employees | Grant and Contract Administration Director | Payroll | Chief Fiscal Officer | Grant and Contract Accountant | Budget Control |
|---|---|---|---|---|---|---|---|---|---|
| 1. Receive record of allocation of total compensation for each employee who has devoted effort to a sponsored agreement | | | | | 2 | 5 | | | |
| 2. Distribute payroll allocation record for certification | | | | | 2 | | | | |
| 3. Receive certification of how employees' effort was actually spent | 5 | 5 | 5 | 5 | 2 | | | | |
| 4. Identify instances where time and effort certification varies from payroll allocation records | | | | | 2 | | | | |
| 5. Receive notification of necessity to revise payroll distribution records | | | | | 5 | | 2 | | |
| 6. Correct accounting and budget control records | | | | | | | 1 | 2 | 2 |

*Participants in Decision-Making Processes*

*Explanation of Decision Matrix 29.*

| Step | Action Responsibility | Action |
|------|----------------------|--------|
| 1 & 2. | Director of Grant and Contract Administration | Receives from payroll, for each employee who has been compensated for some portion of his effort from sponsored agreement funds, a report showing how the employee's total compensation was allocated among sponsored agreement and other activities. Transmits the payroll allocation reports to either the employee, if still employed, or the project or program director or administrator who has personal knowledge of how the former employee's efforts were devoted; requests that he sign, date, and return the report if the actual efforts devoted to the various activities correspond with the way in which compensation has been allocated by payroll, or change the allocations shown on the report to reflect the effort actually devoted to the various activities and then sign, date, and return it. |
| 3 & 4. | Director of Grant and Contract Administration | Receives returned payroll allocation certification reports. Verifies that all reports have been returned, identifies each instance where the allocation |

*Explanation of Decision Matrix 29, Cont'd.*

| Step | Action Responsibility | Action |
|------|----------------------|--------|
| | | of compensation by the payroll department has been changed by the person signing such certifications, and determines the accuracy of the changes identified. |
| 5 & 6. | Chief Fiscal Officer | Receives notification from the director of grant and contract administration of adjustments required to reflect in the accounting records changes identified in payroll allocations. Authorizes the grant and contract accountant and budget control to enter required accounting and budget corrections into the general ledger accounting system. |

*Explanation of Decision Matrix 30.*

| Step | Action Responsibility | Action |
|------|----------------------|--------|
| 1. | Project Director | Identifies the need for a consultant on a project. Identifies the most qualified consultant and negotiates, with input from the chief fiscal officer, the scope of services to be provided and the financial terms under which they will be rendered. |
| 2 & 3. | Director of Grant and Contract Administration | Receives the proposed consulting agreement submitted by the project director and determines whether prior approval by the sponsoring agency is required. If it is, obtains required approval. |
| 4, 5a, & 5b. | Director of Grant and Contract Administration | Determines whether the consultant is an employee. If so, obtains certification from the employee's department head and senior administrator that the employee cannot be given released time to provide the required services. If not, obtains from the project director certification that a consultant's services are essential and cannot be provided by project staff, that the consultant selected is the most qualified available, and that the negotiated agreement properly defines the services |

# Decision Matrix 30. Hiring Consultants.

Legend of decision-making roles
1 – Authorizes action
2 – Action responsibility
3 – Approves recommendation
4 – Recommends action
5 – Provides input

*Participants in Decision-Making Processes*

| Procedural Steps | Senior Administrators | Department Heads | Project or Program Director | Grant and Contract Administration Director | Chief Fiscal Officer | Grant and Contract Accountant | Budget Control | Sponsoring Agency |
|---|---|---|---|---|---|---|---|---|
| 1. Negotiate agreement with consultant | | | 2 | | 5 | | | |
| 2. Receive proposed agreement for review and approval | | 5 | 5 | 2 | | | | |
| 3. Obtain, if required, sponsoring agency's approval | | | | 2 | | | | 5 |
| 4. Determine whether consultant is an employee or an external consultant | | | | 2 | | | | |
| 5(a). If employee, obtain certification that employee cannot be given released time to provide required services | 5 | 5 | | 2 | | | | |
| 5(b). If external consultant, make sure that documentation required by sponsoring agency regulations are on file | | | 5 | 2 | | | | |

| | | | | |
|---|---|---|---|---|
| 6. Execute contract | 2 | 1 | 2 | |
| 7. Receive notification of issuance of contract | | 5 | | 2 | 2 |
| 8. Encumber funds to cover contractual costs | 5 | | | 5 | 2 |
| 9. Receive consultant's invoice | | 2 | | | |
| 10. Verify that documentation showing that services have been rendered and that payment requested is in accord with the consulting contract | | 2 | | | |
| 11. Receive authorization to pay consultant | | 1 | 2 | | |

*Explanation of Decision Matrix 30, Cont'd.*

| *Step* | *Action Responsibility* | *Action* |
|---|---|---|
| | | to be provided. Also obtains the consultant's certification that the rate of compensation specified in the agreement does not exceed rates normally charged. |
| 6 & 7. | Director of Grant and Contract Administration | Issues authorization for the chief fiscal officer to execute the consulting agreement and notifies the project director and grant and contract accountant that authorization has been issued. |
| 8. | Grant and Contract Accountant | Records the receipt of the director of grant and contract administration's notification and notifies budget control to encumber the sponsored agreement budget funds to cover the cost of the consulting services to be provided. |
| 9, 10, & 11. | Director of Grant and Contract Administration | Receives consultant's invoice, approved and transmitted by the project director; verifies that documentation exists showing that the services covered by the invoice have been rendered; and authorizes the chief fiscal officer to pay the consultant. |

*Explanation of Decision Matrix 31.*

| Step | Action Responsibility | Action |
|---|---|---|
| 1. | Project Director | Initiates a request for the reallocation of budgeted funds between line items in a sponsored agreement or between agreements. |
| | Department Head | Reviews the project director's request for reasonableness and appropriateness and recommends approval. |
| | Senior Administrator | Reviews and approves budget transfer request. |
| 2 & 3. | Director of Grant and Contract Administration | Receives transfer request approved by the senior administrator and obtains verification from the grant and contract accountant that the funds requested to be transferred remain unspent and unencumbered. |
| 4. | Grant and Contract Accountant | Instructs budget control to encumber the funds requested to be transferred. |
| 5a & 5b. | Director of Grant and Contract Administration | Determines whether the sponsoring agency's prior approval to transfer requested funds is required. If so, obtains required approval; if not, verifies that documentation justifying the transfer has been provided by the project director. |

## Decision Matrix 31. Sponsored Agreement Budget Reallocation.

Legend of decision-making roles:
1 – Authorizes action
2 – Action responsibility
3 – Approves recommendation
4 – Recommends action
5 – Provides input

| Procedural Steps | Senior Administrators | Department Heads | Project or Program Director | Grant and Contract Administration Director | Chief Fiscal Officer | Grant and Contract Accountant | Budget Control | Sponsoring Agency |
|---|---|---|---|---|---|---|---|---|
| *Participants in Decision-Making Processes* | | | | | | | | |
| 1. Initiate request for budget reallocation | 3 | 4 | 5 | | | | | |
| 2. Receive request for budget reallocation | 5 | | | 2 | | | | |
| 3. Verify that budget funds covered by reallocation request remain unexpended and available for transfer | | | | | | | | |
| 4. Encumber budget funds requested to be transferred | | | | 2 | | 5 | 5 | |
| 5(a). Obtain, if required, sponsoring agency's approval of transfer of budget funds | | | | 2 | | 5 | 2 | 5 |

5(b). Verify that required documentation to support transfer request is on file if sponsoring agency approval is not required    5    2
6. Authorize budget reallocation    2    1
7. Receive notice of approval of reallocation request    2    5    2    2
8. Update budget control records    1    2    2

*Explanation of Decision Matrix 31, Cont'd.*

| Step | Action Responsibility | Action |
|------|----------------------|--------|
| 6 & 7. | Director of Grant and Contract Administration | Issues authorization for the chief fiscal officer to make the requested transfer and notifies the project director that authorization has been issued. |
| 8. | Chief Fiscal Officer | Instructs the grant and contract accountant and budget control to update their records to reflect the authorized transfer of budget funds. |

# Decision Matrix 32. Reallocation of Incurred Costs on Sponsored Agreements.

Legend of decision-making roles
1 – Authorizes action
2 – Action responsibility
3 – Approves recommendation
4 – Recommends action
5 – Provides input

| Procedural Steps | Project or Program Director | Grant and Contract Administration Director | Chief Fiscal Officer | Grant and Contract Accountant | Budget Control |
|---|---|---|---|---|---|
| *Participants in Decision-Making Processes* | | | | | |
| 1. Receive and review budget status report for each sponsored agreement | 2 | 2 | 5 | | |
| 2. Identify coding or charge errors and document justification for reallocation | 5 | 2 | | | |
| 3. Receive request for reallocation of charges and documentation of justification | | 5 | 2 | | |
| 4. Adjust accounting and budget control records | | | 1 | 2 | 2 |
| 5. Review budget underexpenditures to determine if timely completion of the project or program is in jeopardy | 5 | 2 | | | 2 |

*Explanation of Decision Matrix 32.*

| Step | Action Responsibility | Action |
|---|---|---|
| 1 & 2. | Project Director and Director of Grant and Contract Administration | Receive monthly budget status reports for sponsored agreements from the chief fiscal officer. Review reports, identify coding or charging errors, and document justification for the reallocation of erroneous charges. |
| 3 & 4. | Chief Fiscal Officer | Receives request to reallocate erroneous charges, reviews request and documentation of justification for accuracy, and instructs the grant and contract accountant and budget control to update the general ledger and budget control records to reflect the authorized reallocation of charges. |
| 5. | Director of Grant and Contract Administration | Periodically reviews monthly budget status reports with the appropriate project directors to ascertain whether budget underexpenditures indicate that timely completion of the project is in jeopardy. |

# Decision Matrix 33. Equipment Procurement for Sponsored Agreements.

| Legend of decision-making roles |
|---|
| 1 – Authorizes action |
| 2 – Action responsibility |
| 3 – Approves recommendation |
| 4 – Recommends action |
| 5 – Provides input |

**Participants in Decision-Making Processes**

| Procedural Steps | Senior Administrators | Department Heads | Project or Program Directors | Grant and Contract Administration Director | Chief Fiscal Officer | Grant and Contract Accountant | Budget Control | Sponsoring Agency |
|---|---|---|---|---|---|---|---|---|
| 1. Initiate equipment purchase requisition | 3 | 4 | 5 | 2 | | | | |
| 2. Receive equipment purchase requisition | 5 | | | | | | | |
| 3. Determine whether delivery will be timely enough to benefit the project or program | | | 5 | 2 | | | | |
| 4. Determine whether similar equipment that could be used is available | | | 5 | 2 | 5 | | | |
| 5. Obtain, if required, sponsoring agency's approval | | | | 2 | | | | 5 |
| 6. Authorize procurement | | | | 1 | 2 | | | |
| 7. Encumber funds to cover purchase | | | | | 1 | 2 | 2 | |

*Explanation of Decision Matrix 33.*

| Step | Action Responsibility | Action |
|------|----------------------|--------|
| 1. | Project Director | Initiates a purchase requisition for equipment to be acquired for a sponsored agreement. |
|  | Department Head | Reviews requisition for appropriateness to the project and recommends its approval. |
|  | Senior Administrator | Reviews and approves requisition. |
| 2 & 3. | Director of Grant and Contract Administration | Receives equipment purchase requisition approved by the senior administrator. Verifies with the project director that if equipment is purchased, delivery will be timely enough for the equipment to benefit the project; verifies with the chief fiscal officer and the project director that similar equipment owned by the institution is not available for use on the project. |
| 5. | Director of Grant and Contract Administration | Determines whether prior approval from the sponsoring agency is required. If it is, obtains required approval. |
| 6 & 7. | Chief Fiscal Officer | Receives approved equipment purchase requisition from the director of grant and contract |

*Explanation of Decision Matrix 33, Cont'd.*

| Step | Action Responsibility | Action |
|------|----------------------|--------|
|      |                      | administration and instructs the grant and contract accountant and budget control to encumber the budgeted funds under the sponsored agreement. |

**Decision Matrix 34. Travel and Supply Procurement for Sponsored Agreements.**

Legend of decision-making roles
1 – Authorizes action
2 – Action responsibility
3 – Approves recommendation
4 – Recommends action
5 – Provides input

*Participants in Decision-Making Processes*

| Procedural Steps | Senior Administrators | Department Heads | Project or Program Director | Grant and Contract Administration Director | Chief Fiscal Officer | Grant and Contract Accountant | Budget Control | Sponsoring Agency |
|---|---|---|---|---|---|---|---|---|
| 1. Issue request for travel or requisition for supplies | 3 | 4 | 5 | | | | | |
| 2. Receive request or requisition | 5 | | 5 | 2 | | | | |
| 3. For a travel request, obtain, if required, sponsoring agency's approval | | | | 2 | | | | 5 |
| 4. Review requests for travel that do not require the sponsoring agency's approval and supply requisitions for acceptability under terms of the sponsored agreement | | | | 2 | 2 | | | |
| 5. Authorize expenditure | | | | 1 | 1 | | | |
| 6. Encumber funds | | | | | | 2 | 2 | |

*Explanation of Decision Matrix 34.*

| Step | Action Responsibility | Action |
| --- | --- | --- |
| 1. | Project Director | Initiates a travel or supply purchase requisition for a sponsored agreement. |
| | Department Heads | Review the requisition for acceptability and applicability to the project. Recommend its approval. |
| | Senior Administrator | Reviews and approves the requisition. |
| 2, 3, & 4. | Director of Grant and Contract Administration | Reviews the requisition submitted by the senior administrator and determines whether it covers travel or supplies. For travel, determines whether the prior approval of the sponsoring agency is required; if so, obtains required approval. For supplies or travel, where prior approval is not required, determines that the proposed expenditure is acceptable under the terms of the agreement. |
| 5 & 6. | Chief Fiscal Officer | Receives the director of grant and contract administration's authorization to incur the requisitioned expenditure and instructs the grant and contract accountant and budget control to encumber sponsored agreement budgeted funds for the authorized expenditure. |

## Decision Matrix 35. Close-Out of Sponsored Agreements.

Legend of decision-making roles
1 – Authorizes action
2 – Action responsibility
3 – Approves recommendation
4 – Recommends action
5 – Provides input

| Procedural Steps | Project or Program Director | Grant and Contract Administration Director | Chief Fiscal Officer | Grant and Contract Accountant | Sponsoring Agency |
|---|---|---|---|---|---|
| 1. Receive request for final project or program reports | 2 | 5 | | | |
| 2. Prepare final operational report | 2 | | 2 | | |
| 3. Prepare final fiscal report | | 2 | 1 | 2 | |
| 4. Receive final reports | 5 | 2 | 5 | | |
| 5. Review final reports for acceptability | | 2 | | | |
| 6. Transmit reports to sponsoring agency | | | | | |
| 7. Receive sponsoring agency's authorization to close out the project or program | | 2 | | | |
| 8. Receive notification of receipt of authorization to close out the project or program | 2 | | 2 | | 5 |
| 9. Close out accounting records | 2 | 5 | 1 | 2 | |

*Participants in Decision-Making Processes*

*Explanation of Decision Matrix 35.*

| *Step* | *Action Responsibility* | *Action* |
|---|---|---|
| 1. | Director of Grant and Contract Administration | Reviews sponsored agreement reporting dates "tickler" file and determines that final project and fiscal reports need to be prepared. Requests reports from the project director and chief fiscal officer. |
| 2 & 3. | Project Director and Chief Fiscal Officer | Prepare final operational and fiscal reports. |
| 4, 5, & 6. | Director of Grant and Contract Administration | Reviews reports submitted by the project director and chief fiscal officer for acceptability and compatibility. Works out with them any changes required and transmits the reports to the sponsoring agency. |
| 7 & 8. | Director of Grant and Contract Administration | Provides sponsoring agency with any clarifications required on the basis of input from the project director and chief fiscal officer. Receives the sponsoring agency's authorization to close out the project. Notifies the project director and chief fiscal officer of the receipt of authorization to close out the project. |

*Explanation of Decision Matrix 35, Cont'd.*

| *Step* | *Action Responsibility* | *Action* |
|---|---|---|
| 9. | Chief Fiscal Officer | Verifies, if project funds have been received through the Department of Education Federal Assistance Financing Systems Account (DFAFS), that the next DFAFS report reflects the close-out of the project. Authorizes the grant and contract accountant to close out accounting records related to the project. |

# Part Three:
# Student Affairs
# Administration

Part Three covers the management of those activities designed to bring to campus each year the number and mix of new students required to meet the institution's enrollment goals; to assist students in adjusting to campus life and attaining their academic and personal growth objectives; to assist students in planning and carrying out extracurricular programs and activities designed to make their experience at the institution as happy as possible with available resources; and to ensure that their health care, housing, rights protection, and safety needs are met to the best of the institution's ability to do so.

These responsibilities are usually carried out by a series of administrative units reporting to a chief student affairs officer, frequently called a dean of students. In carrying out her responsibilities, it is important that the chief student affairs officer and her staff remember that, as officers and administrators of the institution, their responsibility is to represent the institution to the students in its best light. While she should keep the institution's administration informed regarding student concerns about institutional policies and operations, she does not represent the students.

The essential standards of good management and the decision matrices covering activities related to student affairs are divided into three chapters. Chapter Eight covers all activities other than recruiting and admissions and financial aid, each of which is covered in a separate chapter.

Throughout this book, students are shown participating in an institution's management processes through their student government organizations. This portrayal should not be construed as limiting the administration's involvement of individual students in providing input regarding the formulation of policy or operating decisions. Experience indicates that students can contribute to the formulation of sound management decisions. Their participation, where appropriate, should be encouraged because it will contribute to their acceptance and support of policies that affect them. It will also improve campus morale, contribute to the students' learning, provide the administration with students' perceptions about the institution's operation and campus environment, and possibly head off serious disruption of operations when volatile issues surface. Like faculty, students should participate formally through appointment to recognized faculty organizations, student government organizations, or committees established by the president. In all cases, however, it should be defined clearly whether they may observe, provide input, or participate in debate. In the ensuing chapters of this book, the areas where input from students, through student government organizations, should be a part of the decision-making processes are shown in the decision matrices. Should students be appointed to other committees or to recognized faculty organizations, their role will be reflected in those matrices as part of the role of such organizations or committees.

However, there are decisions in which students, like faculty, should not be involved. These include decisions related to terms of employment or compensation of faculty and staff, budgetary review and approval, academic requirements or grading, accounting and fiscal control policies and procedures, grant and contract policies and procedures, the awarding of financial aid, and the establishment of tuition and room and board charges.

# Managing
# Student Services
# and Activities

The chief student affairs officer is usually responsible for the administration of student disciplinary processes, student health services, nonacademic counseling activities, student activities that include student government, new student orientation activities, the operation of student housing units, the operation of the student union, and recruiting and admission activities. In addition, she is frequently responsible for the administration of student financial aid activities. If she is not, the administration of these activities is assigned to the chief fiscal officer.

Under college and university accounting principles, student housing and the student union are classified as auxiliary enterprises. Further, one frequently finds the responsibility for managing these activities shared between the chief student affairs officer and the chief fiscal officer. Usually, the chief student affairs officer is responsible for matters related to facility operation and utilization, while the chief fiscal officer is responsible for custodial activities, maintenance of the facilities, and fiscal matters related to their operation. Therefore, the essential standards and procedures related to the fiscal control of student housing and student union operation activities are included in Chapter Fifteen. The essential standards of good management and procedures related to the other responsibilities of the chief student affairs officer are set forth in this chapter.

## Student Discipline

The essential standards of good management in the administration of student discipline are set forth below.

★ A campus code of conduct should be developed, published, and effectively communicated to all students. The development of a code of conduct should involve the participation of faculty, students, and administration. The code should be formulated as a recommendation by the chief student affairs officer, reviewed and approved by the president and his advisory committee, and formally adopted by the board of trustees. At a minimum, the code should cover student responsibility for compliance and penalties for failure to comply with regulations about compulsory attendance of classes; academic dishonesty (for example, cheating, misrepresentation, or alteration of records); obstruction, disruption, or interference with regard to any campus activity or campus personnel carrying out lawfully appointed duties; failure to pay properly assessed charges; theft, vandalism, or damage to property; possession, use, or distribution of narcotics or alcoholic beverages; possession of firearms; physical or verbal abuse of others or conduct injuring the rights of others; failure to respond to written notices from college officers; and lewd or obscene conduct or language (see Decision Matrix 36).

★ Disciplinary procedures should be established and adhered to for dealing with violations of the code of conduct that are either repeated or of a serious nature and therefore require the imposition of penalties. In the formulation of these procedures, care should be taken to ensure that they do not violate the student's rights (see Decision Matrix 37).

★ The responsibility and authority for determining the extent and nature of disciplinary action to be imposed on students should be delegated by the president to the committee on faculty and student discipline. Appeals of the committee's decisions should be addressed to the president. The chief student affairs officer should be authorized to determine how to deal with student disciplinary problems that are minor and do not represent repeated violations. Her actions in dealing with such matters should be recorded and retained on file in her office to ensure that they can be documented if subsequent violations by the same student require disciplinary action by the committee on faculty and student discipline. When it is necessary to bring a student before the committee for disciplinary action, the chief student affairs officer should be responsible for seeing that the student's rights are understood and protected.

## Health Care Services

Every institution has the responsibility of ensuring that the basic health care needs of students who are enrolled in programs conducted on its main campus are provided for. This responsibility is normally assigned to the physician or registered nurse who is the director of health care services (see Decision Matrix 38).

The essential standards of good management applicable to the management of health care services are set forth below.

★ All students should be required to provide the institution with a physical examination report or to undergo a physical examination at the time of admission.

★ At a minimum, all full-time students enrolled in programs carried out on the main campus should be covered, at their expense, in a basic medical coverage plan. In addition to this basic coverage, the institution should provide, at its expense, supplemental coverage for athletes participating in intercollegiate sports programs. While not essential, it is desirable that the basic medical insurance plan provide coverage for injuries resulting from student participation in extramural or sport club activities and that coverage under the basic medical insurance plan be made available to part-time students.

★ Facilities or arrangements should exist for providing health services for minor or interim health care needs. These health care services should be available either through an on-campus infirmary, staffed by at least a registered nurse supported by an on-call physician, or through contractual arrangements with a nearby clinic or hospital. The cost of these health care services should be borne by the students through the assessment of a special fee or the allocation of a portion of the institution's general or comprehensive fees.

★   Where an on-campus infirmary exists, facilities for the secure storage of all medication and drugs must be provided.

★   Where an on-campus infirmary exists, infirmary personnel must maintain records of all student visits, diagnoses, prescribed treatments, referrals to physicians, and issuance of medication.

★   Arrangements should exist for transporting students who are seriously ill or injured to a place where they can receive adequate care.

★   Arrangements for providing health care services when the on-campus infirmary or off-campus clinic is closed should be prominently posted.

★   The director of health services, or the administrator of the off-campus clinic that has contracted to provide health services, should be responsible for keeping the chief student affairs officer informed about special situations identified through the review of physical examination reports, through physical examinations, or through the delivery of health care services. Special situations include cases where the student's physical condition requires a special diet or nonparticipation in strenuous sports or activities, the student has a communicable disease that may endanger the health of others, the student's mental health may be dangerous to the student or others, or the student is or has been using illicit drugs. In such situations, it is the responsibility of the chief student affairs officer to see that the appropriate administrators are notified and that appropriate actions are taken by the institution.

### Nonacademic Counseling Activities

Nonacademic counseling should encompass student adjustment to campus life, personal financial counseling, personal understanding and relationships, the improvement of social skills, and emotional support or crisis intervention. The essential standards of good management applicable to these activities are set forth below.

★   All nonacademic counseling activities should be carried out as a unified program and coordinated with academic counseling, regardless of where they are located or how they are funded. Some small institutions receive funding as developing institutions under the U.S. Department of Education's Title III program. Frequently, these grants provide funding for the compensation of counselors to strengthen the institution's nonacademic counseling program. Setting up such counselors' services as separate organizational units can lead to overlapping services and fragmented operations. Also, some institutions have some of their counseling staff live in student dormitories and combine their counseling activities with dormitory supervision responsibilities. Under these circumstances, unless their counseling activities are coordinated with the institution's overall nonacademic counseling program, the same overlapping and fragmentation can occur.

★   The extent and nature of nonacademic counseling services offered by the institution should be documented as an institutional decision, published, and made known to students. The counseling services to be offered should be formulated as a recommendation prepared by the chief student affairs officer on the basis of input from the nonacademic counseling staff (see Decision Matrix 39).

★   Regulations regarding the extent and nature of private counseling services that the professional counseling staff may render to clients should be established and monitored.

★  An annual written report covering the operation of all counseling activities should be prepared by the nonacademic counseling staff for submission to the administration through the chief student affairs officer.

The following standard should be considered essential if foreign students constitute at least 10 percent of the study body.

★  A foreign student adviser should be appointed to assist both foreign students and the administration in dealing with the special problems related to their enrollment. The foreign student adviser should be responsible for assisting the admissions office in evaluating the credentials of foreign students; assisting foreign students with visa, travel, and immigration regulations and problems; assisting the chief fiscal officer in the collection of assessed charges, whether paid by the students or their governments; assisting the students in obtaining academic, career, and personal counseling; assisting the students in obtaining either on-campus or off-campus housing and, if off-campus, assisting in making rental, utility, and service arrangements and in shopping for food or services; advising the administration about special housing, food service, or student activity programs that will attract foreign students to live and eat on campus and enhance their retention; and advising the administration about changes in federal regulations that may affect the foreign students currently enrolled.

## Student Activities and Government

The number and types of student clubs and student activities will vary from campus to campus. All clubs and activities, however, should be authorized by the institution's administration. These clubs and activities, while they provide an enrichment of campus life designed to make the students' campus life as attractive as possible, should also be looked on as providing a part of the students' education. Thus, the manner in which these activities are operated should be designed to teach the students who participate in them the essentials of good management. The essential standards of good management applicable to student activity and government are set forth below.

★   Policies and procedures covering the operation of student government and activities should be published and made known to the students. At a minimum, such policies and procedures should encompass the identification of authorized student organizations, the signatory authority required to disburse funds, approvals necessary to carry out activities or programs, supervision or monitoring required of activities or programs, approvals necessary to permit students to collect additional revenue for an activity through advertisement sales, solicitation, or the assessment of charges, responsibility for covering activity or program losses, disposition of unexpended program or activity funds at the end of the year, accounting required for revenue and expenditures for an approved program or activity, eligibility requirements for candidates for student government offices, and the timing and duration of elections to fill such offices. Where student activities include the publication of a student newspaper, institutional policies should also cover limitations, if any, on the subject matter that may be published and the institution's right of censorship (see Decision Matrix 40).

★   Students should be advised by the chief fiscal officer, as soon as possible after completion of registration, of the amount of revenue available to cover the costs of student government and student activities. The revenue may come from special fees assessed for these activities, an allocation for these activities from the comprehensive or general fees assessed by the institution, or budgetary allocations for these activities made available to the chief student affairs officer. Fees assessed for these purposes from students enrolled in the evening and weekend college or in off-campus programs should take into consideration their limited ability to participate in or benefit from on-campus student government and activities.

★   Each student organization should be required to submit and obtain institutional approval for an annual budget covering its operations.

★   Fees specifically assessed for student activities and agreed-on allocations from general or comprehensive fees for these activities should not be used for any other purpose unless specific written authorization to do has been obtained from the student organization involved. Unfortunately, many institutions facing financial difficulties have used student fee revenue specifically assessed for student government or student activities for other institutional operating purposes. Needless to say, these institutions have had to contend with bad student relations when their actions became known to the students.

★   The chief student affairs officer should be responsible for maintaining a master calendar of campus events and for scheduling student activity events within this calendar.

### New Student Orientation

Institutions usually require first-time students to arrive on campus for orientation about a week before registration for the term to which they have been admitted. The essential standard of good management applicable to new student orientation is this:

★   Before registration, a new student orientation program should be conducted that all first-time students are required to attend. At a minimum, the new student orientation program should cover the academic and administrative processes required to become enrolled, student responsibilities covered by the code of conduct, financial regulations and procedures, the layout of the campus and the location of offices with which students are likely to have direct contact or whose services they may need, and the identification of student organizations, programs, and activities in which they may wish to participate. While not essential, it is desirable that parents be invited to attend the new student orientation program (see Decision Matrix 41).

Readers wishing more information about student affairs should contact the National Association of Student Personnel Administrators (NASPA), One Dupont Circle, Washington, D.C. 20036.

# Decision Matrix 36. Developing Student Code of Conduct.

Legend of decision-making roles:
1 – Authorizes action
2 – Action responsibility
3 – Approves recommendation
4 – Recommends action
5 – Provides input

*Participants in Decision-Making Processes*

| Procedural Steps | Board of Trustees | Legal Counsel | President | Advisory Committee | Chief Academic Officer | Faculty | Chief Student Affairs Officer | Chief Fiscal Officer | Student Government | Other Administrators | Publications Director |
|---|---|---|---|---|---|---|---|---|---|---|---|
| 1. Authorize revision or development of student code of conduct | | | 1 | | | | 2 | | | | |
| 2. Develop recommended code of conduct | | 5 | 3 | | 5 | 5 | 4 | 5 | 5 | 5 | |
| 3. Review and approve code of conduct | | 5 | 4 | 4 | | | 5 | | | | |
| 4. Obtain board approval for code of conduct | 2 | | 4 | | | | 5 | | | | |
| 5. Authorize publication and implementation of code of conduct | | | 1 | | | | 2 | | | | |
| 6. Finalize content of code of conduct | | | | | | | 2 | | | | 5 |
| 7. Authorize printing of code of conduct | | | | | | | 1 | | | | 2 |

*Explanation of Decision Matrix 36.*

| Step | Action Responsibility | Action |
|------|----------------------|--------|
| 1. | Chief Student Affairs Officer | Receives the president's authorization to develop or revise a student code of conduct. |
| 2. | Chief Student Affairs Officer | Develops a recommended student code of conduct with input regarding its content and provisions from the chief fiscal and academic officers, student government organizations, faculty, and other administrators. |
| 3. | Advisory Committee | Reviews the recommended student code of conduct submitted by the chief student affairs officer for reasonableness, clarity, enforceability, and impact. Recommends its approval to the president. |
| | President | Obtains legal counsel's input to ensure that the recommended student code of conduct does not violate any student's legal rights. Approves advisory committee's recommendation. |
| 4. | President | Submits the student code of conduct to the board of trustees with a recommendation for its adoption. |

*Explanation of Decision Matrix 36, Cont'd.*

| Step | Action Responsibility | Action |
|------|----------------------|--------|
| | Board of Trustees | Reviews the recommended student code of conduct, obtaining clarification from the chief student affairs officer and legal counsel, and authorizes its adoption. |
| 5. | Chief Student Affairs Officer | Receives the president's authorization to publish and implement the approved student code of conduct. |
| 6 & 7. | Chief Student Affairs Officer | Finalizes the content and authorizes the director of publications to print the required number of copies of the student code of conduct. |

## Decision Matrix 37. Administration of Student Discipline.

Legend of decision-making roles
1 – Authorizes action
2 – Action responsibility
3 – Approves recommendation
4 – Recommends action
5 – Provides input

| Procedural Steps | President | Chief Student Affairs Officer | Committee on Faculty and Student Discipline | Complainant | Student | Witnesses |
|---|---|---|---|---|---|---|
| 1. Receive notification of student's infraction of code of conduct | | 2 | | | | |
| 2. Establish the facts of the case | | 2 | | 5 | 5 | 5 |
| 3. (a) Resolve problem with student or | | 2 | | 5 | 2 | 5 |
| (b) Determine that discipline hearing is required | | 2 | | | | |
| 4. Establish time, date, and place of hearing | | 5 | 2 | | | |
| 5. Receive written notification of hearing | | 5 | 2 | 2 | 2 | 2 |
| 6. Conduct hearing | | 5 | 2 | 5 | 5 | 5 |
| 7. Receive discipline decision | | 2 | 5 | | 2 | |
| 8. Receive student's appeal of decision | 2 | | | | 5 | |
| 9. Review case | 2 | 5 | 5 | | 5 | |
| 10. Receive written notification of appeal decision | | 2 | | | 2 | |
| 11. Implement decision of committee or president | 5 | 2 | | | | |

*Participants in Decision-Making Processes*

*Explanation of Decision Matrix 37.*

| Step | Action Responsibility | Action |
|------|----------------------|--------|
| 1. | Chief Student Affairs Officer | Receives complaint of a student's infraction of the code of conduct. |
| 2 & 3. | Chief Student Affairs Officer | Obtains the facts of the case from the complainant, the student, and witnesses, if any. If the infraction is minor and the student does not have a history of repeated infractions, determines appropriate disciplinary action to be taken. If the infraction is serious, or if prior warnings have not been effective, determines that it is necessary to bring the student before the committee on faculty and student discipline for a hearing. |
| 4. | Faculty and Student Discipline Committee | The chairperson, upon the receipt of notification from the chief student affairs officer, notifies her of the scheduled date, time, and place for the hearing. |
| 5. | Chief Student Affairs Officer | Issues written notification of the date, time, and place of the scheduled hearing to the complainant, the student, witnesses, and members of the committee on faculty and student discipline. Also notifies the student of his right to be |

*Explanation of Decision Matrix 37, Cont'd.*

| *Step* | *Action Responsibility* | *Action* |
|---|---|---|
| | | represented by legal counsel, if he so desires. |
| 6 & 7. | Committee on Faculty and Student Discipline | Conducts hearing to ascertain the facts of the case from the complainant, the student, and witnesses. Reaches a decision on disciplinary action to be imposed and notifies the chief student affairs officer and the student of its decision in writing. |
| 8. | President | Receives the student's written appeal to reverse or modify the decision of the committee on faculty and student discipline. |
| 9 & 10. | President | Reviews the discipline committee's written summary of its proceedings and obtains clarification from the complainant, witnesses, or the student. Notifies the student and the chief student affairs officer in writing of his decision on the appeal. |
| 11. | Chief Student Affairs Officer | Initiates steps to implement the disciplinary action determined by the committee on faculty and student discipline, if no appeal was involved, or by the president, if an appeal was involved. |

# Decision Matrix 38. Revising Health Care Program.

| Legend of decision-making roles |
| --- |
| 1 – Authorizes action |
| 2 – Action responsibility |
| 3 – Approves recommendation |
| 4 – Recommends action |
| 5 – Provides input |

**Participants in Decision-Making Processes**

| Procedural Steps | President | Legal Counsel | Advisory Committee | Chief Student Affairs Officer | Health Care Director | Contract Physicians | Chief Fiscal Officer | Student Government | Students |
|---|---|---|---|---|---|---|---|---|---|
| 1. Formulate revised health care regulations, delivery systems, and health emergency plan recommendations | 1 | | | 4 | 5 | 5 | 5 | 5 | |
| 2. Approve recommended regulations, systems, and plans | 3 | 5 | 4 | 5 | | | | | |
| 3. Authorize implementation of health care program | | | | 2 | | | | | |
| 4. Publish regulations | 1 | | | 2 | | | | | |
| 5. Negotiate new or revised student medical care insurance contract | | | | 5 | 5 | 5 | 4 | | |
| 6. Approve student medical care insurance contract | 3 | | 4 | | | | 5 | | |
| 7. Execute student medical care insurance contract | 1 | | | | | | 2 | | |
| 8. Negotiate new or revised physician service contract | | | | 4 | 5 | 2 | 2 | | |
| 9. Approve physician service contract | 3 | | 4 | | | | 5 | | |
| 10. Execute physician service contract | 1 | | | | | | 2 | | |
| 11. Implement health care program | | | | | 2 | 2 | | | |
| 12. Process student medical insurance claims | | | | | 5 | 2 | | | 2 |
| 13. Report major health problems | | | | | 2 | 5 | | | |
| 14. Institute health emergency plans | | | | 2 | 5 | 5 | | | |
| 15. Evaluate health service operations | | | | 2 | 5 | 5 | | 5 | |

*Explanation of Decision Matrix 38.*

| Step | Action Responsibility | Action |
|------|----------------------|--------|
| 1. | Chief Student Affairs Officer | Upon the receipt of presidential authorization, formulates recommended revisions to the existing health care program on the basis of input from the director of health care, contract physicians, student government organizations, and the chief fiscal officer. |
| 2 & 3. | Advisory Committee | Reviews recommended health care programs submitted by the chief student affairs officer for reasonableness, appropriateness, and impact. Recommends their approval to the president. |
| | President | Obtains input from legal counsel regarding the potential legal ramifications of the recommended health care program. Approves the advisory committee's recommendation and authorizes implementation of the health care program. |
| 4. | Chief Student Affairs Officer | Publishes and promulgates the approved health care regulations and health care service program. |
| 5. | Chief Fiscal Officer | Contacts insurers and obtains proposals for a student health care insurance program. |

*Explanation of Decision Matrix 38, Cont'd.*

| Step | Action Responsibility | Action |
|------|----------------------|--------|
| | | Reviews proposals with the chief student affairs officer, the director of health care, and contract physicians; negotiates proposed changes with insurers; and selects the insurance proposal recommended for approval. |
| 6. | Advisory Committee | Reviews recommended insurance coverage and proposed rates and recommends approval to the president. |
| | President | Approves the recommendation of the advisory committee. |
| 7. | Chief Fiscal Officer | Upon the receipt of the president's authorization, executes an insurance agreement with the insurer, notifying other insurers of the rejection of their proposals. |
| 8. | Chief Fiscal Officer | On the basis of input from the director of health care and recommendations from the chief student affairs officer, negotiates the terms of a physican service contract. |
| 9. | Advisory Committee | Reviews the physician service contract recommended by the chief fiscal officer for adequacy of proposed services |

*Explanation of Decision Matrix 38, Cont'd.*

| Step | Action Responsibility | Action |
|------|----------------------|--------|
| | | and proposed fees. Recommends its approval to the president. |
| | President | Approves the advisory committee's recommendation. |
| 10. | Chief Fiscal Officer | Upon the receipt of the president's authorization, executes the physician service contract. |
| 11, 12, & 13. | Director of Health Care and Contract Physicians | Provide agreed-on health care services and assist students in the preparation of claims under the insured health care program. Report major health care problems to the chief student affairs officer. |
| 14. | Chief Student Affairs Officer | Prepares, for posting around campus, arrangements available for emergency health treatment on the basis of input from the director of health care and contract physicians. |
| 15. | Chief Student Affairs Officer | Obtains a written report on health care operations from the director of health care. Obtains input from student government, the chief fiscal |

*Explanation of Decision Matrix 38, Cont'd.*

| Step | Action Responsibility | Action |
|------|----------------------|--------|
|      |                      | officer, and contract physicians regarding the effectiveness of the health care program and identifies ways in which the program could be improved. |

**Decision Matrix 39. Establishing Nonacademic Counseling Program.**

| Legend of decision-making roles | |
|---|---|
| 1 | Authorizes action |
| 2 | Action responsibility |
| 3 | Approves recommendation |
| 4 | Recommends action |
| 5 | Provides input |

| Procedural Steps | President | Advisory Committee | Chief Student Affairs Officer | Counselors | Chief Academic Officer | Faculty | Student Government |
|---|---|---|---|---|---|---|---|
| _Participants in Decision-Making Processes_ | | | | | | | |
| 1. Recommend scope of nonacademic counseling program | | | 2 | 5 | 5 | 5 | 5 |
| 2. Recommend organizational structure for nonacademic counseling activities | | | 2 | 5 | | | |
| 3. Recommend regulations regarding counselor's right to private practice | | | 2 | 5 | | | |
| 4. Approve scope, organization, and regulations | 3 | 4 | 5 | | | | |
| 5. Authorize implementation of program | 1 | | 2 | | | | |
| 6. Implement program | | | 1 | 2 | | | |
| 7. Receive report of results of program operations | | | 2 | 5 | | | |
| 8. Review report and identify any desirable changes in scope, organizational structure, or regulations | | | 2 | 5 | 5 | 5 | 5 |

*Explanation of Decision Matrix 39.*

| Step | Action Responsibility | Action |
|---|---|---|
| 1 & 2. | Chief Student Affairs Officer | Develops recommendations covering the scope of services to be provided by each area of nonacademic counseling, the organizational structure under which such services will be provided, and how such services can most effectively be coordinated with academic counseling activities. Her recommendations should be based on input from counseling staff, student government organizations, the chief academic officer, and faculty. |
| 3. | Chief Student Affairs Officer | Develops regulations covering the terms and circumstances under which counseling staff may provide private counseling services to third parties. Her recommendations should be based on input from professional counseling staff. |
| 4 & 5. | Advisory Committee | Reviews recommendations from steps 1, 2, and 3 submitted by the chief student affairs officer for appropriateness and impact. Recommends approval of the nonacademic counseling program to the president. |
| | President | Approves the nonacademic counseling program and |

*Explanation of Decision Matrix 39, Cont'd.*

| *Step* | *Action Responsibility* | *Action* |
|--------|------------------------|----------|
| | | authorizes its implementation by the chief student affairs officer. |
| 6 & 7. | Counselors | Carry out the authorized nonacademic counseling program under the supervision of the chief student affairs officer. Submit to her a written annual report on counseling activities. |
| 8. | Chief Student Affairs Officer | Reviews the annual report and obtains input from student government organizations, faculty, and the chief academic officer regarding the effectiveness of the program. Identifies ways in which the nonacademic counseling program can be improved. |

*Explanation of Decision Matrix 40.*

| Step | Action Responsibility | Action |
|------|----------------------|--------|
| 1. | Chief Student Affairs Officer | Formulates recommended policies and procedures to be followed in carrying out student government and other student organization activities on the basis of input from student government and student organization representatives and the chief fiscal officer. |
| 2. | Advisory Committee | Reviews the policy and procedure recommendations submitted by the chief student affairs officer for acceptability and appropriateness and recommends their approval to the president. |
|    | President | Approves the advisory committee's recommendation. |
| 3. | President | Submits policy recommendations to the board of trustees for approval. |
|    | Board of Trustees | Reviews recommended policies, obtaining clarification from the president and chief student affairs officer, and adopts the policies. |
| 4. | Chief Student Affairs Officer | Receives the president's authorization to implement policies and procedures. |

# Decision Matrix 40. Student Activities and Government.

Legend of decision-making roles
1 – Authorizes action
2 – Action responsibility
3 – Approves recommendation
4 – Recommends action
5 – Provides input

| Procedural Steps | Board of Trustees | President | Advisory Committee | Chief Student Affairs Officer | Chief Fiscal Officer | Student Government | Student Organizations | Budget Control | Cashier |
|---|---|---|---|---|---|---|---|---|---|
| 1. Develop recommended policies and procedures to be followed by student government and activity organizations | | 3 | 4 | 2 | 5 | 5 | 5 | | |
| 2. Approve policies and procedures | | 4 | | 5 | | | | | |
| 3. Obtain trustee approval of policies | 2 | | | 5 | | | | | |
| 4. Authorize implementation of policies and procedures | | 1 | | 2 | | | | | |
| 5. Notify student government and organizations of amount of revenue that will be available to support their activities and request that they prepare expenditure budget requests | | | | 2 | 5 | | | | |

*Participants in Decision-Making Processes*

| | | | | |
|---|---|---|---|---|
| 6. Prepare expenditure budget requests | 5 | 5 | 2 | 2 |
| 7. Approve expenditure budget requests | 3 | 5 | 4 | 2 | 4 |
| 8. Receive notification of authorized budgets | 5 | | 2 | 2 |
| 9. Schedule activities | 2 | | 4 | 4 |
| 10. Encumber funds for scheduled activities | 5 | | | 2 |
| 11. Conduct activities and | | | | |
| (a) disburse necessary funds | 3 | 2 | 4 | 4 |
| (b) collect activity revenues | | 1 | 2 | 2 |
| 12. Receive revenues collected together with required accounting support documentation | 5 | 5 | 2 |

*Explanation of Decision Matrix 40, Cont'd.*

| Step | Action Responsibility | Action |
|------|----------------------|--------|
| 5. | Chief Student Affairs Officer | On the basis of data obtained from the chief fiscal affairs officer, notifies student government and student activity officers of the amount of student fee revenue that will be available to support their activities and instructs them to prepare their expenditure budget requests. |
| 6. | Student Government and Student Organizations | Prepare, with assistance from the chief fiscal officer and chief student affairs officer, their expenditure budget requests. |
| 7. | Chief Student Affairs Officer | Approves budget requests and includes them in the annual operating budget request for her area of operations. |
| 8. | Student Government and Student Organizations | Receive, from the chief student affairs officer, notification of approved expenditure budgets. |
| 9. | Chief Student Affairs Officer | Works with student government and organization officers in planning, budgeting for, and scheduling activities. Approves activities and updates master calendar. |
| 10. | Budget Control | Encumbers budgeted student activity funds when notified by the chief student affairs officer that they have been authorized. |

*Explanation of Decision Matrix 40, Cont'd.*

| Step | Action Responsibility | Action |
|------|----------------------|--------|
| 11a. | Chief Fiscal Officer | Disburses funds for student activities when such disbursements have been requested by authorized student government and student activity officers and approved by the chief student affairs officer. |
| 11b. | Student Government and Student Organizations | Collect revenue from the sale of tickets, the sale of advertising, and the like for student activities in accordance with controls authorized by the chief fiscal officer. |
| 12. | Cashier | Receives funds collected in step 11b with required accounting documentation and issues cashier's receipt. |

## Decision Matrix 41. New Student Orientation Program.

Legend of decision-making roles

1 – Authorizes action
2 – Action responsibility
3 – Approves recommendation
4 – Recommends action
5 – Provides input

*Participants in Decision-Making Processes*

| *Procedural Steps* | President | Advisory Committee | Chief Student Affairs Officer | Administrators | Recruiting and Admissions Director | Student Government | Students |
|---|---|---|---|---|---|---|---|
| 1. Develop recommended timetable and content of new student orientation program | 3 | | 2 | 5 | | 5 | |
| 2. Approve timetable and content | | 4 | 5 | | | | |
| 3. Authorize implementation of program | 1 | | 2 | | | | |
| 4. Notify director of recruiting and admissions of timetable and requirement that all new students must attend | | | 2 | | | | |
| 5. Notify new students | | | | | 2 | | |
| 6. Schedule program and obtain any material to be used or distributed | | | 2 | 5 | | | |
| 7. Conduct program | | | 2 | 2 | | | |
| 8. Evaluate program | | | 2 | 5 | | | |
| 9. Review results of evaluation and determine desirable changes, if any | | | 2 | | | | 5 |

*Explanation of Decision Matrix 41.*

| Step | Action Responsibility | Action |
|------|----------------------|--------|
| 1. | Chief Student Affairs Officer | Develops recommendations for timetable and identification of subject matter to be covered by a new student orientation program on the basis of input from the chief academic officer and faculty, the chief fiscal officer, the director of financial aid, the registrar, the director of student housing, the director of food services, the director of the bookstore, the librarian, the director of health services, and student government and student organizations. |
| 2 & 3. | Advisory Committee | Reviews the chief student affairs officer's recommended timetable and areas of coverage for timing and adequacy of orientation program and recommends presidential approval. |
| | President | Approves the program and authorizes the chief student affairs officer to arrange for its implementation. |
| 4. | Chief Student Affairs Officer | Notifies the director of recruiting and admissions of the scheduled timetable and the requirement that all new students attend the orientation program. |

*Explanation of Decision Matrix 41, Cont'd.*

| Step | Action Responsibility | Action |
|------|----------------------|--------|
| 5. | Director of Recruiting and Admissions | Notifies admitted applicants of the scheduled timetable and the necessity to attend the new student orientation program. |
| 6. | Chief Student Affairs Officer | Arranges for space and facilities required for the program, updates the master calendar to reserve space for the required period, and obtains from each operational area to be covered by the program any material that is to be handed out to the new students during the program. |
| 7. | Chief Student Affairs Officer | Supervises the conduct of the orientation program and sees that the heads of operational areas to be covered have their material for distribution available when needed and adequate time to make their presentations. |
| 8 & 9. | Chief Student Affairs Officer | Obtains input regarding the program's effectiveness from students and the heads of operational areas who have made presentations during the program; identifies ways in which future programs can be improved. |

# Recruiting
# and Admissions

The recruiting and admissions functions are administered as separate organizational units at some institutions. However, operations are more efficient and effective, particularly at smaller institutions, when these activities are combined into an integrated operation administered by a director of recruiting and admissions. This chapter, therefore, deals with both activities as though they were consolidated into one function. Decision Matrix 42 shows the processes that should be followed in the operation of the recruiting and admissions office. An admissions committee should assist the director in formulating admission policies and procedures and in making admission decisions for marginal applicants. This committee also should be involved in reviewing and evaluating the operation of the recruiting and admissions office.

The essential standards of good management applicable to the conduct of recruiting and admissions activities are set forth below.

★   The director of recruiting and admissions should be responsible for the development and implementation of a recruiting plan designed to ensure that the proper number of applicants from each category of student is recruited and admitted to achieve the institution's enrollment goals in both overall numbers and student mix. Failure to adhere to this standard can cause serious financial problems, identified in Chapter Five. The number of new students required to meet the institution's enrollment goals is defined in its multi-year plan, as are the mixes of students required to do so. These mixes include not only upper- and lower-division students but also male and female, residential and nonresidential, in-state and out-of-state, married and single, and the like. In addition, the number of foreign students, the limits on the number of upper-division students to be admitted to various academic programs, the number that are capable of meeting their financial obligations without financial aid, and a desirable racial mix may also be defined.

These numbers are determined not only by the institution's academic aspirations and mission but also by the availability of student housing, including accommodations for married students, the availability of financial aid funds, and the like. Every effort must be made to achieve recruiting goals to ensure academic balance, full dormitories, sufficient financial aid funding to minimize unanticipated costs, the ability to collect assessed charges, and the availability of revenues for planned expenditures.

The appointment of designated faculty and student recruiters can help the institution's professional recruiting staff in meeting the institution's enrollment goals. The procedures to be followed in recruiting and admissions should include a regular system of follow-up communication with each applicant, before and after admission, to reinforce the student's ultimate decision to matriculate. Further, the director of financial aid should notify the director of recruiting and admissions regularly of the names and addresses of applicants who have submitted an application for financial aid to the financial aid office but whose names do not appear on listings of applicants provided to the financial aid office by the admissions office. Should the admissions office find that it has no record of contact with such applicants, it should establish such contact as quickly as possible. Where the records of both the admissions office and the financial aid office are maintained in the computer, the applicants' name and address files should be linked. This linkage will permit a computer program to be written that provides each office with the names and addresses of applicants appearing in one file but not in the other file.

★ Recruiters should be familiar with the institution's financial aid plan, policies, and application and award requirements; provided with financial aid material and forms; and directed to communicate policies and requirements to prospective applicants. Recruiters should be authorized to discuss with potential applicants the amount of aid to which they may be entitled. They should not be authorized, however, to commit the institution to providing a stipulated amount of financial aid. They, and all recruiting material, should make it clear that the amount of aid that applicants can receive can be determined only after their financial aid documentation is completed, their enrollment status is finalized, and their need for financial aid has been determined.

★ Recruiters should be familiar with the institution's planned academic programs to avoid recruiting students whose career objectives cannot be met.

★ Each recruiter should be required to provide the director of recruiting and admissions, immediately after each recruiting visit or activity, with a written report of the results of the visit or activity. These reports should identify, at the least, the places visited, the nature of the activity, the name and title of the person responsible for conducting the activity, the type of reception the recruiter received, the number of applicants contacted, the number of applications for admission and financial aid given out, the number of completed applications received, and the recruiter's assessment of the results of the visit or activity.

★ The director of recruiting and admissions should be responsible for the coordination of recruiting activities carried out by or through alumni or sponsoring churches (if the institution is church-related). The director should be guided by the director of alumni relations and whoever is responsible for the maintenance of church relations as to the best way to achieve the desired recruiting objectives.

★   The director of recruiting and admissions should be responsible for maintaining records that identify which recruiting activities have been successful and productive and which have not. This information should be used in the development of future recruiting plans. Activities that have not been successful and productive should be abandoned or modified.

★   While the director of recruiting and admissions should be responsible for specifying how much can be spent on recruitment advertising, the message to be communicated, and the target locations, the director of public relations should be responsible for the execution of the agreed-on advertising program.

★   The director of recruiting and admissions should maintain current and historical records that provide the administration, and through the president the board of trustees, with reports of current and prior-year data about the results of recruiting and admissions activities for each month of the recruiting and admissions period. Such data should include, at a minimum, the number of inquiries received, the number of complete and incomplete applications received, the number of completed applications that have been processed, the number of applicants admitted, and the number of admitted applicants who have accepted admission.

★   The director of recruiting and admissions should be responsible for supplying the registrar with lists of the names of applicants who have been admitted and their high school or college transcripts, their admission applications, and their test scores. No student should be allowed to matriculate who has not been admitted by the admissions office. Students' personal data to be maintained in the registrar's records should be derived from information provided by the applicants on the application for admission form, since that is likely to be the most accurate source of such data. Where the admissions office records and registrar records are both maintained in the computer, the files should be linked. This linkage permits the automatic updating of the registrar's files with data on applicants who have been accepted for admission (see Decision Matrix 21 in Chapter Six).

★ The admissions office should be responsible for notifying the director of financial aid of the names and addresses of applicants for admission who have requested financial aid. The admissions office is also responsible for seeing that all admission documents required to establish eligibility for financial aid awards are obtained and retained on file.

★ The admissions office should be responsible for notifying the director of housing of the number of applicants, both those already admitted and those in the process of being admitted, who have indicated on their applications a desire to live on campus.

★ The admissions office should assist the director of health services in obtaining health certifications and scheduling physical examinations for admitted students.

★ The applicability of transfer credits to general education requirements should be determined by the registrar in accordance with established policies. The acceptability of transfer credits in the student's major should be determined by the appropriate faculty in accordance with established policies. The number of credits granted for externally acquired experiential learning should be determined by the chief academic officer on the basis of recommendations from appropriate faculty members. The director of recruiting and admissions should notify the applicant promptly regarding the number and nature of transfer or experiential learning credits that have been accepted for transfer and the remaining course requirements the student will have to meet in order to obtain a degree.

★ The policies and procedures adopted for recruiting and admissions should include special policies and procedures applicable to the admission of foreign students, U.S. students applying for admission to satellite programs, nondegree programs, or weekend or evening college programs, and transfer, readmit, and walk-in applicants. Chapter Six states that no student should be permitted to matriculate unless the student holds a permit to register issued by the admissions office. Walk-in applicants are those who have not applied for admission prior to their appearance at the time of registration. If the institution wishes to accept such students for admission, a permit to register must be issued on the spot. If the walk-in applicant does not have all of the documentation required to make an admit decision, any permit to register should be made conditional on the student's providing the required documentation by a specific date and the ultimate acceptability of that documentation. Further, no permit to register should be issued to an applicant for readmission until the admissions office has obtained verification from the registrar that no encumbrance exists in the applicant's record that would prevent the applicant from matriculating. Should an encumbrance exist, any permit to register should be conditional on the applicant's having the encumbrance removed prior to registration (see Chapter Six for information on the encumbrance system maintained by the registrar).

★   Unless adequate on-campus expertise exists, the evaluation of the credentials of foreign applicants should be referred to professional organizations that are qualified to provide such services.

★   Payments received by the admissions office for application fees and tuition or room deposits should be transmitted to the business office daily, together with the data necessary for that office to properly record such payments. If an institution has a policy that requires the payment of an application fee before a permit to register can be issued but does not adhere to that policy, the institution should consider abandoning the policy.

★   At least once every three years, the director of recruiting and admissions should conduct a study to evaluate the correlation of admissions standards with students' satisfactory academic performance.

Readers desiring additional information about recruiting and admissions should contact the American Association of Collegiate Registrars and Admissions Officers (AACRAO), One Dupont Circle, Washington, D.C. 20036.

*Explanation of Decision Matrix 42.*

| Step | Action Responsibility | Action |
|------|----------------------|--------|
| 1. | Director of Recruiting and Admissions | Receives and reviews multi-year plan and identifies changes in admission policies, academic policies, academic programs, and the mixes and characteristics of student enrollment on which the multi-year plan is based. |
| 2. | Director of Recruiting and Admissions | Formulates recommended recruiting and admissions plans and procedures. Bases recommendations on an analysis of historical data about the results of prior recruiting efforts and attrition factors applicable to the number of applications received and the number of applicants admitted, the number of applicants admitted and the number of admission acceptances received, and the number of admission acceptances received and the number of new matriculants. Also bases recommendations on input from the chief academic officer, regarding the number of current students likely to be denied readmission for academic reasons, the number who will advance in grade, and the level of faculty involvement in recruiting that can be counted on; the chief fiscal officer, regarding the number of students likely to be denied readmission for financial |

## Decision Matrix 42. Conducting Recruiting and Admissions Operations.

Legend of decision-making roles
1 – Authorizes action
2 – Action responsibility
3 – Approves recommendation
4 – Recommends action
5 – Provides input

Participants in Decision-Making Processes

| Procedural Steps | Trustees | President | Advisory Committee | Chief Academic Officer | Chief Fiscal Officer | Registrar | Financial Aid Director | Student Housing Director | Public Relations Director | Alumni Relations Director | Church Relations Director | Recruiting and Admissions Director | Publications Director | Students | Faculty | Campus-Based Recruiters | Alumni Recruiters | Church Recruiters | Applicants |
|---|---|---|---|---|---|---|---|---|---|---|---|---|---|---|---|---|---|---|---|
| 1. Receive multi-year plan and become familiar with changes in admission policies, student characteristics desired, academic program plans, and enrollment and student mixes desired | | | | | | | | | | | | 2 | | | | | | | |
| 2. Formulate recruiting and admission plans and procedures | | | | 5 | 5 | 5 | 5 | 5 | | 5 | 5 | 2 | | | | | | | |
| 3. Review and approve plans and procedures | | 3 | 4 | | | | | | | | | 5 | | | | | | | |
| 4. Authorize implementation of plan and procedures | | 1 | | | | | | | | | | 2 | | | | | | | |
| 5. Receive financial aid material to be used in recruiting | | | | | | | 5 | | | | | 2 | | | | | | | |
| 6. Prepare recruiting material | | | | | | | | | | | | 2 | | 5 | | | | | |
| 7. Conduct orientation program for campus-based recruiters | | | | 5 | 5 | | | 5 | | | | 1 | 2 | | | 5 | | | |
| 8. Arrange alumni recruiting efforts | | | | | 5 | 5 | 5 | | | 5 | | 2 | | | | 5 | | | |
| 9. Arrange church recruiting efforts | | | | | 5 | | | | | | 5 | 2 | | | | | | | |
| 10. Arrange and schedule campus-based recruiting efforts | | | | | | | | | | | | 2 | | | | 5 | | | |

| # | Activity | Values |
|---|---|---|
| 11. | Arrange for advertising campaign | 5 |
| 12. | Conduct recruiting activities | 2, 2, 2, 2 |
| 13. | Receive recruiting activity result reports | 5, 5, 5 |
| 14. | Adjust recruiting activities if warranted by recruiting activity reports | 2 |
| 15. | Receive applications or applicant contact identification | 5, 5, 5, 5, 2 |
| 16. | Follow up incomplete applications and contacts until required documentation is complete | 5 |
| 17. | Receive and process payments | 2, 2, 5 |
| 18. | Obtain decision on award of experiential learning credits | 3, 2, 2, 4 |
| 19. | Obtain decisions on acceptability of transfer credits | 2, 2 |
|  | (a) applicable to general education requirements | 1, 2, 2 |
|  | (b) applicable to the student's major | 2, 1 |
| 20. | Make admission decisions | 2, 2 |
| 21. | Receive notification of |  |
|  | (a) admission decision and request for acceptance | 2, 2, 5, 2 |
|  | (b) admitted applicants requesting housing | 2, 5 |
|  | (c) admitted applicants requesting financial aid | 2, 5 |
|  | (d) admission documents of admitted applicants | 2, 2, 5 |
|  | (e) admitted applicants' academic areas of interest | 5 |
| 22. | Receive notification of acceptance of admission | 2, 5, 2, 2 |
| 23. | Maintain records required for management reporting and future evaluation | 2, 2 |
| 24. | Receive regular, periodic reports on status of recruiting and admissions operations | 2, 2, 2, 2, 5 |
| 25. | Receive president's report on status of recruiting and admissions operations | 2, 5, 2, 5 |
| 26. | Evaluate recruiting and admissions activities and identify desirable changes | 5, 5, 5, 5, 5, 5, 5, 5, 5, 5, 5, 5 |

*Explanation of Decision Matrix 42, Cont'd.*

| Step | Action Responsibility | Action |
|------|----------------------|--------|
| | | reasons and the involvement of coaches in recruiting; the registrar, regarding current enrollment statistics, the estimated attrition loss, and the number of students expected to graduate; the director of financial aid, regarding the anticipated ability to meet the financial assistance needs of new students; the director of student housing, regarding the projected number of housing spaces that will be available; the directors of alumni and church relations, regarding the level of recruiting assistance expected from alumni and churches; and students, regarding expected improvements if the changes authorized by the multi-year plan are successfully implemented. |
| 3 & 4. | Advisory Committee | Reviews the recommended recruiting plan and procedures and recommends presidential approval. |
| | President | Approves the recruiting and admissions plan and authorizes its implementation by the director of recruiting and admissions. |

*Explanation of Decision Matrix 42, Cont'd.*

| Step | Action Responsibility | Action |
|------|----------------------|--------|
| 5. | Director of Recruiting and Admissions | Receives financial aid material to be used in recruiting efforts from the director of financial aid. |
| 6. | Director of Recruiting and Admissions | Determines content and number of copies of recruiting brochures, forms, and other material required on the basis of input from the chief academic officer and faculty, the chief fiscal officer, and students. |
| | Director of Publications | Prints required material in accordance with the instructions and authorization received from the director of recruiting and admissions. |
| 7. | Director of Recruiting and Admissions | Conducts, with the assistance of the chief fiscal officer, registrar, director of financial aid, and director of student housing, an orientation workshop to familiarize campus-based recruiters with the recruiting procedures to be followed, financial and fiscal policies, housing constraints, and recruiting goals. |
| 8 & 9. | Director of Recruiting and Admissions | Makes arrangements, with the advice and assistance of the directors of alumni and church relations, for the involvement of alumni and churches in recruiting. |

*Explanation of Decision Matrix 42, Cont'd.*

| Step | Action Responsibility | Action |
|------|----------------------|--------|
| 10. | Director of Recruiting and Admissions | Schedules the efforts of campus-based recruiters and briefs them on their contact person and the results of prior recruiting efforts from that source. |
| 11. | Director of Recruiting and Admissions | Determines target areas for and recruiting message to be included in an advertising campaign, on the basis of advice and cost estimates obtained from the director of public relations. Obtains budgetary clearance from the chief fiscal officer. |
| | Director of Public Relations | Arranges for the advertising campaign authorized by the director of recruiting and admissions. |
| 12. | Recruiters | Conduct recruiting activities. Submit activity results report following each activity showing the number of applicants contacted, the number of contacts who took applications, the number of completed applications received and transmitted with the report, and comments regarding the reception received, the adequacy of arrangements, |

*Explanation of Decision Matrix 42, Cont'd.*

| Step | Action Responsibility | Action |
|------|----------------------|--------|
| | | the types of questions asked, and the desirability of including the activity in future recruiting efforts. |
| 13 & 14. | Director of Recruiting and Admissions | Analyzes the reports received from recruiters and adjusts the recruiting activity program, if deemed desirable. Notes pertinent comments for follow-up. |
| 15 & 16. | Director of Recruiting and Admissions | Receives application forms submitted by students or recruiters and names and addresses of potential applicants, contacted by recruiters, who have expressed an interest in receiving an application or more information about the institution. Processes applications and follows up with applicants whose application documentation is complete and prospects who have requested information or application forms. Continues follow-up until documentation is complete or notification is received that no further follow-up is desired. |

*Explanation of Decision Matrix 42, Cont'd.*

| Step | Action Responsibility | Action |
| --- | --- | --- |
| 17. | Chief Fiscal Officer | Receives and processes application fees and tuition and room deposit payments received from applicants and transmitted daily by the director of recruiting and admissions. Issues cashier's receipt to be transmitted to applicant. |
| 18. | Director of Recruiting and Admissions | Obtains from the chief academic officer a decision, based on faculty recommendations, about experiential learning credit to be awarded to applicants who have applied for such credit. |
| 19. | Director of Recruiting and Admissions | Obtains data required to advise applicants regarding the acceptability of transfer credits within established policy from the registrar, for credits applicable to general education requirements, and from the faculty of the departments from which the applicants will receive their degree, for credits applicable to major requirements. |
| 20. | Director of Recruiting and Admissions | Makes admission decisions for applicants whose application documentation is complete. |

*Explanation of Decision Matrix 42, Cont'd.*

| Step | Action Responsibility | Action |
|------|----------------------|--------|
| 21. | Director of Recruiting and Admissions | Issues the following notification of admission decisions: notifies applicants of acceptance for admission with a request that they return notification of acceptance of admission; notifies the director of housing of the names of admitted applicants who have indicated a desire to live on campus; notifies the director of financial aid of the names and addresses of admitted applicants who have indicated a need for financial assistance; notifies the registrar of personal and transcript data for each admitted applicant; and notifies the chief academic officer of the names of students who have expressed interest in particular areas of academic concentration. |
| 22. | Director of Recruiting and Admissions | Receives admitted applicants' notification of acceptance of admission. |
| 23. | Director of Recruiting and Admissions | Maintains records to identify the number of contacts made and inquiries received, the number of applications received, the |

*Explanation of Decision Matrix 42, Cont'd.*

| Step | Action Responsibility | Action |
|------|----------------------|--------|
| | | number of applications completed, the number of applicants admitted, and the number of acceptances of admissions received. These records should be sufficiently detailed to identify the success of various recruiting activities, the male-female mix, the full-time–part-time mix, the residential-commuting mix, the U.S.-foreign mix, the racial mix, the in-state–out-of-state mix, the ages of applicants, the number of handicapped applicants, the class to which applicants have been admitted, and the programs to which they have been admitted (regular, evening or weekend, or alternative education off campus). |
| 24. | Director of Recruiting and Admissions | Periodically submits recruiting and admissions status reports to the president, the chief academic officer, the chief fiscal officer, the registrar, and the director of financial aid. The frequency of reporting should increase as the cycle gets closer to registration. |

*Explanation of Decision Matrix 42, Cont'd.*

| Step | Action Responsibility | Action |
|------|----------------------|--------|
| 25. | President | Informs the board of trustees of the results of recruiting and admissions activity at board meetings during the recruiting period. |
| 26. | Director of Recruiting and Admissions | Evaluates the results of recruiting and admissions activities, obtaining input from all who have participated in the process or are affected by the results. Identifies ways in which the recruiting and admissions programs can be improved. |

# Financial Aid
# Programs

Administering an institution's student financial aid program can be defined briefly as promoting the most effective use of grant, loan, or employment opportunity funds to help students defray the cost of attending the institution. These funds include resources provided by both public and private sources as well as institutional resources earmarked for this purpose. Funds provided by private sources include income from endowed scholarships, both restricted and unrestricted, restricted and unrestricted scholarship gifts and grants, donated loan funds, and third-party payments of assessed charges for specific students. Restricted scholarships, both endowed funds and gifts and grants, are those where the donor has specified the type of student to whom the scholarship is to be awarded. Unless otherwise specified by the donor, such scholarships may be awarded on a "need" or "no-need" basis. The funds from public sources can include grants from both state and federal programs. Some states will even make grants for students who are residents of that state but attend colleges and universities located in other states. Some states also have both "need" and "no-need" student financial aid funding programs. State-funded programs include equalization grants, incentive grants, scholarships, and loans. Federal student financial aid programs, on the other hand, are all need-based. Federal programs that are administered by the federal government include Pell Grants, known as Basic Educational Opportunity Grants (BEOG), the Guaranteed Student Loan program (GSL), and the Veterans Cost of Instruction Payment Program (VCIPP). Federal programs administered by the institution include the Supplemental Education Opportunity Grants (SEOG), both initial and continuing, National Direct Student Loans (NDSL), and the College Work Study Programs (CWSP). Institutions receiving NDSL and CWSP grants must provide matching funds for those programs. Institutional resources allocated for student financial aid are unfunded programs that include merit scholarships, athletic, band, and music scholarships, tuition remission, and work aid grants.

The financial aid funds available to an institution should be considered a tool for achieving enrollment goals. While the day-to-day administration of such funds should be delegated to the director of financial aid, her applications for funding from state and federal programs and her administration of award decisions should be carefully reviewed by the administration and the board of trustees. Their reviews should evaluate whether the financial aid office's activities are using available funds as effectively as possible to assist the institution in achieving its mission, goals, and enrollment objectives, whether they are designed to bring to the institution the maximum funding possible, and whether the funds are equitably used in helping all eligible students meet the cost of attending the institution. Further, the administration and the board of trustees should be kept apprised of potential changes in eligibility requirements and levels of funding so they can evaluate the potential impact of such changes on institutional operations. The director of financial aid thus has a formidable administrative task; meeting her responsibilities to the students and the institution requires extensive record keeping and meticulous planning.

The essential standards of good management in the administration of student financial aid activities are set forth below.

★ The director of financial aid should prepare an annual plan for the utilization of projected financial aid funds and submit it to the administration and the board of trustees for their review and approval. The plan should identify the total financial aid resources expected from each funding source and the total from all sources, the projected cost of attending the institution for each category of student (main campus, remote sites, residential, commuting, married, single, in-state, out-of-state, and the like), the demand for financial aid likely to be generated by each category of student, and an allocation of available resources against the projected demand for financial assistance. The cost of attending the institution should include not only institutionally assessed charges for tuition, fees, room, board, and books but also costs such as transportation, clothing, health care, and laundry (see Decision Matrix 43).

★   Financial aid awards should not be made from unfunded institutional scholarships or grant-in-aid programs to any student whose need for financial assistance can be met legitimately from programs funded by third parties. To ensure the director's ability to adhere to this standard, she should be an ex officio member of all committees whose activities involve making recommendations for the awarding of or actually awarding financial assistance. In this capacity, she should be responsible for advising the committees of instances where the contemplated award will have a negative effect on third-party funded assistance that has been awarded to the student or to which the student is entitled. Further, regardless of how award determinations are made, the notification, record keeping, and administration of all awards, whatever their source, should be handled by the financial aid office. If any portion of the financial aid awarded to a student is provided from need-based funds and the total award meets the student's total calculated need, any subsequent awards from non-need-based funds or unanticipated third-party payments will require the reduction of the amount awarded from need-based funds. For example, if a student has been awarded the maximum aid possible and receives a portion of that aid from need-based funds, an additional non-need-based award for academic attainment or athletic participation will compel the director of financial aid to reduce the amount of the original award. Such additional non-need-based awards may appear to be assisting the students in meeting the cost of attending the institution; however, unless the total awarded from non-need-based funds is greater than that awarded from need-based funds, the students will not benefit. In addition, such awards will reduce the revenue the institution is entitled to from need-based funding sources, since this revenue is limited to the amount that the students need to cover their costs after deducting the amount their "need analysis" says they, or their parents, should be required to pay and the amount of assistance available to them from other sources.

★   The director of financial aid should be informed promptly of changes that affect either the availability of financial aid funding or the student's eligibility to receive financial aid. Notification may come from the registrar, regarding changes in enrollment status, residential status, withdrawal or dismissal, and unsatisfactory academic status; from the development office, regarding the receipt of new scholarship gifts, grants, and loans, including the identification of donor-imposed restrictions on the use of such funds; from the business office, regarding changes in the level of NDSL collections, increases or decreases in charges assessed to students receiving financial aid, and payments received from third parties for the assessed charges to students receiving financial aid; from either the personnel or payroll office, regarding the employment of students on the institution's regular payroll; and from principal investigators or project directors, regarding the appointment of students to a sponsored agreement in which a stipend is involved.

★   Policies and procedures should exist covering the application for funding under state and federal student financial aid programs, the award and disbursement of all student aid funds, the administration of student employment, and the preparation of reports required by federal and state funding agencies. These policies and procedures should include those related to the processing of students who are accepted for admission at the time of registration where the data necessary to make financial aid award decisions are incomplete. Any award data provided the student under these circumstances must be understood by the student, and clearly identified on any documents given to the student, to be conditional on the submission of required documentation that substantiates the amount awarded (see Decision Matrices 44, 45, and 46). The policies adopted also should include a policy on the percentage of campus-based, federally funded financial aid program funding that can be awarded prior to the receipt of final award notification letters by the institution. Such a policy is necessary because the government frequently does not decide how much money will be appropriated to each of its student financial aid programs or how much of the appropriated funds will be made available to each institution until long after the time when institutions must begin notifying applicants for admission of the amount of financial aid they can count on if they enroll. Failure to have such a policy and to permit the director of financial aid to begin notifying applicants about the amount and packaging of awards can significantly hamper the institution's ability to achieve its enrollment objectives. Further, by using prudent judgment, the director of financial aid can commit expected funds prior to the receipt of notification of final awards with little risk of financial loss. This is true because the amount of funding can be estimated on the low side from data obtained by following the news and maintaining contact with the funding agency; because of the processing time required to determine awards; and because the percentage of anticipated funding that may be committed can be limited to 60, 70, or 80 percent of the low estimate.

★  The procedures to be followed by the financial aid office should ensure the maintenance of all records necessary to meet all internal and external reporting requirements and internal control requirements. Further, they should ensure compliance with all policies, regulations, rules, and restrictions related to or imposed by each source of financial aid funds. The internal control requirements should include those necessary to control awards to ensure that the funds available are maximally utilized without overexpenditure and to reconcile the amounts awarded from each funding source with the fiscal records of the institution. Although it cannot be said to be an essential standard, the volume of data that must be recorded by a financial aid office warrants the maintenance of such records in the institution's computer. Further, where such records are automated, the files related to them should be linked with the files of the admissions office, the registrar's office, and the student accounts receivable file.

★   The financial aid office should maintain a student financial aid file for each student who has applied for or has been awarded financial aid. The file should be maintained for the entire period of the student's enrollment. It should contain the annual financial aid application; the annual need analysis form; a cumulative master record of all awards; the annual statement of educational purpose; the annual statement of independent status; all annual award or revised award letters properly executed by the student; a financial aid transcript, if appropriate, of awards made by other institutions; CWSP job referrals, employment records, and time sheets; and correspondence or any other records related to the determination of eligibility, need, or awards. The federal government requires institutions to withhold federally funded financial aid awards from students who are required by law to register with the Selective Service for the draft but have not done so. Several cases are now being considered by the United States Supreme Court concerning the issues raised by this requirement. Pending the Court's judgment, institutions have been relieved of the necessity of obtaining verification that students have in fact registered; they may grant federally funded financial aid awards to students who provide them with a written certification that they have complied with the registration requirements.

★   All documents related to the NDSL program — notes, disclosure statements, repayment agreements, and the like — must be maintained in a secure, fireproof facility.

★   Financial aid award records should be reconciled periodically with the registrar's and accounting office's records. Reconciliations should be made at least once before the expiration of each term. The reconciliation with the records of the registrar's office should verify that the student's eligibility data are the same in both files. The reconciliation with the accounting office's records should verify that the amounts awarded and the amounts expended from each funding source are in agreement.

★    The financial aid office should be responsible for the administration of student employment covered by awards from the CWSP or Institutional Work Aid (IWA) grants. The administration of student employment should ensure that all students who received a CWSP or IWA award as a part of their financial aid package are employed either on or off campus, work up to but not more than the number of hours required to earn the amount awarded, have minimal conflict between their class hours and work schedule, have the data necessary to compensate them for such work properly entered into the payroll system, and are properly compensated for the hours they work. The director of financial aid should also formulate and receive the administration's approval for a student employment compensation plan. The compensation of students should be as much as possible like that of regular employees; for example, differentials in rates of pay for job difficulty and the skill and experience of the student should be taken into consideration when compensation rates are established for various jobs (see Decision Matrix 47).

★    The financial aid application process for continuing students should be undertaken as early as practical while the students are still enrolled. This will permit the financial aid office to obtain the information and documentation necessary to process these applications and provide better information for multi-year planning. It will also enhance the institution's ability to retain enrolled students.

★    A biennial compliance audit of each campus-based, federally funded financial aid program should be conducted by the institution's external auditors, unless such audits have been conducted by the Department of Education auditors.

★ The chief fiscal officer should conduct periodic audits of financial aid award records to determine whether students have received the maximum award to which they are entitled within available resources. This is particularly important for students whose awards are based on need. If students who have met the need eligibility requirements do not obtain awards equal to their need when funding is available to meet such need, the fiscal office is bound to have difficulty in collecting the student accounts receivable from such students.

While it cannot be cited as an essential standard, the director of financial aid's ability to carry out her responsibilities is enhanced when she has a financial aid committee to work with. The size and composition of such a committee may vary from institution to institution. It is recommended, however, that it include, in addition to the director of financial aid, the director of recruiting and admissions, the chief student affairs officer, and the chief fiscal officer, at the least. Further, applicants should be encouraged to take advantage of the federally funded Guaranteed Student Loan (GSL) program to minimize the drain on institutional resources.

Readers desiring additional information regarding the conduct of student financial aid activities should contact the National Association of Student Financial Aid Administrators (NASFAA), 1812 H Street Northwest, Washington, D.C. 20006.

# Decision Matrix 43. Developing and Implementing Financial Aid Plan.

Legend of decision-making roles:
1 – Authorizes action
2 – Action responsibility
3 – Approves recommendation
4 – Recommends action
5 – Provides input

| Procedural Steps | Board of Trustees | President | Advisory Committee | Chief Student Affairs Officer | Chief Development Officer | Chief Fiscal Officer | Planning Director | Financial Aid Director | Recruiting and Admissions Director | Publications Director | Registrar | Students |
|---|---|---|---|---|---|---|---|---|---|---|---|---|
| 1. Provide copy of approved multi-year plan and request development of financial aid plan | | | | | | 2 | | 5 | | | | |
| 2. Project revenue availability | | | | | 5 | 5 | | 2 | | | | |
| 3. Project student costs of attending institution | | | | 5 | | 5 | | 2 | | | 5 | 5 |
| 4. Project demand for financial aid | | | | 5 | | 5 | | 2 | | | 5 | 5 |
| 5. Develop recommended financial aid award and allocation policies and plan | | | | 5 | | 5 | | 2 | 5 | | | |
| 6. Review and approve policies and plan | | 3 | | | | | | 5 | | | | |
| 7. Obtain board of trustees' approval for policies and plan | 2 | 4 | 4 | | | | | 5 | | | | |
| 8. Authorize implementation of policies and plan | | 2 | | | | 5 | | | 5 | | | |
| 9. Develop material to assist recruiters | | | | 5 | | | | 1 | 5 | 2 | | 5 |

*Participants in Decision-Making Processes*

| |  | | | |
|---|---|---|---|---|
| 10. | Communicate plan to recruiters and provide them with forms and financial aid materials | | | 2 |
| 11. | Prepare funding applications | 2 | 2 | 2 |
| 12. | Review and approve applications | 2 | 4 | 4 |
| 13. | Submit applications | | 2 | 2 |
| 14. | Receive notification of awards | | 2 | 2 |
| 15. | Receive notification of new gifts and grants | | 5 | 2 |
| 16. | Update plan | | | 2 |
| 17. | Establish required internal controls | | 2 | 2 |

*Explanation of Decision Matrix 43.*

| Step | Action Responsibility | Action |
|------|----------------------|--------|
| 1. | Chief Fiscal Officer | Provides director of financial aid with a copy of the multi-year plan approved by the board of trustees and requests that she prepare a recommended financial aid utilization plan. |
| 2. | Director of Financial Aid | Projects financial aid funds to be available on the basis of her own knowledge of federal and state legislative actions on proposals related to student financial assistance programs, input from the chief fiscal officer regarding the likely level of NDSL repayments, carryover funds from restricted scholarship loan gifts and grants and projected income from endowed scholarship loan funds, and input from the chief development officer regarding anticipated receipts of new scholarship gifts and grants. |
| 3. | Director of Financial Aid | Projects per-student cost of attending the institution for each category of student, using input from the chief fiscal officer regarding assessed charges for tuition, fees, room, and board and input from the chief student affairs |

*Explanation of Decision Matrix 43, Cont'd.*

| Step | Action Responsibility | Action |
|------|----------------------|--------|
| | | officer and students regarding other costs students will incur for transportation, laundry, clothing, and the like. |
| 4. | Director of Financial Aid | Projects student demand for financial aid, using input from the registrar and students, regarding the number of students of each category that are likely to return; the director of recruiting and admissions, regarding anticipated intake of new students who are U.S. citizens; the chief student affairs officer, regarding the anticipated number of residential students; and the chief fiscal officer, regarding the anticipated number of students who will not be permitted to reregister because of failure to meet financial obligations. |
| 5. | Director of Financial Aid | Reviews the results of steps 2, 3, and 4 and the problems identified with the existing financial aid program with the chief fiscal officer and chief student affairs officer. From the results of the review, develops recommended changes in financial aid policies and a plan for the |

*Explanation of Decision Matrix 43, Cont'd.*

| *Step* | *Action Responsibility* | *Action* |
|---|---|---|
| | | utilization of available financial aid funds among categories of students to maximize their usefulness in achieving planned enrollment goals and objectives. |
| 6. | Director of Financial Aid | Submits the plan and recommended policy changes to the advisory committee. |
| | Advisory Committee | Reviews recommended policies for their effects on other areas of operation, reviews the plan for consistency with planned goals and objectives, and recommends their approval to the president. |
| | President | Approves recommended plan and policies. |
| 7 & 8. | President | Recommends the adoption of the plan and policies to the board of trustees. |
| | Director of Financial Aid | Provides answers to any board questions regarding plan and policy recommendations. |
| | Board of Trustees | Adopts the recommended plan and policies. |

*Explanation of Decision Matrix 43, Cont'd.*

| Step | Action Responsibility | Action |
|------|----------------------|--------|
| | President | Authorizes the implementation of the approved policies and financial aid plan. |
| 9. | Director of Financial Aid | Obtains input from the chief student affairs officer, the director of recruiting and admissions, and students regarding the content of financial aid brochures; reviews the content requirement with the director of publications and authorizes the printing of a brochure; arranges for the revision and printing of financial aid applications, if necessary. |
| 10. | Director of Financial Aid | Conducts a workshop to familiarize recruiters with new policies and planned utilization of financial aid funds and provides them with financial aid brochures and application forms for use during their recruiting activities. |
| 11. | Director of Financial Aid and Chief Fiscal Officer | Jointly prepare Fis-Op report—a combined report on the use of the prior year's funding from federal financial aid programs and an application for next year's funding under these programs. |

*Explanation of Decision Matrix 43, Cont'd.*

| Step | Action Responsibility | Action |
|------|----------------------|--------|
| 12. | President | Reviews the Fis-Op report and approves its submission. |
| 13 & 14. | Director of Financial Aid, Chief Fiscal Officer, and President | Sign and submit Fis-Op report. Receive notification of the amount awarded under each program from the federal government. |
| 15. | Director of Financial Aid and Chief Fiscal Officer | Receive from the director of development notification of new scholarship and loan gifts and grants received. |
| 16. | Director of Financial Aid | Updates financial aid utilization plan to give consideration to changes in funds available resulting from steps 14 and 15. |
| 17. | Director of Financial Aid | Establishes master control record required to control awards from each source of funds to prevent over-expenditures. |
|  | Chief Fiscal Officer | Establishes accounts to account for expenditures from each source of funding. |

*Explanation of Decision Matrix 44.*

| Step | Action Responsibility | Action |
|------|----------------------|--------|
| 1 & 2. | Director of Financial Aid | As soon as possible, but not later than January 31, provides Pell Grant (BEOG) and financial aid application forms to current students receiving aid. Maintains a record of those who have picked up forms and follows up on those who have not. Assists current students in completing applications and encourages early mailing of Pell Grant (BEOG) applications. Files financial aid applications, maintaining a log of those received. |
| 3. | Director of Financial Aid | Receives notification from the admissions officer of applicants who have indicated on their application for admission form the need for financial aid but who have not submitted a financial aid application form. Sends forms and financial aid brochures to those students. |
| 4 & 5. | Director of Financial Aid | Receives financial aid application documents from applicants or admissions office. Opens a file for each student. Notifies admissions office of financial aid applications received directly from |

**Decision Matrix 44. Initial Financial Aid Award Process.**

Legend of decision-making roles
1 – Authorizes action
2 – Action responsibility
3 – Approves recommendation
4 – Recommends action
5 – Provides input

*Participants in Decision-Making Processes*

| Procedural Steps | President | Chief Fiscal Officer | Chief Student Affairs Officer | Academic Scholarship Committee | Athletic Scholarship Committee | Band/Music Scholarship Committee | Financial Aid Director | Nonacademic Counselors | Recruiting and Admissions Director | Registrar | Cashier | Cash Disbursements | Student Accounts Receivable | Students and Parents |
|---|---|---|---|---|---|---|---|---|---|---|---|---|---|---|
| 1. Distribute application forms to continuing students | | | 5 | | | | 2 | 5 | | | | | | 2 |
| 2. Complete application form | | | | | | | 5 | | | | | | | 5 |
| 3. Distribute applications and information to applicants for admission | | | | | | | 2 | | | | | | | |
| 4. Receive applications | | | | | | | 2 | | | | | | | |
| 5. Follow up until all required documentation is received | | | | | | | 2 | | | | | | | |
| 6. Receive student registration and residential status data | | | | | | | | | | 5 | | | | |
| 7. Receive institutional aid and restricted scholarship award data | 5 | | 5 | 5 | 5 | 5 | 2 | | | | | | | |
| 8. Compute need and award package and update control log | | | | | | | 2 | | | | | | | |
| 9. Prepare and send award letter to students | | | | | | | 2 | | | | | | | |

|  |  | | | | | |
|-----|----------|---|---|---|---|---|
| 10. | Receive student acceptance of awards | 2 | 2 | | | |
| 11. | Receive copies of accepted award letters | 2 | 5 | | 2 | 5 |
| 12. | Prepare journal vouchers for noncash awards | 1 | | | | |
| 13. | Prepare checks covering cash awards | | | 2 | | |
| 14. | Obtain students' endorsement of cash awards | | | 2 | | 5 |
| 15. | Post awards to students' accounts | 5 | | 5 | | |
| 16. | Reconcile student accounts receivable subsidiary records with control account | 2 | | 2 | | |
| 17. | Reconcile fiscal and financial aid records | 2 | 2 | | | |
| 18. | Audit award records to ensure that students have been awarded the maximum amount to which they are entitled | 2 | | | | |

*Explanation of Decision Matrix 44, Cont'd.*

*Step          Action Responsibility    Action*

students for its follow-up if
applications for admission
have not been received.
Determines whether financial
aid application documentation is complete and, if not,
follows up with applicants
until documentation is
complete.

6, 7,        Director of              Receives data required to
& 8.         Financial Aid            determine amount and
                                      packaging of awards, includ-
                                      ing the number of credits for
                                      which students are regis-
                                      tered, from the registrar; the
                                      number of residential stu-
                                      dents, from the chief student
                                      affairs officer; and the number
                                      of scholarship or grant-in-aid
                                      awards, from various com-
                                      mittees. Computes need,
                                      based on either need analysis
                                      reports or Pell Grant
                                      (BEOG) classifications, and
                                      the amount and types of aid
                                      to be awarded. Updates con-
                                      trol log to reduce the amount
                                      of unawarded funds remain-
                                      ing in each source of funds
                                      after the award.

9 & 10.      Director of              Prepares award letter and
             Financial Aid            sends or presents it to stu-
                                      dent for acceptance. Obtains

*Explanation of Decision Matrix 44, Cont'd.*

| Step | Action Responsibility | Action |
|------|----------------------|--------|
| | | student's signed acceptance of award letter. |
| 11, 12, & 13. | Chief Fiscal Officer and Cash Disbursement Clerk | Receive copies of accepted award letters from the director of financial aid. Prepare journal vouchers concerning noncash awards and enter them into the appropriate general ledger accounts. Prepare checks covering cash awards. Send checks covering cash awards to the cashier. |
| 14. | Cashier | Obtains students' endorsement of cash award checks and issues cash receipt to students. |
| 15. | Student Accounts Receivable Clerk | Receives copy of receipts covering cash awards and journal vouchers covering noncash awards and enters award data into students' accounts in student accounts receivable subsidiary records. |
| 16. | Chief Fiscal Officer and Student Accounts Receivable Clerk | Reconcile student accounts receivable subsidiary records with general ledger control account. |
| 17. | Chief Fiscal Officer and Director of | Reconcile record of amount of awards authorized with award expenditure |

*Explanation of Decision Matrix 44, Cont'd.*

| *Step* | *Action Responsibility* | *Action* |
|--------|------------------------|----------|
|        | Financial Aid          | control accounts for each source of funding. |
| 18.    | Chief Fiscal Officer   | Once each academic term, audits a sampling of student financial aid files to determine whether student costs and need have been properly computed and whether students have been awarded the maximum amount to which they are entitled within the limitation of funding availability. |

*Explanation of Decision Matrix 45.*

| Step | Action Responsibility | Action |
|------|----------------------|--------|
| 1. | Director of Financial Aid | In cooperation with the chief fiscal officer and the director of recruiting and admissions, formulates policies and procedures for making conditional decisions regarding potential financial aid award amounts for students who show up at registration without prior contact with the institution or with incomplete financial aid application documentation. |
| 2. | Advisory Committee | Reviews policies and procedures developed and recommends their approval by the president. |
| | President | Approves policies and procedures. |
| 3. | President | Submits policies to the board of trustees with a recommendation for adoption. |
| | Board of Trustees | Adopts recommended policies. |
| 4. | President | Authorizes the director of recruiting and admissions, director of financial aid, and chief fiscal officer to |

**Decision Matrix 45. Conditional Financial Aid Award Process.**

Legend of decision-making roles
1 – Authorizes action
2 – Action responsibility
3 – Approves recommendation
4 – Recommends action
5 – Provides input

Participants in Decision-Making Processes

| Procedural Steps | Board of Trustees | President | Advisory Committee | Chief Fiscal Officer | Financial Aid Director | Recruiting and Admissions Director | Registrar | Registration Personnel | Students and Parents |
|---|---|---|---|---|---|---|---|---|---|
| 1. Formulate policy and procedures for granting conditional financial aid to applicants with incomplete documentation | | 3 | 4 | 5 | 2 | 5 | | | |
| 2. Review and approve policy and procedures | | 4 | | 5 | 5 | | | | |
| 3. Obtain board approval for policy | 2 | 1 | | | | | | | |
| 4. Authorize implementation of policy and procedures | | | | | 2 | | | | |
| 5. Refer nonadmitted students to admissions office | | | | | | | | 2 | 5 |
| 6. Have student provide completed admission documents | | | | | | 2 | | | 5 |
| 7. Admit student | | | | | | 2 | | | |
| 8. Complete academic and housing forms | | | | | | | | 2 | 5 |
| 9. Compute assessed charges and send students to financial aid desk | | | | | | | 2 | | 5 |

|  |  | | | |
|---|---|---|---|---|
| 10. | Have student complete application and determine if other required documentation is completed | | 2 | 5 |
| 11. | If not, require student to sign agreement to provide missing documents within 30 days | | | |
| 12. | Calculate need using student's input | | 2 | 5 |
| 13. | Calculate conditional award, provide student with form showing estimated financial aid eligibility | | 2 | 5 |
| 14. | Make admit decision and financial arrangements with student | 2 | 2 | 5 |
| 15. | Follow up until student provides missing documentation, then follow procedures shown in Matrix 43, step 8 | 2 | | |
| 16. | Institute dismissal procedures for students who fail to provide required documentation and cannot pay their assessed charges | 2 | 2 | 5 |

*Explanation of Decision Matrix 45, Cont'd.*

| *Step* | *Action Responsibility* | *Action* |
|---|---|---|
| | | implement policies and procedures. |
| 5. | Registration Personnel | Send students who appear for registration without having been accepted for admission to the admissions office. |
| 6 & 7. | Director of Recruiting and Admissions | Has the student complete application for admission and arranges for student submission of other required documents, if the student does not have them. Admits the student. |
| 8. | Registration Personnel | Complete registration for courses and, if applicable, housing arrangements; send the student to the registrar. |
| 9. | Registrar | Computes assessed charges and sends students needing financial aid to the director of financial aid. |
| 10 & 11. | Director of Financial Aid | Determines missing financial aid documentation. If there has been no prior contact, requires that the student complete the financial aid application and the Pell Grant (BEOG) application. Requires students to |

*Explanation of Decision Matrix 45, Cont'd.*

| *Step* | *Action Responsibility* | *Action* |
|--------|------------------------|----------|
| | | execute the following documents: an agreement stipulating their understanding that, unless missing documentation is provided within thirty days, they will be dismissed unless they are able to pay assessed charges; and notification to the parents of dependent student that their child's enrollment is conditional and will be revoked in thirty days unless missing financial aid documents are provided and that such dismissal does not eliminate the obligation to pay assessed charges. |
| 12 & 13. | Director of Financial Aid | Using data available or provided by the student, calculates tentative need and financial aid entitlement. Provides the student with a form showing tentative calculations for delivery to the chief fiscal officer. |
| 14. | Chief Fiscal Officer | Audits the registrar's calculations of assessed charges and reviews the director of financial aid's tentative entitlement |

*Step*          *Action Responsibility*      *Action*

calculations. Reviews financial obligations with
students and has them sign
deferred payment agree-
ments for total assessed
charges. Authorizes conditional admission.

15.           Director of                    Follow up to determine
              Financial Aid and             whether conditionally
              Chief Fiscal                  admitted students have pro-
              Officer                       vided missing financial aid
                                            documentation within
                                            thirty-day grace period.
                                            (For students who have
                                            done so, follow procedures
                                            starting at step 8 on Deci-
                                            sion Matrix 43.)

16.           Chief Fiscal                   Notifies the chief academic
              Officer                       officer and chief student
                                            affairs officer to institute
                                            dismissal of students who
                                            have failed to provide
                                            missing financial aid docu-
                                            mentation and have not
                                            otherwise arranged to pay
                                            assessed charges.

## Decision Matrix 46. Revision of Financial Aid Awards.

Legend of decision-making roles

1 – Authorizes action
2 – Action responsibility
3 – Approves recommendation
4 – Recommends action
5 – Provides input

*Participants in Decision-Making Processes*

| Procedural Steps | Chief Fiscal Officer | Chief Student Affairs Officer | Chief Development Officer | Financial Aid Director | Registrar | Payroll | Personnel Director | Principal Investigator | Program Director | Funding Agencies |
|---|---|---|---|---|---|---|---|---|---|---|
| 1. Receive notice of change in student's | | | | | | | | | | |
| (a) enrollment status | | 5 | | 2 | | | | | | |
| (b) residential status | | | | 2 | 5 | | | | | |
| (c) eligibility because of receipt of third-party payments | 5 | | | 2 | | | | | | |
| (d) eligibility because of employment on regular payroll or appointment to work on sponsored agreement | | | | 2 | | 5 | 5 | 5 | 5 | |
| 2. Reduce awards, where necessary, because of step 1 | | | | 2 | | | | | | |
| 3. Receive notification of | | | | | | | | | | |
| (a) receipt of new loan or scholarship gifts and grants | 2 | | 5 | 2 | | | | | | |
| (b) supplemental awards from funding agency | 2 | | | 2 | | | | | | 5 |
| 4. Identify additional funds available as a result of step 2 | | | | 2 | | | | | | |
| 5. Identify students with unmet needs and revise their awards | | | | 2 | | | | | | |
| 6. Prepare and send revised award letter resulting from steps 3 and 5 to affected students; then follow procedures shown in Matrix 43 at step 10 | | | | 2 | | | | | | |

*Explanation of Decision Matrix 46.*

| Step | Action Responsibility | Action |
|---|---|---|
| 1 & 2. | Director of Financial Aid | Reviews and, if necessary, revises financial aid awards to students as a result of change in students' enrollment status notification from the registrar, change in students' residential status notification from the chief student affairs officer, receipt of third-party payment of student charges from the chief fiscal officer, or student employment notification received from a principal investigator, a program director, payroll, or personnel. |
| 3, 4, & 5. | Director of Financial Aid | Identifies students whose financial aid awards were not sufficient to meet their need entitlement and revises their awards when additional financial aid funds are made available as the result of receipt of notification of or knowledge of new scholarship gifts and grants from the chief development officer, supplemental awards from funding agencies, or funds that revert to various sources of funding from adjustment or cancellation of prior awards. |

*Explanation of Decision Matrix 46, Cont'd.*

| Step | Action Responsibility | Action |
|------|----------------------|--------|
| 6. | Director of Financial Aid | Prepares and issues revised award letters to students whose awards need to be adjusted as a result of steps 1 through 5. (For remaining steps, follow the procedures starting at step 10 on Decision matrix 43.) |

## Decision Matrix 47. Student Employment.

*Participants in Decision-Making Processes*

Legend of decision-making roles
1 – Authorizes action
2 – Action responsibility
3 – Approves recommendation
4 – Recommends action
5 – Provides input

| Procedural Steps | President | Advisory Committee | Chief Fiscal Officer | Financial Aid Director | Personnel Director | Department Heads | Payroll | Student Employees | Student Accounts Receivable Clerk | Cashier |
|---|---|---|---|---|---|---|---|---|---|---|
| 1. Formulate student employment compensation plan | 3 | 4 | 5 | 2 | 5 | | | | | |
| 2. Review and approve compensation plan | | | | 5 | | | | | | |
| 3. Authorize implementation of plan | 1 | | | 2 | | | | | | |
| 4. Receive budget data on student employment authorized | | | 5 | 2 | | | | | | |
| 5. Obtain job specifications from departments authorized to employ students | | | | 2 | | 5 | | | | |
| 6. Obtain identification of students departments would like to reemploy | | | | 2 | | 5 | | | | |
| 7. Obtain identification of skills or job preference from students awarded CWSP or IWA | | | | 2 | | | | 5 | | |
| 8. Match students' skills or job preferences with departmental needs and reemployment desires | | | | 2 | | | | | | |
| 9. Counsel students on job opportunities and refer them to department heads for job interviews | | | | 2 | | | | | | |
| 10. Interview and select students for employment | | | | 2 | | 2 | | 5 | | |
| 11. Receive notification of departmental selections | | | | 2 | | 5 | | 5 | | |

|  |  | | | | | | |
|-----|------|---|---|---|---|---|---|
| 12. | Notify students and obtain payroll data | 2 | | | | | 5 |
| 13. | Enter data into the payroll system | 5 | 2 | | | | 2 |
| 14. | Perform required services | | | | | | 5 |
| 15. | Input number of hours worked on student's time sheet | | | | | | |
| 16. | Certify time sheet and submit it to financial aid | | 2 | | | | |
| 17. | Audit time sheet for compliance with terms of award | | 2 | 2 | | | |
| 18. | Notify department heads of cases where hours of work need to be increased or decreased | 2 | | | | | |
| 19. | Enter time sheet data into payroll system | 5 | 2 | 2 | | | |
| 20. | Produce student employee payroll register | | 2 | | | | |
| 21. | Audit payroll register for consistency with time sheets | 2 | | 5 | | | |
| 22. | Enter adjustments, if any, into payroll system | 5 | 2 | 5 | | | |
| 23. | Prepare payroll checks | 1 | 2 | 2 | | | |
| 24. | Sign payroll checks | 2 | 2 | 5 | | | |
| 25. | Determine amount of check student should apply to any unpaid balances | | 5 | | | 2 | |
| 26. | Obtain student's agreement to amount to be applied to unpaid balances | | | | | 5 | 2 |
| 27. | Authorize disbursement of remaining amount of check after withholding amount to be applied to unpaid balances | | | | | | 2 |
| 28. | Obtain student's endorsement of payroll checks | | | | | 5 | 2 |
| 29. | Issue student a cash receipt for the amount to be applied to unpaid balances and cash to cover remainder of payroll check | | | | | | 2 |

*Explanation of Decision Matrix 47.*

| Step | Action Responsibility | Action |
|------|----------------------|--------|
| 1, 2, & 3. | Director of Financial Aid | Formulates, using input from the chief fiscal officer and director of personnel, an hourly wage rate compensation plan for student CWSP and IWA employees and submits plan to administration for approval. |
| | Advisory Committee | Reviews recommended compensation plan for equity and potential impact on other areas of operations and recommends that the president approve it. |
| | President | Approves compensation plan and authorizes its implementation. |
| 4. | Director of Financial Aid | Receives from the chief fiscal officer the identification of departmental allocations of funding provided in the annual operating budget to cover student employment. |
| 5 & 6. | Director of Financial Aid | Obtains from department heads information regarding the number of student employees required, the hours of coverage required, the skill requirements of each position, and preferences for reassignment of prior student employees. |

*Explanation of Decision Matrix 47, Cont'd.*

| Step | Action Responsibility | Action |
|---|---|---|
| 7, 8, & 9. | Director of Financial Aid | Obtains from all students awarded CWSP or IWA as part of their financial aid award package identification of the skills they possess, their class schedules, and their areas of employment preference. To the extent possible, the director of financial aid matches student skills and employment preferences with departmental need and desire for reassignment of prior student employees and refers students to appropriate department heads for an interview. |
| 10 & 11. | Department Heads | Interview student employee applicants, discuss job requirements, select students for employment, and notify the director of financial aid of authorization to hire students. |
| 12. | Director of Financial Aid | Prepares and executes with student an employment agreement specifying the periods (hours and days) of employment required, the maximum number of hours of employment authorized, and the rate of pay. |

*Explanation of Decision Matrix 47, Cont'd.*

| *Step* | *Action Responsibility* | *Action* |
|---|---|---|
| 13. | Director of Financial Aid | Obtains from student the data required to process payroll. |
| | Payroll | Receives payroll data from the director of financial aid and enters data into the student payroll system. |
| 14, 15, & 16. | Department Heads | Monitor student performance of services, enter hours worked each day on the student employee's time sheet, certify at the end of a payroll period that the hours of work reflected on the time sheet are accurate, and submit the student employee's time sheet to the director of financial aid. |
| 17 & 18. | Director of Financial Aid | Verifies that time sheets for all student employees have been received from each department. Audits time sheets against employment agreements and class assignments. Notifies departmental chairpersons and students of instances where students have worked more or fewer hours than were authorized |

*Explanation of Decision Matrix 47, Cont'd.*

| Step | Action Responsibility | Action |
|------|----------------------|--------|
| | | and the corresponding increase or decrease in hours required for subsequent pay periods. |
| 19 & 20. | Payroll | Enters the hours of work for each student, received from the director of financial aid, into the payroll system and prepares the student employee payroll register. Submits the register to the director of financial aid. |
| 21. | Director of Financial Aid | Audits register against time sheets and notifies payroll of any change required. |
| 22. | Payroll | Enters adjustments required and repeats steps 20 and 21 until the student employee payroll register is accurate. |
| 23. | Payroll | Receives the director of financial aid's authorization to cut payroll checks, cuts checks, and submits them to the chief fiscal officer for signature. |
| 24. | Chief Fiscal Officer | Signs checks and sends them to the cashier. Notifies the student |

*Explanation of Decision Matrix 47, Cont'd.*

*Step            Action Responsibility    Action*

|  |  |  |
|---|---|---|
|  |  | accounts receivable clerk of the amounts of checks being issued to students. |
| 25, 26, & 27. | Student Accounts Receivable Clerk | Reviews account balances of students who are to receive payroll checks, determines the portion of checks students should apply to their account balance, and obtains students' authorization to do so. Notifies the cashier of the portion of checks to be applied to students' accounts and sends students to the cashier with authorization to issue checks. |
| 28 & 29. | Cashier | Has students endorse checks, pays students the authorized amount, and issues students cashier's receipts for the amount being applied to their account balance. |

# Part Four:
# Institutional
# Advancement

The development activities of private colleges and universities are normally subdivided into four categories: fund raising, alumni affairs, public relations, and publications. Usually, the chief development officer is directly responsible for managing fund-raising activities and for supervising the other activities, which are carried out by directors who report to him. All these activities should be carefully coordinated and designed to present the institution in the best light to each of its supporting constituencies, the better to convert the constituencies' interest in the institution to financial support of the institution.

Unfortunately, many smaller, private institutions, whose need for financial support is greater than that of their sister institutions with greater resources, fail to invest the resources necessary to carry out properly a carefully planned and coordinated fund-raising program. In these cases, one finds that the development office is understaffed, especially with skilled employees, lacks supplies and equipment, and is not properly utilized to coordinate all fund-raising activities taking place on campus. A multiplicity of fund-raising efforts of which the development office has no knowledge are carried out by individual faculty members or administrators, frequently addressing the same potential donors. Sometimes the development office is not

even informed of gifts or grants received as a result of these activities. These uncoordinated fund-raising activities frequently
result in the failure to receive gifts that might otherwise have
been obtained or in the receipt of gifts or grants that do not
support planned or budgeted activities but rather require the
institution to carry out unplanned activities or programs, perhaps
diverting resources budgeted for planned activities. Further, fund
raisers frequently desire to represent the cost of the program
for which they are soliciting funds as being as low as possible
in the hope of increasing the chances of getting funding; in addition, they often fail to take some costs into consideration. As
a result, the gifts or grants obtained frequently are inadequate
to carry out the program or activities for which they were
solicited.

   These problems can be avoided if an institution instills
in its operation the essential standards and processes of good
management set forth in this part. It is also to be hoped that
those institutions that cannot fill all the positions identified in
this book will fill as many as they can afford. At a minimum,
they should see that the standards of good management are incorporated into their developmental programs and activities
through available personnel.

   The integration and coordination of fund raising, alumni
relations, public relations, and publications are of prime importance to a successful developmental effort; therefore, all four
activities are presented in a single chapter. The integration of
the four developmental activities will enhance an institution's
ability to attract the financial support it needs from its various
constituencies. Since a number of smaller colleges and universities have a church relationship, this chapter also discusses the
maintenance of such relationships.

   Two axioms are relevant to all institutions seeking financial support from their constituencies. First, no one gives you
money because you need it; they give you money because they
believe you can do something they wish to see done more effectively than someone else. Second, nobody wants to be left holding
the baby. Potential donors, particularly larger donors such as

foundations and corporations, do not wish to see an institution become unduly dependent on their support. Therefore, they want to see that the trustees, alumni, community, and other constituencies are making reasonable contributions to the institution before they commit major resources. They also want to know that the institution is well managed and will utilize their contributions prudently and properly.

# Fund Raising,
# Institutional Relations,
# and Publications

Institutional advancement or development encompasses fund
raising, public relations, alumni relations, and publications.
These activities should be organized under a senior administrator, referred to in this book as the chief development officer;
ideally, each activity should be administered by a director. If
an institution does not have the resources to staff itself in this
manner, the development activities should still be organized
along these functional lines, and the personnel assigned to the
development office should have among them the skills necessary
to carry them out.

The chief development officer should be responsible for
the administration of all four development functions and the
orchestration and integration of their activities and staff talents
to make them as efficient and effective as possible. She should
also be responsible for interpreting the institution's mission,
goals, objectives, programs, and need for financial support to
its constituencies for the purpose of nurturing their interest in
the institution and their willingness to support it. Finally, she
should be responsible for seeing to it that the activities of the
development office are designed to transform the willingness to
support the institution into gifts, grants, and contracts from both
public and private sources.

The chief development officer should have the confidence
of and be able to rely on the cooperation of trustees, adminis-

trators, faculty, staff, students, and alumni in providing input and carrying out development activities. She should be responsible for identifying and recommending the person or group whose talents best meet the needs of each development activity or fund-raising effort. Appeals or applications for or solicitation of funds, whether from public or private sources, should not be made until the chief development officer has been consulted.

The chief development officer is responsible for providing the administration, and through it the board of trustees, with data about the institution's ability to generate gift, grant, and contract income to support its operating and capital needs. Such income includes, in addition to unrestricted gifts and grants, program gifts, grants, and contracts that will underwrite operating costs, student financial aid to supplement that available from federal or state programs, and capital funds for investment in physical plant or as part of the institution's endowment funds.

It is important to remember that restricted funds or gifts in kind that support current or future operating costs can be as beneficial to the institution's financial health as unrestricted gifts, provided they cover operating expenditures that otherwise would have to be made from unrestricted funds in the current year or future years, do not expand the operations of the programs or activities they are given to support beyond the planned level, and do not require the institution to commit itself to carrying on the expanded programs or activities beyond the period covered by the restricted funds. Further, institutional policy should require that, when restricted funds that support current operations become available, the annual operating budget be revised to reflect their receipt and the expenditures required to cover the program and activity costs for which they were donated. This should be done before any unrestricted funds made available by the existent authorized operating budget are expended for programs or activities now covered by the new gift or grant. Such policy should also provide that the approval of the board of trustees should be obtained for the acceptance of any restricted gift, grant, or contract that does not meet the criteria set forth above.

The remainder of this chapter is devoted to the essential standards of good management that should be adhered to in carrying out the activities of fund raising, public relations, alumni relations, and publication.

## Fund Raising

If the funding available does not make it possible for the chief development officer to have a director of fund raising on her staff, she should assume the responsibility for these activities in addition to her responsibility for supervising the other development office activities. The essential standards applicable to fund-raising activities are set forth below.

★ The director of fund raising should prepare and obtain the chief development officer's approval for an annual fund-raising plan that identifies the fund-raising appeals to be carried out during the year, when each will be implemented, the targeted audience of each, and the amount of income each is expected to produce. The plan is not expected to identify efforts devoted to the submission of applications for program gifts, grants, or contracts from public and private sources, but it should identify all regularly conducted activities designed to generate unrestricted gifts, supplemental student aid gifts or grants, and deferred giving.

★ The director of fund raising should also prepare and obtain the administration's and the board of trustees' approval for a statement of standards to be adhered to in such matters as the minimum amount of gifts or grants required to name buildings, endow professorships or chairs, establish named scholarships, and the like.

★ The director of fund raising should be a central source of information about all private and public sources of program gifts, grants, and contracts. If the institution has sufficient federal, state, or private grants or contracts to warrant it, the director should have a director of program gifts on her staff. The responsibilities of the director of program gifts should not be confused with those of the director of grant and contract administration; this administrator is responsible for keeping the institution informed regarding opportunities and actions that need to be taken to obtain new or increased program funding to support institutional activities, whereas the director of grant and contract administration is responsible for seeing to it that the institution adheres to the rules and regulations applicable to federal, state, and private grants and contracts that have already been awarded.

The director of program gifts should maintain current records on each private, federal, and state agency, foundation, and corporation that is a potential source of funding regarding its areas of program interest, the limits it sets on the amount of awards, the length of program support commitment, the types of expenditure allowed, its indirect cost allowance and matching cost policies, its application processes and content requirements, its application submission deadlines, its application review and approval policies, the key personnel involved in its decision-making processes, and its response to prior contacts made or applications submitted by the institution.

★   The director of fund raising should be responsible for informing appropriate administrators of opportunities to obtain program support funds from public or private sources, working with them in identifying faculty members or others who should be involved in the preparation of proposals for such funding, and following up with administrators and proposal preparers to be sure that deadlines and application submission requirements are adhered to.

★   The director of fund raising also should have available to her a grant and contract review committee to screen applications for program funding. This committee should include the chief academic officer, the chief development officer, the chief fiscal officer, and the director of grant and contract administration. The committee should review all applications for program funding resulting from information provided by the director of program gifts or by other sources. If the committee authorizes the applicants to prepare the documentation necessary for the submission of an application for a grant or contract, it should also review the submission documentation before the application is submitted to the potential funding agency, whether public or private. These reviews will assure the administration that the purposes for which the funding is sought are consistent with approved institutional goals, objectives, and policies; the institution is capable of carrying out the proposed programs or activities for which funding is sought under the rules and regulations of the funding agency; the applications do not overlap or duplicate applications that have been submitted to other funding agencies; they have been adequately costed; they are consistent with what is known about the interest, funding limitations, submission requirements, and policies of the organization or agency to which they are to be submitted; they do not require matching cost, use of facilities, or released time of faculty or staff that the institution cannot provide; and they do not require a commitment to carry on the programs or activities involved beyond the period to be covered by the gift, grant, or contract.

★   All gifts, grants, and contracts, for whatever purpose, from whomever received, and by whomever received, should be processed through the office of the director of fund raising. The director should be responsible for seeing to it that for all gifts, grants, and contracts, the date of receipt, the amount or type of gift in kind received, from whom it was received, the donor's relationship to the institution, the activity that generated the gift, and the purpose, if any, of the gift are properly recorded. The director should also be responsible for ensuring that a gift receipt or an acknowledgment of grant or contract receipt is issued and that gift payments received are batch-totaled daily and transmitted to the fiscal office for processing. She should also see to it that an acknowledgment of receipt of the gift and a copy of the gift receipt are sent to each donor, or that signatures required for acceptance of grants and contracts are obtained and that copies of acceptance of award documents are sent to the appropriate funding agencies.

Part of the responsibility for processing gifts is to inform donors systematically of the contribution their gifts have made to the institution's ability to accomplish its goals and objectives or to the students' ability to complete their education. The objective of such notification is to encourage the donors' continuing support. The responsibility of informing donors is distinct from the responsibility of rendering reports required by restricted grants and contracts, whether public or private; the latter is the responsibility of the director of grant and contract administration. Finally, the director of fund raising should see to it that the chief fiscal officer maintains accounts in which the receipt and use of such gifts are properly recorded. For restricted grants and contracts, this responsibility is assigned to the director of grant and contract administration.

★   Gift receipts issued for gifts in kind should not reflect any dollar value assigned by the institution. While the director should obtain from the chief fiscal officer a dollar value that will be used by both the accounting office and the development office to record the receipt of a gift in kind, it should not be reflected on the gift receipt issued to the donor. Rather, the information on the gift-in-kind receipt should be limited to the identification of the nature of the item or service received as a gift in kind. The value of the gift in kind, for tax purposes, should be determined by the donor and the Internal Revenue Service.

★   Third-party payments toward the cost of education of particular students identified by the donor should not be treated as gifts and should not be included in reports on the results of fund-raising activities. The Internal Revenue Service has determined that payments of this nature do not qualify as gifts. The institution must carefully adhere to Internal Revenue Service regulations regarding gifts in order to protect its own tax-exempt status.

★   The director of fund raising should maintain records that permit her to periodically submit reports covering the results of fund-raising activities to the administration and, through it, to the board of trustees. Such reports should identify not only the amounts raised by each activity, but also the number of contributions received, the percentage of those solicited who contributed, and the number of donors who contributed specific amounts (for example, over $10,000, over $5,000, over $2,500, over $1,000, over $500, over $100, and under $100), as well as the percentage of the total represented by each category.

★    Where professional fund-raising counsel is retained by the institution, the director of fund raising should be responsible for liaison required for effective and efficient fulfillment of the counsel's professional services. Processes related to the preparation of fund-raising projections for multi-year planning, submission of applications for restricted grants and contracts, and activities related to processing of gifts are set forth in Decision Matrices 48, 49, and 50.

## Public Relations

The director of public relations should be an information and communications specialist, competent in interpreting the institution to its constituencies and interpreting the perceptions and concerns of the constituencies to the institution. She should be responsible for assisting all segments of campus in communicating to internal and external constituencies, through appropriate media and forums, an image of the institution in its fullest and richest dimension — its strengths, its programs, its contributions to education and the public good, and its need for financial support.

The standards of good management applicable to carrying out the public relations function are set forth below.

★    The director should be responsible for maintaining cordial working relationships with the representatives of each unit of the media through which the institution desires to communicate its messages. She should be familiar with the type of items that each medium is most apt to cover and with the medium's operating requirements — its deadlines, the person to whom copy is to be submitted, its preference in the format of news releases, and the like.

★   When the institution desires to buy advertising for recruiting or special events, the director should be consulted about the selection of the vehicle to be utilized and the type of presentation through which the institution's message can be conveyed most effectively.

★   The director should be kept informed by all segments of the campus community of news or events that would be of interest to any of its supporting constituencies. For example, she should be informed of students who attain academic honors or receive other recognition for their achievements; faculty who make significant contributions to higher education, the advancement of knowledge in their disciplines, or public service; alumni who receive honors or make significant advances in their profession; the receipt of important gifts, grants, or contracts; on-campus visits by distinguished people; and the selection of trustees, administrators, faculty, or staff to participate in important events.

★   The director should also be kept advised of information and events that may have an adverse effect on public perception of the institution. Under these circumstances, her function is to assist in mitigating the negative effect. While she should not necessarily be the spokesperson for the institution, her knowledge of the media and her communication expertise should be consulted in identifying who should be the spokesperson, what questions he should expect, and how he might best respond.

★   The director should be responsible for maintaining current and accurate mailing lists or contact information of persons or media units who should be receiving news releases or other institutional information.

★   The director should have available to her a competent photographer to serve both her needs and the needs of the director of publications. She should also be responsible for maintaining a file of properly identified photographs that might be useful to either function. The services of a photographer can be supplied by having such a person on the staff, contracting with a local professional photographer, or employing a skilled student under work-study.

## Alumni Relations

The director of alumni relations should be responsible for recommending and carrying out programs designed to foster continuing alumni interest in and support of the institution's programs and needs. Alumni programs should be targeted not only at graduates and those who have left the institution without graduating but also at currently enrolled students so as to encourage them to become active alumni after they leave the institution. Though alumni can contribute to the institution's welfare in many ways, such as by assisting in recruiting students, the amount of current and future financial support they can provide should be a prime consideration in determining how much the institution should invest in alumni programs beyond the amount required for basic office staff, alumni publications, and maintenance of alumni records.

There are two basic types of alumni organizations, independent and dependent. The independent alumni organization is created by the alumni, formulates its own policy, obtains its own tax-exempt status, hires and fires its own personnel, generates its own funds to support its activities, and determines for itself how its activities should best be used to meet institutional needs. The dependent organization is created by the institution, operates under the institution's tax-exempt status, is managed by the institution, and is funded by the institution as a part of its annual operating budget. A dependent alumni organization best meets the needs of smaller colleges and universities; the material that follows, therefore, focuses on dependent organizations. However, one aspect of the relationship with an independent alumni organization should be considered here. At a number of institutions with independent alumni organizations, the collection of alumni dues is handled through the director of alumni relations and the institution's accounting system. Unless these dues payments may be used by the institution to cover costs it incurs in providing services to the independent alumni organization, such dues payments should not be treated as gifts. Rather, the institution's acknowledgment of receipt of alumni membership dues payments should merely inform the alumni that the payments received are being turned over to the independent alumni organization to cover the cost of its operation and activities.

The essential standards of good management applicable to alumni relations are set forth below.

★ The director of alumni relations should be responsible for providing each geographical association with the names and addresses of graduates, students leaving the institution without graduating, alumni living in the area, and, to the extent possible, alumni moving into the area. Keeping the geographical associations so informed fosters their ability to solicit membership and participation in their activities in support of the institution.

★ Currently enrolled students should be informed regularly that even though they have met all their financial obligations to the institution, the charges they have been assessed do not cover the cost of providing them with their education. They should be told that the institution's ability to provide the services from which they are benefiting is the result of the generosity of alumni and other supporting constituencies. Further, it should be stressed that the institution's ability to survive and provide educational opportunities to future generations of students will be significantly influenced by the students' financial support when they become alumni.

★ Although recruiting students is the responsibility of the director of recruiting and admissions, all efforts to involve alumni in such activities should be coordinated by the director of alumni relations.

★ The director should be responsible for coordinating all efforts at obtaining alumni input to assist the institution in its decision-making processes. Alumni input should be considered in arriving at decisions about the evaluation of presidential performance, the selection of a president, addition or deletion of degrees to be offered, revision of the student code of conduct and student life or activity programs, religious attendance requirements (for a church-related institution), and the conduct of special events such as homecoming, class reunions, convocation, and commencement. It is also recommended that the alumni association be involved in institutional government through, at the least, ex officio, nonvoting membership on the board of trustees.

★   The director should be responsible for the publication of an alumni newsletter or alumni magazine through which the alumni can be kept informed of matters of interest to them. Such matters include changes in alumni's names, addresses, academic attainments, employment, special honors, and the like; the activities of various alumni groups or geographical organizations; the results of alumni fund-raising activities; campus developments; and the dates of events that they might be interested in attending. All campus constituencies, all alumni, and all alumni organizations should be advised of the importance of providing the director with material of interest to the alumni so that it can be included in this publication.

★   The institution's fund-raising efforts should include an annual fund-raising drive. During such a drive, the alumni should be reminded that, while they are encouraged to contribute as much as they can, they should not feel that small contributions, if that is all they can afford, are not welcomed. A small contribution is better than none because other constituencies that are considering providing financial support frequently are interested in the alumni's willingness to provide support. The percentage of alumni supporting the institution is as important as the amount of support they provide. Further, even though the initial contribution may be small, giving to the annual campaign becomes a habit and the amount contributed annually tends to increase as the alumnus's earning capacity grows.

★   The director should make alumni employed by firms that have a matching contribution program aware that such a program exists and urge them to follow up with their employers to make sure that matching payments are made. Alumni employed by firms that do not have such matching contribution programs should be urged to encourage their employers to establish such a program.

★   The director should be responsible for maintaining records of all contributions received from an alumnus. These records should include not only contributions made to an alumni appeal but also identifiable alumni contributions received as a result of a community-based drive, a capital fund drive, a trustee's contribution, or fund-raising activities conducted by supporting church groups, if the institution is church-related. Under no circumstances, however, should alumni contributions be double-counted in either gift reporting or accounting records.

## Publications

The administration of the institution should define the audiences the institution's publications program is designed to reach, the institutional message and impression it seeks to convey, and the type, quality, and style of publications it will issue. Even though the director of publications should be responsible for working with other administrators in the production of institutional publications, the chief development officer should be responsible for reviewing all publications for consistency with defined objectives before they are issued. If the resource limitations of the institution make it impossible to provide the chief development officer with a director of publications, he or she should be provided through either development office staff, contracted services, or a faculty member with the services of personnel skilled in writing, graphic arts, layout, and printing.

The essential standards of good management of a publications program are set forth below. It is assumed that institutional resources permit the chief development officer to have a director of publications on his staff.

★   Provision for all costs of preparing and printing publications, excluding the cost of services provided by the director of publications, should be made in the annual operating budgets of the departments for which publications are to be prepared. The heads of these departments should seek the advice of the director of publications in preparing their budgets, but they should be held responsible for determining the audience to which their publication is directed, the publication's subject and content, the number of copies required, and the people to whom copies should be distributed; they should also be responsible for controlling the cost of producing the publication. In carrying out their responsibilities, the department heads should be able to rely on the director of publications to write copy; edit copy written by themselves or members of their staff; oversee layout; select graphics; select type, paper stock, and ink; select a printer; and oversee the distribution of publications to the recipients they have identified. Names and addresses required for the distribution of publications directed to students, their parents, faculty, and staff should be obtained by the director from the records of the registrar or the payroll records of the institution. The director should be held responsible for maintaining the records necessary for distribution to other constituencies. In carrying out this responsibility, the director must be able to count on the department heads, who are responsible for identifying the people to whom their publications are to be distributed, and keeping him informed of changes in name or address and additions and deletions to the list of recipients.

★ The director should be held responsible for working with all administrators in the preparation of publications and the determination of printing requirements related to their areas of operation. At a minimum, this responsibility should include working with the director of recruiting and admissions for all recruiting and admissions material; the director of financial aid for all student financial aid material; the development office directors for fund-raising and alumni material, campus newsletters, public relations material, and special events programs; the chief academic officer for the catalogue and faculty handbook; the chief student affairs officer for the student handbook and student activities or events announcements; and the athletic director for game programs and press guides.

   ★   After the annual operating budget has been approved by
the board of trustees, the director should prepare and obtain
the chief development officer's approval for a publications activities plan. The director's activity plan should identify for each
publication to be produced the administrator responsible for its
publication, the dates and frequency of publication, and the lead
time necessary for its preparation.

   ★   Whether the actual printing of publications is to be done
in house or by an outside contractor, the director should be
responsible for providing the printer with specifications for the
publication project. The specifications provided should include
the publication's title, the number of copies required, the col-
ors of ink to be used, the paper stock to be used for the cover
and the text, the print time allowed and the required date of
completion, the number and size of photographs or graphic ex-
hibits to be included, the type of proofs required and the time
allowance necessary for their review and approval, binding instructions, packaging and delivery instructions, the name of the
person to be contacted for clarification of specifications or questions that arise during production, and the printing standards
that are to be adhered to.

   ★   A publication review committee charged with reviewing
all publications and formulating recommendations about how
they can be improved. The committee should be composed of
administrators responsible for the preparation of publications
and student and alumni representatives.

   Processes to be followed in the preparation of institutional
publications are set forth in Decision Matrix 51. Readers who
desire more detailed information about any aspect of institutional advancement or development activities, either publications available or training programs, should contact the Council
for Advancement and Support of Education (CASE), 11 Dupont
Circle, Washington, D.C. 20036.

*Explanation of Decision Matrix 48.*

| Step | Action Responsibility | Action |
|---|---|---|
| 1. | Chief Development Officer | Reviews the institution's records of annual giving and formulates recommended annual giving expectations, for each year to be covered by the institution's multi-year plan, for program gifts and grants from private and public sources, using input from the director of program grants and the director of grant and contract administration; for unrestricted gifts and grants from corporations, foundations, alumni, friends, and churches, using input from the director of alumni relations and the director of public relations; and for private (nongovernmental) gifts and grants restricted for scholarship or financial aid purposes, using input from the director of alumni relations and the director of public relations. |
| 2. | Planning Committee | Reviews the chief development officer's proposal that a capital gifts campaign be conducted during the period covered by the multi-year plan and recommends that the president seek the board of trustees' authorization to have a feasibility study conducted for such a campaign. |
|  | President | Concurs with the planning committee's recommendations. |

## Decision Matrix 48. Fund-Raising Projections for Multi-Year Planning.

Legend of decision-making roles
1 – Authorizes action
2 – Action responsibility
3 – Approves recommendation
4 – Recommends action
5 – Provides input

*Participants in Decision-Making Processes*

| Procedural Steps | Board of Trustees | President | Planning Committee | Chief Development Officer | Alumni Relations Director | Program Grants Director | Public Relations Director | Grant and Contract Administration Director | Chief Academic Officer | Chief Student Affairs Officer | Chief Fiscal Officer | Fund-Raising Consulting Firm |
|---|---|---|---|---|---|---|---|---|---|---|---|---|
| 1. Review historical records of giving and assess potential for attracting, during the period covered by the plan, | | | | | | | | | | | | |
| (a) program grants and contracts | | | | 2 | | 5 | | 5 | | | | |
| (b) unrestricted gifts and grants | | | | 2 | 5 | | 5 | | | | | |
| (c) private student aid gifts and grants | | | | 2 | 5 | | 5 | | | | | |
| 2. Determine that during the period covered by the plan, the feasibility of conducting a capital gifts campaign should be explored | | 3 | 4 | 5 | | | | | | | | |
| 3. Authorize the conduct of a capital gifts campaign feasibility study | 2 | 4 | | 5 | | | | | | | | |
| 4. Solicit proposals for conducting feasibility study | | 1 | | 2 | | | | | | | | |
| 5. Review proposals and recommend firm to be selected to conduct feasibility study | | 3 | | 4 | | | | | | | | 5 |

| | | | | | | | |
|---|---|---|---|---|---|---|---|
| 6. Authorize award of feasibility study and contract | 2 | 3 | 5 | | | 2 | 2 |
| 7. Execute feasibility study contract | | 1 | 5 | | | 5 | 2 |
| 8. Conduct feasibility study | 5 | 5 | 5 | 5 | 5 | 5 | 5 |
| 9. Review results of consultants study | | 5 | 2 | | | 5 | 5 |
| 10. Determine that a capital gifts campaign should be included in multi-year plan | | 3 | 4 | 5 | | | 5 |
| 11. Provide chief fiscal officer with projections of operating and capital gift and grant income to be used in preparing multi-year plan | | | 2 | | | | |

*Explanation of Decision Matrix 48, Cont'd.*

| Step | Action Responsibility | Action |
|------|----------------------|--------|
| 3. | Board of Trustees | Reviews the president's request for authorization to engage the services of a fund-raising consulting firm to conduct a capital gifts campaign feasibility study, obtaining input from the chief development officer. Approves the president's request. |
| 4. | Chief Development Officer | Solicits proposals for a feasibility study from fund-raising consulting firms when authorized to do so by the president. |
| 5. | Chief Development Officer | Reviews proposals received from fund-raising consulting firms and recommends to the president the engagement of the firms she considers most qualified. |
|  | President | Reviews the chief development officer's recommendation and, in consultation with her, selects the firm to be awarded the engagement. |
| 6. | Board of Trustees | Reviews the president's report on the results of proposal solicitation efforts and his recommendation for a firm to be awarded the engagement. Obtains input from the chief development officer and authorizes the president to engage the services of the fund-raising consulting firm. |

*Explanation of Decision Matrix 48, Cont'd.*

| Step | Action Responsibility | Action |
|------|----------------------|--------|
| 7. | Chief Fiscal Officer | Executes a consulting contract with the fund-raising consulting firm when authorized to do so by the president. |
| 8. | Fund-Raising Consulting Firm | Conducts a feasibility study, considering the needs to which capital gifts campaign funds would be applied and the feasibility of raising the funds to cover such needs. Obtains input from the trustees, president, chief academic, student affairs, and fiscal officers, chief development officer, and directors of alumni and public relations. |
| 9. | Chief Development Officer | Reviews the feasibility study report with the fund-raising consultant and the chief fiscal officer and recommends its acceptance. |
| 10. | Planning Committee | Reviews the feasibility study report recommended for acceptance by the chief development officer and recommends that the results shown therein be included in the multi-year plan being formulated. |
|  | President | Concurs with the planning committee's recommendation and authorizes the chief development officer to act on it. |

*Explanation of Decision Matrix 48, Cont'd.*

| Step | Action Responsibility | Action |
|------|----------------------|--------|
| 11. | Chief Development Officer | Provides the chief fiscal officer with a projection of revenue to be derived from fund-raising activities for each year to be covered by the multi-year plan. |

*Explanation of Decision Matrix 49.*

| Step | Action Responsibility | Action |
|------|----------------------|--------|
| 1. | Chief Development Officer | Updates his information file of public and private sources of program grants, using input from the director of program grants about what has been learned from recent relationships with such sources and from a review of corporate, governmental, and foundation publications. |
| 2. | Director of Program Grants | Reviews the annual operating budget, multi-year plan, and program grant source information file. Identifies operational funding needs that could be met with program grants and recommends that applications for such grants be submitted. |
| | Chief Development Officer | Reviews and approves the director's recommendation. |
| 3. | Director of Program Grants | Reviews recommendations for submission of applications for program grants with appropriate senior administrators when authorized to do so by the chief development officer. Obtains from senior administrators the identification of faculty or staff members selected to prepare such applications. |
| 4. | Proposal Writer | Develops a conceptual approach for the project to be covered by |

**Decision Matrix 49. Application for Restricted Grants or Contracts.**

Legend of decision-making roles:
1 – Authorizes action
2 – Action responsibility
3 – Approves recommendation
4 – Recommends action
5 – Provides input

*Participants in Decision-Making Processes*

| Procedural Steps | Board of Trustees | President | Advisory Committee | Chief Development Officer | Program Grants Director | Grant and Contract Review Committee | Senior Administrators | Proposal Writers | Chief Fiscal Officer | Funding Agency |
|---|---|---|---|---|---|---|---|---|---|---|
| 1. Obtain input and update federal, state, foundation, and corporate program interest records | | | | 2 | 5 | | | | | |
| 2. Review multi-year plan and annual operating budgets and identify potential grantees whose program interests match institutional support needs | | | | | 2 | | | | | |
| 3. Review results of step 2 with senior administrators and identify proposal writers | | | | | 5 | | 2 | | | |
| 4. Conceptualize project or program and submit a request for authorization to submit a grant or contract application | | | | | 5 | | 3 | 4 | 5 | |
| 5. Review and approve request for authorization to submit application | | | | | | 3 | 4 | 5 | | |
| 6. Finalize application | | | | | 5 | | 3 | 4 | | |
| 7. Review and approve application for submission | | | | | | 3 | 4 | 5 | | |

| No. | Activity | Values |
|---|---|---|
| 8. | Sign application | 2 |
| 9. | Negotiate grant or contract | 2 |
| 10. | Receive notification of award of grant or contract | 2, 2, 3, 5, 4, 2 |
| 11. | Determine whether to accept grant or contract where grantee's terms require activity expansion beyond that planned or future commitment to continue the program | 4, 5, 5, 5 |
| 12. | Authorize acceptance of grant or contract recommended for acceptance as a result of step 11 | 2, 4, 3 |
| 13. | Accept grant or contract (authorized by board, if such authorization is required) | 2, 2 |

| Step | Action Responsibility | Action |
|------|----------------------|--------|
| | | the grant application and determines the resources required to carry it out, obtaining input from the director of program grants regarding the targeted source's interests, policies, and practices and from the chief fiscal officer regarding cost estimates for the resources required to carry out the project. Prepares a request for authorization to submit an application. |
| | Senior Administrator | Reviews and approves the proposal writer's request for authorization to submit an application. |
| 5. | Grant and Contract Review Committee | Reviews the request for authorization to submit an application for consistency with approved goals or objectives; adherence to institutional policy; feasibility of successful completion; adequacy of funding requested; consistency with what is known about the grantee's interests and policies; institutional capability of meeting requirements for matching cost, use of facilities, and released time of personnel required by the project; and ongoing commitments. Approves the proposal writer's request. |

*Explanation of Decision Matrix 49, Cont'd.*

| *Step* | *Action Responsibility* | *Action* |
|---|---|---|
| 6. | Proposal Writer | Prepares a grant application for submission to the targeted funding source, obtaining assistance from the director of program grants. |
| | Senior Administrators | Review the application and authorize its submission to the grant and contract review committee. |
| 7. | Grant and Contract Review Committee | Reviews the application for adherence to the conceptual proposal covered by the approved request for authorization to submit an application. Approves submission of the application. |
| 8. | President and Chief Fiscal Officer | Review the application submitted by the proposal writer for acceptability and, when satisfied, sign the application. |
| 9. | Director of Program Grants | Conducts any required grant negotiations with the targeted funding source, obtaining the concurrence of the proposal writer and the appropriate senior administrator for proposed changes in project approach or resource requirements and obtaining the concurrence of the chief fiscal officer for proposed changes in project funding. |

*Explanation of Decision Matrix 49, Cont'd.*

| Step | Action Responsibility | Action |
|------|----------------------|--------|
| 10. | Chief Development Officer | Receives notification of the award of a grant from the funding agency. |
| 11. | Director of Program Grants | Reviews grant award notification to determine whether the funding agency has included terms that require expanding the activities of the organizational unit that must execute the project beyond its planned level of operation, or a commitment to carry on the program beyond the period covered by the funding provided. If so, the director submits the grant to the advisory committee for review. |
| | Advisory Committee | Reviews the terms of the grant award, obtaining input from the proposal writer, the appropriate senior administrator, and the director of program grants regarding the grant's effect on institutional operations. Determines whether to recommend accepting the grant. |
| | President | Concurs with the advisory committee's recommendation. |
| 12. | President | Reports to the board of trustees the receipt of grant awards, notifies it of grants that are being rejected because of |

*Explanation of Decision Matrix 49, Cont'd.*

| Step | Action Responsibility | Action |
|------|----------------------|--------|
| | | unacceptable terms, and requests authorization to accept grants that will contribute to institutional strength and growth even though their terms require expanding program activities beyond the planned level or a commitment to carry on the program beyond the period covered by the funding made available. |
| | Board of Trustees | Determines whether to accept grants recommended for acceptance by the president. |
| 13. | President and Chief Fiscal Officer | Accept grants authorized by the board of trustees and grants the acceptance of which does not require such authorization. |

**Decision Matrix 50. Nonprogram Fund Raising and Gift and Grant Processing.**

Legend of decision-making roles
1 – Authorizes action
2 – Action responsibility
3 – Approves recommendation
4 – Recommends action
5 – Provides input

*Participants in Decision-Making Processes*

| Procedural Steps | Board of Trustees | President | Advisory Committee | Senior Administrators | Chief Development Officer | Alumni Relations Director | Public Relations Director | Publications Director | Fund-Raising Director | Chief Fiscal Officer |
|---|---|---|---|---|---|---|---|---|---|---|
| 1. Formulate plan and schedule for fund-raising activities to be conducted during the year | | 3 | | | 2 | 5 | 5 | 5 | 5 | |
| 2. Review and approve fund-raising plan and schedule | | | 4 | | | | | | | |
| 3. Implement planned fund-raising activities | | 5 | | | 1 | 2 | 2 | 2 | 2 | |
| 4. Receive nonprogram gifts and grants | | | | 5 | 5 | | | | | |
| 5. Record receipt in development office records | | | | | | | | | 2 | |
| 6. Record alumni gifts in alumni records | | | | | | 2 | | | | |
| 7. Prepare gift receipts for | | | | | | | | | | |
| (a) cash gifts | | | | | | | | | 2 | |
| (b) gifts in kind | | | | | | | | | 2 | 5 |

| |  | | | | |
|---|---|---|---|---|---|
| 8. | Transmit gift receipts to donors | | | | 2 |
| 9. | Batch-total daily payments received and gift receipts, making sure that batch totals are reconciled | | | | 2 |
| 10. | Transmit payments, batch totals, and a copy of each gift receipt to the cashier | | | | 2 |
| 11. | Follow up communications with donors regarding the value of their contributions to the institution | | | | 2 |
| 12. | Reconcile development office and accounting office gift and grant records | | | | 2 |
| 13. | Prepare periodic fund-raising status report | | | 2 | 5 |
| 14. | Review periodic fund-raising status report | | 3 | 5 | |
| 15. | Receive and accept fund-raising status report | 2 | 4 | 5 | |

*Explanation of Decision Matrix 50.*

| Step | Action Responsibility | Action |
| --- | --- | --- |
| 1. | Chief Development Officer | Formulates recommended fund-raising activity plan and schedule with the assistance of development office staff. |
| 2. | Advisory Committee | Reviews and recommends presidential approval of the fund-raising activity plan and schedule proposed by the chief development officer. |
| | President | Approves fund-raising activity plan and schedule. |
| 3. | Chief Development Officer | Supervises the implementation by his directors of fund-raising activities as scheduled and planned. |
| 4, 5, & 6. | Director of Fund Raising | Receives nonprogram gifts and grants from donors or from others to whom such gifts and grants were sent by the donor. Records receipt of gifts and grants in development office records and sees that the director of alumni relations updates the alumni gift records. |
| 7 & 8. | Director of Fund Raising | Prepares and transmits to the donors gift receipts and acknowledgment letters covering their contributions, obtaining from the chief fiscal officer valuations to |

*Explanation of Decision Matrix 50, Cont'd.*

| Step | Action Responsibility | Action |
|---|---|---|
| | | be used for recording gifts in kind in the development office records. |
| 9 & 10. | Director of Fund Raising | At the end of each day, batch-totals gift receipts issued and gift payments received, reconciles batch totals, and transmits batch-totaled payments and accounting office copy of gift receipts to the cashier for processing. |
| 11. | Director of Fund Raising | Periodically communicates with donors to advise them of the contribution their donations have made to institutional strength and progress, so as to cultivate and encourage their continuing support. |
| 12. | Director of Fund Raising and Chief Fiscal Officer | Reconcile development office records of the results of fund-raising activity with the accounting records of gift, grant, and contract receipts. |
| 13. | Chief Development Officer | Prepares periodic fund-raising status reports with input from the directors of fund raising and alumni relations. |

*Explanation of Decision Matrix 50, Cont'd.*

| Step | Action Responsibility | Action |
|------|----------------------|--------|
| 14.  | Advisory Committee | Reviews and recommends acceptance of the periodic fund-raising status report. |
|      | President | Accepts the fund-raising status report and periodically advises the board of trustees of the results of fund-raising activities to date. |
|      | Board of Trustees | Receives and accepts the fund-raising status report. |

*Explanation of Decision Matrix 51.*

| Step | Action Responsibility | Action |
|---|---|---|
| 1. | Director of Publications | Prepares recommended statement of publication program objectives, obtaining input from the administrators for whom such publications will be prepared. |
| | Chief Development Officer | Reviews and approves statement of publication program objectives. |
| 2. | Advisory Committee | Reviews statement of publication program objectives submitted by the chief development officer and recommends its approval to the president. |
| | President | Approves statement of publication program objectives and authorizes the chief development officer to monitor all publications for adherence to the objectives. |
| 3. | Director of Publications | Prepares recommended publication plan and schedule using input from the administrators for whom publications will be prepared. |
| | Chief Development Officer | Reviews and approves publication plan and schedule. |

# Decision Matrix 51. Publications.

Legend of decision-making roles
- 1 – Authorizes action
- 2 – Action responsibility
- 3 – Approves recommendation
- 4 – Recommends action
- 5 – Provides input

| Procedural Steps | President | Advisory Committee | Administrators* | Chief Development Officer | Publications Director | Chief Fiscal Officer | Printer |
|---|---|---|---|---|---|---|---|
| *Participants in Decision-Making Processes* | | | | | | | |
| 1. Develop recommended statement of publication program objectives | | | 5 | 3 | 4 | | |
| 2. Review and approve statement and authorize implementation | 3 | 4 | | | 4 | | |
| 3. Plan and schedule publication program | | | 5 | 5 | | | |
| 4. Determine audience, subject, and budget limitations for publications to be produced | | | 2 | | 5 | | |
| 5. Write draft copy | | | | | 2 | | |
| 6. Review copy for acceptability | | | 2 | | 5 | | |
| 7. Review copy for consistency with statement of publication program objectives | | | 5 | 2 | 5 | | |
| 8. Prepare rough layout and printing specifications | | | 5 | 3 | 4 | | |
| 9. Assemble dummy | | | 5 | 3 | 4 | | |

| | 1 | 2 | 3 | 4 | 5 |
|---|---|---|---|---|---|
| 10. Select printer | | | 3 | | 5 |
| 11. Execute printing contract | | 2 | 1 | 2 | 2 |
| 12. Edit and correct galley proofs | | | | 2 | 5 |
| 13. Approve key art to be printed | | | | 2 | 5 |
| 14. Approve vandykes to be printed | | | | 2 | 5 |
| 15. Print required copies | | | | 1 | 2 |
| 16. Receive and store completed publications | | | | 2 | 5 |
| 17. Distribute publications | 1 | | | 2 | |
| 18. Evaluate publications produced and determine whether any changes in statement of publications program objectives should be made | 5 | | 3 | 4 | |

*The administrators of operating areas for which publications are to be prepared and who are responsible for the use of such publications.

*Explanation of Decision Matrix 51, Cont'd.*

| Step | Action Responsibility | Action |
|------|----------------------|--------|
| 4. | Administrators | Each administrator responsible for the preparation of a publication determines the audience to which the publication is to be addressed, its subject, the number of copies required, and the amount of money available for its printing, obtaining input from other administrators whose activities are to be covered in the publication and from the director of publications. |
| 5. | Director of Publications | Prepares draft copy based on determinations arrived at as a result of step 4. |
| 6. | Administrators | Review draft copy for adequacy and acceptability of subject coverage, obtaining input from other administrators of activities covered by the publication. |
| 7. | Chief Development Officer | Reviews draft copy for consistency with approved publication program objectives and reviews suggested changes with the director of publications and appropriate administrators. |

*Explanation of Decision Matrix 51, Cont'd.*

| Step | Action Responsibility | Action |
|---|---|---|
| 8 & 9. | Director of Publications | Prepares recommended rough layout and printing specifications and assembles dummy. |
| | Administrators | Review and approve the director of publication's recommendations. |
| | Chief Development Officer | Reviews and approves recommendations. |
| 10. | Chief Development Officer | Approves the selection of the printer recommended by the director of publications. |
| 11. | Chief Fiscal Officer | Executes contract with the selected printer when authorized to do so by the chief development officer. |
| 12. | Director of Publications | Edits and corrects galley proofs submitted by the printer |
| 13. | Director of Publications | Approves key art to be included in the publication. |
| 14. | Director of Publications | Approves vandykes submitted by the printer. |
| 15. | Director of Publications | Authorizes printer to print publication. |

*Explanation of Decision Matrix 51, Cont'd.*

| Step | Action Responsibility | Action |
|------|----------------------|--------|
| 16 & 17. | Director of Publications | Receives completed publication from the printer. Distributes copies to audiences identified by the responsible administrator and stores copies not required for immediate distribution. |
| 18. | Chief Development Officer | Evaluates publications produced during the year, obtaining input from administrators for whom publications have been prepared. Determines whether any changes in the statement of publication program objectives should be proposed on the basis of recommendations from the director of publications. |

# Part Five:
# Business and
# Financial
# Operations

$P$art Five covers the business and fiscal management activities of college and university administration that are usually administered by a senior administrator carrying a title such as vice president for business and fiscal affairs, business manager, controller, or comptroller. Because of the diversity of titles used to identify this senior administrator, this book identifies him simply as the chief fiscal officer.

The chief fiscal officer's responsibilities involve the supervision of activities as broad as those supervised by the chief academic officer. These activities usually employ the majority of a campus's nonacademic staff, and the expenditure budgets for these activities, excluding auxiliary enterprises, are very close to equaling the budget for an institution's academic program activities. In general, the chief fiscal officer has the following responsibilities. First, he must see that the business affairs of the institution are well managed and designed to protect and preserve the institution's assets. Second, he must see that the institution receives all the monies due to it from all sources. Third, he must see that other administrators delegated the authority to authorize expenditures use the resources allocated to them in accordance with the limits of their operating budgets and institutional policies and procedures. Fourth, he must maintain fiscal records that account properly for all institutional assets, liabilities, receipts, and disbursements and provide the institution's management and external agencies with accurate and timely fiscal reports required to show the status of the institution's financial affairs. Fifth, he must advise management regarding the potential impact of changes in the internal or external environment on the institution's financial health. Sixth, he must assure management of the reasonableness and mathematical accuracy of revenue and expenditure forecasts contained in the multi-year plan, the annual operating and capital budgets, and budgets prepared for applications for restricted grants and contracts. Finally, he must see that the institution's business and fiscal operations are conducted in accordance with state and federal laws and the principles of prudent management.

The chief fiscal officer thus can have a powerful influence on the institution's decision-making processes. In exercising this influence, a prudent chief fiscal officer should bear in mind that in his role as an administrator he should seek to help the trustees, the president, and other administrators carry out authorized programs and activities, provided he can do so without violating his responsibilities. Therefore, before saying no to requests for assistance that require his authorization, he should first seek to work out a legitimate way of saying yes. In addition, he should bear in mind that his role encompasses carrying out his responsibilities in such a manner as to create an operating environment that is most conducive to permitting the institution to accomplish its mission, goals, and objectives with the minimum amount of internal stress.

# Business
# and Administrative
# Services

The chief fiscal officer is responsible for the administration of a large number of activities. These activities include central services — post office and mail delivery and collection, the switchboard and telephone services, centralized printing and duplicating services, and data-processing services, excluding those whose sole purpose is to support instructional or research programs. Data processing may be administered by someone other than the chief fiscal officer, but on smaller campuses, the chief fiscal officer is the most qualified person to assume that responsibility. In addition, the chief fiscal officer usually administers directly the risk management and insurance program, purchasing and inventory control, cash and investment management, NDSL and student accounts receivable collections, and records management. The essential standards applicable to these activities are set forth in this chapter. The chief fiscal officer also supervises department heads administering personnel activities, plant operation and maintenance activities, auxiliary enterprise operations, and fiscal records and reporting systems. The essential standards for these activities are covered in later chapters. Finally, the chief fiscal officer is responsible for managing the preparation of the annual operating and capital budgets. Because this activity is an institutionally broad one and because of its relationship to multi-year planning, its essential standards have been covered in Chapter Four. At some institutions, the chief fiscal officer may also be responsible for supervising student financial aid activities, the essential standards of which were covered in Chapter Ten.

The following essential standard of good management is applicable to all of the activities that the chief fiscal officer is responsible for administering or supervising.

★ The chief fiscal officer should see to it that the procedures followed in carrying out these activities contain the necessary checks and balances to ensure that no one person has control over all aspects of a financial transaction. For example, persons who receive cash should not be responsible for or have access to general ledger cash accounts, bank reconciliations, or financial aid or registration records; the payroll clerk should not authorize payroll documents or issue paychecks; and the purchasing clerk should not issue requisitions, receive invoices and receiving documents, or prepare and mail checks to vendors.

## Central Services

The essential standards of good management applicable to central services are set forth below.

★ If the institution has a post office, the postmaster should be bonded. Several institutions where the postmaster was not bonded have suffered defalcations in post office operations. The cost of adding the postmaster to the list of bonded employees should be minimal and it is well worth the small investment involved.

★ A postage meter should be used to frank all official mail. Under no circumstances should the postage meter be used to frank the personal mail of employees or students.

★ The institution's need for telephone communication services and the availability of installations to meet its need should be assessed periodically. The type of installation, the number of lines, the number and type of instruments installed, and access to placing long-distance calls should be limited to what is required to conduct operations efficiently and economically.

★ Long-distance and toll calls should be charged to the departments initiating the calls. The departmental charges should be supported by a listing of the date, time, duration, number called, and charges associated with each call. Department heads should be held responsible for the supervision of the proper use of telephone communication services by the employees of their departments.

★ The institution's need for centralized printing and duplication services and the availability of equipment to meet its need should be assessed periodically. Where centralized services are deemed adequate to meet printing or duplicating services needs, other on-campus installations or use of off-campus services should not be permitted unless it can be demonstrated that user requirements cannot be met through the centralized services.

★ Job records of labor and material used to provide printing or duplicating services requested by users should be maintained; users should be charged for the cost of providing the requested services. These job-cost records should be compared periodically with the costs that would have been incurred had the services been provided by an off-campus source to evaluate the performance of the manager of the centralized services and determine whether the continuation of the centralized services is warranted.

★ The specifications on which the institution's computer programs are based should be established by the users for whom such programs are written. User specifications should include the format, content, frequency, and timing of records to be produced; the controls and audit procedures required to ensure the accuracy and completeness of data entered into the system; and the processing rules to be used in the production of the required reports. An example of the latter is found in the user inputs required to generate the number of full-time-equivalent (FTE) students enrolled in the institution. In this case, the users must identify the sources of data to be used in computing the total number of credit hours of instruction for which all students are registered and the division to be used in converting the total number of credits into an FTE count.

★   The development of the program required to store, access, and massage the inputted data to produce the required reports should be the responsibility of the data-processing manager. If the entry of data into the system is performed by data-processing staff from data-entry forms provided by the users, the data-processing staff should not guess about or change such data. If they are unsure about the data provided by the users, they should seek clarification before entering the data into the system. In addition to the capability of developing and operating the programs required to generate the regularly required reports, the staff of the data-processing center should have the capability of developing report-generating routines, using stored data, to produce special reports that may be requested from time to time by the administration or other users.

★   All data-processing systems should be documented to permit technically qualified new personnel to understand and learn to operate the system. In small institutions with limited technically qualified data-processing staff, failure to document systems adequately can present serious problems if the institution loses the key data-processing staff members who have the knowledge to operate the system. To ensure adequate systems documentation, institutions should have their external auditors examine the existing documentation and verify its adequacy.

★   The priorities and deadlines for all output from data-processing systems should be clearly defined. The data-processing manager should be responsible for scheduling the workload to meet priorities and deadlines. The effectiveness of the data-processing center should be judged by its performance in doing so.

★   The data-processing manager should maintain records of the computer time used for each application for each user. Although many institutions do not do so, experience indicates that user departments should be charged for the cost of services provided by the data-processing center in order to make them aware of the costs the institution incurs in meeting their demand for data-processing services.

Although they cannot be said to be essential, the following standards for data-processing operations should be considered for adoption.

★   An agreed-on plan for the development of management information and data-processing systems should exist. Such a plan should cover at least the next two to three years and should be based on input obtained from all potential users regarding their anticipated information and data-processing needs. Once such a plan has been formulated and agreed on, it should be promulgated to all potential users.

★   Data-processing systems should be designed to link files that use common data or where data that can be used by processing in one file can be used as data input to another file.

★   Backup transaction tapes should be maintained and stored in a site other than the data-processing center.

### Risk Management

The essential standard of good management applicable to risk management is set forth below.

★   The institution should have a risk management and insurance program that has been approved by its board of trustees. Such a program should be developed by the chief fiscal officer and recommended to the board by the president for adoption. The program should identify the risk involved and the insurance that should be carried to cover such risk resulting from the loss of each building and its contents; accidents involving owned, leased, or rented vehicles; personal injury to faculty, staff, students, and visitors from occurrences for which the institution could be held liable; criminal acts of employees; and personal indemnification of board members and college officials. The program should also identify the types and limits of insurance coverage that should be carried against each such risk, including the amount of the deductible provision acceptable under each.

Although they cannot be said to be essential, the following are considered to be desirable standards for risk management activities.

★ The chief fiscal officer should seek the assistance of insurance consultants or brokers in assessing the institution's risk exposure and acceptable deductibles when formulating the risk management and insurance program for submission to the board of trustees. The types of coverage that should be considered include fire and extended coverage, peril or "all-risk" coverage, transit insurance, data-processing system coverage, boiler and machinery coverage, general liability coverage, worker's compensation, and unemployment insurance.

★ Insurance coverage should include the bonding of all employees involved in handling cash or accounting for financial resources and their utilization. It should be adequate to cover the risk involved in normal operations and should be increased during periods of high risk, such as at registration time.

★ The amount of deductible acceptable should be limited to the amount of loss the institution can sustain without jeopardizing its continued operation.

### Purchasing and Inventory Control

The essential standards of good management applicable to purchasing and inventory control are set forth below.

★ All purchases other than food, library acquisitions, and bookstore or student store materials purchased for resale should be made through a centralized purchasing function.

★ All purchases should be initiated by a requisition. Requisitions should be prepared by people requesting the procurement of goods and should be approved by their supervisor, the senior administrator to whom the supervisor reports, the director of grant and contract administration (if payment for any part of the goods being requested is to be made from sponsored agreement funds), and the person responsible for the budget control function. The requisition should identify the type, quantity, and quality of goods to be procured, estimated costs, suggested vendors, and the title and code numbers of the account to be charged. When an institution has an experienced, competent purchasing agent, she should be responsible for the actual selection of the vendor from which requisitioned goods are to be purchased.

★ All purchases other than small purchases made through petty cash should be covered by a purchase order. Purchase orders should be numbered, used in sequence, and controlled. Since they represent a contract, purchase orders should identify all conditions of purchase that must be adhered to by the vendor. All employees should be notified that they will be held personally responsible for payment to the vendor for any goods they purchase that are not covered by a valid purchase order issued by the centralized purchasing office. The requisitioner should be provided with a copy of the purchase order. It is also recommended that bulk buying through standing purchase orders be used when the quantity required will result in a saving.

★ All vendor invoices should be received by the accounts payable clerk. The accounts payable clerk should be responsible for verifying that the invoice is covered by a valid purchase order and that acknowledgment of the receipt and acceptability of the goods covered by the invoice has been received from the requisitioner, for auditing the invoice for proper pricing and the extension of unit prices, and for entering the accounts payable encumbrance transaction covering the invoice into the accounting records.

★   A central stores facility should exist for warehousing commonly used items. The central stores facility should provide secure storage, protect the inventory from deterioration, be located (if possible) at a site that will permit deliveries to be made with minimal delivery traffic on campus, and be operated by a central stores manager.

★   The chief fiscal officer should be responsible for seeing that issuance procedures, valuation and pricing regulations, and proper inventory control procedures are followed by the central stores manager.

★   All issuances from central stores should be covered by an issuance slip signed by the requisitioner. Issuance slips should be numbered, used in sequence, and controlled. The issuance slip should identify the types and quantities of goods issued, unit prices and extension prices for the quantity issued, and the account title and code to be charged.

★   Issuance slips should be batched and transmitted to the accounting office at least once a week.

★   The central stores manager should be responsible for the maintenance of perpetual inventory records for each item warehoused. The perpetual inventory records should identify, for each item, its name, description, and inventory number; the quantity ordered, received, issued, and on hand; transaction dates for receipts and issuances; annual normal usage quantity; normal reorder point and quantity; and cost and pricing data.

★   In addition to the physical inventory taken annually by the external auditors, the chief fiscal officer should have his staff conduct a physical inventory at least once each term. Both inventory control records and accounting records should be adjusted to reflect any shortages or overages discovered as a result of the physical inventory.

★ The chief fiscal officer should be responsible for formulating a policy that establishes the type of equipment items and dollar value limitations that should be considered capitalized movable equipment. This policy should be approved by the president and adopted by the board of trustees.

★ A current inventory of all movable equipment that meets the established policy criteria should be maintained by the business office. The inventory records to be maintained should include, at a minimum, each item's type, description, and inventory number, location by building and room number, original cost, and custodian — that is, the name of the person responsible for its safekeeping.

★ Each piece of equipment included in the inventory should be tagged with its assigned inventory number.

★ Items of inventoried equipment that are lost, stolen, traded, scrapped, or considered obsolete should be deleted from the inventory records and the investment in plant accounting records should be adjusted accordingly.

★ A physical inventory of movable equipment should be taken at least once every five years.

Decision Matrices 52 and 53 cover purchasing, accounts payable, and central stores operation.

### Cash and Investment Management

The essential standards of good management applicable to cash and investment management are set forth below.

★ No bank account should be opened or closed without authorization by the board of trustees.

★   The number of bank accounts should be held to a minimum. Because each bank account requires the maintenance of a cash balance, excess bank accounts tie up cash that could be invested. One of the institution's bank accounts should be maintained at a national bank to enable wire transfers to be made from DFAFS. Such transfers provide more rapid reimbursement of expenditures made for sponsored agreement or financial aid programs and funding to cover anticipated expenditures for such purposes.

★   The chief fiscal officer should be responsible for the preparation of cash flow projections. Such projections should cover a six-month period, at a minimum, and be updated and extended monthly.

★   All cash receipts should be deposited intact daily and expenditures should be made as late as possible to maximize the availability of funds for temporary investment. The chief fiscal officer should receive a daily report of the cash balance in each bank account. With the authorization of the board of trustees, he should invest any operating funds not required to meet the next few days' cash disbursement needs.

★   Unless the board of trustees determines that on-campus talent qualified to make investment decisions exists, the investment of endowment funds should be managed by a professional investment manager under policies established and authority delegated by the board of trustees. When a professional investment manager is retained, he must keep the chief fiscal officer informed of investment actions so that they can be entered into the institution's accounting system.

★   The chief fiscal officer should have on file documentation that identifies the principal donated and any restrictions on the use of either principal or income imposed by the donor. Preferably, such documentation should be the original source documents. Legal opinion should be obtained and retained on file regarding any situation where the donor's intent cannot be clearly established from the original source documents, the original source documents have been lost, or the purposes specified by the donor can no longer be carried out by the institution because of program changes or legal restrictions. The chief fiscal officer should be responsible for informing the investment manager of any donor-imposed restrictions that would affect investment decisions.

★ The chief fiscal officer should advise the board's finance committee and the investment manager when stock dividends are received or when a portion of cash dividends received represents a return of capital. The amount of cash dividends received that represent a return of capital should be remitted to the investment manager for reinvestment. If the finance committee or the investment manager decides that shares received as stock dividends should be retained, the investment manager should be required to purchase them at the fair market value on the date they were received.

★ The chief fiscal officer should be responsible for verifying that the institution has received all the investment income to which it is entitled, seeing that all such income and the profits or losses on the sale of securities are equitably distributed among the various endowments, and seeing that income allocations from restricted endowments are used for the purposes specified by the donor. While it cannot be cited as an essential standard, fairness indicates that where an institution follows a "pooled" investment policy, a unit fund method of accounting should be followed to ensure the equitable distribution of income and profits or losses on security sale transactions among the various endowments. It should also be pointed out that some institutions that are financially able to do so have adopted a policy of distributing endowment income among the various endowments according to a predetermined rate of return, setting aside any excess income received during the year in a reserve for endowment income shortfall. This practice facilitates the projection of the amount of endowment income that will be available for each purpose covered by the endowment funds and stabilizes the amount of such income.

★   The chief fiscal officer should have on file records identifying funds held in trust by others for the benefit of the institution, if any, and any restriction imposed by the donors of such funds on the income derived from their investment. The amount of each fund should be recorded in the institution's accounting records and the institution should receive regular reports from the organization holding and managing the funds showing the amount of income received and distributed and the results of investment actions taken.

★   The chief fiscal officer should be responsible for seeing that the finance committee of the board and the president are provided with reports at least annually showing the results of endowment investment management. Such reports should show the rate of return (yield plus or minus market-value change) achieved by the investment of endowment funds during the period covered by the report and a comparison of the rate of return achieved with those achieved by widely quoted indexes such as the Standard & Poor's 500-stock index, the Dow Jones industrial average, the National Association of College and University Business Officers (NACUBO) annual investment performance study, and the Common Fund.

★   The chief fiscal officer should be responsible for the proper classification of the endowment fund's principal accounts in the institution's accounting records. An account may be classified as true endowment — unrestricted as to the use of income; true endowment — restricted as to the use of income; term endowment — unrestricted; term endowment — restricted; quasi endowment — unrestricted; or quasi endowment — restricted. True endowments are those where the donor has restricted the use of the principal in perpetuity. Term endowments are those where the donor has restricted the use of the principal for a specified number of years. Quasi endowments are those that have been set aside by the board of trustees to function as endowments even though the donor has not placed any restriction on the use of the principal. Knowing the amount of quasi endowment held by the institution can be extremely important because the restrictions imposed by the board of trustees on the use of the principal can be removed by the board at any time, making the principal available for operating purposes.

Decision Matrices 54 and 55 cover the management of operating cash and the investment of endowment funds.

### NDSL Management

The collection of NDSL loans is extremely important for two reasons. First, the funds collected remain available to the institution for relending; second, if the amount of uncollected loans get too high, the federal government will withdraw the institution's eligibility for participation in the program. Therefore, while the chief fiscal officer is ultimately responsible for the disbursement and collection of NDSL loans awarded by the director of financial aid, he should have an NDSL loan officer on his staff to administer the loan disbursement and collection activities.

The essential standards applicable to the management of the NDSL program are set forth below.

★ The funds necessary for the institution's required contribution to match the federal government's contribution to the NDSL program should be deposited in the NDSL bank account that the institution is required to maintain. All receipts, from both contributions and collections, and disbursements must be processed through this bank account.

★ Student borrowers should be fully informed by the director of financial aid at the time they accept an NDSL as part of their financial aid package of the conditions of the loan and the repayment requirements.

&#9733;   The NDSL loan officer, under the supervision of the chief fiscal officer, should be responsible for all activities related to the disbursement and collection of NDSL loans. The activities related to disbursement include obtaining, each time a loan is made, the signatures of the borrowers on a promissory note that identifies the amount of the loan, their obligation to repay, the terms of the loan, and the regulations and policies that govern the NDSL program; providing the borrowers, each time a loan is made, with a copy of a Truth in Lending statement that they have signed; and having the borrowers endorse, each time a loan is made, the loan disbursement check, which should be made jointly payable to the borrowers and the institution. All NDSL documents are required to be retained in locked, fireproof or fire-resistant storage facilities.

Prior to the end of each term, the NDSL loan officer should obtain verification from the registrar of the borrowers' status as at least half-time students and of the expected date of separation. Before they leave campus, if possible, or by mail, if necessary, the NDSL loan officer should conduct exit interviews with the borrowers who will be leaving or who have left the institution. The loan officer should make sure the borrowers understand the terms and conditions of their loans and their repayment responsibilities and obtain the borrowers' agreement as to the amounts borrowed, the interest rate, and the repayment schedule, including the date of the first payment and the frequency of subsequent payments. In addition, the borrowers should be informed regarding skip tracing collection requirements and required to provide the name, address, and telephone number of someone who will know where they can be reached; advised of the advantages of prepayment; advised of requirements to pay promptly or provide notification of inability to pay; advised of requirements to provide notification of change of address; notified of documents required for and provisions applicable to loan deferment, postponement, or cancellation; and informed of the billing system that will be used. The borrowers at this time should be provided with a copy of the Truth in Lending form and the repayment agreement that they have signed.

The NDSL loan officer must contact the borrowers three

times during the grace period allowed by the NDSL program and must seek to locate borrowers whose contact letters are returned by the post office. The loan officer is responsible for seeing that the monthly, bimonthly, or quarterly billings, as agreed on with the borrower, are mailed. Billings are required to identify the amount due, the date due, and to whom the check should be made payable. The loan officer is required to use due diligence in attempting to collect payments due from borrowers who are in arrears on their payments. Due diligence is defined as the use by the lender, in making, servicing, and collecting loans, of practices at least as extensive and forceful as those generally used by financial institutions for consumer loans. The NDSL loan officer is responsible for approving the cancellation, deferment, postponement, or forbearance of loan payments, in accordance with NDSL regulations, after verifying that the borrower has provided adequate documentation to support such actions. The loan officer is also responsible for maintaining all records related to such actions, records of collection of payments made, and duly diligent efforts made to collect past due payments. The loan officer should also see that all payments made are deposited in the NDSL bank account, that the chief fiscal officer and the director of financial aid are kept informed regarding the amount of repayments collected, and that the chief fiscal officer is provided with a monthly aged listing of past due accounts.

★ Loans that remain past due after two years of diligent efforts at collection should be written off (assigned) to the Department of Education. For such assignments to be acceptable, the promissory notes must be valid instruments, the collection efforts must be documented, the borrower' payment histories must be documented, and all documents for each of the above must be the originals.

★ Verification that the promissory note form used for an NDSL loan is a valid instrument should be obtained from either the regional office of the Department of Education or the institution's legal counsel.

Decision Matrix 56 covers NDSL loan management activities.

## Student Accounts Receivable Management

The essential standards of good management applicable to student accounts receivable management activities are set forth below.

★ The chief fiscal officer should be responsible for the formulation of policies covering student accounts receivable management. Such policies should be approved by the president and adopted by the board of trustees. They should include policies covering the admission of students who require a deferred payment plan to cover the cost of attending the institution, the right of readmission or right to participate in commencement exercises for students with prior-year balances, the assessment of interest charges to students who are delinquent in meeting deferred payment plan obligations, and the penalties to be imposed on students who are delinquent in meeting deferred payment plan obligations or who have given the institution a bad check. Such penalties might involve withdrawal of the right to continue on the institution's meal plan, withdrawal of the right to take examinations, suspension, or dismissal. All policies adopted by the board should be strictly adhered to.

★ The assessed charges and financial aid awards posted to students' accounts should be reconciled each term with the records of the registrar and the financial aid office.

★ Students, and the parents of dependent students, with unpaid balances should be provided with a monthly statement of the balances and payments due in accordance with the institution's deferred payment plan.

★ The students' responsibility to pay assessed charges, the terms of the institution's deferred payment plan, and penalties for the failure to make required payments when due should be clearly set forth in the institution's catalogue, recruiting material, and student handbook and reaffirmed during the new student orientation program.

★ All faculty, administrators, and staff should provide support and assistance to the chief fiscal officer, when requested, in the collection of past due student accounts receivable and the enforcement of related institutional policies.

★ An aged listing of student accounts receivable should be prepared at least annually.

★ Payment schedules and arrangements should be made with foreign governments sponsoring students who wish to enroll before such students are permitted to matriculate.

★ The chief fiscal officer is responsible for seeing that the registrar is notified of the need to place an encumbrance on the academic records of students who are delinquent in meeting their financial obligations and to remove such encumbrances when the obligations have been met.

## Records Management

The essential standards of good management applicable to records management activities are set forth below.

★ The chief fiscal officer should be responsible for seeing that each office has established policies and procedures for the creation, movement, retention, retrieval, safekeeping, emergency protection, and destruction of records. He should also be responsible for providing adequate and well-organized facilities for the storage of records that are to be retained but are not needed on a ready-access basis for day-to-day operations.

★ The number of forms and the number of copies of each form should be controlled and limited to the number required for institutional information flow. All forms should be numbered and used in sequence.

★   After transaction processing of forms received or used by the business office has been completed, the forms should be stored in an organized manner.

★   A person in the business office should be designated as responsible for record retention. This person should control and issue all receipt forms and checks; store all documents received or used by the business office; retrieve and provide documents and records from storage, maintaining records to identify the person to whom they were provided and to ensure their return; transfer to dead storage records not required for current use; and destroy records after the required period of retention has passed.

Readers wishing more information on the business activities covered in this chapter should contact the National Association of College and University Business Officers (NACUBO), One Dupont Circle, Washington, D.C. 20036.

**Decision Matrix 52. Purchasing and Accounts Payable Activities.**

Legend of decision-making roles
1 – Authorizes action
2 – Action responsibility
3 – Approves recommendation
4 – Recommends action
5 – Provides input

*Participants in Decision-Making Processes*

| Procedural Steps | President | Chief Fiscal Officer | Purchasing | Accounts Payable | Cash Disbursement | Requisitioner | Vendor |
|---|---|---|---|---|---|---|---|
| 1. Receive requisitions and verify that they contain required approvals and account coding | | | 2 | | | 5 | |
| 2. Determine acceptability of source of supply and prepare purchase order | | | 2 | | | | |
| 3. Sign purchase order | | 2 | 5 | | | | |
| 4. Receive copy of purchase orders issued | | | 5 | 2 | | 2 | 2 |
| 5. Receive verification of delivery of material ordered | | | | 2 | | 5 | 5 |
| 6. Receive and audit vendor's invoice | | | | 2 | | | |
| 7. Match vendor's invoice, purchase order, and receiving documentation and update accounts payable subsidiary ledger and general ledger control accounts | | | | 2 | | | |
| 8. Authorize payment of accounts payable | | 2 | | 4 | | | |
| 9. Receive payment instructions and support documentation and cut checks | | | | 5 | 2 | | |
| 10. Obtain required signatures | 2 | 2 | | | 5 | | |
| 11. Mail checks and update accounts payable subsidiary and general ledger control accounts | | | | | 2 | | |

*Explanation of Decision Matrix 52.*

| Step | Action Responsibility | Action |
|------|----------------------|--------|
| 1. | Purchasing | Receives purchase requisitions and verifies that they contain required approval signatures and are properly coded. |
| 2. | Purchasing | Determines acceptability of suggested source of supply and prepares purchase order. |
| 3. | Chief Fiscal Officer | Signs purchase orders submitted by purchasing. |
| 4. | Purchasing | Issues purchase order to vendor, providing copies to requisitioner and accounts payable. |
| 5. | Accounts Payable | Receives verification from requisitioner that material ordered has been received and is satisfactory as to quantity and quality. |
| 6 & 7. | Accounts Payable | Receives and audits vendor's invoice; matches invoice with corresponding purchase order and receiving documentation; updates accounts payable subsidiary records and control accounts. |
| 8. | Chief Fiscal Officer | Reviews aged accounts payable listing and cash |

*Explanation of Decision Matrix 52, Cont'd.*

| *Step* | *Action Responsibility* | *Action* |
|---|---|---|
| | | situation with accounts payable and determines which vendor accounts are to be paid. |
| 9. | Cash Disbursement | Receives, from accounts payable, vendor invoices authorized for payment with supporting documentation and prepares payment checks. |
| 10 & 11. | Cash Disbursements | Obtains required signatures from the chief fiscal officer and president (or their authorized representative), issues checks, and updates accounts payable subsidiary and control records to reflect payments made. |

**Decision Matrix 53. Central Stores Operation.**

Legend of decision-making roles
1 – Authorizes action
2 – Action responsibility
3 – Approves recommendation
4 – Recommends action
5 – Provides input

| Procedural Steps | Participants in Decision-Making Processes | | | | |
|---|---|---|---|---|---|
| | Chief Fiscal Officer | Central Stores Manager | Accounting | Requisitioner | Vendor |
| 1. Receive material ordered, check quantity and quality, sign receiving documents, and send them to accounts payable | | 2 | | | 5 |
| 2. Store material and update perpetual inventory records | | 2 | | | |
| 3. Issue material requisitioned, complete interdepartmental supply slip, obtain requisitioner's signature for receipt of material issued, and update perpetual inventory records | | 2 | | 5 | |
| 4. Receive batched interdepartmental charge slips and update accounting records | | 5 | 2 | | |
| 5. Identify that stock on hand has been reduced to the reorder point and issue purchase order to replenish stock | | 2 | | | |
| 6. Conduct physical inventory and identify discrepancies | 1 | 2 | 2 | | |
| 7. Update accounting records to reflect discrepancies | 1 | 2 | 2 | | |
| 8. Update perpetual inventory records to reflect discrepancies | 1 | 2 | | | |

*Explanation of Decision Matrix 53.*

| Step | Action Responsibility | Action |
|------|----------------------|--------|
| 1. | Central Stores Manager | Receives ordered material from vendors, verifies acceptability of its quantity amd quality, signs receipt documentation, and sends notification of receipt to accounts payable. |
| 2. | Central Stores Manager | Stores material received and updates perpetual inventory records to reflect date, quantity, and price of material received. |
| 3. | Central Stores Manager | Receives requisition to issue supplies from inventory, withdraws requested material from stock, completes interdepartmental charge slip, obtains requisitioner's signature on charge slip acknowledging receipt of material, issues material, and updates perpetual inventory records to reflect date, quantity, and price of material issued. |
| 4. | Accounting | Receives, at least once a week, batched transmittal of interdepartmental charge slips covering material issued from inventory, audits them, and updates accounting records. |
| 5. | Central Stores Manager | Monitors perpetual inventory records, determines when supply on hand has been reduced to the reorder point, and issues requisition to replenish stock. |

*Explanation of Decision Matrix 53, Cont'd.*

| *Step* | *Action Responsibility* | *Action* |
|--------|-------------------------|----------|
| 6. | Accounting and Central Stores Manager | Conduct a physical inventory when instructed to do so by the chief fiscal officer and identify any discrepancies between perpetual inventory records, physical count, or valuation of inventory on hand and accounting inventory control records. |
| 7. | Accounting | Adjusts inventory control account for the difference between it and the physical inventory count valuation when authorized to do so by the chief fiscal officer. |
| 8. | Central Stores Manager | Adjusts perpetual inventory records for the differences between them and the physical inventory count when authorized to do so by the chief fiscal officer. |

*Explanation of Decision Matrix 54.*

| Step | Action Responsibility | Action |
|------|----------------------|--------|
| 1. | Chief Fiscal Officer | Formulates recommendations, after obtaining the president's input, as to the bank accounts that should be maintained and the policies that should be followed in short-term investment of excess operating funds. |
| | Finance Committee | Reviews and approves the chief fiscal officer's recommendations. |
| 2. | Finance Committee | Recommends board approval for opening or closing bank accounts, establishing short-term investment policies, and delegating authority to the chief fiscal officer to make short-term investment decisions. |
| | Board of Trustees | Reviews and approves the finance committee's recommendations. |
| 3. | Chief Fiscal Officer | Opens or closes bank accounts, in accordance with the board of trustees' authorization, when instructed to do so by the president. |
| 4. | Chief Fiscal Officer | Develops cash flow projections covering each of the ensuing six months on the basis of revenue and expenditure projection data obtained from the chief development officer, the director of |

## Decision Matrix 54. Cash Management of Operating Funds.

Legend of decision-making roles

1 – Authorizes action
2 – Action responsibility
3 – Approves recommendation
4 – Recommends action
5 – Provides input

Participants in Decision-Making Processes

| Procedural Steps | Board of Trustees | Finance Committee | President | Advisory Committee | Chief Development Officer | Chief Fiscal Officer | Financial Aid Director | Grant and Contract Administration Director | Cashier | Accounting | Accounts Payable | Payroll | Cash Disbursements | Bank Reconciliations | Banks |
|---|---|---|---|---|---|---|---|---|---|---|---|---|---|---|---|
| 1. Formulate recommendations on bank accounts to be maintained and policies to govern short-term investment of excess operating funds | | 3 | 5 | | | 4 | | | | | | | | | |
| 2. Approve opening or closing bank accounts and short-term investment policies | 2 | 4 | 5 | | | 5 | | | | | | | | | |
| 3. Open or close bank accounts | | | 1 | | | 2 | | | | | | | | | |
| 4. Develop cash flow projections | | | | | 5 | | 5 | 5 | 5 | 5 | 5 | 5 | | | |
| 5. Review and approve cash flow projections | | 4 | 3 | | | 5 | 5 | 5 | | 5 | 5 | 5 | | | |
| 6. Receive and deposit daily cash collections, receive cash disbursement data, update accounting records, and prepare daily cash report | | | | | | | | | 5 | 2 | 5 | 5 | 5 | | 5 |

|  | | | | | | | | |
|---|---|---|---|---|---|---|---|---|
| 7. Receive and reconcile bank statements | | | | | 5 | | 2 | 5 |
| 8. Enter adjustments identified by bank reconciliations into accounting records | | | | | 2 | | 5 | |
| 9. Determine that excess funds are available for short-term investments | | | 2 | | | | | |
| 10. Invest excess funds | 1 | | 2 | 5 | 5 | | | |
| 11. Revise and extend cash flow projections | 2 | 5 | 2 | 5 | 5 | 5 | | |
| 12. Review results of short-term investment actions | 2 | 5 | 5 | | | | | |

*Explanation of Decision Matrix 54, Cont'd.*

| Step | Action Responsibility | Action |
|------|-----------------------|--------|

|      |                       | grant and contract administration, the director of financial aid, accounting, accounts payable, payroll, and cash disbursements. |

5.   Advisory
     Committee

Reviews the chief fiscal officer's cash flow projections and recommends presidential approval.

     President

Approves cash flow projections.

6.   Accounting

Receives, audits, and deposits daily cash collections submitted by cashiers. Receives and audits cash disbursements made that day. Receives bank advisories covering charges or credits for returned checks, investments made or liquidated, and service charges.

Updates accounting records to reflect daily receipts, bank charges and credits, and disbursements. Prepares daily cash report showing for each bank account the balance on hand at the beginning of the day, deposits and disbursements, bank charges and credits, bank reconciliation adjustments, and the balance on hand at the end of the day.

*Explanation of Decision Matrix 54, Cont'd.*

| Step | Action Responsibility | Action |
|------|----------------------|--------|
| 7. | Bank Reconciliation | Receives bank statements and reconciles them with balances reflected in accounting records. |
| 8. | Accounting | Enters bank reconciliation entries into the accounting records. |
| 9. | Chief Fiscal Officer | Reviews the daily cash report submitted by accounting and cash flow projections and determines the amount of excess funds available for investment and the periods for which they can be invested. |
| 10. | Chief Fiscal Officer | Reviews current cash and projected cash needs with the president and obtains his authorization to invest excess funds in accordance with policies established by the board of trustees. |
| 11. | Chief Fiscal Officer | Revises and extends cash flow projections each month on the basis of the latest daily cash report and current revenue and expenditure projection data obtained from the chief development officer, the director of grant and contract administration, the director of financial aid, accounting, accounts payable, payroll, and cash disbursements. |

*Explanation of Decision Matrix 54, Cont'd.*

| Step | Action Responsibility | Action |
|------|----------------------|--------|
| 12.  | Chief Fiscal Officer | Reviews the results of short-term investment decisions with the president and the finance committee of the board of trustees. |

*Explanation of Decision Matrix 55.*

| Step | Action Responsibility | Action |
|------|----------------------|--------|
| 1. | Finance Committee | Formulates recommended policies to be followed in the investment of endowment funds and recommends the appointment of an investment manager with delegated authority to manage the portfolio, basing its recommendations on input from legal counsel, the president, and the chief fiscal officer. |
| 2. | Finance Committee | Recommends that the board of trustees adopt the formulated policies and approve the appointment of the investment manager. |
| | Board of Trustees | Reviews the finance committee's recommendations, obtaining clarification from legal counsel. Adopts policies, appoints the investment manager, and authorizes the delegation of authority for him to manage the portfolio. |
| 3. | President | Notifies the investment manager of his appointment, the investment policies approved by the board of trustees, and the authority it has delegated to manage the portfolio. |

## Decision Matrix 55. Endowment Fund Investment Management.

| Legend of decision-making roles |
|---|
| 1 – Authorizes action |
| 2 – Action responsibility |
| 3 – Approves recommendation |
| 4 – Recommends action |
| 5 – Provides input |

_Participants in Decision-Making Processes_

| Procedural Steps | Board of Trustees | Finance Committee | Legal Counsel | President | Chief Development Officer | Chief Fiscal Officer | Investment Manager | Accounting |
|---|---|---|---|---|---|---|---|---|
| 1. Formulate recommendations for policies to be followed in the investment of endowment fund assets and the delegation of authority to manage the portfolio | | 2 | 5 | 5 | | 5 | | |
| 2. Adopt policies and authorize delegation of authority | 2 | 4 | 5 | | | | | |
| 3. Receive authorization to manage portfolio | | | | 1 | | | 2 | |
| 4. Receive identification of donor restrictions that could affect investment decisions | | | 5 | | | 5 | 2 | |
| 5. Receive identification of donor restrictions on use of principal and income | | 2 | 5 | | | 5 | | |
| 6. Enter dividend and interest income data into accounting records | | | | | | 1 | | 2 |
| 7. Receive identification of receipt of stock dividends and cash dividends that represent a return of capital | | 2 | | | | 5 | 2 | |

|  |  | | | | | | | |
|-----|----------|---|---|---|---|---|---|---|
| 8. | Receive identification of endowment gifts or unrestricted bequests received | 2 | | | 2 | | 2 | |
| 9. | Enter receipt of endowment gifts or unrestricted bequests into accounting records | | 2 | 5 | 1 | | | 2 |
| 10. | Approve acceptance of endowment gifts and authorize transfer of unrestricted bequests to quasi-endowment funds | 2 | 4 | 5 | 5 | 1 | | |
| 11. | Receive notification of additions to the portfolio | | | 5 | 1 | 5 | 2 | |
| 12. | Adjust accounting records to reflect board's decisions | | | | 1 | | | 2 |
| 13. | Receive investment transaction data and enter data into the subsidiary and general ledger accounting records | | | | | 1 | 5 | 2 |
| 14. | Review and accept investment manager's report on portfolio investments | 2 | 4 | | | 1 | 5 | 2 |
| 15. | Verify that the institution has received all the dividend and interest income to which it is entitled | | 4 | | | | 5 | |
| 16. | Determine and enter into the accounting records the equitable distribution of gains and losses on security transactions and income received among the various funds | | | | 1 | | | 2 |
| 17. | Evaluate the investment manager's performance in managing the portfolio | 2 | 5 | 5 | 1 | 5 | 2 | |

*Explanation of Decision Matrix 55, Cont'd.*

| *Step* | *Action Responsibility* | *Action* |
| --- | --- | --- |
| 4. | Chief Fiscal Officer | Advises the investment manager, after obtaining legal counsel's concurrence, of any donor-imposed restrictions that might affect his investment decisions. |
| 5. | Chief Fiscal Officer | Advises the finance committee, after obtaining legal counsel's concurrence, of donor-imposed restrictions on the use of the principal or income of each endowment fund. |
| 6 & 7. | Chief Fiscal Officer | Receives dividend and interest income. Instructs accounting to enter receipts in the subsidiary and general ledger accounting records. Advises the investment manager of the receipt of stock dividends and of cash dividends a portion of which represents a return of capital. |
| 8. | Chief Development Officer | Advises the finance committee, president, and chief fiscal officer of the receipt of new endowment gifts and unrestricted bequests. Provides the chief fiscal officer with original documentation covering such gifts and bequests. |

*Explanation of Decision Matrix 55, Cont'd.*

| Step | Action Responsibility | Action |
|------|----------------------|--------|
| 9. | Chief Fiscal Officer | Updates endowment gift documentation records, opens required new accounts, and instructs accounting to enter gifts and bequests received into the appropriate subsidiary and general ledger accounts. |
| 10. | Finance Committee | Formulates recommendations for the acceptance of new endowment fund gifts and for the use of unrestricted bequests as quasi endowment, after obtaining input from legal counsel, the president, and the chief fiscal officer regarding the institution's need for cash or alternative use of unrestricted bequests. |
| | Board of Trustees | Reviews the finance committee's recommendations and determines the appropriate course of action. |
| 11. | Investment Manager | Receives, when authorized by the president, additions to the portfolio and transfer of donated assets from the chief fiscal officer. |
| 12. | Chief Fiscal Officer | Updates endowment gift documentation records to record the board of trustees' |

*Explanation of Decision Matrix 55, Cont'd.*

| *Step* | *Action Responsibility* | *Action* |
|---|---|---|
| | | decision to add unrestricted bequests to quasi endowment, opens the required new accounts, and instructs accounting to adjust the subsidiary and general ledger accounting records to reflect the board of trustees' decision. |
| 13. | Chief Fiscal Officer | Receives the investment manager's notification of security transactions entered into and instructs accounting to enter the results of such transactions into the accounting records. |
| 14. | Finance Committee | Receives periodic reports from the investment manager showing the composition of portfolio assets by type of investment, their book value, and their current market value. Submits a report on the status of the portfolio to the board of trustees. |
| | Board of Trustees | Discusses and accepts the finance committee's report. |
| 15. | Accounting | When authorized to do so by the chief fiscal officer, compares records of dividend and interest payments received |

*Explanation of Decision Matrix 55, Cont'd.*

| Step | Action Responsibility | Action |
|------|----------------------|--------|
| | | with Standard and Poor's or Moody's published data to verify that the institution has received all the income to which it is entitled. Follows up on discrepancies with corporations or the investment manager. |
| 16. | Accounting | When authorized to do so by the chief fiscal officer, calculates the allocation of profits and losses on security transactions and investment income among the funds that make up the portfolio and enters such allocations into the accounting records. |
| 17. | Chief Fiscal Officer | Computes the rate-of-return results of the investment manager's investment decisions and develops a comparative report of his rate-of-return performance with widely quoted indexes such as Standard and Poor's 500-stock index, the Common Fund, NACUBO's annual investment performance study, and the Dow Jones industrial average. Provides comparative reports to the president and the finance committee. |

*Explanation of Decision Matrix 55, Cont'd.*

| *Step* | *Action Responsibility* | *Action* |
|---|---|---|
| | Finance Committee | Reviews and evaluates the investment manager's comparative performance results, obtaining input from the investment manager, the president, and the chief fiscal officer. |

*Explanation of Decision Matrix 56.*

| *Step* | *Action Responsibility* | *Action* |
|---|---|---|
| 1. | Chief Fiscal Officer | Receives payment of new award of NDSL funds and deposits it, together with required matching funds, in the NDSL bank account. |
| 2. | Director of Financial Aid | Makes NDSL awards and advises borrowers of the terms and conditions under which the award is made. |
| 3. | Chief Fiscal Officer | Obtain concurrence from legal counsel that the promissory note being used by the institution represents a valid instrument. |
| 4. | NDSL Loan Officer | Has the borrower sign a promissory note for the amount of the new award and a Truth in Lending statement and endorse the check disbursing the new loan. Updates the borrower's loan record file. |
| 5. | Accounting | Enters loan disbursement transaction data into accounting records according to input from the NDSL loan officer. |
| 6. | NDSL Loan Officer | Receives from the registrar a listing of students whose enrollment status has dropped to less than half-time, who are withdrawing, or who are expecting to graduate. |

# Decision Matrix 56. National Direct Student Loan Management.

Legend of decision-making roles
1 – Authorizes action
2 – Action responsibility
3 – Approves recommendation
4 – Recommends action
5 – Provides input

*Participants in Decision-Making Processes*

| Procedural Steps | Chief Fiscal Officer | Legal Counsel | NDSL Loan Officer | Financial Aid Director | Borrowers | Collection Agency | Skip Tracing Firm | Registrar | Accounting | Alumni Relations Director | Career Placement Officer |
|---|---|---|---|---|---|---|---|---|---|---|---|
| 1. Receive NDSL payment, deposit it and matching funds in the NDSL bank account | 2 | | | | | | | | | | |
| 2. Make NDSL awards, advising borrowers of their terms and conditions | | | | 2 | 5 | | | | | | |
| 3. Obtain legal opinion on validity of NDSL promissory note to be used | 2 | 5 | | | | | | | | | |
| 4. Have borrowers sign promissory note and Truth in Lending statement and endorse loan check; update borrower's file | | | 2 | | 5 | | | | | | |
| 5. Enter loan transaction into student accounts receivable, subsidiary, general ledger control, and NDSL control accounts | | | 5 | | | | | | 2 | | |
| 6. Receive notification of expected date of graduation or change in enrollment status to less than half-time status | | | 2 | | | | | 5 | | | |
| 7. Conduct exit interview with borrower | | | 2 | | 5 | | | | | | |
| 8. Send borrower follow-up notices during grace period | | | 2 | | | | | | | | |
| 9. Bill borrower | | | 2 | | | | | | | | |
| 10. Receive borrower's payments and update borrower's loan record | | | 2 | | 5 | | | | 2 | | |

|  |  | | | | | | | |
|---|---|---|---|---|---|---|---|---|
| 11. | Receive and determine acceptability of borrower's request for loan cancellation, deferment, postponement, or forbearance and update borrower's file and loan record | | | 2 | 5 | | | |
| 12. | Process loan payments and cancellation transactions | | | 5 | | 2 | | |
| 13. | Identify delinquent accounts, institute due-diligence procedures, and provide chief fiscal officer with an aged listing of delinquent accounts | | | 2 | | | | |
| 14. | Instruct skip tracing firm to locate borrower with whom contact has been lost and update borrower's file | | | | | | | |
| 15. | Receive new addresses and update borrower's file | 1 | | 2 | | | | |
| 16. | Turn collection problems over to a collection agency and update borrower's file | 1 | | 2 | 5 | | 5 | 5 |
| 17. | Receive payments collected by collection agency and update loan record | 1 | | 2 | 5 | | | |
| 18. | Process payments received from collection agency | | | 2 | | | | |
| 19. | Request legal counsel to institute suit against borrower and update borrower's file | 1 | | 5 | | 2 | | |
| 20. | Receive notification from legal counsel of results of suit and update borrower's file and loan record | | 5 | 2 | | | | |
| 21. | Process collections made as a result of suit | | | 5 | | | | |
| 22. | Transfer accounts delinquent for more than two years to the department of education | 1 | | 2 | | 2 | | |
| 23. | Update accounting records to reflect write-off of accounts transferred to the department of education | | | 5 | | 2 | | |

*Explanation of Decision Matrix 56, Cont'd.*

| Step | Action Responsibility | Action |
|------|----------------------|--------|
| 7. | NDSL Loan Officer | Conducts exit interviews with borrowers identified as a result of step 6. Updates each borrower's loan file and notifies accounting to transfer the amount of the borrower's debt from "advances to students — in school" to "advances to students — out of school." |
| | Accounting | Makes the required transfer in accounting records. |
| 8 & 9. | NDSL Loan Officer | Sends the borrower follow-up notices during the grace period and sends the borrower billings for payments due ten days before the date each payment is due. |
| 10 & 11. | NDSL Loan Officer | Receives the borrower's payment or request for cancellation, deferment, postponement, or forbearance of payment due. Determines the acceptability of the borrower's request, updates the borrower's loan record and file, and transmits payments and authorized loan cancellation data to the accounting office. |

*Explanation of Decision Matrix 56, Cont'd.*

| Step | Action Responsibility | Action |
|------|----------------------|--------|
| 12. | Accounting | Processes NDSL loan payment and enters payment and cancellation data into the accounting records. |
| 13. | NDSL Loan Officer | Reviews loan collection records and identifies delinquent accounts. Institutes due-diligence procedures. Provides the chief fiscal officer with an aged listing of delinquent accounts. |
| 14. | NDSL Loan Officer | Reviews delinquent accounts with the chief fiscal officer and, in accordance with his instructions, engages a skip tracing firm to locate borrowers with whom contact has been lost and updates borrowers' files to record that such action has been taken. |
| 15. | NDSL Loan Officer | Receives new addresses, point of contact data, and telephone numbers from the skip tracing firm, the registrar (from requests for transcripts of encumbered records), the career placement office (from requests for assistance in obtaining employment), or the alumni |

*Explanation of Decision Matrix 56, Cont'd.*

| *Step* | *Action Responsibility* | *Action* |
|---|---|---|
| | | office (from alumni membership records). |
| 16. | NDSL Loan Officer | Turns collection of delinquent accounts over to a collection agency when instructed to do so by the chief fiscal officer. Updates borrower's file to record that such action has been taken. |
| 17 & 18. | NDSL Loan Officer | Receives payments collected by the collection agency and the agency's charges. Updates borrower's loan records and transmits collection and charge data to accounting. |
| | Accounting | Records collections and collection agency charges in the accounting records. |
| 19. | NDSL Loan Officer | Requests legal counsel to institute suit to collect delinquent accounts when authorized to do so by the chief fiscal officer. Updates borrower's file to record that such action has been taken. |
| 20 & 21. | NDSL Loan Officer | Receives from legal counsel payments collected as a |

*Explanation of Decision Matrix 56, Cont'd.*

| *Step* | *Action Responsibility* | *Action* |
|--------|------------------------|----------|
| | | result of the suit, if any, and notification of the results of suit. Updates borrower's loan record and file and transmits collections to accounting. |
| | Accounting | Processes collections and updates the accounting records. |
| 22 & 23. | NDSL Loan Officer | Transfers, when authorized to do so by the chief fiscal officer, accounts that have been delinquent for more than two years to the Department of Education, after verifying that the borrower's file reflects that all due-diligence requirements have been complied with and that all documents contained therein are the original copies. |
| | Accounting | Adjusts accounting records to reflect the write-off of accounts transferred to the Department of Education when advised that the transfer has been made by the NDSL loan officer. |

# Personnel
# Administration

Personnel administration frequently is not given the attention it deserves in smaller institutions. Employee turnover and dissatisfaction are as costly and disruptive to the operation of a small institution as they are to that of a larger institution or industrial enterprise. For this reason, it is recommended that any institution employing more than 200 faculty, administrators, and staff have a personnel administrator on its payroll. Institutions with a smaller number of employees should have at least one person assigned to perform the personnel administration functions on a part-time basis. In either case, the personnel office should maintain all personnel records related to compensation, fringe benefits, and employment history for all employees, including faculty, and provide other essential personnel services for all employees other than faculty. As set forth in Chapter Five, the responsibility for providing faculty with essential personnel services not provided by the personnel office should be the responsibility of the chief academic officer.

For the purposes of this book, it is assumed that the institution has a full-time director of personnel. The essential standards of good management applicable to her operations are set forth below.

★ Written personnel policies and procedures should be promulgated and adhered to. These policies and procedures should cover, for nonacademic personnel, their employment, change in employment status, and termination. Additional policies and procedures that should be considered include a probationary period, the employer's religious preference in employment, if any, the employment of relatives, working hours and schedules, including rest periods, compensatory time off, overtime pay, layoffs and recalls, and discipline and grievances. These policies and procedures should be formulated as recommendations by the director of personnel and should be in compliance with state and federal regulations (see Decision Matrices 57, 58, 59, and 60).

★  The director of personnel should be responsible for verifying that established policies and procedures are being adhered to. The administration should be informed promptly if established policies or procedures are violated.

★  Personnel policies and information about the institution's employee benefit program should be published and made available to all employees. Where institutional policies make participation in certain benefit programs voluntary, the employees should be encouraged to participate. While employee benefit programs are primarily established to assist in attracting and retaining employees, they should also be viewed from the perspective of protecting the institution's image. If an employee is injured, dies, or retires with inadequate income, the institution's image can be damaged if it does not offer benefit programs to help the employee or his or her heirs. Where such programs are voluntary and contributory, every effort should be made to see that employees enroll. To encourage enrollment, institutions might consider sending employee benefit program information to the employees' homes where it can be reviewed by the employees with their spouses. In any event, if employees choose not to enroll in a voluntary or contributory program, their signatures should be obtained on a form, which should be retained in their personnel files, on which they acknowledge that the benefits of the program have been explained to them and they have chosen not to participate.

★   A basic wage and salary administration program for non-academic employees should be administered by the director of personnel. This program should be designed to ensure equity of compensation within the institution and, to the extent it is financially feasible, a competitive position with other employers in the marketplace. The formulation of such a program can involve techniques that range from fairly simple to complex, including the use of personnel administration consultants. It is to an institution's advantage to seek outside expertise in the formulation of its wage and salary administration program if on-campus expertise does not exist and the institution is financially able to do so. If not, an institution should use its best efforts to establish such a program. The administration of the compensation program for academic employees is the responsibility of the chief academic officer. The job classifications to be used in formulating the wage and salary administration program for nonacademic employees should be consistent with those utilized in the institution's payroll system to facilitate subsequent monitoring of the program's administration. If it is determined that the existing classifications should be changed to formulate an acceptable wage and salary administration program, the classification coding maintained in the payroll system should be revised to conform with that required for wage and salary administration (see Decision Matrix 61).

★   The director of personnel should maintain, for nonacademic employees, records that provide the affirmative action officer with such data or reports as are required to verify that the institution's personnel activities are in compliance with equal employment opportunity and affirmative action policies, procedures, and regulations. Similar records should be maintained by the chief academic officer regarding personnel activities related to academic staff (see Decision Matrix 62).

★   The director of personnel should be provided with written notification of all disciplinary actions taken with regard to nonacademic employees and should maintain such records in the employees' personnel files. The chief academic officer should be responsible for the maintenance of similar records for the academic staff.

★ The director of personnel should maintain in each academic and nonacademic employee's personnel file a chronological record of the employee's employment history at the institution, from the date of employment to the date of termination, and copies of all documents necessary to verify the accuracy of that record. The chronological record should identify the date of each change in compensation or employment status and the nature of the change.

★ The director of personnel should be responsible for providing payroll with personal, compensation, and fringe benefit data necessary to compute payroll disbursements, except for data about the number of hours worked by employees whose compensation is based on an hourly wage rate. Payroll should not change the payroll computation data of any employee, whether academic or nonacademic, without authorization from the director of personnel.

★ The director of personnel should be responsible for the administration and maintenance of records related to the institution's employee benefit program. Administrative and record-keeping responsibilities include those related to noninsured benefits — such as vacations, sick leave, and emergency leave — as well as those related to insured programs.

While they cannot be said to be essential, the following standards for personnel administration are considered desirable.

★ Position descriptions should exist for each nonacademic administrative or professional position. These descriptions should identify the position's title, to whom the employee reports and who reports to him or her, the responsibilities and authority associated with the position, its education and skill requirements, and its compensation range. Position descriptions should be reviewed and updated, if necessary, each year.

★ The president should delegate to the chief fiscal officer the authority to commit the institution to the employment of nonacademic personnel, except for the employment of senior or key administrators.

★ Orientation programs should be held to inform new employees about the institution, its personnel policies, procedures, and practices, and its employee benefit programs.

★ Employee training and development programs should exist to improve employees' performance and enhance their opportunities for advancement.

★ Nonacademic employees' performance evaluations should be conducted annually. The employees should be apprised of their evaluation and the evaluation made a part of their personnel file (see Decision Matrix 63).

Readers desiring more information regarding the conduct of personnel administration activities should contact the College and University Personnel Association (CUPA), Suite 120, 11 Dupont Circle, Washington, D.C. 20036.

# Decision Matrix 57. Formulating Nonacademic Personnel Policies and Procedures.

Legend of decision-making roles:
1 – Authorizes action
2 – Action responsibility
3 – Approves recommendation
4 – Recommends action
5 – Provides input

Participants in Decision-Making Processes

| Procedural Steps | Board of Trustees | Legal Counsel | President | Advisory Committee | Senior Administrators | Department Heads | Nonacademic Staff | Personnel Director | Grant and Contract Administration Director | Chief Fiscal Officer |
|---|---|---|---|---|---|---|---|---|---|---|
| 1. Formulate new or revised nonacademic personnel policies and procedures recommendation | | | | | 5 | 5 | 5 | 4 | 5 | 3 |
| 2. Review and approve recommended policies and procedures | | 5 | 3 | | 5 | 5 | 5 | 5 | 5 | 5 |
| 3. Adopt recommended policies | | 5 | 4 | 4 | | | | | | |
| 4. Authorize implementation of new or revised policies and procedures | 2 | | 1 | | | | | | | |
| 5. Update personnel policies and procedures manual | | | | | | | | 2 | | 2 |
| 6. Review and approve revisions to manual | | | | | 2 | 2 | | 5 | | 2 |
| 7. Receive copy of revised manual | | | | | | | | | | 5 |
| 8. Inform employees of new or revised policies and procedures | | | | | | | | 2 | | |

*Explanation of Decision Matrix 57.*

| Step | Action Responsibility | Action |
|------|----------------------|--------|
| 1. | Senior Administrators, Department Heads, and Nonacademic Staff | Provide the director of personnel with input regarding nonacademic personnel administration problems encountered as a result of existing policies, procedures, or practices and suggest changes that would improve operations. |
| | Director of Personnel | Develops and documents recommended changes in policies and procedures. |
| | Chief Fiscal Officer | Reviews and approves recommended changes. |
| 2. | Chief Fiscal Officer | Submits recommended changes for review and approval. |
| | Advisory Committee | Reviews recommended changes to ensure that their potential impact on all aspects of institutional operation is considered. When satisfied, recommends their adoption. |
| | Legal Counsel | Reviews recommended changes to ensure that proposed policies and procedures do not violate state or federal laws or regulations. |
| | Director of Grant and Contract Administration | Reviews recommended changes to ensure that proposed policies and |

*Explanation of Decision Matrix 57, Cont'd.*

| Step | Action Responsibility | Action |
|------|----------------------|--------|
| | | procedures do not violate terms or requirements of existing grants and contracts. |
| | President | When satisfied, approves proposed changes. |
| 3. | President | Recommends adoption of new or revised policies to the board of trustees. |
| | Director of Personnel and Legal Counsel | Provides any clarification the board of trustees may request. |
| | Board of Trustees | When satisfied, adopts revised or new policies. |
| 4. | President | Authorizes the chief fiscal officer to implement revised or new policies and procedures. |
| 5. | Director of Personnel | Develops, with the assistance of the director of publications, a new or revised personnel policy and procedures manual. |
| 6 & 7. | Chief Fiscal Officer | Distributes copies of manual to all department heads and senior administrators. |
| 8. | Personnel | Prepares and posts personnel information bulletin notifying staff of approved changes. |

# Decision Matrix 58. Employment of Nonacademic Staff.

Legend of decision-making roles:
1 – Authorizes action
2 – Action responsibility
3 – Approves recommendation
4 – Recommends action
5 – Provides input

| Procedural Steps | President | Senior Administrators | Department Heads | Chief Fiscal Officer | Budget Control | Payroll | Personnel Director | Grant and Contract Administration Director | Applicants |
|---|---|---|---|---|---|---|---|---|---|
| 1. Receive authorized position list for each department | | | | 5 | | | 2 | | |
| 2. Prepare staffing forecast | | | | | | | 2 | | |
| 3. Approve staffing forecast | | | | 3 | | | 4 | | |
| 4. Update position control system | | | | | | | 2 | | |
| 5. Initiate personnel requisition | | 3 | 4 | | | | | 3 | |
| 6. Verify availability of funds | | 5 | | | 2 | | | | |
| 7. Receive approved personnel requisition | | | | | 5 | | 2 | | |
| 8. Prepare position description, if necessary | | | 5 | | | | 2 | | |
| 9. Approve position descriptions, if new or revised | | 2 | | | | | 4 | | |

*Participants in Decision-Making Processes*

| | | | | | | |
|---|---|---|---|---|---|---|
| 10. Recruit applicants | | | | | 2 | 5 |
| 11. Conduct preliminary screening | | | | | 2 | 5 |
| 12. Conduct reference checks | | | | | 2 | |
| 13. Refer qualified candidates to requisitioner for interview | | | | | 2 | 5 |
| 14. Conduct interviews and recommend employment | | | 2 | | | 5 |
| 15. Approve hiring related to own area of responsibility | | | | | | |
| 16. Initiate personnel action form | | 3 | 4 | | | |
| 17. Approve personnel action form | 2 | 1 | 2 | | | |
| 18. Receive approved form and obtain acceptance of employment | 5 | 3 | 5 | | | |
| 19. Notify rejected applicants | | 5 | | | 2 | 5 |
| 20. Obtain forms and data required for input into payroll system and other personal data required for personnel administration | | | | | 2 | |
| 21. Enter data into payroll system | | | | 2 | 5 | 5 |

*Explanation of Decision Matrix 58.*

| Step | Action Responsibility | Action |
|------|----------------------|--------|
| 1. | Chief Fiscal Officer | Provides the director of personnel with an authorized position list for each department as established by the annual operating budget adopted by the board of trustees. |
| 2. | Director of Personnel | Analyzes the authorized position list, projects turnover, promotions, and positions to be filled during the year, and prepares staffing forecast. |
| 3. | Director of Personnel | Obtains the chief fiscal officer's approval of staffing forecast. |
| 4. | Director of Personnel | Updates position and employee control system for either new positions authorized by the budget or vacancies that result from employee turnover or change in employment status. |
| 5. | Department Heads | Initiate the process of filling vacant positions by preparing a personnel requisition form. |
|  | Director of Grant and Contract Administration | For personnel requisitions where any portion of the employee's salary is to be paid from a restricted grant or contract, determines whether the position, salary range, and percentage of restricted effort are acceptable under the terms of the applicable grant or contract. |

*Explanation of Decision Matrix 58, Cont'd.*

| Step | Action Responsibility | Action |
|------|----------------------|--------|
| | Senior Administrators | Determine whether to approve the personnel requisition form initiated by a subordinate. |
| 6. | Senior Administrators | Transmit approved personnel requisitions to budget control. |
| | Budget Control | Determines whether the department's budget, or the grant or contract budget, if applicable, has an unfilled position and sufficient unspent funds to cover the requisition. If so, approves requisition and records budget encumbrance. |
| 7. | Director of Personnel | Receives approved personnel requisition from budget control. |
| 8. | Director of Personnel | If requisition covers a new position or a change in duties for an existing position, revises or prepares a position description on the basis of input from the administrator to whom the employee will report. |
| 9. | Senior Administrators | Review and approve new or revised position description recommended by the director of personnel. |
| 10. | Director of Personnel | Recruits internal transfer applicants or new applicants for position. |

*Explanation of Decision Matrix 58, Cont'd.*

| Step | Action Responsibility | Action |
|------|----------------------|--------|
| 11. | Director of Personnel | Conducts preliminary screening, and testing, if applicable, of applicants for qualifications, experience, and general acceptability. |
| 12. | Director of Personnel | Checks prior employer references of acceptable screened applicants possessing required skills. |
| 13. | Director of Personnel | Sends the most highly qualified applicants to the hiring department head for interviews. Provides the department head with applicant referral form, employment application form, and results of reference checks. |
| 14. | Department Heads | Interview applicants and select one recommended for employment. |
| 15. | Senior Administrators | Review and approve hiring recommendation of subordinate department heads. |
| 16. | Department Head | Completes personnel action form when authorized to do so. |
| 17. | Senior Administrators | Review and approve personnel action forms prepared by subordinate department heads. |
| | President | Reviews hiring recommendation of department head and senior administrator and authorizes employment. |

*Explanation of Decision Matrix 58, Cont'd.*

| Step | Action Responsibility | Action |
|------|----------------------|--------|
| 18. | Director of Personnel | Receives employment authorization (the completed personnel action form) from the senior administrator and executes employment agreement with applicant. |
| 19. | Director of Personnel | Updates employee and position control system records and notifies unsuccessful applicants that the position has been filled. |
| 20. | Director of Personnel | Has new employee complete employee benefit forms and other forms required to compute payroll and provide required personnel information. |
| 21. | Payroll | Receives from the director of personnel and enters into the payroll system the data required to compute payroll. |

# Decision Matrix 59. Change in Status of Nonacademic Employee.

Legend of decision-making roles
- 1 – Authorizes action
- 2 – Action responsibility
- 3 – Approves recommendation
- 4 – Recommends action
- 5 – Provides input

Participants in Decision-Making Processes

| Procedural Steps | President | Senior Administrators | Department Heads | Grant and Contract Administration Director | Budget Control | Payroll | Personnel Director | Employee |
|---|---|---|---|---|---|---|---|---|
| 1. Initiate change-in-status recommendation | | | 2 | | | | 5 | 5 |
| 2. Review and approve changes that affect employees devoting efforts to sponsored agreement activities | | | 4 | 2 | | | | |
| 3. Review and approve changes recommended by subordinates | | 2 | 4 | | | | | |
| 4. Verify availability of funds | | 5 | | | 2 | | | |
| 5. Authorize change in status for employee | 2 | 4 | | | | | | |
| 6. Receive notification of authorized change in status | | 5 | | | | | 2 | |
| 7. Execute revised employment agreement with employee | | | 2 | | | | 2 | 5 |
| 8. Receive notification of change in status | | | | | | 2 | 5 | |
| 9. Enter change-in-status data into payroll system | | | | | | 2 | | |

*Explanation of Decision Matrix 59.*

| Step | Action Responsibility | Action |
|------|----------------------|--------|
| 1. | Department Heads | Review their plans to change a nonacademic employee's status with the employee and the director of personnel for acceptability and any negative effect the proposed change might have on other areas of institutional operation. Recommend a change in status in the form of a promotion, transfer, change between full-time and part-time employment, salary increase, or reallocation of effort. |
| 2. | Director of Grant and Contract Administration | Reviews and approves changes in status that affect employees' efforts being devoted to restricted grant or contract activities. |
| 3. | Senior Administrators | Review and approve changes in status recommended by subordinate department heads. |
| 4. | Budget Control | Determines whether the departmental budget, and the grant or contract budget, if applicable, has sufficient unexpended funds to cover any increased cost that results from implementing the recommended change in status. If so, or if a decrease in cost results from the implementation, |

| *Step* | *Action Responsibility* | *Action* |
|--------|------------------------|----------|
| | | approves the change in status and records either a budget encumbrance or an increase in encumbered budget funds. |
| 5. | President | Reviews change in status recommended by department heads and their senior administrators and authorizes implementation. |
| 6 & 7. | Director of Personnel | Receives authorization for change in status and executes revised employment agreement with the affected employee. |
| 8. | Department Head and Payroll | Receives notification from the director of personnel that the change in status has been implemented. |
| 9. | Payroll | Enters change-in-status data received from the director of personnel into the payroll system. |

*Explanation of Decision Matrix 60.*

| Step | Action Responsibility | Action |
|------|----------------------|--------|
| 1. | Department Heads | Upon the identification of an infraction of institutional rules or regulations or of unsatisfactory performance, discuss the problem with the employee and determine the extent and nature of disciplinary action to be taken. |
| 2. | Director of Personnel | Receives department head's written notification of disciplinary actions and updates employee's personnel file. |
| 3. | Payroll | Receives the director of personnel's written notification of disciplinary actions when a fine, suspension, or demotion is involved; updates the payroll system. |
| 4. | Department Heads | Decide to recommend dismissal of an employee because of continued infraction of rules or unsatisfactory performance, for which previous disciplinary action has been imposed, or because the infraction is of such a serious nature that it warrants dismissal. |
| 5. | Senior Administrators | Review dismissal recommendations initiated by subordinate department heads, obtaining the employee's side of the story and his or her employment record |

# Decision Matrix 60. Employee Discipline and Termination.

Legend of decision-making roles
1 – Authorizes action
2 – Action responsibility
3 – Approves recommendation
4 – Recommends action
5 – Provides input

*Participants in Decision-Making Processes*

| *Procedural Steps* | Board of Trustees | Legal Counsel | President | Senior Administrators | Department Heads | Grant and Contract Administration Director | Budget Control | Payroll | Personnel Director | Employee |
|---|---|---|---|---|---|---|---|---|---|---|
| 1. Notify employee of unsatisfactory performance or violation of published policy, rules, or regulations and determine disciplinary action if other than dismissal | | | | | 2 | | | | | 5 |
| 2. Receive notification of disciplinary action other than dismissal | | | | | 5 | | | | 2 | |
| 3. Receive director of personnel's notification of disciplinary actions | | | | | | | | 2 | 5 | |
| 4. Decide to recommend dismissal | | | | | 2 | | | | | |
| 5. Review and approve dismissal recommendations of subordinates | | | | 2 | 5 | | | | 5 | |
| 6. Review and approve dismissal decision | | | 2 | 4 | 5 | | | | 5 | |
| 7. Notify employee of dismissal decision | | | 1 | | | | | | 2 | |

|  | | | | | |
|---|---|---|---|---|---|
| 8. Receive employee's appeal of dismissal decision | 2 | | | | 5 |
| 9. Conduct appeal hearing | 2 | 5 | 5 | 5 | 5 |
| 10. Receive notification of board of trustees' decision | 5 | 2 | 2 | 2 | 2 |
| 11. Receive notification of resignation | | | | | 5 |
| 12. Conduct exit interview with resigning or dismissed employees | | | | | |
| 13. Process employee benefit transfer or cancellation | | | | 2 | 5 |
| 14. Enter termination data into payroll system | | | 2 | 2 | 5 |
| 15. Restore position and fund availability to affected budgets | | 2 | 2 | 5 | 5 |

*Explanation of Decision Matrix 60, Cont'd.*

*Step   Action Responsibility   Action*

|  |  |  |
|---|---|---|
|  |  | information from the director of personnel. Decide whether to approve dismissal recommendation. |
| 6. | President | Reviews the dismissal recommendations of senior administrators and their subordinate department heads to obtain the facts of the case. Obtains from the director of personnel additional data regarding the employee's personal situation and employment record. Decides whether to approve dismissal recommendation. |
| 7. | Director of Personnel | Upon the receipt of the president's authorization, notifies the employee of dismissal decision. |
| 8. | Board of Trustees | Receives the dismissed employee's appeal of the dismissal decision. |
| 9. | Board of Trustees | Conducts a hearing of the employee's appeal, obtaining from the employee the reason for appeal, from the president, senior administrator, and department head their justification for the dismissal decision, from personnel any desired employment history or personal data, and |

*Explanation of Decision Matrix 60, Cont'd.*

| Step | Action Responsibility | Action |
|------|----------------------|--------|
| | | from legal counsel advice regarding any pertinent legal aspects of the case. Decides whether to uphold dismissal. |
| 10. | Director of Personnel | Receives written notification of the board's decision. |
| 11. | Department Heads or Director of Personnel | Receive written notification of resignation from an employee. If such notification is received by a department head, he transmits it to the director of personnel for processing. If it is received by the director of personnel, he informs the department head of its receipt and of the pertinent related details. |
| 12. | Director of Personnel | Conducts exit interview with dismissed or resigning employees to ascertain and document any employee relations problems the correction of which would reduce turnover problems. |
| 13. | Director of Personnel | Determines actions to be taken and acts to cancel or transfer fringe benefit entitlements. |
| 14. | Payroll | Enters termination data provided by the director of personnel into the payroll system. |

*Explanation of Decision Matrix 60, Cont'd.*

| Step | Action Responsibility | Action |
|------|----------------------|--------|
| 15. | Budget Control and Director of Grant and Contract Administration | Restore unexpended funds and position vacancy data resulting from termination to the appropriate departmental and restricted grant or contract budgets. |

*Explanation of Decision Matrix 61.*

| Step | Action Responsibility | Action |
|---|---|---|
| 1. | President | Authorizes the chief fiscal officer to develop a basic (minimal) wage and salary administration plan for nonacademic staff. |
| 2. | Director of Personnel | Recommends job classifications to be used on the basis of input from department heads (including senior administrators). The classifications should include, at a minimum, senior administrators, managers and professional staff, senior clerical, technicians, and skilled trades, and staff. |
| | Chief Fiscal Officer | Approves the director of personnel's job classification recommendations. |
| 3. | Director of Personnel | Assigns existing positions (employees) to appropriate job classifications on the basis of input from department heads. |
| | Chief Fiscal Officer | Approves the director of personnel's assignment of positions to job classifications. |
| 4. | Director of Personnel | Determines, on the basis of the current compensation levels of employees filling positions assigned to each job classification, the minimum compensation for each job classification. |

## Decision Matrix 61. Basic Nonacademic Wage and Salary Administration Program.

Legend of decision-making roles:
1 – Authorizes action
2 – Action responsibility
3 – Approves recommendation
4 – Recommends action
5 – Provides input

| Procedural Steps | Board of Trustees | President | Advisory Committee | Department Heads | Chief Fiscal Officer | Chief Academic Officer | Personnel Director | Payroll | Employees |
|---|---|---|---|---|---|---|---|---|---|
| 1. Authorize formulation of basic nonacademic wage and salary administration program | | 1 | | | 2 | | 4 | | |
| 2. Establish job classifications to be used | | | | 5 | 3 | | 4 | | |
| 3. Assign positions to appropriate job classifications | | | | 5 | 3 | | 4 | | |
| 4. Determine current minimum and maximum compensation range for each job classification | | | | | | | 4 | 5 | |
| 5. Review and approve classifications, position assignment, and minimum and maximum compensation ranges | | 3 | 4 | | 5 | | 5 | | |
| 6. Develop comparative data about minimum and maximum compensation ranges being paid by competitors for each classification and ranges being paid in the academic area | | | | | 3 | 5 | 4 | | |

|  |  | | | | |
|---|------|---|---|---|---|
| 7. | Recommend competitive position to be maintained and revised minimum and maximum range for each classification | | | 3 | 4 |
| 8. | Review and approve new minimum and maximum ranges | 3 | 4 | 5 | 5 |
| 9. | Develop recommended compensation adjustments to implement new program | 3 | | 4 | 5 |
| 10. | Authorize adoption of new salary ranges and budget necessary to implement compensation adjustment program | 2 | 4 | 5 | 5 |
| 11. | Receive notification of wage and salary administration program and implementation plan | 2 | 5 | 5 | 2 |

*Explanation of Decision Matrix 61, Cont'd.*

| *Step* | *Action Responsibility* | *Action* |
|---|---|---|
| | Payroll | Verifies the accuracy of the current compensation levels of employees used in the calculation. |
| 5. | Chief Fiscal Officer and Director of Personnel | Submit job classification, position assignment, and minimum and maximum compensation range recommendations and data for review and approval. |
| | Advisory Committee | Reviews recommendations and data and recommends that the president approve them. |
| | President | Approves recommendations and data. |
| 6. | Director of Personnel | Obtains from published sources, telephone communication with competing institutions, communication with local employers, and so on, the minimum and maximum ranges others are paying for each job classification. Also obtains from the chief academic officer the minimum and maximum ranges being paid for each faculty rank. Develops tables showing how current minimums and maximums for each job classification compare with competitors' ranges and faculty ranges. |

*Explanation of Decision Matrix 61, Cont'd.*

| Step | Action Responsibility | Action |
|------|----------------------|--------|
| | Chief Fiscal Officer | Reviews and approves the data developed, the methodology used in developing comparative tables, and the result reflected in the tables. |
| 7. | Director of Personnel | Recommends minimum and maximum compensation ranges that should be adopted for each job classification to permit the institution to remain competitive and attract and retain competent nonacademic staff. |
| | Chief Fiscal Officer | Reviews and approves the director of personnel's recommendations. |
| 8. | Chief Fiscal Officer and Director of Personnel | Submit comparative competitive compensation tables and recommended changes in minimum and maximum ranges for each job classification to the advisory committee. |
| | Advisory Committee | Reviews data and recommendations and recommends that the president approve the recommended changes. |
| | President | Approves recommended changes. |
| 9. | Director of Personnel | Formulates a plan to adjust current compensation to bring |

*Explanation of Decision Matrix 61, Cont'd.*

| Step | Action Responsibility | Action |
|------|----------------------|--------|
|      |                      | employees' salaries and wages into line with new minimum and maximum ranges for each job classification and calculates the costs of such adjustments. |
|      | Chief Fiscal Officer | Reviews and approves the plan and recommends its approval to the president. |
|      | President | Reviews and approves the plan. |
| 10.  | President | Recommends adoption of new minimum and maximum ranges for each job classification and compensation adjustment plan. |
|      | Chief Fiscal Officer and Director of Personnel | Provide board with any clarification it may wish. |
|      | Board of Trustees | Approves new compensation ranges and authorizes implementation of compensation adjustment plan. |
| 11.  | Chief Fiscal Officer | Publishes notification to department heads and employees of the wage and salary administration program and the board's actions adopting the new minimum and maximum ranges for each job classification and its authorization to implement a compensation adjustment plan. |

## Decision Matrix 62. Affirmative Action Compliance—Nonacademic Staff.

Legend of decision-making roles:

1 – Authorizes action
2 – Action responsibility
3 – Approves recommendation
4 – Recommends action
5 – Provides input

*Participants in Decision-Making Processes*

| *Procedural Steps* | Board of Trustees | President | Advisory Committee | Senior Administrators | Department Heads | Affirmative Action Officer | Personnel Director |
|---|---|---|---|---|---|---|---|
| 1. Appoint affirmative action officer | | 2 | 5 | | | | 5 |
| 2. Review existing affirmative action program | | | | | | 2 | 5 |
| 3. Obtain existing staffing report | | | | | | 2 | 5 |
| 4. Obtain personnel action reports | | | | | | 2 | |
| 5. Determine affirmative action deficiencies | | | | 5 | 5 | 2 | 5 |
| 6. Develop corrective action recommendations | | | | | 5 | 2 | |
| 7. Review and approve corrective action recommendations | | 3 | 4 | | | | |
| 8. Authorize implementation of corrective actions | 2 | 4 | | | | 5 | |
| 9. Implement corrective actions | | 1 | | 2 | 2 | 5 | 2 |

*Explanation of Decision Matrix 62.*

| Step | Action Responsibility | Action |
|------|----------------------|--------|
| 1. | President | On the basis of input from advisory committee and the director of personnel, designates a person to whom the responsibility of an affirmative action officer is assigned. |
| 2. | Affirmative Action Officer | Familiarizes herself with the existing affirmative action program. |
| 3. | Affirmative Action Officer | Obtains from the director of personnel current nonacademic staff complement report. |
| 4. | Affirmative Action Officer | Obtains from the director of personnel nonacademic staff personnel action reports identifying applicant flow, new hires, terminations, promotions, salary inceases, and leaves. |
| 5. | Affirmative Action Officer | Analyzes data provided by the director of personnel and identifies areas where institutional practices or actions do not meet affirmative action program requirements. |
| 6. | Affirmative Action Officer | Confers with department heads, senior administrators, and the director of personnel to determine why deficiencies in meeting affirmative action program requirements have occurred and develops recommendations for |

*Explanation of Decision Matrix 62, Cont'd.*

| Step | Action Responsibility | Action |
|------|----------------------|--------|
| | | changes in policies and procedures to eliminate deficiencies. |
| 7. | Affirmative Action Officer | Submits recommendations for corrective action. |
| | Advisory Committee | Reviews recommendations and recommends that the president approve them. |
| | President | Approves recommendations. |
| 8. | President | Submits recommendations to the board of trustees with his recommendation for adoption. |
| | Affirmative Action Officer | Responds to questions the board may have regarding recommendations. |
| | Board of Trustees | Approves recommendations. |
| 9. | President | Authorizes senior administrators, department heads, and the director of personnel to implement recommended actions to eliminate affirmative action deficiencies. |

## Decision Matrix 63. Performance Evaluation of Nonacademic Employees.

Legend of decision-making roles
1 – Authorizes action
2 – Action responsibility
3 – Approves recommendation
4 – Recommends action
5 – Provides input

| Procedural Steps | President | Advisory Committee | Senior Administrators | Department Heads | Chief Fiscal Officer | Personnel Director | Employees — Exempt | Employees — Nonexempt |
|---|---|---|---|---|---|---|---|---|
| 1. Authorize formulation of an annual performance evaluation program for nonacademic employees | 1 | | | | | | | |
| 2. Develop program plan, timetable, and forms to be used | | | | | 2 | | | |
| 3. Review and approve program plan | 3 | 4 | | 5 | 3 | 4 | | |
| 4. Authorize implementation of program | 1 | | | | 5 | | | |
| 5. Conduct evaluation program orientation workshops | | | | | 2 | 2 | | |
| 6. Prepare statements of objectives for exempt employees | | | | | | | | |
| 7. Review objectives with exempt employees | | | | 5 | 3 | 4 | | |
| 8. Observe employees' performance | | | | 2 | | | 5 | |
| 9. Complete evaluation forms for all employees | | | | 2 | | | | |
| 10. Review evaluations with employees | | | | 2 | | | 5 | 5 |
| 11. Review evaluations prepared by subordinate department heads | | | 2 | 2 | | | | |
| 12. Receive completed, signed evaluation forms for inclusion in employee personnel files | | | 5 | 5 | | 2 | | |
| 13. Conduct workshop to analyze results of the program | | | 5 | 5 | 2 | 5 | 5 | 5 |

*Participants in Decision-Making Processes*

*Explanation of Decision Matrix 63.*

| Step | Action Responsibility | Action |
|------|----------------------|--------|
| 1. | President | Instructs the chief fiscal officer to develop a performance evaluation program for all nonacademic employees. |
| 2. | Director of Personnel | Obtains input from department heads employing nonacademic staff. On the basis of this input, formulates an evaluation plan, including the timetable to be followed and forms to be used. |
|  | Chief Fiscal Officer | Reviews and approves the plan, timetable, and forms. |
| 3 & 4. | Chief Fiscal Officer | Submits the plan to the advisory committee for approval. |
|  | Advisory Committee | Reviews the plan and recommends to the president that he approve its implementation. |
|  | President | Approves the plan and authorizes its implementation. |
| 5. | Director of Personnel | Conducts a workshop for department heads to acquaint them with the program, its timetable, and the use of the forms developed. |
| 6. | Director of Personnel | Works with department heads in developing statements of performance objectives for each exempt employee. |

*Explanation of Decision Matrix 63, Cont'd.*

| *Step* | *Action Responsibility* | *Action* |
|---|---|---|
| | Chief Fiscal Officer | Reviews and approves statements of objectives. |
| 7. | Department Heads | Review, with all exempt employees, their performance objectives, provide them with a copy, and advise them that their performance in meeting these objectives during the year will be evaluated. |
| 8 & 9. | Department Heads | Observe the performance of all employees during the year and at the appropriate time, toward the end of the year, record the result of their evaluations on the appropriate employee performance evaluation forms. |
| 10 & 11. | Department Heads | Conduct performance evaluation interview with each employee, identifying why ratings recorded on evaluation form were assigned, suggest ways performance could be improved, and obtain employees' signatures on forms verifying that the evaluation results have been reviewed with them. |
| | Senior Administrators | Review, with subordinate department heads, the |

*Explanation of Decision Matrix 63, Cont'd.*

| *Step* | *Action Responsibility* | *Action* |
|--------|--------------------------|----------|
| | | evaluations of their employees for reasonableness and equity. |
| 12. | Director of Personnel | Receives completed evaluation forms transmitted by senior administrators and files them in each employee's personnel file jacket. Verifies that the evaluation of all employees has been completed and follows up where it has not. |
| 13. | Chief Fiscal Officer | Obtains input from senior administrators, department heads, and employees regarding the evaluation process and identifies ways in which it can be improved. |

# Plant Operation
# and Management

The primary role of the physical plant department is to assist in planning, creating, maintaining, and operating a physical environment that is conducive to learning, teaching, and research. This environment should be as attractive, safe, and free of operating difficulties as the efficient and effective use of the available resources will permit. Thus, the director of these activities is normally responsible for managing the transportation, energy conservation, campus safety, and campus security activities of an institution, as well as the custodial, maintenance, and grounds care services required to protect and preserve the useful life of its physical plant. While it can be said that the teaching-learning process can take place with the teacher sitting at one end of a log and the student at the other, neither students nor teachers desire this in today's era of technological revolution. Thus, even the campuses of the smaller colleges and universities are minicommunities encompassing transportation networks, utility services, housing facilities, eating and health care facilities, a library, security and police protection, and a working environment that includes offices, classrooms, laboratories, and recreational facilities, which serve not only the institution's residential and working population but also the community in which the institution is located. All these facilities in a living, learning, and research environment involve the utilization of sophisticated, complex operating and support systems that must be maintained to be kept operational twenty-four hours a day.

The task of the director of physical plant will be made easier if the assistance of students, faculty, and staff can be enlisted in keeping the campus clean and safe. Obtaining their assistance will be easier if the director, together with the chief fiscal officer and chief student affairs officer, takes the opportunity presented by student, faculty, and staff orientation programs to acquaint each group with its responsibility to assist the institution in the maintenance and preservation of a clean and safe campus. Unfortunately, many institutions, when facing the necessity of finding ways to reduce operating expenditures in order to balance their budgets, have chosen to constrain the resources allocated for plant operation and maintenance activities. Although this might solve their fiscal problems for a short time, in the long run the deferred maintenance problems that resulted from such decisions will cost more to correct than the budgetary savings realized.

The physical plant operations and maintenance activities should be administered by a competent director experienced in providing custodial and maintenance services to large, complex installations. He should be supported by adequate staff to meet the installation's need for in-house service. The number of employees required is affected by the number, size, and operating systems complexity of campus structures and the overall size of the campus itself. The number of employees required will also be affected by the extent to which the institution is able to use student employees to perform routine maintenance, custodial, and groundskeeping tasks. The number of skilled craftspersons required also will be affected by the extent to which the institution is able and willing to rely on contracted services and by how effectively the director plans, schedules, and supervises the work of in-house maintenance personnel, as well as by the quality, training, and experience of those personnel. The director should have the opportunity to attend workshops and programs designed to provide him with training in modern techniques applicable to custodial, maintenance, energy conservation, and campus safety and security programs.

With the foregoing points in mind, the essential standards

of good management applicable to conducting plant operation and maintenance activities are set forth below.

★   All facilities should be inspected periodically to identify any existing or potential maintenance service requirements or safety hazards that should be eliminated. On such inspections, the director of physical plant should be accompanied by the chief fiscal officer and, if possible, a member of the board of trustees who ideally should have a construction or engineering background. The results of these inspections should be recorded in a maintenance log and reported to the board of trustees. They should also be used as the basis for formulating the repair and replacement component of the institution's plant operation and maintenance operating budget. It is then up to the administration and the board of trustees to determine how much of the required repairs and replacement expenditures they can fund and how much of a deferred maintenance problem they are willing to live with. Once these decisions have been made, the director's maintenance log should be updated and should become the basis for establishing the priority and advance scheduling of the tasks to be performed by the in-house maintenance or grounds crews and the tasks that require the use of contract services by outside contractors. During the year, custodial and grounds crews should be responsible for reporting to the director unanticipated potential maintenance needs they observe in the performance of their duties. This input should be recorded in the maintenance log and should also be scheduled for corrective action to the extent that the director of physical plant has available staff and budgeted funds.

★   The director of physical plant also should maintain for each facility a record of the actual delivery of all scheduled and unscheduled maintenance services, preventive maintenance services, scheduled and unscheduled service of operating support systems, and user-requested alterations and improvements.

★   The director of physical plant should have on file up-to-date campus layout drawings showing the location of all utility services—that is, electrical, water, sewage, storm drainage, telephone, heating, air conditioning, and lighting systems. In addition, to the extent possible, the director should have on file as-built working drawings for all buildings on campus and service manuals for all operating support systems contained in them. Changes that result from maintenance services or alteration and improvement projects should be recorded on these drawings.

★   Maintenance services to be provided by in-house plant operations and maintenance staff should be covered by a work-order system. Work orders should identify the scheduled date and time the work is to be performed, the estimated number of man-hours of each skill required, all materials, parts, and equipment required for the completion of the work, and the reporting of actual time and materials used on the job (see Decision Matrix 64).

★   Work standards should be established for the performance of custodial and groundskeeping tasks. To the extent possible, repetitive custodial and grounds care services should be covered by standing work orders (see Decision Matrices 67 and 68).

★   The director of physical plant should maintain records showing all custodial supplies and equipment issued for use in each building. He should also be responsible for seeing that a secure area is provided in each building for the storage of issued, but unused, supplies and equipment.

★   Any costs incurred by the plant operations and maintenance department in providing services required for special events or for user-requested alterations and improvements should be charged to the budgets of the activity or department requesting the work or services.

★   The director of physical plant should be responsible for the formulation of plans to provide emergency services. These plans, once formulated and approved by the administration, should be prominently posted throughout campus and should identify the person to contact and how to contact him or her for services required during off-duty hours or in the event of fire, storm damage, and the like.

★   The director of physical plant and the chief fiscal officer should periodically conduct joint surprise inspections of work sites of scheduled custodial, grounds, and maintenance activities to evaluate the performance of employees.

★   The director of physical plant should be responsible for the supervision of any custodial, maintenance, groundskeeping, or campus security services performed by outside contractors. In carrying out this responsibility, the director should approve the job specifications, monitor the contractor's performance for adherence to specifications, and approve the contractor's invoice for payment. He should also be involved in the selection of the contractors who will perform the required services.

★   The director of physical plant should be responsible for the maintenance and use scheduling of campus-owned vehicles. Maintenance, service, and use records should be maintained for each vehicle.

★   The director of physical plant should be responsible for the formulation of a campus safety and security program designed to maximize the protection of people and property. The director should obtain input from campus personnel regarding safety and security needs in the formulation of such a program, which should be approved by the administration and the board of trustees. Once the program has been approved, the custodial and grounds crew should be informed of the security regulations agreed on and should be held responsible for reporting instances of noncompliance observed during the performance of their duties (see Decision Matrix 65).

★   Campus security personnel should be provided with the names and duty station assignments of off-hour custodial personnel and be required to ascertain their adherence to established security regulations.

★ The director of physical plant should be responsible for the formulation and monitoring of an energy conservation plan. The plan should take into consideration the operating environmental conditions required by classrooms, laboratories, research facilities, and offices. The plan should be approved by the administration and the board of trustees. Once approved, the plan should be published and promulgated so that all campus personnel are aware of their responsibilities in helping to achieve its energy conservation objectives. Further, custodial staff should be held responsible for reporting instances of noncompliance observed in the performance of their duties (see Decision Matrix 66). Institutions that have sufficient student employees under the College Work-Study Program should consider assigning some of those employees to assist in monitoring compliance with the regulations of the energy conservation plan.

Readers desiring additional information regarding plant operations and maintenance activities should contact the Association of Physical Plant Administrators of Universities and Colleges (APPA), 11 Dupont Circle, Washington, D.C. 20036.

# Decision Matrix 64. Maintenance Services.

Legend of decision-making roles
1 – Authorizes action
2 – Action responsibility
3 – Approves recommendation
4 – Recommends action
5 – Provides input

Participants in Decision-Making Processes

| Procedural Steps | Board of Trustees | Legal Counsel | President | Advisory Committee | Senior Administrators | Department Heads | Chief Fiscal Officer | Physical Plant Director | Maintenance Crew | Custodial Staff | Grounds Crew | Outside Contractors |
|---|---|---|---|---|---|---|---|---|---|---|---|---|
| 1. Inspect all facilities | | | | | | | 2 | 2 | 5 | | | |
| 2. Formulate preventive maintenance program | | | | | | | 3 | 4 | 5 | | | |
| 3. Obtain list of renovation, repair, alteration, and improvement projects covered by authorized budget | | | | | | | 5 | 2 | | | | |
| 4. Establish priority schedule of routine and special projects that can be performed by in-house maintenance crew | | | | | | | 3 | 4 | | | | |
| 5. Establish specifications and schedule for projects to be performed by outside contractors | | | | | | | 3 | 4 | | | | |
| 6. Prepare listing of needed maintenance, identified in step 1, that cannot be carried out with existing resources | | | | | | | 3 | 4 | | | | |
| 7. Review and accept list of maintenance needs that cannot be met | | | 3 | 4 | | | 5 | 5 | | | | |
| 8. Receive president's report of maintenance needs that cannot be met | 2 | | 5 | | | | 5 | 5 | | | | |
| 9. Develop maintenance work orders for ensuing week | | | | | | | | 2 | 5 | | | |
| 10. Obtain approval of cost estimates for work orders to be charged to benefiting department's budget | | | | | 3 | 4 | | 2 | | | | |

|  |  | | | | | | |
|---|---|---|---|---|---|---|---|
| 11. | Receive identification of unforeseen maintenance needs | 5 | 5 | | 2 | | 5 5 |
| 12. | Determine priority of unforeseen needs and revise work-order schedule as necessary | | | 3 | 2 | 5 | 5 5 |
| 13. | Carry out assigned work orders | | | 1 | 1 | 2 | |
| 14. | Solicit bids for work to be performed by outside contractors | 5 | | | | | |
| 15. | Review bids and recommend award of contract | 5 | 2 | | 5 | | |
| 16. | Approve award of contract | | 3 | 4 | 3 | | 5 |
| 17. | Execute contract with successful bidder | | 1 | | 5 | | |
| 18. | Execute contracted work | | | | 2 | | 2 |
| 19. | Monitor contractor's performance and approve contractor's invoices for payment | | | | 2 | | |
| 20. | Log completion of maintenance services provided by in-house staff and contractors in building maintenance log | | | | 2 | | |
| 21. | Prepare interdepartmental charge slips to charge benefiting departments with the cost of special project services provided by in-house staff | | | | 2 | | |
| 22. | Enter interdepartmental charges into accounting records | | | | 5 2 | | |
| 23. | Conduct surprise performance evaluation visits | | | | 2 | | |
| 24. | Evaluate maintenance program and identify ways in which it can be improved | | 3 | | 4 | 5 | |

*Explanation of Decision Matrix 64.*

| *Step* | *Action Responsibility* | *Action* |
|--------|------------------------|----------|
| 1. | Chief Fiscal Officer, Director of Physical Plant, and Maintenance Crew | Inspect all building and grounds facilities and identify nonroutine current or preventive maintenance that should be carried out for their preservation or for safety and security. |
| 2. | Director of Physical Plant and Maintenance Crew Foreman | Formulate recommended routine preventive maintenance programs that should be carried out to keep all utility and building services installations in good working order. |
| | Chief Fiscal Officer | Reviews and approves recommended routine preventive maintenance program. |
| 3. | Director of Physical Plant | Obtains, from the chief fiscal officer, identification of any special maintenance, renovation, alteration, or improvement projects that have been funded through approval of the annual operating budget. |
| 4, 5, & 6. | Director of Physical Plant | Reviews data derived from steps 1, 2, and 3, and prepares a recommended, prioritized schedule of routine maintenance activities and special projects that can be carried out by the in-house maintenance crew, recommended specifications and a prioritized schedule for carry- |

*Explanation of Decision Matrix 64, Cont'd.*

| *Step* | *Action Responsibility* | *Action* |
|--------|------------------------|----------|
| | | ing out authorized special projects that require the services of outside contractors, and a recommended listing of current or preventive maintenance needs, identified in step 1, that cannot be carried out with currently budgeted funding. |
| | Chief Fiscal Officer | Reviews and approves the director of physical plant's recommendation. |
| 7. | Advisory Committee | Reviews listing of unfunded current and preventive maintenance needs prepared by the director of physical plant and the chief fiscal officer. Recommends presidential approval and submission to the board of trustees. |
| | President | Approves the advisory committee's recommendations. |
| 8. | Board of Trustees | Reviews list of unfunded current and preventive maintenance needs, obtaining clarification from the president, the chief fiscal officer, and the director of physical plant, and determines what actions to take to obtain or provide funds to meet these needs. |

*Explanation of Decision Matrix 64, Cont'd.*

| Step | Action Responsibility | Action |
|------|----------------------|--------|
| 9 & 10. | Director of Physical Plant | Prepares, with the assistance of the foreman of the maintenance crew, work orders covering routine or special maintenance tasks to be carried out by the maintenance crew during the ensuing week. Obtains acceptance of cost estimates for special maintenance projects from the department head whose budget is to be charged with the cost of such special maintenance services. |
| 11 & 12. | Director of Physical Plant | Receives identification of unexpected emergency or routine maintenance needs identified by the custodial, grounds, and maintenance staff or department heads in carrying out their responsibilities. Prioritizes the need to meet these unexpected service requirements and revises work schedule and work orders as necessary. |
| 13. | Maintenance Crew | Executes work orders issued by the director of physical plant. |
| 14. | Chief Fiscal Officer | Prepares bid documents for funded special projects to be |

*Explanation of Decision Matrix 64, Cont'd.*

| *Step* | *Action Responsibility* | *Action* |
|---|---|---|
| | | carried out by outside contractors, obtaining agreement as to their completeness and acceptability from legal counsel and the director of physical plant. Solicits bids from qualified contractors. |
| 15. | Chief Fiscal Officer | Reviews bids for special projects received from contractors with legal counsel and the director of physical plant; approves the selection of the successful bidder on the basis of the director of physical plant's recommendation. |
| 16. | Advisory Committee | Reviews bidding results and contract award recommendation submitted by the chief fiscal officer and recommends presidential approval of award of contract. |
| | President | Approves award of contract. |
| 17. | Chief Fiscal Officer | Executes contract with successful bidder when authorized to do so by the president. |
| 18 & 19. | Contractor | Performs work covered by the contract. |

*Explanation of Decision Matrix 64, Cont'd.*

| Step | Action Responsibility | Action |
|------|----------------------|--------|
| | Director of Physical Plant | Monitors contractor's performance and approves contractor's invoices for payment. |
| 20. | Director of Physical Plant | Maintains a log for each building and major utility installation in which he records all routine and special maintenance services provided by either in-house staff or contracted services. |
| 21 & 22. | Director of Physical Plant | Prepares and submits to the chief fiscal officer interdepartmental charge records to charge the cost of special projects to the benefiting department. |
| | Chief Fiscal Officer | Enters special project interdepartmental charges into the accounting records. |
| 23 & 24. | Chief Fiscal Officer and Director of Physical Plant | Periodically conduct joint surprise visits to sites where maintenance crews are assigned to evaluate their effectiveness and efficiency. Develop, with input from the foreman of the maintenance crew, ways in which the delivery of maintenance services can be improved. |

# Decision Matrix 65. Campus Security and Safety.

Legend of decision-making roles:
1 – Authorizes action
2 – Action responsibility
3 – Approves recommendation
4 – Recommends action
5 – Provides input

Participants in Decision-Making Processes

| Procedural Steps | Board of Trustees | Legal Counsel | President | Advisory Committee | Senior Administrators | Department Heads | Student Government | Chief Fiscal Officer | Physical Plant Director | Security Force | Custodial Staff |
|---|---|---|---|---|---|---|---|---|---|---|---|
| 1. Formulate campus security and safety policies and program | | 5 | | | 5 | 5 | 5 | 3 | 4 | 5 | |
| 2. Review and approve recommended policies and program | | 5 | 3 | 4 | | | | 5 | 5 | | |
| 3. Approve policies and program | 2 | | 4 | | | | | 5 | | | |
| 4. Authorize implementation of policies and program | | | 5 | | | | | | | | |
| 5. Plan and schedule implementation | | | | | | | | 1 | 2 | | |
| 6. Carry out security policies and program | | | | | 5 | 5 | 5 | 2 | 2 | 5 | 5 |
| 7. Receive notification of instances of noncompliance with security and safety policies and program | | | | | | | | | 1 | 2 | |
| 8. Determine how corrective action should be taken | | | | | 5 | 5 | 5 | 2 | 4 | 5 | 5 |
| 9. Conduct surprise inspections to evaluate effectiveness of security and safety policies and program | | | | | | | | 2 | 2 | | |
| 10. Evaluate program and identify ways in which it can be improved | | | | | | | | 3 | 4 | 5 | |

*Explanation of Decision Matrix 65.*

| Step | Action Responsibility | Action |
|------|----------------------|--------|
| 1. | Director of Physical Plant | Formulates recommended campus safety and security program based on input from all segments of campus and the chief of the security force. |
| | Chief Fiscal Officer | Reviews and approves recommended campus safety and security program after obtaining legal counsel's input and recommendations. |
| 2. | Advisory Committee | Reviews safety and security program, obtaining clarification from the chief fiscal officer and the director of physical plant. Recommends presidential approval. |
| | President | Approves safety and security program for submission to the board of trustees. |
| 3. | Board of Trustees | Reviews and approves safety and security program recommended by the president, obtaining clarification from legal counsel and the chief fiscal officer. |
| 4. | Director of Physical Plant | Receives, through the chief fiscal officer, the president's authorization to implement approved program. |

*Explanation of Decision Matrix 65, Cont'd.*

| Step | Action Responsibility | Action |
|------|----------------------|--------|
| 5. | Chief Fiscal Officer and Director of Physical Plant | Jointly conduct workshops to acquaint all campus constituencies with the requirements of the approved campus safety and security program, the planned implementation schedule, and each constituency's related responsibilities. |
| 6. | Security Force | Carries out the safety and security program under the direction of the director of physical plant. |
| 7 & 8. | Director of Physical Plant | Receives notification of violations of safety and security program requirements and advises the chief fiscal officer of those where corrective action beyond the director of physical plant's authority is required. |
| | Chief Fiscal Officer | Determines how required corrective action should be taken after obtaining the director of physical plant's recommendations. |
| 9 & 10. | Chief Fiscal Officer and Director of Physical Plant | Jointly conduct surprise inspection of security force operations and such other inspections as are needed to evaluate the effectiveness of the security and safety program, and identify ways in which the program can be improved. |

**Decision Matrix 66. Energy Conservation.**

Legend of decision-making roles
1 – Authorizes action
2 – Action responsibility
3 – Approves recommendation
4 – Recommends action
5 – Provides input

| Procedural Steps | Board of Trustees | President | Advisory Committee | Senior Administrators | Department Heads | Faculty and Staff | Student Government | Chief Fiscal Officer | Physical Plant Director | Security Force | Custodial Staff | Maintenance Crew | Grounds Crew |
|---|---|---|---|---|---|---|---|---|---|---|---|---|---|
| 1. Review energy usage records | | | | 5 | 5 | 5 | 5 | 5 | 2 | 5 | 5 | 5 | 5 |
| 2. Formulate plan for energy conservation | | 3 | 4 | 5 | 5 | 5 | 5 | 3 | 4 | | | | |
| 3. Review and approve recommended plan | 2 | 4 | | | | | | 5 | 5 | | | | |
| 4. Approve implementation of plan | | 5 | | | | | | 5 | 2 | | | | |
| 5. Receive authorization to implement plan | | | | | | | | 1 | 2 | | | | |
| 6. Promulgate plan to all campus constituencies | | | | 5 | 5 | 5 | 5 | 2 | 2 | 5 | 5 | 5 | 5 |
| 7. Monitor energy usage records | | | | | | | | 5 | | 5 | 5 | 5 | 5 |
| 8. Receive notification of instances of noncompliance with plan | | | | 5 | 5 | 5 | 5 | | 2 | 5 | 5 | 5 | 5 |
| 9. Determine how corrective action should be taken | | | | | | | | 2 | 4 | | | | |

*Explanation of Decision Matrix 66.*

| Step | Action Responsibility | Action |
|------|----------------------|--------|
| 1 & 2. | Director of Physical Plant | Reviews energy usage history data provided by the chief fiscal officer. Formulates a recommended energy conservation plan after obtaining input from all campus constituencies. |
| | Chief Fiscal Officer | Reviews and approves recommended energy conservation plan. |
| 3. | Advisory Committee | Reviews recommended energy conservation plan and recommends presidential approval. |
| | President | Approves energy conservation plan. |
| 4. | President | Presents energy conservation plan to the board of trustees and recommends its adoption. |
| | Board of Trustees | Reviews energy conservation plan, obtaining such clarification as it deems appropriate, and approves its adoption. |
| 5. | Director of Physical Plant | Receives, through the chief fiscal officer, the president's authorization to implement the approved energy conservation plan. |

*Explanation of Decision Matrix 66, Cont'd.*

| Step | Action Responsibility | Action |
|------|----------------------|--------|
| 6. | Chief Fiscal Officer and Director of Physical Plant | Jointly conduct workshops to acquaint all campus constituencies with the requirements of the energy conservation plan, its schedule of implementation, and their related responsibilities. |
| 7. | Director of Physical Plant | Monitors implementation of the energy conservation plan and energy usage records and evaluates its effectiveness. |
| 8 & 9. | Director of Physical Plant | Receives notification of violations of the energy conservation plan requirements and advises the chief fiscal officer of those where corrective action beyond the director of physical plant's authority is required. |
| | Chief Fiscal Officer | Determines how required corrective action should be taken, having obtained the director of physical plant's recommendations. |

## Decision Matrix 67. Custodial Services.

Legend of decision-making roles
1 – Authorizes action
2 – Action responsibility
3 – Approves recommendation
4 – Recommends action
5 – Provides input

| Procedural Steps | President | Advisory Committee | Senior Administrators | Department Heads | Chief Fiscal Officer | Physical Plant Director | Custodial Staff |
|---|---|---|---|---|---|---|---|
| 1. Formulate custodial standards for each building on campus | 2 | | 5 | 5 | 3 | 4 | 5 |
| 2. Review and approve standards | 5 | 4 | 5 | 5 | 5 | | |
| 3. Receive authorization to implement standards | | | | | 1 | 2 | |
| 4. Train custodial staff | | | | | | 2 | 5 |
| 5. Provide custodial services | | | | | | 1 | 2 |
| 6. Conduct surprise visits to monitor performance of custodial staff | | | | | 2 | 2 | |
| 7. Evaluate custodial services and identify ways in which they can be improved | | | 5 | 5 | 3 | 4 | 5 |

*Participants in Decision-Making Processes*

*Explanation of Decision Matrix 67.*

| Step | Action Responsibility | Action |
|------|----------------------|--------|
| 1. | Director of Physical Plant | Formulates custodial standards applicable to each building after obtaining input regarding the service requirements of its occupants. |
| | Chief Fiscal Officer | Reviews and approves recommended custodial standards. |
| 2. | Advisory Committee | Reviews recommended custodial standards and recommends presidential approval. |
| | President | Approves recommended custodial standards. |
| 3 & 4. | Director of Physical Plant | Receives, through the chief fiscal officer, the president's authorization to implement approved custodial standards and trains the custodians regarding what they must do to meet the standards. Also trains the custodians regarding their responsibility to report maintenance, safety, and security problems they observe while carrying out their assigned tasks. |
| 5. | Custodial Staff | Provide required custodial services under the direction of the director of physical plant. |

*Explanation of Decision Matrix 67, Cont'd.*

| Step | Action Responsibility | Action |
|------|----------------------|--------|
| 6 & 7. | Chief Fiscal Officer and Director of Physical Plant | Jointly conduct surprise visits to sites where custodial services are being performed to evaluate the efficiency and effectiveness of custodial staff. Formulate ways in which the delivery of such services can be improved after obtaining input regarding satisfaction with custodial services from the building occupants. |

**Decision Matrix 68. Grounds Care Services.**

Legend of decision-making roles
1 - Authorizes action
2 - Action responsibility
3 - Approves recommendation
4 - Recommends action
5 - Provides input

| Procedural Steps | President | Advisory Committee | Chief Fiscal Officer | Physical Plant Director | Grounds Crew |
|---|---|---|---|---|---|
| | | | Participants in Decision-Making Processes | | |
| 1. Formulate grounds care program | 2 | 4 | 3 | 4 | 5 |
| 2. Review and approve recommended program | 5 | | | 5 | 5 |
| 3. Receive authorization to implement program | | | 1 | 2 | |
| 4. Train grounds care crew | | | | 2 | 5 |
| 5. Provide grounds care services | | | | 1 | 2 |
| 6. Conduct surprise inspections to evaluate performance of grounds crew | | | 2 | 2 | |
| 7. Evaluate program and identify ways in which it can be improved | | | 3 | 4 | 5 |

*Explanation of Decision Matrix 68.*

| Step | Action Responsibility | Action |
|---|---|---|
| 1. | Director of Physical Plant | Formulates recommended program and schedule for the care of campus grounds after obtaining input from the foreman of the grounds crew. |
| | Chief Fiscal Officer | Reviews and approves grounds care program. |
| 2. | Advisory Committee | Reviews recommended grounds care program and recommends presidential approval. |
| | President | Approves grounds care program. |
| 3 & 4. | Director of Physical Plant | Receives, through the chief fiscal officer, the president's authorization to implement the approved grounds care program and trains grounds crew personnel regarding the schedule and standards to be maintained and their responsibility to report maintenance, safety, or security problems they observe while performing their assigned tasks. |
| 5. | Grounds Crew | Provides scheduled grounds care services under the direction of the director of physical plant. |

*Explanation of Decision Matrix 68, Cont'd.*

| Step | Action Responsibility | Action |
|------|----------------------|--------|
| 6 & 7. | Chief Fiscal Officer and Director of Physical Plant | Jointly conduct surprise visits to sites where grounds crew personnel are working to evaluate their performance and identify ways in which delivery of grounds care services can be improved. |

# Auxiliary
# Enterprises

Auxiliary enterprises sell services that are required to support the institution's basic educational purpose. They include the bookstore or student store, the student union, student housing, faculty and staff housing, food service, and intercollegiate athletics. Each of these activities is administered by a director or a manager who, except for the director of student housing, reports to the chief fiscal officer. As Chapter Eight shows, the responsibility for the management of student housing operations is normally divided, the chief student affairs officer's staff being responsible for housing assignments and dormitory supervision and the chief fiscal officer for fiscal, maintenance, and custodial matters related to dormitory operation. Essential standards of good management applicable to all of the aforementioned auxiliary enterprise activities are presented first in this chapter; essential standards specifically related to each activity's operation follow.

Auxiliary enterprise revenues and expenditures are reported as separate subsections of the institution's operating statements. This permits easy identification of whether or not they are at least breaking even. Auxiliary enterprise operations as a group should be designed, at a minimum, to be self-sustaining so that they do not become a drain on other operating resources.

## General Essential Standards

The following essential standards of good management are applicable to all auxiliary enterprise operations.

★   Revenue projections and expenditure budgets should be prepared for each auxiliary enterprise and included as a separately identified component in the institution's annual operating budget. These expenditure budgets should include all elements of the expected cost of operations — that is, those that are directly controllable by the directors or managers of the enterprise as well as the allocated cost of utilities, services, insurance, debt service, and the like, which are not under their direct control. The revenue projections and expenditure budgets should reflect, if applicable, the gross cost of goods purchased for resale and the gross revenue derived from such resale.

★   All expenditures attributable to the operation of auxiliary enterprises should be accounted for as part of the cost of their operation. Expenditures that can be directly attributed to such operations should be accounted for as direct costs. Other costs, where the enterprise contributes to the total cost incurred by the institution, should be allocated to the cost of its operation. Such allocations should be made periodically, at least once each semester or school term. The bases for each such allocation should account for 100 percent of the cost incurred by the institution to ensure that the total cost incurred is equitably shared by all activities that contributed to the cost. The bases of allocation should be reviewed and revised, if necessary, each year. They should also be documented and maintained on file in the accounting office.

★   Policies and procedures for the provision by auxiliary enterprises of special services to other institutional users or external users should be adhered to. The director or manager of the enterprise involved should be required to obtain the approval of the chief fiscal officer for the prices to be charged for such special services (see Decision Matrix 69).

★ Where costs are incurred by an auxiliary enterprise as the result of providing services to another operating unit of the institution, the cost of providing the services should be borne by the operating unit that requested the services. For example, should the president request the director of food services to provide a special meal for visiting dignitaries, the cost of so doing should be charged to the budget of the president's office.

★ The chief fiscal officer should be responsible for formulating policies and procedures to be followed by the directors or managers of auxiliary enterprises in their direct purchasing of goods for resale. All other equipment or material required in the operation of the enterprise should be purchased in the regular manner through the institution's central purchasing operation.

★ All proceeds from cash sales made by auxiliary enterprise operations should be transmitted daily by the director or manager to the cashier, together with the documentation required to record the receipts properly in the institution's accounting records. The chief fiscal officer is responsible for determining the extent and nature of the documentation required for such transactions. It is also desirable that the chief fiscal officer or his representative conduct periodic surprise audits of auxiliary enterprise cash operations.

★ Operating imprest funds required by auxiliary enterprises to conduct their operations should be returned each day to the business office for safekeeping unless the chief fiscal officer is satisfied that adequate facilities for the safekeeping of such funds exist under the control of the director or manager of the unit involved.

★ The chief fiscal officer should be responsible for seeing that adequate, secure storage areas are available for the storage of goods purchased for resale and that adequate inventory control records are maintained to account properly for their use or sale. Such records should be similar to those required in central stores operation. A physical inventory count and valuation of auxiliary enterprise inventories likewise should be conducted at least once a year.

★ The directors or managers of auxiliary enterprise units should be responsible for maintaining statistical and operating records that permit the fiscal office to account properly for the revenues, expenditures, and financial results of their operations. They should also be responsible for providing the chief fiscal officer with management information that enables him to evaluate the enterprises' performance properly.

★ All auxiliary enterprise operations that are carried out by a third party should be covered by a contract. Such contracts, at a minimum, should identify the costs, performance, and services for which each party is responsible; the pricing of services and the procedures to be followed in agreeing on the pricing of services not specifically covered by the contract; the extent, nature, format, content, and frequency of the reports to be submitted to the institution by the contractor; and how the profits realized by the contractor will be shared with the institution.

★ Whether auxiliary enterprise operations are conducted on an in-house or contract basis, consumer input regarding satisfaction with services being provided should be obtained regularly. To facilitate obtaining such input, an institution should consider formulating a campus-based committee, representative of all consumer groups, to be charged with the responsibility of providing the administration with a periodic assessment of the operation of each major auxiliary enterprise.

### Bookstore or Student Store

Bookstore or student store operations are, for many smaller institutions, difficult to operate on a break-even basis. This is often the result of circumstances beyond the bookstore manager's control. Adherence to the following essential standards of good management, however, should enhance the institution's ability to make this operation self-sustaining.

★ Policies and procedures for the determination of text-books to be acquired to support the institution's instructional programs, as well as their retention and return, should be adhered to. For smaller institutions, the handling of textbook ordering and sales is frequently the cause of bookstore or student store operating losses. Causes for such losses include the failure of faculty to specify textbooks to be ordered in time for the manager to have them in stock at the beginning of classes, when they are most needed and easiest to sell; faculty decisions to change a textbook when the stock of a previously specified textbook has been retained because it was to be used for more than one term or year; the failure of faculty to require students actually to obtain textbooks that are required for a course; competition from nearby bookstores that sell used copies of required textbooks; overestimating the number of students that will enroll in various courses; and the failure to return unsold books for credit within the time limit allowed by the publishers.

★ A policy should exist regarding the extent to which the bookstore or student store will compete with nearby noncampus vendors of nontextbook items. This standard is not intended to preclude such competition but rather to point out that its extent should be considered with regard to the institution's town-gown relationship. The taxable nature of such transactions should be considered in the formulation of such a policy.

★ All persons entering the bookstore or student store should be required to leave briefcases, bookbags, and packages outside the store area. Facilities for the temporary storage of such items should be provided immediately outside the entrance to the bookstore or student store.

★ Faculty and staff should not be granted special discounts for purchases made through the bookstore or student store.

★ The bookstore or student store should not extend credit, other than as authorized by the business office for student purchase of required textbooks and classroom supplies, to faculty, staff, or students.

★  The records maintained by the manager for accounting or operational reporting should identify transactions related to the sale of textbooks separately from the sale of other items.

The recommended processes to be followed in bookstore or student store operations are set forth in Decision Matrix 70.

### Food Service

Many institutions have opted to have their food service operations conducted by an outside contractor, while others still run their own campus-based food service. Very successful examples of both types of operation exist; therefore, I cannot recommend one type over the other. However, regardless of whether the delivery of food service is conducted as an in-house or contracted operation, the administration has a responsibility to see that it is properly managed. The following essential standards are applicable to either type of operation.

★  The chief fiscal officer should be responsible for the administration of all activities related to the control and issuance of meal tickets. Where food service is conducted as an in-house operation, the chief fiscal officer should see that periodic surprise audits of food service operations are conducted to ensure that meals are not being served to unauthorized students.

★  The chief fiscal officer and the chief student affairs officer, acting jointly, should be responsible for establishing the criteria for food service operation. The establishment of these criteria should be based on input from the director of food services or the contractor's manager. They should include quality standards for food to be served, meal cycles, the number of entrees to be served at each meal, a policy on serving second helpings, and the hours of food service operation.

★  Food service facilities should be inspected periodically for sanitary conditions by the director of health services.

★ Food service operations should not be required to provide special meals or additional food for athletes unless the additional cost is borne by the intercollegiate athletic budget.

★ Credit should not be extended to faculty, staff, or students for food service provided in the regular dining room or snack bars.

★ Where certain employees are provided with free meals as a part of their compensation, the value of the meals should be reported to the director of personnel for inclusion as a non-cash benefit when the employees' compensation is considered for the purpose of wage and salary administration.

The recommended processes to be followed in food service operations are set forth in Decision Matrix 71.

## Student Housing

The responsibility for managing student housing facilities should be shared by the chief student affairs officer and the chief fiscal officer. In general, the chief student affairs officer should be responsible for occupancy assignments, dormitory supervision, and specifying the level of custodial and maintenance services to be provided. The chief fiscal officer should be responsible for administering the delivery of custodial and maintenance services through the director of physical plant and for the fiscal affairs related to student housing operations. The essential standards of good management related to student housing operations are set forth below.

★ The chief fiscal officer and the chief student affairs officer, acting jointly, should be responsible for the formulation of policies related to student housing operations. These policies should be approved by the administration, adopted by the board of trustees, published and promulgated, and enforced by the board. They should cover, at the least, requirements related to room deposits prior to registration, visitation privileges, penalties related to unauthorized occupancy, requirements for student residents to check in and check out, what constitutes unacceptable behavior, the use of public areas, and students' rights to have food storage or preparation appliances in their room. Adequate on-site, around-the-clock supervision should be provided in each dormitory unit to monitor adherence to the established policies. While it cannot be said to be essential, if an institution requires certain categories of students to live in on-campus housing, that requirement should be adopted as a policy. For example, many institutions require that all noncommuting freshmen and sophomores live in on-campus dormitories. However, a number of campuses that have such a policy also have a substantial number of foreign students who do not desire to live in on-campus dormitories for a variety of reasons. Under these circumstances, the institution should carefully consider the extent to which it can or wishes to enforce such a policy. If the institution determines that it cannot or does not wish to enforce such a policy, its policy statement should be amended to exclude foreign students from the categories of students to which the policy is applicable.

★ A policy also should be formulated regarding the use of student housing facilities by off-campus groups when such facilities are not being occupied by students or when housing units are not required to meet student demand for housing.

★ Students residing in campus-owned or -operated housing facilities should be required to provide the institution with a damage deposit to cover the cost of repairing damage caused by vandalism, carelessness, or malicious mischief. The institution's right to use such deposits to cover costs in cases where the students responsible for causing the damage cannot be identified should be established as a policy.

★ The cost of providing student housing to athletes during periods when dormitory occupancy is not covered by the regular housing fee should be charged to the intercollegiate athletic budget.

The processes to be followed in conducting student housing operations are set forth in Decision Matrix 72.

## Faculty and Staff Housing

Many institutions own housing units that they rent to certain faculty and staff. Such units may be required to house staff whose services may be required on an emergency or around-the-clock basis (such as the director of physical plant), faculty on their initial term of appointment until they can make other housing arrangements, or faculty on short-term appointments who should not be expected to make their own housing arrangements. Housing provided the president or other key administrators as a part of their compensation package is not covered by this section. The essential standards of good management in the operation of faculty and staff housing units are set forth below.

★ The chief fiscal officer should be responsible for managing all aspects of faculty and staff housing units except for the determination of who should be entitled to occupy them. The determination of who should be entitled to occupy the units should be made by the president.

★ Policies governing the operation of faculty and staff rental housing units should be formulated by the chief fiscal officer. The policies should be approved by the administration and adopted by the board of trustees. They should cover the purposes for which such housing is to be used, the limit on the duration of occupancy by any one tenant, and the occupancy rights of faculty or staff whose appointments are terminated, for any reason, prior to the expiration of the duration limit of occupancy they were given at the time of appointment.

★ The conditions of occupancy of each faculty or staff housing unit should be covered by a lease or rental agreement executed by the occupant and the chief fiscal officer. The terms and conditions of the lease or rental agreement should be competitive with those applicable to similar units in the competitive marketplace. They should not be used as a subsidization or a means of circumventing the compensation range agreed on for a position. Each faculty and staff housing unit should be separately metered for utilities and the occupant required to pay for utility services. Occupants should also be required to arrange for the installation of telephone services, which should not go through the campus switchboard. The institution, however, should render such assistance as the occupant may require in obtaining the installation desired.

★ Faculty and staff occupying institutionally owned rental housing units should be required to authorize the deduction of required rent payments from their paychecks if they fail to make such payments.

Although housing provided the president and other key administrators as part of their compensation package is excluded from this section because it does not constitute an auxiliary enterprise operation, the following essential standards of good management should be followed with regard to such housing.

★ The cost of operating and maintaining such units should be budgeted and accounted for as a part of the cost of the operational entity for which the occupant is responsible.

★ The chief fiscal officer and the president, acting jointly, should be responsible for formulating policies related to the occupants' or their families' right of continued occupancy in the event of death or retirement.

The recommended processes to be followed in the operation of faculty and staff housing units are set forth in Decision Matrix 73.

### Student Union

Like the operation of student housing, the operation of the student union should be shared between the chief student affairs officer and the chief fiscal officer. The director of the student union, who should report to the chief student affairs officer, should be responsible for scheduling the use of the facilities, monitoring activities that take place in the facilities, and specifying the level of custodial care and maintenance required. The chief fiscal officer should be responsible for all fiscal matters related to the student union's operation and, through the director of physical plant, for seeing that the specified custodial and maintenance services are delivered.

The essential standards of good management applicable to the student union are set forth below.

★   Charges to cover the cost of the use of the student union by students and student organizations should be covered by either a special student union fee or an allocation of a portion of the assessed comprehensive fee to the student union revenue account.

★   The chief fiscal officer and the chief student affairs officer, acting jointly, should be responsible for the formulation of policies and procedures covering the use of the student union facilities by campus-based organizations or third-party organizations. The policies formulated should be approved by the administration and adopted by the board of trustees.

★   Third-party users and the budgets of campus-based users should be charged for the use of the student union at rates jointly established by the chief fiscal officer and the chief student affairs officer.

The processes that should be followed in the operation of the student union are set forth in Decision Matrix 74.

## Parking

The essential standards of good management applicable to the control of campus parking are set forth below.

★   No student, faculty member, or staff member should be permitted to park on campus without authorization. Authorization should be covered by a parking sticker showing the period for which authorization has been granted. This sticker should be required to be prominently displayed on the vehicle. The campus security force should be assigned the responsibility of seeing that unauthorized vehicles do not park on campus.

★ Students, faculty, and staff should be required to register their vehicles with the business office and provide proof that third-party liability insurance is in force before they are granted authorization to park on campus.

★ Vehicular access to campus should be controlled and designated parking places for visitors to campus should be provided.

★ A fee should be charged each semester or academic term for on-campus parking privileges.

The processes applicable to the management of on-campus parking are set forth in Decision Matrix 75.

### Intercollegiate Athletics

Intercollegiate athletics are an expensive operation that is seldom self-supporting for smaller institutions. Each institution that has an intercollegiate athletic program should evaluate the contribution the program makes to its educational goals and objectives and determine whether that contribution is worth the investment of resources required to operate the program. The intercollegiate athletic program should be administered by a director of athletics, who should report to the chief fiscal officer.

The essential standards of good management applicable to intercollegiate athletics are set forth below.

★ Policies related to the operation of the intercollegiate athletic program should be formulated by a standing committee. This committee should be chaired by the director of athletics and its membership should include student, faculty, and administration representatives, who should be appointed for terms varying from two to five years. Such varying term appointments will permit both change in membership and continuity of program. The committee's policy recommendations should be approved by the administration and adopted by the board of trustees. Policies should cover the definition of prioritized, joint use of equipment, facilities, and staff by the intercollegiate athletic program, the physical education academic program, intramural sports, and student recreational programs; the number and types of sports in which the institution will compete; the identification of the conference with which the institution will be affiliated or whether it will maintain an independent status; how the program will be staffed; criteria and procedures of employment where coaching staff also serve as physical education faculty members, including their eligibility for tenure; scheduling events to minimize conflicts with registration and examinations; academic standards for student athletes, including requirements for eligibility to participate in athletic competition; athletic scholarships; fiscal policies; special health care and insurance requirements; and indemnification against lawsuits resulting from accidents or injuries suffered by student athletes. With regard to the employment of coaching staff, the policy should require joint concurrence in selecting people to be employed. The director of financial aid should participate in the formulation of athletic scholarship policies and the administration of the award of scholarships. The fiscal policies related to the intercollegiate athletic program should be consistent with those required for other institutional operating units, including the requirement that the intercollegiate program bear all direct and indirect costs associated with its activities (see Decision Matrix 76).

★ The director of athletics should be responsible for the administration of the intercollegiate athletic program in accordance with approved policies and procedures. The director should see that checklists are prepared for each sport identifying the many details involved in the management of athletic contests. The checklists should include, at the least, the identification of equipment and supplies required; transportation, housing, and meal arrangements; and medical care and transportation arrangements. The head coach of each sport should be assigned the responsibility of seeing that all required details are taken care of before each contest (see Decision Matrix 77).

★ Fund-raising activities to support the intercollegiate athletic program should be coordinated with the chief development officer and all gifts received should be processed through the development office.

★ The fiscal office should be responsible for the accounting of all receipts and disbursements related to the operation of the intercollegiate athletic program. Any additional costs incurred by the fiscal officer in carrying out this responsibility — such as for staffing ticket sales booths at the gate or making special deposit arrangements — should be charged to the intercollegiate athletic program budget. The intercollegiate athletic program budget should also bear its share of the cost of operating and maintaining the plant and equipment it uses.

★ The head coaches, under the supervision of the director of athletics, should be responsible for inventory control of athletic equipment and supplies. A physical inventory of equipment and supplies should be prepared annually and transmitted to the chief fiscal officer by the director of athletics.

Readers wishing additional information regarding the operation of auxiliary enterprises should contact the National Association of College and University Business Officers (NAC-UBO), One Dupont Circle, Washington, D.C. 20036.

*Explanation of Decision Matrix 69.*

| Step | Action Responsibility | Action |
|------|----------------------|--------|
| 1. | Chief Fiscal Officer | Formulates recommended policies and procedures to be followed in the use of campus facilities by either internal or external organizations or users on the basis of input from the chief academic affairs officer, the chief student affairs officer, the chief development officer, the director of the student union, the director of food service, the director of student housing, and the director of physical plant. |
| 2. | Advisory Committee | Reviews recommended policies and procedures for adequacy and potential impact on operations. Recommends presidential approval. |
|  | President | Approves the advisory committee's recommendation. |
| 3. | President | Submits recommended policies to the board of trustees with his recommendation for adoption. |
|  | Board of Trustees | Reviews and approves recommended policies, obtaining clarification from the president and chief fiscal officer. |

## Decision Matrix 69. Delivery of Special Services by Auxiliary Enterprise Units.

Legend of decision-making roles
1 – Authorizes action
2 – Action responsibility
3 – Approves recommendation
4 – Recommends action
5 – Provides input

*Participants in Decision-Making Processes*

| Procedural Steps | Board of Trustees | President | Advisory Committee | Chief Academic Officer | Chief Student Affairs Officer | Chief Fiscal Officer | Chief Development Officer | Student Union Director | Food Service Director | Housing Director | Physical Plant Director | Cashier | Department Heads | External Organizations |
|---|---|---|---|---|---|---|---|---|---|---|---|---|---|---|
| 1. Formulate policies and procedures covering delivery of special services by auxiliary enterprise units | | 3 | 4 | 5 | 5 | 2 | 5 | 5 | 5 | 5 | 5 | | | |
| 2. Review and approve policies and procedures | | 4 | | | 5 | 5 | | | | | | | | |
| 3. Adopt recommended policies | 2 | | | | | 5 | | | | | | | | |
| 4. Authorize implementation of policies and procedures | | 1 | | | | | | | | | | | | |
| 5. Distribute policies and procedures | | | | | 2 | 2 | | | | | | | | |
| 6. Make preliminary arrangements for special services | | | | | 2 | 2 | | | | | | | 5 | |
| 7. Review and approve arrangements | | | | | 4 | 3 | 5 | 5 | 5 | 5 | 5 | | 5 | 5 |

8. Update master calendar for approved events    2

9. Execute written agreement covering special services requested    2

10. Provide special services and prepare charge slips    1   2   2   2   2

11. Approve charge slips    2   5   5   5   5

12. Enter internal charge slips into the accounting records    2

13. Prepare and transmit invoices to external organizations    2

14. Receive and issue receipt for payment    1   2   5

*Explanation of Decision Matrix 69, Cont'd.*

| Step | Action Responsibility | Action |
|------|----------------------|--------|
| 4. | President | Authorizes the chief fiscal officer to implement approved policies and procedures. |
| 5. | Chief Fiscal Officer | Distributes approved policies and procedures to those administrators who may be involved in providing special services. |
| 6. | Chief Student Affairs Officer | Receives request for special services from internal or external organizations and verifies against the master calendar that the requested date for the event does not conflict with other scheduled events. Obtains input, from the directors of the auxiliary enterprise units and the director of physical plant who will be involved in delivery of the requested services, regarding the arrangements required and projected cost. |
| 7. | Chief Fiscal Officer | Reviews and approves proposed special services arrangements and cost estimates recommended by the chief student affairs officer. |
| 8. | Chief Student Affairs Officer | Schedules the special services events on the master calendar. |

*Explanation of Decision Matrix 69, Cont'd.*

| Step | Action Responsibility | Action |
|------|----------------------|--------|
| 9. | Chief Fiscal Officer | Executes written agreement with the internal or external requester setting forth the services to be provided and the related terms and conditions. |
| 10. | Directors of Auxiliary Enterprise Units and Director of Physical Plant | Receive copies of the agreement executed and provide agreed-on services. Prepare charge slips covering services rendered. |
| 11. | Chief Fiscal Officer | Approves charge slips submitted by those who have provided special services. |
| 12 & 13. | Chief Fiscal Officer | Enters charges to internal users of special services into the accounting records as charges against their budgets. Prepares and transmits invoice covering special services to external users. |
| 14. | Chief Fiscal Officer | Receives payment from external users and instructs cashier to issue receipt for payment. |

# Decision Matrix 70. Bookstore or Student Store Operations.

**Legend of decision-making roles**
1 – Authorizes action
2 – Action responsibility
3 – Approves recommendation
4 – Recommends action
5 – Provides input

*Participants in Decision-Making Processes*

| Procedural Steps | Board of Trustees | President | Advisory Committee | Chief Academic Officer | Department Heads | Faculty | Chief Fiscal Officer | Bookstore Manager | Students | Other Purchasers | Cashier | Student Accounts Receivable Clerk | Registrar |
|---|---|---|---|---|---|---|---|---|---|---|---|---|---|
| 1. Develop bookstore or student store operating policies and procedures | | 3 | 4 | 5 | 5 | 5 | 2 | 5 | 5 | | | | |
| 2. Review and approve policies and procedures | | 4 | 4 | 5 | 5 | 5 | 5 | 5 | | | | | |
| 3. Adopt recommended policies | 2 | | | | | | 5 | | | | | | |
| 4. Authorize implementation of policies and procedures | | 1 | | | | | | | | | | | |
| 5. Distribute policies and procedures | | | | | | | 2 | | | | | | |
| 6. Identify textbooks to be purchased | | | | 3 | 4 | 5 | 2 | 5 | | | | | |
| 7. Purchase textbooks | | | | 1 | 1 | | | 2 | | | | | |
| 8. Identify other items to be purchased | | | | | | | 3 | 4 | 5 | | | | |
| 9. Purchase other items for resale | | | | | | | 1 | 2 | | | | | |
| 10. Issue authorization for students to buy books on credit | | | | | | | 2 | | | | | | |
| 11. Advise students regarding textbooks required for class | | | | | | 2 | | | | | | | |

|  |  | | | | | | | | |
|-----|------|--|--|--|--|--|--|--|--|
| 12. | Provide bookstore manager with class enrollment rosters | | | | | | | | 2 |
| 13. | Operate bookstore | 5 | | 2 | 2 | 5 | 5 | | |
| 14. | Maintain sales activity and fiscal records | | | 2 | | | | | |
| 15. | Receive daily cash receipts and activity and fiscal records | | | 5 | 5 | | 2 | | |
| 16. | Update student accounts receivable records for credit and purchases | | 2 | 5 | 5 | | | 2 | |
| 17. | Update accounting records and issue monthly budget status report | | 2 | 2 | 5 | | | | |
| 18. | Receive unsold textbook inventory listing | 2 | | 5 | 5 | | | | |
| 19. | Return unsold textbooks to suppliers | 1 | 4 | 5 | 2 | 2 | | | |
| 20. | Receive periodic bookstore or student store management report | | 2 | 2 | 5 | | | | |
| 21. | Conduct surprise audits of bookstore or student store operations | | 2 | 2 | | | | | |
| 22. | Evaluate bookstore or student store operations | 5 | 5 | 5 | 5 | 5 | 5 | 5 | |

*Explanation of Decision Matrix 70.*

| Step | Action Responsibility | Action |
|------|----------------------|--------|
| 1. | Chief Fiscal Officer | Formulates recommended policies and procedures covering bookstore or student store operations with input from the chief academic officer, academic department heads, faculty, the bookstore manager, and students. |
| 2. | Advisory Committee | Reviews recommended policies and procedures submitted by the chief fiscal officer for appropriateness and potential impact on other operations. Recommends presidential approval. |
| | President | Approves the advisory committee's recommendations. |
| 3. | President | Submits recommended policies to the board of trustees with his recommendation for adoption. |
| | Board of Trustees | Reviews and approves recommended policies, obtaining clarification from the president and the chief fiscal officer. |
| 4 & 5. | Chief Fiscal Officer | Receives the president's authorization to implement |

*Explanation of Decision Matrix 70, Cont'd.*

| Step | Action Responsibility | Action |
|------|----------------------|--------|
| | | policies and procedures and distributes them to academic administrators, faculty, and the bookstore manager. |
| 6. | Chief Academic Officer | On the basis of faculty requests submitted through and recommended by department heads, approves textbooks to be purchased after reviewing existing textbook inventory with the bookstore manager. |
| 7. | Bookstore Manager | Purchases textbooks authorized by the chief academic officer. |
| 8. | Chief Fiscal Officer | Reviews and approves purchase of nontextbook items for resale as recommended by the bookstore manager after receiving input from students regarding items they desire to have stocked. |
| 9. | Bookstore Manager | Purchases nontextbook items for resale when authorized to do so by the chief fiscal officer. |
| 10. | Chief Fiscal Officer | Issues purchase authorization forms to students requiring credit to buy textbooks. |

*Explanation of Decision Matrix 70, Cont'd.*

| Step | Action Responsibility | Action |
|------|----------------------|--------|
| 11. | Faculty | Advises students of the textbooks they are required to have for courses for which they are enrolled. |
| 12. | Bookstore Manager | Receives roster of classes for which each student is enrolled from the registrar. |
| 13 & 14. | Bookstore Manager | Operates the bookstore and maintains required sales activity, inventory control, and fiscal records. |
| 15. | Cashier | Processes daily cash receipts and related fiscal reports received from the bookstore manager. Issues cashier receipt for cash received from the bookstore manager. |
| 16. | Chief Fiscal Officer | Receives from the bookstore manager a daily accounting of textbooks issued to students against credit authorizations and records transactions in appropriate general ledger control accounts. |
| | Student Accounts Receivable Clerk | Receives student account charge slips from the bookstore manager and enters charges into the |

*Explanation of Decision Matrix 70, Cont'd.*

| Step | Action Responsibility | Action |
|------|----------------------|--------|
| | | students' accounts in the student accounts receivable subsidiary records. |
| 17. | Chief Fiscal Officer | Processes bookstore receipt and disbursement transactions and provides the bookstore manager with a monthly budget status report reflecting such transactions and credit sale transactions for textbooks issued to students. |
| 18 & 19. | Chief Academic Officer | Receives inventory of unsold textbooks from the bookstore manager. Obtains recommendations from department heads, based on input from their faculty, regarding which textbooks should be retained and which should be returned to the supplier. Approves departmental recommendations. |
| | Bookstore Manager | Returns unneeded textbooks to suppliers on the receipt of the chief academic officer's authorization to do so. |
| 20 & 21. | Chief Fiscal Officer | Receives periodic bookstore activity reports prepared by |

*Explanation of Decision Matrix 70, Cont'd.*

| Step | Action Responsibility | Action |
|------|----------------------|--------|
|      |                      | the bookstore manager. Conducts periodic surprise audits of bookstore operations. |
| 22.  | Chief Fiscal Officer | Analyzes bookstore operations, obtaining input regarding services provided from students, faculty, and academic administrators, and identifies ways in which services can be improved. |

*Explanation of Decision Matrix 71.*

| Step | Action Responsibility | Action |
|------|----------------------|--------|
| 1. | Chief Fiscal Officer and Chief Student Affairs Officer | Formulate recommended policies and procedures covering food service operations, using input from the director of food service, users (students, faculty, and staff), and the director of physical plant (for custodial and maintenance requirements). |
| 2. | Advisory Committee | Reviews recommended policies and procedures submitted by the chief fiscal officer and chief student affairs officer for appropriateness and recommends presidential approval. |
| | President | Approves the advisory committee's recommendation. |
| 3. | President | Submits policies to the board of trustees with his recommendation for their adoption. |
| | Board of Trustees | Reviews and adopts recommended policies, obtaining clarification from the president, the chief fiscal officer, and the chief student affairs officer. |
| 4 & 5. | Chief Fiscal Officer | Receives the president's authorization to implement approved policies and procedures and distributes them |

## Decision Matrix 71. Food Service Operations.

Legend of decision-making roles
1 – Authorizes action
2 – Action responsibility
3 – Approves recommendation
4 – Recommends action
5 – Provides input

| Procedural Steps | Board of Trustees | President | Advisory Committee | Chief Student Affairs Officer | Chief Fiscal Officer | Food Service Director | Students | Faculty and Staff | Cashier | Accounts Payable | Purchasing | Physical Plant Director |
|---|---|---|---|---|---|---|---|---|---|---|---|---|
| 1. Develop food service operating policies and procedures | | | | 2 | 2 | 5 | 5 | 5 | | | | |
| 2. Review and approve policies and procedures | | 3 | 4 | 5 | 5 | | | | | | | |
| 3. Adopt recommended policies | 2 | 4 | | 5 | 5 | | | | | | | |
| 4. Authorize implementation of policies and procedures | | 1 | | | 2 | 2 | | | | | | |
| 5. Distribute approved policies and procedures | | | | | 2 | 2 | | | | | | |
| 6. Purchase food | | | | | | 2 | | | | | | |
| 7. Purchase nonfood items | | | | | 1 | 4 | | | | | 2 | |
| 8. Receive vendor invoices and director of food service's acknowledgment of receipt documentation | | | | | | 5 | | | | 2 | | |

| | | | | | | |
|---|---|---|---|---|---|---|
| 9. Issue meal tickets | 2 | | | | | 5 |
| 10. Operate food service | | 2 | | | | |
| 11. Maintain statistical and fiscal records | | 2 | | | | |
| 12. Receive daily cash receipts and related fiscal records | | 5 | 2 | | | |
| 13. Process accounting transactions and issue monthly budget status report | 2 | | | | | |
| 14. Receive director's periodic management reports | 2 | 5 | | | | |
| 15. Conduct surprise audit of food service operations | 2 | 5 | | 5 | | |
| 16. Evaluate food service operations | 2 | 5 | | 5 | | 5 |

*Explanation of Decision Matrix 71, Cont'd.*

| Step | Action Responsibility | Action |
|------|----------------------|--------|
|      |                      | to the appropriate administrators. |
| 6.   | Director of Food Service | Purchases food directly from suppliers. |
| 7.   | Purchasing Clerk     | Purchases nonfood items requisitioned by the director of food service and approved by the chief fiscal officer. |
| 8.   | Accounts Payable     | Receives verification from the director of food service that ordered supplies have been received and are of satisfactory quality and quantity; receives and audits vendor's invoice; matches invoice with either corresponding purchase order issued by purchasing clerk or open purchase order under which purchase was initiated by director of food service and with receiving documentation; updates accounts payable subsidiary records and control accounts. |
| 9.   | Chief Fiscal Officer | Issues meal tickets to students who have been charged the boarding fee |

*Explanation of Decision Matrix 71, Cont'd.*

| Step | Action Responsibility | Action |
|------|----------------------|--------|
| | | or who purchase them on a monthly basis. |
| 10 & 11. | Director of Food Service | Conducts food service operations. Monitors custodial and maintenance services provided by the director of physical plant. Maintains required statistical, fiscal, and inventory control records. |
| 12. | Cashier | Receives daily cash receipts and accounting data from the director of food service. Issues cashier's receipt to the director for the cash received. |
| 13. | Chief Fiscal Officer | Processes all receipt and disbursement transactions for food service operations and provides the director with monthly budget status reports. |
| 14 & 15. | Chief Fiscal Officer | Receives periodic management reports covering food service operations from the director and conducts periodic surprise audits of such operations. |

*Explanation of Decision Matrix 71, Cont'd.*

| Step | Action Responsibility | Action |
|------|----------------------|--------|
| 16. | Chief Fiscal Officer and Chief Student Affairs Officer | Analyze food service operations, obtaining input regarding satisfaction with its services from students, faculty, and staff users, the director of food service, and the director of physical plant. Identify ways in which services can be improved. |

*Explanation of Decision Matrix 72.*

| Step | Action Responsibility | Action |
|---|---|---|
| 1. | Chief Student Affairs Officer and Chief Fiscal Officer | Formulate recommended student housing policies and procedures, using input from dormitory supervisors, students, and the director of physical plant (for custodial and maintenance service requirements). |
| 2. | Advisory Committee | Reviews recommended policies and procedures submitted by the chief student affairs officer and chief fiscal officer for appropriateness and recommends presidential approval. |
| | President | Approves the advisory committee's recommendation. |
| 3. | President | Submits policies to the board of trustees with his recommendation for their adoption. |
| | Board of Trustees | Reviews and adopts recommended policies, obtaining clarification from the president, the chief student affairs officer, and the chief fiscal officer. |
| 4. | Chief Student Affairs Officer and Chief Fiscal Officer | Receive the president's authorization to implement approved policies and procedures. |

## Decision Matrix 72. Student Housing Operations.

Legend of decision-making roles
1 – Authorizes action
2 – Action responsibility
3 – Approves recommendation
4 – Recommends action
5 – Provides input

*Participants in Decision-Making Processes*

| Procedural Steps | Board of Trustees | President | Advisory Committee | Chief Student Affairs Officer | Chief Fiscal Officer | Dormitory Supervisors | Students | Purchasing | Recruiting and Admissions Director | Physical Plant Director | Registrar | Accounts Payable |
|---|---|---|---|---|---|---|---|---|---|---|---|---|
| 1. Develop student housing policies and procedures | | 3 | | 2 | 2 | 5 | 5 | | | 5 | | |
| 2. Review and approve policies and procedures | | 4 | 4 | 5 | 5 | | | | | | | |
| 3. Adopt recommended policies | 2 | | | 5 | 5 | | | | | | | |
| 4. Authorize implementation of policies and procedures | | 1 | | | | | | | | | | |
| 5. Distribute approved policies and procedures | | | | 2 | 2 | | | | | | | |
| 6. Receive applications for housing | | | | 2 | 2 | | | | | | | |
| 7. Assign students to housing units | | | | 2 | | | 5 | | 5 | | | |
| 8. Issue occupancy authorization | | | | | 2 | | | | | | | |
| 9. Issue keys to students who have received business office authorization | | | | 1 | | 2 | 5 | | | | | |

|  | | | | | | |
|---|---|---|---|---|---|---|
| 10. Audit and control occupancy | 1 | | | 2 | | |
| 11. Receive notification of authorized housing assignments | 5 | | | 5 | | 2 |
| 12. Operate and maintain dormitories | 1 | | | 2 | | |
| 13. Purchase supplies, furniture, and so on | 4 | 1 | | 5 | 2 | |
| 14. Receive invoices and acknowledgment of receipt | | 1 | | 5 | 2 | |
| 15. Process accounting transactions and issue monthly budget status reports | | 2 | | | | 2 |
| 16. Receive periodic housing management reports | 2 | 2 | | 5 | 5 | |
| 17. Evaluate student housing operations | 2 | 2 | | 5 | 5 | |

*Explanation of Decision Matrix 72, Cont'd.*

| *Step* | *Action Responsibility* | *Action* |
|--------|-------------------------|----------|
| 5. | Chief Fiscal Officer | Distributes approved policies and procedures to appropriate administrators. |
| 6 & 7. | Chief Student Affairs Officer | Receives notification from the director of recruiting and admissions of students who have indicated on their applications for admission that they desire to live on campus. Receives requests for housing from students at registration. Assigns students to appropriate student housing units and sends students to the chief fiscal officer to get financial clearance to occupy assigned housing. |
| 8. | Chief Fiscal Officer | Makes financial arrangements with students and issues authorization to occupy assigned housing. |
| 9 & 10. | Dormitory Supervisors | Issue room keys to students authorized to occupy assigned housing and help them move in. Make sure students understand housing rules and regulations. Audit and control occupancy to ensure that unauthorized students are not living in the dormitories. |

*Explanation of Decision Matrix 72, Cont'd.*

| Step | Action Responsibility | Action |
|------|----------------------|--------|
| 11. | Registrar | Receives notification from the chief student affairs officer of student housing assignments and updates students' personal data files. |
| 12. | Dormitory Supervisors | Monitor and supervise dormitory operations, including the delivery of required custodial and maintenance services provided by the director of physical plant. |
| 13. | Purchasing Clerk | Buys required furniture, fixtures, and supplies against requisitions initiated by dormitory supervisors and approved by the chief student affairs officer and the chief fiscal officer. |
| 14. | Accounts Payable | Receives vendor invoices and dormitory supervisors' acknowledgment of receipt of material ordered. |
| 15. | Chief Fiscal Officer | Processes receipt and disbursement transactions related to student housing operations and provides the chief student affairs officer with monthly budget status reports. |

*Explanation of Decision Matrix 72, Cont'd.*

| Step | Action Responsibility | Action |
|------|----------------------|--------|
| 16 & 17. | Chief Student Affairs Officer and Chief Fiscal Officer | Receive periodic student housing management reports from dormitory supervisors. Evaluate operations, obtaining input regarding satisfaction with services provided from student occupants, dormitory supervisors, and the director of physical plant. Identifies ways in which student housing programs can be improved. |

# Decision Matrix 73. Faculty and Staff Housing.

| Legend of decision-making roles | |
|---|---|
| 1 – Authorizes action | 2 – Action responsibility |
| 3 – Approves recommendation | 4 – Recommends action |
| 5 – Provides input | |

Participants in Decision-Making Processes

| Procedural Steps | Board of Trustees | President | Advisory Committee | Chief Academic Officer | Chief Student Affairs Officer | Chief Development Officer | Chief Fiscal Officer | Department Heads | Personnel Director | Faculty | Physical Plant Director | Occupants | Payroll |
|---|---|---|---|---|---|---|---|---|---|---|---|---|---|
| 1. Formulate faculty and staff housing policies and procedures | | 3 | | 5 | | | 2 | | 5 | 5 | 5 | 5 | |
| 2. Review and approve policies and procedures | | 4 | 4 | | | | 5 | | | 5 | 5 | 5 | |
| 3. Adopt recommended policies | 2 | | | | | | 5 | | | | | | |
| 4. Authorize implementation of policies and procedures | | 1 | | | | | 2 | | | | | | |
| 5. Promulgate approved policies and procedures | | | | | | | 2 | | | | | | |
| 6. Authorize faculty occupancy | | 2 | | 4 | | | 5 | | | | | | |
| 7. Authorize staff occupancy | | 2 | | | 4 | 4 | 4 | | | | | | |
| 8. Receive authorization for occupancy | | 5 | | | | | 2 | 5 | | | | | |
| 9. Execute lease and payroll deduction authorization | | | | | | | 2 | | | | | 2 | |
| 10. Receive notification of occupancy | | | | | | | 5 | | 2 | | | | |
| 11. Update personnel records | | | | | | | | | 2 | | | | |
| 12. Enter deduction data into payroll system | | | | | | | | | 5 | | | | 2 |
| 13. Provide custodial and maintenance services for common areas | | | | | | | 1 | | | 2 | 2 | | |
| 14. Receive requests for renovations or repairs | | | | | | | 2 | | | 4 | 4 | 5 | |
| 15. Make renovations or repairs | | | | | | | 1 | | | 2 | 2 | | |
| 16. Evaluate faculty and staff housing operations | | | | 5 | | | 2 | | | 5 | 5 | 5 | |

*Explanation of Decision Matrix 73.*

| Step | Action Responsibility | Action |
|------|----------------------|--------|
| 1. | Chief Fiscal Officer | Formulates recommended policies and procedures to be followed in administering faculty and staff housing units owned by the institution, using input from the chief academic officer, the director of personnel, current occupants, faculty, and the director of physical plant. |
| 2. | Advisory Committee | Reviews recommended policies and procedures submitted by the chief fiscal officer for appropriateness and impact on other operations and recommends presidential approval. |
| | President | Approves the advisory committee's recommendation. |
| 3. | President | Submits policies to the board of trustees with his recommendation for adoption. |
| | Board of Trustees | Reviews and adopts policies, obtaining clarification from the president and the chief fiscal officer. |
| 4 & 5. | Chief Fiscal Officer | Receives the president's authorization to implement |

*Explanation of Decision Matrix 73, Cont'd.*

| Step | Action Responsibility | Action |
|------|----------------------|--------|
| | | approved policies and procedures and distributes them to the appropriate administrators. |
| 6 & 7. | President | Approves senior administrators' recommendations for occupancy of faculty and staff housing after obtaining verification from the chief fiscal officer that requested housing will be available for the occupancy recommended. |
| 8 & 9. | Chief Fiscal Officer | Upon receipt of the president's authorization, executes leases covering occupancy of available housing units with faculty or staff members and obtains their written authorization to deduct rental payments from payroll checks. |
| 10 & 11. | Director of Personnel | Receives from the chief fiscal officer notification of housing assignments and faculty or staff members' authorization to deduct rent from their payroll checks; updates employees' personnel records. |

*Explanation of Decision Matrix 73, Cont'd.*

| *Step* | *Action Responsibility* | *Action* |
|---|---|---|
| 12. | Payroll | Updates payroll file for deduction of rental payment on receiving the director of personnel's notification to do so. |
| 13. | Director of Physical Plant | Provides required custodial and maintenance services for common areas of faculty and staff housing units. |
| 14. | Chief Fiscal Officer | Receives requests from occupants for renovation or repair of facilities occupied. Obtains the director of physical plant's recommendation regarding the request and an estimate of the cost of making the requested repairs or renovations. |
| 15. | Director of Physical Plant | Makes requested repairs or renovations when authorized to do so by the chief fiscal officer. |
| 16. | Chief Fiscal Officer | Evaluates faculty and staff housing operations, using input from occupants, the chief academic officer, and the director of physical plant, and identifies ways in which operations can be improved. |

## Decision Matrix 74. Student Union Operations.

Legend of decision-making roles:
1 – Authorizes action
2 – Action responsibility
3 – Approves recommendation
4 – Recommends action
5 – Provides input

*Participants in Decision-Making Processes*

| *Procedural Steps* | Board of Trustees | President | Advisory Committee | Chief Academic Officer | Chief Student Affairs Officer | Chief Fiscal Officer | Student Union Director | Student Organizations | Counselors | Physical Plant Director | Purchasing |
|---|---|---|---|---|---|---|---|---|---|---|---|
| 1. Formulate student union operating policies and procedures | | | | 5 | 2 | 2 | 5 | 5 | 5 | | |
| 2. Review and approve policies and procedures | | 3 | 4 | | 5 | 5 | | | | | |
| 3. Adopt recommended policies | 2 | 4 | | | 5 | 5 | | | | | |
| 4. Authorize implementation of policies and procedures | | 1 | | | | | | | | | |
| 5. Promulgate approved policies and procedures | | | | | 2 | 2 | | | | | |
| 6. Operate the student union | | | | | 1 | 2 | 2 | | | | |
| 7. Purchase supplies and equipment | | | | | 4 | 1 | 5 | | | 5 | 2 |
| 8. Process accounting for receipts and disbursements and provide monthly budget status reports | | | | | | 2 | | | | | |
| 9. Receive periodic activity reports | | | | | 2 | 2 | 5 | 5 | 5 | | |
| 10. Evaluate student union operations | | | | 5 | 2 | 2 | 5 | 5 | 5 | 5 | |

*Explanation of Decision Matrix 74.*

| Step | Action Responsibility | Action |
|---|---|---|
| 1. | Chief Student Affairs Officer and Chief Fiscal Officer | Formulate recommended policies and procedures for the operation of the student union, using input from the chief academic officer, the director of the student union, student organizations, and counselors. |
| 2. | Advisory Committee | Reviews recommended policies and procedures submitted by the chief student affairs officer and the chief fiscal officer for appropriateness and impact on other operations. Recommends presidential approval. |
|  | President | Approves the advisory committee's recommendation. |
| 3. | President | Submits policies to the board of trustees with his recommendation for their adoption. |
|  | Board of Trustees | Reviews and adopts recommended policies, obtaining clarification from the president, the chief student affairs officer, and the chief fiscal officer. |
| 4 & 5. | Chief Student Affairs Officer and Chief Fiscal Officer | Receive the president's authorization to implement approved polices and pro- |

*Explanation of Decision Matrix 74, Cont'd.*

| *Step* | *Action Responsibility* | *Action* |
|--------|------------------------|----------|
| | | cedures; the chief fiscal officer distributes them to appropriate administrators. |
| 6. | Director of the Student Union | Operates the student union and monitors the delivery of custodial and maintenance services provided by the director of physical plant. |
| 7. | Purchasing Clerk | Buys furniture, fixtures, equipment, and supplies requisitioned by the student union manager and approved by the chief student affairs officer when authorized to do so by the chief fiscal officer |
| 8. | Chief Fiscal Officer | Processes all receipt and disbursement transactions related to student union operations and provides the director of the student union and the chief student affairs officer with monthly budget status reports. |
| 9 & 10. | Chief Student Affairs Officer and Chief Fiscal Officer | Receive periodic activity reports submitted by the student union manager. Evaluate student union operations, obtaining input from the chief academic officer, the director of the |

*Explanation of Decision Matrix 74, Cont'd.*

*Step*        *Action Responsibility*    *Action*

                                        student union, student
                                        organizations, counselors,
                                        and the director of physical
                                        plant. Identify ways in which
                                        student union operation can
                                        be improved.

# Decision Matrix 75. Campus Parking Operations.

Legend of decision-making roles
1 – Authorizes action
2 – Action responsibility
3 – Approves recommendation
4 – Recommends action
5 – Provides input

*Participants in Decision-Making Processes*

| Procedural Steps | Board of Trustees | President | Advisory Committee | Chief Fiscal Officer | Senior Administrators | Faculty | Staff | Students | Security Force | Cashier |
|---|---|---|---|---|---|---|---|---|---|---|
| 1. Formulate campus parking policies and procedures | | | | 2 | 5 | 5 | 5 | 5 | 5 | |
| 2. Review and approve policies and procedures | | 3 | 4 | 5 | | | | | | |
| 3. Adopt recommended policies | 2 | 4 | | 5 | | | | | | |
| 4. Authorize implementation of policies and procedures | | 1 | | | | | | | | |
| 5. Promulgate approved policies and procedures | | | | 2 | | | | | | |
| 6. Receive parking applications | | | | 2 | 5 | 5 | 5 | 5 | | |
| 7. Receive proof of insurance coverage | | | | 2 | 5 | 5 | 5 | 5 | | |
| 8. Authorize issuance of parking stickers | | | | 1 | | | | | | |
| 9. Receive parking fee payments and issue parking stickers | | | | | | | | | | 2 |
| 10. Receive notification of parking stickers issued | | | | | 5 | 5 | 5 | 5 | 2 | 2 |
| 11. Monitor parking | | | | | | | | | 2 | 5 |

*Explanation of Decision Matrix 75.*

| *Step* | *Action Responsibility* | *Action* |
|---|---|---|
| 1. | Chief Fiscal Officer | Formulates recommended campus parking policies and procedures, using input from other senior administrators, faculty, staff, and students, and the security force. |
| 2. | Advisory Committee | Reviews recommended policies and procedures submitted by the chief fiscal officer for appropriateness and recommends presidential approval. |
| | President | Approves the advisory committee's recommendation. |
| 3. | President | Submits policies to the board of trustees with his recommendation for adoption. |
| | Board of Trustees | Reviews and adopts recommended policies, obtaining clarification from the president and the chief fiscal officer. |
| 4 & 5. | Chief Fiscal Officer | Receives the president's authorization to implement approved policies and procedures and distributes them to appropriate admin- |

*Explanation of Decision Matrix 75, Cont'd.*

| *Step* | *Action Responsibility* | *Action* |
|--------|------------------------|----------|
| | | istrators. Posts them to advise students of parking regulations. |
| 6 & 7. | Chief Fiscal Officer | Receives applications for parking privileges and proof of insurance coverage from students, faculty, staff, and senior administrators. |
| 8 & 9. | Cashier | Receives notification from the chief fiscal officer of student, faculty, and staff authorized to park on campus. Collects required parking fees and issues parking stickers. |
| 10 & 11. | Security Force | Receives listing of vehicles authorized to park on campus from the cashier, monitors parking, and enforces parking restrictions. |

## Decision Matrix 76. Formulating Intercollegiate Athletics Policies and Procedures.

Legend of decision-making roles

1 – Authorizes action
2 – Action responsibility
3 – Approves recommendation
4 – Recommends action
5 – Provides input

*Participants in Decision-Making Processes*

| Procedural Steps | Board of Directors | President | Advisory Committee | Athletics Director | Intercollegiate Athletics Committee | Head Coaches | Chief Academic Officer | Department of Physical Education | Chief Student Affairs Officer | Financial Aid Director | Health Services Director | Recruiting and Admissions Director | Registrar | Chief Fiscal Officer | Academic Requirements Committee | Students | Alumni | Chief Development Officer |
|---|---|---|---|---|---|---|---|---|---|---|---|---|---|---|---|---|---|---|
| 1. Appoint director of athletics | 2 | 2 | 4 | | | | | | | | | | | | | | | |
| 2. Appoint intercollegiate athletics committee | 2 | 2 | 3 | 5 | | | | 5 | 5 | | | | | 4 | | 5 | 5 | |
| 3. Formulate intercollegiate athletics policies related to | | | | | | | | | | | | | | | | | | |
| (a) relationship with academic and student life programs | | | | | | | | | | | | | | | | | | |
| (b) scope of programs | | | | 4 | 2 | 5 | 5 | 5 | 5 | | | 5 | | 5 | | 5 | | |
| (c) athletic organization affiliation | | | | 4 | 2 | 5 | 5 | 5 | | | | 5 | | 5 | | 5 | 5 | |
| (d) criteria and processes for selecting staff | | | | 4 | 2 | 5 | 5 | 5 | 5 | | | | | 5 | | | | |
| (e) scheduling of events | | | | 4 | 2 | 5 | 5 | 5 | 5 | | | | 5 | 5 | | | | |
| (f) academic standards for student athletes | | | | 5 | 2 | 5 | 2 | | | 5 | | 5 | | 5 | 4 | | | |
| (g) athletic scholarships | | | | 5 | 2 | 5 | | | | 5 | | 5 | | 5 | | | | |
| (h) fiscal policies | | | | 4 | 2 | 5 | | | | | | | | 2 | | | | 5 |
| (i) health care | | | | 4 | 2 | 5 | | | | | 5 | | | 5 | | | | |
| (j) indemnification of administrators and staff | | | | 4 | 2 | 5 | | | | | | | | 5 | | | | |

|  |  | | | | | | | |
|---|------|---|---|---|---|---|---|---|
| 4. | Review and approve recommended policies | 2 | 4 | 5 | 3 | 3 | 3 | 3 |
| 5. | Adopt recommended policies | 2 | 4 | 5 | 5 | 5 | 5 | 5 |
| 6. | Authorize implementation of policies | | 1 | 2 | 2 | 2 | 2 | 2 |
| 7. | Formulate fiscal control procedures | | | 5 | 5 | 5 | | 2 |
| 8. | Approve fiscal control procedures | | 3 | 4 | | 5 | | 5 |
| 9. | Authorize implementation of fiscal control procedures | | | | | | | |
| 10. | Develop intercollegiate athletic budget | | 1 | 2 | | | | 2 |
| 11. | Consolidate intercollegiate athletic budget into operating budget | | 3 | 5 | | | | 2 |

*Explanation of Decision Matrix 76.*

| *Step* | *Action Responsibility* | *Action* |
|--------|------------------------|----------|
| 1. | President | Appoints a director of athletics on the basis of recommendations from the advisory committee. |
| 2. | Chief Fiscal Officer | Recommends changes in the composition of the intercollegiate athletics committee on the basis of input from students, alumni, the director of athletics, the chairperson of the department of physical education, and the chief student affairs officer. |
| | Advisory Committee | Reviews recommended changes and recommends presidential appointment. |
| | President | Appoints new or replacement members to the intercollegiate athletics committee. |
| 3a-e, g, i, j. | Director of Athletics | Formulates recommendations, based on input from all appropriate campus constituencies, for adopting or revising all policies governing the operation of the intercollegiate athletics program, except those dealing with academic standards for |

*Explanation of Decision Matrix 76, Cont'd.*

| Step | Action Responsibility | Action |
|------|----------------------|--------|
| | | student athletes and fiscal control. |
| | Intercollegiate Athletics Committee | Reviews and approves intercollegiate athletic policy recommendations submitted by the director of athletics. |
| 3f. | Academic Requirements Committee | Recommends academic standards for student athletes after considering input from coaches, the director of recruiting and admissions, and the director of financial aid. |
| | Chief Academic Officer | Reviews and approves the recommendations of the academic requirements committee. |
| 3h. | Chief Fiscal Officer | Formulates fiscal control policy recommendations to govern the operation of the intercollegiate athletic program, after obtaining input from the director of athletics and head coaches. |
| 4. | Advisory Committee | Reviews recommendations for policies to govern the operation of the intercollegiate athletic program submitted to it by the chief academic officer, the chief |

*Explanation of Decision Matrix 76, Cont'd.*

| Step | Action Responsibility | Action |
|------|----------------------|--------|
| | | fiscal officer, and the intercollegiate athletics committee chairperson and recommends their approval by the president, after obtaining clarification from the director of athletics and director of financial aid. |
| | President | Approves recommended policies. |
| 5. | President | Submits approved policies for governing the intercollegiate athletic program to the board of trustees with his recommendation that they be adopted. |
| | Board of Trustees | Reviews recommended policies and acts on their adoption, obtaining clarification from the director of athletics, chairperson of the intercollegiate athletics committee, chief academic officer, chief fiscal officer, and the director of financial aid. |
| 6. | President | Authorizes the director of athletics, the chief academic and fiscal officers, and the director of financial aid to implement the policies |

*Explanation of Decision Matrix 76, Cont'd.*

| Step | Action Responsibility | Action |
|------|----------------------|--------|
| | | adopted by the board of trustees. |
| 7. | Chief Fiscal Officer | Formulates any special fiscal control procedures required for the intercollegiate athletic program. |
| 8 & 9. | Advisory Committee | Reviews and recommends presidential approval of special fiscal control procedures submitted for approval by the chief fiscal officer. |
| | President | Approves special fiscal control procedures and authorizes the chief fiscal officer and the director of athletics to see that they are implemented. |
| 10 & 11. | Director of Athletics | Formulates recommended annual operating budget for the intercollegiate athletic program after obtaining input from each of the head coaches. |
| | Chief Fiscal Officer | Reviews and approves budget request and incorporates it into the auxiliary enterprise section of the institution's annual operating budget. |

# Decision Matrix 77. Implementing Intercollegiate Athletic Program.

Legend of decision-making roles
1 – Authorizes action
2 – Action responsibility
3 – Approves recommendation
4 – Recommends action
5 – Provides input

Participants in Decision-Making Processes

| Procedural Steps | President | Advisory Committee | Intercollegiate Athletics Committee | Athletics Director | Coaches | Chief Academic Officer | Department of Physical Education | Chief Student Affairs Officer | Health Services Director | Financial Aid Director | Recruiting and Admissions Director | Public Relations Director | Publications Director | Chief Fiscal Officer | Accounting | Cashier | Physical Plant Director | Purchasing |
|---|---|---|---|---|---|---|---|---|---|---|---|---|---|---|---|---|---|---|
| 1. Promulgate approved intercollegiate athletic policies | | | 2 | | | | | | | | | | | | | | | |
| 2. Promulgate approved intercollegiate athletic procedures | | | | | | | | | | | | | | 2 | | | | |
| 3. Select staff | | | | 3 | 5 | 3 | 5 | 3 | | | | | | | | | | |
| 4. Negotiate athletic events contracts | | | | 2 | 5 | | | | | | | | | 5 | | | | |
| 5. Review and approve contracts | 3 | 4 | | 5 | | | | | | | | | | | | | | |
| 6. Execute approved contracts | 1 | | | 2 | | | | | | | | | | | | | | |
| 7. Recruit and admit student athletes | | | | 4 | 5 | | | | | | 2 | | | | | | | |
| 8. Make athletic scholarship awards | | | | 4 | 5 | | | | | 2 | | | | | | | | |
| 9. Purchase equipment and supplies | | | | 4 | 5 | | | | | | | | | 1 | | | | 2 |

10. Include game schedules on calendar of events — 5   2
11. Obtain physician's certification of eligibility for competition — 2
12. Formulate checklist for athletic events — 2
13. Prepare for events — 1   2
14. Prepare game programs and press guides — 4   5   2
15. Obtain publicity for games and game results — 4   5   2
16. Control ticket sales and accounting for operation of program — 1   2
17. Process receipts — 2
18. Provide custodial and maintenance services — 4   5   1   2
19. Control equipment and supply inventories — 1   2   2
20. Evaluate intercollegiate athletic programs — 2   3   5   5   5

*Explanation of Decision Matrix 77.*

| *Step* | *Action Responsibility* | *Action* |
|--------|-------------------------|----------|
| 1. | Director of Athletics | Promulgates adopted policies governing the operation of the intercollegiate athletic program. |
| 2. | Chief Fiscal Officer | Promulgates special fiscal control procedures for the intercollegiate athletic program. |
| 3. | Director of Athletics | Interviews and recommends employment of coaches, jointly with the chief academic officer or the chief student affairs officer if dual appointment in either area of operation is involved (see Decision Matrix 58 for follow-up employment procedures). |
| 4, 5, & 6. | Director of Athletics | Negotiates athletic event contracts with competing institutions, obtaining appropriate input from the chief fiscal officer and head coaches, and submits them for review and approval. |
| | Advisory Committee | Reviews and recommends presidential approval of athletic event contracts. |
| | President | Approves athletic event contracts and authorizes their execution by the director of athletics. |

*Explanation of Decision Matrix 77, Cont'd.*

| Step | Action Responsibility | Action |
|------|----------------------|--------|
| 7. | Coaches | Recruit student athletes. |
| | Director of Athletics | Reviews qualifications of recruited student athletes and recommends that they be admitted. |
| | Director of Recruiting and Admissions | Makes admission decision. |
| 8. | Coaches | Make recommendations for non-need-based athletic scholarship awards. |
| | Director of Athletics | Reviews and approves coaches' recommendations and notifies the director of financial aid of non-need-based scholarship awards. |
| | Director of Financial Aid | Makes need-based and non-need-based financial aid awards. |
| 9. | Coaches | Prepare requisitions for intercollegiate athletic program equipment and supplies. |
| | Director of Athletics | Reviews equipment and supply requisitions for appropriateness and conformity with the approved budget and recommends approval. |
| | Chief Fiscal Officer | Reviews requisitions, determines availability of |

*Explanation of Decision Matrix 77, Cont'd.*

| *Step* | *Action Responsibility* | *Action* |
|--------|------------------------|----------|
|        |                        | budgetary funds, and authorizes purchases. |
|        | Purchasing             | Procures requisitioned equipment and supplies. |
| 10.    | Chief Student Affairs Officer | Receives notification of the schedule of athletic events from the director of athletics and updates the master calendar. |
| 11.    | Director of Health Services | Makes arrangements to obtain a physician's certification of eligibility for competition for student athletes. |
| 12.    | Director of Athletics  | Formulates checklist of required pre-game preparation activities that must be carried out before each athletic event. |
| 13.    | Coaches                | Acting with authority delegated by the director of athletics, sees that all pre-game preparations required by the checklist are arranged for and accomplished before each athletic event. |
| 14.    | Director of Publications | Obtains required input from coaches and the director of athletics and prepares game programs and press guides for each event. |

*Explanation of Decision Matrix 77, Cont'd.*

| Step | Action Responsibility | Action |
|------|----------------------|--------|
| 15. | Director of Public Relations | Seeks to obtain maximum publicity for athletic events, using input obtained from the coaches and the director of athletics. |
| 16. | Accounting | Controls the sale of tickets, both pre-game and at the gate, for all athletic events, under the supervision of the chief fiscal officer. |
| 17. | Cashier | Processes all cash receipts for intercollegiate athletic events. |
| 18. | Director of Physical Plant | Provides all custodial, grounds care, and maintenance services required by the intercollegiate athletic program. |
| 19. | Coaches | Maintain inventory control over all intercollegiate athletic program equipment and supplies. Annually, provide the chief fiscal officer, through the director of athletics, with a physical inventory report of equipment and supplies. |
| 20. | Intercollegiate Athletics Committee | Evaluates the intercollegiate athletic program; identifies and recommends changes in policies or procedures that will improve its effectiveness or efficiency. |

# Fiscal
# Management

Seeing that an adequate fiscal control and reporting system exists is probably an institution's most important task in maintaining its fiscal viability. An adequate fiscal control system includes planning, budgeting, accounting, and reporting among its subsystems. Since planning and budgeting were covered in earlier chapters, this chapter is limited to the essential standards of good management applicable to accounting and fiscal reporting operations. Nevertheless, the efficient and effective management of the other institutional activities is not to be overlooked, since all such activities are related to fiscal control. The proper operation of an institution's fiscal control system is a part of the management responsibility of all its administrators. The chief fiscal officer cannot and should not be looked on as the only administrator responsible for exercising fiscal control responsibility. However, through the accounting system, he should be held responsible for maintaining fiscal records that permit the issuance of regular or special reports to provide the other administrators with the fiscal information they need to manage the activities for which they are responsible and to provide their superiors with the information they require to monitor their subordites' fiscal management performance. The chief fiscal officer should also be responsible for seeing that the fiscal records maintained are adequate to meet the institution's external reporting requirements. In addition, the fiscal records must provide for the management of the assets, liabilities, and fund balances of each fund group of accounts the institution is required to maintain.

The institution's accounting records should be maintained in accordance with generally accepted accounting principles established by the American Institute of Certified Public Accountants' (AICPA) *Audit Guide for Colleges and Universities* and the National Association of College and University Business Officer's publication *College and University Business Administration-82 (CUBA-82)*. These publications are consistent in their definitions of generally accepted accounting principles.

Among these principles is the identification of the fund groups that should be maintained as self-balancing funds. These include unrestricted operating funds, restricted operating funds, endowment and similar funds, loan funds, agency funds, and investment in plant funds. The investment in plant funds group should be subdivided into four self-balancing funds: unexpended plant funds, reserves for retirement of indebtedness funds, reserves for repairs and replacement funds, and invested in plant funds. These fund groups are designed to identify for the reader of an institution's financial statements the nature of the restrictions that exist on the use of assets available to an institution to conduct its operations. While interfund borrowing is not prohibited, it should be kept to the minimum required by the institution's operating needs and properly recorded in each fund's accounts; provision should be made for repayment as quickly as possible.

Generally accepted accounting principles also require the maintenance of accounting records on a modified accrual basis. Some institutions, with more sophisticated accounting systems, have encumbrance accounting as a feature of their accounting system. Where such a feature is not a part of the system, accrued expense data covering open purchase orders and travel advances should be entered into the system at the end of each month, before budget status reports are issued, and reversed at the beginning of the following month. Further, if payments of debt obligations are not made when they are due, accrued expense data should be entered into the accounting records to cover the unpaid obligations.

Another generally accepted accounting principle is that the revenues and expenditures related to summer school operations should be accounted for in the fiscal year in which the majority of summer school instruction takes place. Revenue and expenditure transactions for summer school operations recorded in the prior fiscal year should be classified for the purpose of financial reporting as "prepaid expense" and "deferred income."

Institutional account systems consist of a general ledger system and a number of subsystems; control accounts are maintained in the general ledger system for each subsystem. The subsystems normally found include a payroll system, an accounts payable system, a student accounts receivable system, an endowment investment system, and a movable equipment inventory system. In addition, supply inventory subsystems are maintained by the bookstore, food service, central stores, the print shop, and physical plant. Control accounts are maintained in the general ledger system for each off-line inventory control system. Off-line subsystems are also maintained for financial aid awards from each source of financial aid funding and NDSL loans outstanding with control accounts maintained in the general ledger system.

With the foregoing general principles established, the following essential standards of good management are applicable to fiscal management.

★   A chart of accounts adequate to meet the institution's internal reporting, external reporting, and asset, liability, and fund balances control requirements should exist. The chart of accounts should identify whether each account is an asset, liability, fund balance, revenue, or expense account. It also should identify the organizational unit to which each revenue and each expense account is applicable and should be reported. The level of detail of the accounting information recorded through the chart of accounts should be greater than that required for reporting and control purposes. For example, an institution may have several general operating cash accounts the transactions of which need to be separately recorded, but whose balances, for financial reporting purposes, will be aggregated and shown as "cash in banks." An institution may also record separately the compensation cost of each rank of faculty or classification of staff employed in order to be able to determine the impact of a proposed salary increase or rates determined to be required for each. For fiscal control purposes, however, these accounts would normally be aggregated and reported as "salary expense," or possibly as "faculty salary expense" and "staff salary expense." The coding of these salary expense accounts may also require subcode identifications to permit the identification of the portion of each covered by each sponsored agreement. The subcoding used to identify the sponsored agreements to which some portion of salary expense incurred is applicable should be the same as that used for the other categories of expense of which a portion is chargeable to such sponsored agreements.

Once the chart of accounts has been established, each administrator who is responsible for entering revenue or expense data into the accounting system should be provided with the account codes and titles of the accounts that are to be used to record the transactions applicable to the activities for which he or she is responsible. These administrators should then be held responsible for coding the transactions to be recorded; the accounting office should be responsible for auditing their coding for appropriateness and acceptability. Accounts should not be added to or deleted from the chart of accounts without the chief fiscal officer's authorization.

Finally, the chart of accounts should follow the organizational structure of the institution and the budgeted categories of revenue and expense. This is necessary in order to permit the issuance of budget status reports to the proper administrators and to ensure that such reports properly reflect the comparison of actual revenues and expenditures recorded to date with the budgeted projections for such revenue and expense categories. If the institution changes its organizational structure, the chart of accounts should be revised to reflect the changes.

★   The processing of all receipts and disbursements should be handled through the central accounting office in accordance with established policies and procedures (see Decision Matrix 78).

★  All receipt and disbursement transactions processed by the accounting officer should be entered into the accounting records by the end of the workday following the day on which the transactions were processed.

★  All transactions processed should be properly documented to identify each transaction being recorded and the reason it is being made so as to have a clear audit trail. Particular care should be given to the proper documentation of cash receipts issued and journal vouchers used to enter transactions into the accounting system.

★  All payments received should be covered by a cash receipt that identifies from whom the payment was received, the amount that was received, what the payment represents, and the title and account code number of the account to which it is to be credited. Cash receipts should be numbered, retained in a secure storage area, and issued to the cashier in numerical sequence. The person issuing the receipts to the cashier should maintain a log showing the receipt numbers issued, used, and returned each day. Copies of all receipts used, including the original copy of voided receipts, should be batch-totaled and reconciled with cash received by the cashier each day. The cash and batch-totaled receipts should be turned over to another person in the accounting department for auditing, depositing of cash, and updating of the accounting records.

★  Noncash gifts received should be entered into the accounting system at the appraised or determinable fair market value established by independent appraisals or other data sources obtained by the chief fiscal officer. Gift receipts issued to the donors of such gifts should not reflect any dollar value but should simply identify the gift received. The determination of the value of the gift for tax purposes should be left to the donor and the Internal Revenue Service.

★  Contributed services should be recorded as an expense, with an offsetting credit to contributed service revenue, at the fair market value determined by the chief fiscal officer.

★  Sponsored agreement awards received that extend over
more than one fiscal year should be recorded in the accounting
system at the full amount awarded in the restricted current fund
section of the accounting system balance sheet, even if the full
amount awarded is not paid to the institution at the time of the
award. Such a transaction would involve establishing an "account
receivable" from the sponsoring agency with an offsetting credit
to a "fund balance" account. Payment received from the sponsoring agency would then be recorded as a reduction of the account receivable amount. This practice will permit the institution
to reflect in its published financial statements the amount of
restricted sponsored agreement funds it has available to cover
such sponsored activities in future years.

★  The amount of income from restricted gifts, grants, or
contracts and restricted endowment funds recorded in the accounting system (or reported in budget status reports or any
published financial reports) should not exceed the expenditures
incurred in carrying out the purposes for which they were given
or awarded plus the recovery of related indirect costs for the
fiscal period covered by such accounting records or reports. The
unexpended and unearned portion of such restricted income
should be classified as unexpended restricted fund balances until they are earned by meeting the donor's requirements for their
use.

★  Cash transfers to the unrestricted current fund from the
restricted fund, endowment fund, loan fund, agency fund, or
plant fund bank accounts should be limited to the amount required to reimburse the unrestricted current fund for expenditures it has incurred in carrying out the purposes for which
such funds were made available plus any authorized recovery
of related indirect costs. Expenditures incurred by the unrestricted current fund for such restricted purposes should be offset
in the accounting records by a credit to the appropriate restricted
revenue accounts and a charge to a "due from" account for the
fund groupings from which reimbursement is due. An offsetting entry should be made simultaneously in the appropriate
fund group accounts to record its "due to unrestricted

current fund" and a charge to the appropriate "unexpended fund balance" account. In some institutions that have sophisticated "table-driven" automated accounting systems, the offsetting entry in the affected fund group account will be generated automatically by the entries made in the unrestricted current fund accounts. When such a "table-driven" system does not exist, it is the responsibility of the chief fiscal officer to see that such offsetting entries are entered into the accounting system. In either case, the amount of cash transferred from the other fund groups to the unrestricted current fund should then be the amount necessary to clear its "due to unrestricted current fund" account. Any transfers made in excess of the amount necessary to clear the account represents an interfund borrowing. When such interfund borrowing occurs, a schedule for its repayment should be adhered to. Further, to ensure that all interfund transactions have been properly recorded, the chief fiscal officer should see that all interfund account balances are reconciled at least monthly.

★   An indirect cost rate, applicable to federal grants and contracts that allow reimbursement of such costs, should be negotiated annually. As set forth above, the amount of reimbursement from restricted fund groups that should be made is limited to the amount of direct expenditures actually incurred plus authorized recovery of related indirect costs. Authorized recovery of indirect costs, in the case of some federal student financial aid programs and other programs, is limited to a fixed percentage of expenditures incurred in carrying out the program. In other federally sponsored agreements, it is limited to a percentage of either the direct salary costs or the total cost of carrying out the agreed-on activities. The percentage and the base to which it is applicable are negotiated by the institution and its designated sponsoring agency. These negotiated arrangements are intended to provide a way of reimbursing the institution for costs that must be incurred in carrying out the agreed-on purpose of the grant or contract but that cannot be identified by the institution as direct costs. Thus, the extent to which an institution's accounting system enables it to direct-charge for support services will influence its indirect cost rate. In general, those who are involved in the negotiation of indirect cost rates say that the more the institution is able to direct-charge costs, the greater is its overall dollar recovery from carrying out sponsored agreement activities. Direct-charging sponsored agreements for the cost of support services, however, requires the institution not only to charge sponsored agreements for the use of such support services but also to charge other internal and external users of such services. Institutions, therefore, must weigh the cost of record keeping related to support service usage against the benefits accruing from being able to direct-charge such costs to federally sponsored agreements. Regardless of the extent to which an institution is willing and able to account for direct charging of support services, there will always be items of indirect costs that cannot be directly charged. These indirect costs are recoverable through indirect cost rates that must be negotiated annually. The calculations that support the institution's negotiating position and subsequent agreement to an indirect cost rate must account for the allocation of 100 percent of each item of indirect cost involved and must be retained as a matter of record in the fiscal office.

★  The institution's accounting records must document its compliance with the matching expenditure or cost-sharing requirements of the federally sponsored agreements it enters into. Failure to adhere to this standard may result in the institution's receiving reimbursement to which it is not entitled for direct and indirect costs related to sponsored agreements. When this occurs, the institution's financial reports will misrepresent its fiscal position to the administration, the board of trustees, and external sources of funding that rely on such financial reports.

★  All disbursements, except those made through petty cash, should be made with numbered checks, which should be used in numerical sequence. All checks should be stored in a secure place. The person responsible for issuing blank checks for daily use should maintain a log in which should be recorded the numbers of the checks issued, used, and returned each day. Copies of the checks used, including the original copy of voided checks, together with their supporting documentation should be batch-totaled each day and turned over to another person in the accounting department for audit and entry into the accounting system.

★   Two signatures should be required on all checks. The board of trustees should specify the persons to whom check-signing authority is delegated. Where signature plates are used to sign checks, no one person should have control of more than one plate. Where signatures are placed on checks as a part of a data-processing routine, a person from the accounting office should be present when data processing is applying the signatures.

★   The accounting, reserve establishment, and repayment provisions of an institution's indenture agreements should be strictly adhered to. If an institution anticipates that it will be unable to meet the debt service requirements of its indenture agreements, it should notify the debt holder and seek to negotiate a payment deferral agreement.

★   DFAFS reporting of actual expenditures should be in agreement with, or reconciled with, the related accounting records. Where such reporting is on a reconciled basis, the reconciliation documentation should be maintained on file for future program review or audit. The amount of DFAFS advances drawn by the institution should be sufficient to permit it to meet the expenditure needs of the covered sponsored programs without having to use unrestricted funds, but it should not be such that the balance on hand at the end of a month is greater than the projected expenditures for the ensuing month.

★   Accounts payable should be accounted for on an accrued basis. Accounts payable records should be maintained in a subsidiary ledger or data-processing file in which should be recorded, at the least, the vendor's name, address, and assigned vendor number; the date, number, and amount of each invoice received; and, for each payment made to a vendor, the date, check number, amount paid, and numbers of the vendor's invoices covered by the payment. The chief fiscal officer should establish the dates in each month when accounts payable payments are to be made. Prior to each payment date, he should be provided with an aged accounts payable listing. At that time, he should identify which vendor invoices are to be paid on the next payment date.

★ Travel regulations and procedures should be adhered to. Where employees are provided with a travel advance, they should be required to sign an authorization to withhold the amount advanced from their paychecks if they do not submit the required accounting for travel expenses actually incurred within the specified time allowed for them to do so. The major expenditures for which the traveler is accounting should be supported by receipts. A person in the accounting office should be assigned the responsibility of auditing travel expense reports for mathematical accuracy, adherence to travel policy, and reasonableness as well as the responsibility of entering travel expense data into the accounting system. Any unexpended travel advance funds should be returned with the submission of the travel expense report (see Decision Matrix 34 in Chapter Seven for the procedures that should be followed for obtaining travel authorization).

★ The dates and manner in which the earnings of employees are paid should be standardized and not deviated from for the personal convenience of the employees. Adherence to this standard is required to minimize payroll processing complexities and maximize the reliability and accuracy of budget status reporting. A calendar of dates for payroll processing and payment, including cutoff dates for submission of payroll data, should be established, published, and adhered to. It is recommended that all regular faculty, administrators, and salaried staff be paid in twelve equal installments, that wage earners be paid twice monthly, and that student employees be paid monthly. The processing of voluntary deductions from payroll should be discouraged and held to the minimum required for good employee relations.

★ Time reports should be required for all wage earners and attendance reports should be required for all other employees. Attendance reports should identify days not worked by employees for which they are to be compensated under an employee benefit plan, such as vacation days, sick leave, and emergency leave.

★ A log should be maintained in which should be recorded the date and nature of all documents received for entry into the payroll system.

★ Data processing should provide the payroll clerk with a payroll register of the regular employees to be paid prior to each established pay date. (A payroll register for student employees should also be provided to the director of financial aid prior to the date on which their earnings are to be paid.) The payroll clerk should be responsible for auditing the payroll register and for entering any required corrections into the payroll system before authorization is given for data processing to prepare the payroll checks. Payroll checks should be drawn on a separate bank account established for that purpose. The chief fiscal officer should be responsible for the transfer of funds to the payroll accounts in amounts necessary to cover the checks that have been issued. Payroll checks should be stored in a secure place that is not under the control of either data processing or the payroll clerk. Payroll checks should be numbered and issued in numerical sequence. Once prepared, payroll checks should be distributed to the employees by someone other than the person who is responsible for certifying the hours or days for which they are to be paid (see Decision Matrix 79).

★ If it is not accomplished as a part of an automated payroll/personnel system, the payroll clerk should be responsible for providing the accounting office with the data necessary to enter into the accounting system the distribution of payroll charges, payroll deductions, the required matching of withheld taxes, and fringe benefit costs.

★ The payroll clerk should be responsible for the preparation of all quarterly and annual reports required to meet federal and state payroll and payroll tax reporting requirements.

★ All bank accounts should be reconciled with the accounting records each month. This reconciliation should be performed by someone other than the cashier, the payroll clerk, or the person responsible for depositing cash receipts. This person should maintain a log showing, for each bank account, the date of receipt of the bank statement and the date on which the reconciliation was completed. The reconciled bank statements, canceled checks, and bank charge documentation should be transmitted to the person responsible for record retention as soon as the reconciliation has been completed. The person responsible for bank reconciliation should provide the accounting office with the data, if any, required for entry into the accounting system to adjust the accounting records to agree with the bank statement.

★ A general ledger trial balance should be prepared and submitted to the chief fiscal officer at the end of each month. The chief fiscal officer should be responsible for reviewing the trial balance and seeing that each fund is self-balancing, all interfund account balances are in agreement, all subsidiary ledgers are reconciled to their general ledger control account, all required accrual entries have been made in the accounting system, all transactions related to the month's activity have been entered into the accounting system, no obvious errors have been made in account coding or entry of data into the accounting system, and all income earned from restricted funds and all related indirect cost recovery have been entered into the unrestricted current fund accounting records.

★ Budget status reports should be issued by the tenth working day after the chief fiscal officer has completed his review of the month's-end trial balance. Two types of budget status reports should be issued for each organizational unit for which a separate

budget has been prepared. The first is a summary report showing, for each line item of budget expense, the authorized budget,
the amount of actual and accrued expenditures charged during
the prior month, the amount of actual and accrued expenditures
charged for the year to date, and the unexpended balance or
overruns of the authorized budget. The second is a listing of
all actual and accrued expenditure transactions charged against
each line item of the authorized budget during the prior month.
A copy of both reports should be sent to each administrator who
is responsible for administering an operational unit or a sponsored agreement for which a budget was prepared. The director of grant and contract administration should also receive a
copy of each budget status report provided to the principal investigators or project directors of sponsored agreements. Each
administrator who is responsible for the supervision of budgetary
units for which other administrators are directly, operationally
responsible should also receive a copy of the summary reports
provided to the administrators, principal investigators, or project directors reporting to her and a consolidated summary report
covering all the units or activities for which she is responsible.
The president should receive, in addition to the summary budget
status report and transaction listing report for each budget unit
under his direct control, a copy of the consolidated budget summary report provided to each senior administrator and a summary revenue budget status report. The summary revenue
budget status report should show, for each budgeted category
of revenue, the amount budgeted, the amount collected during
the prior month, the amount collected for the year to date, and
the amount by which collections exceeded or fell short of
budgeted expectations. The chief fiscal officer should retain a
copy of all budget status reports issued each month.

    ★   Each administrator, principal investigator, and project
director who receives a budget status report should be responsible for reviewing such reports, advising the accounting office
of any errors discovered, and determining what actions need
to be taken when budgetary overruns or significant underex-

penditures are identified. Significant underexpenditures can mean that a planned activity that is important to the institution's ability to achieve its objectives has not been carried out.

Readers wishing additional information about fiscal control and fiscal management processes should contact the National Association of College and University Business Officers (NACUBO), One Dupont Circle, Washington, D.C. 20036.

# Decision Matrix 78. Processing Cash Receipts and Disbursements.

**Legend of decision-making roles**
1 – Authorizes action
2 – Action responsibility
3 – Approves recommendation
4 – Recommends action
5 – Provides input

*Participants in Decision-Making Processes*

| Procedural Steps | Chief Fiscal Officer | Chief Development Officer | Auxiliary Enterprise Directors | Students | Cashier | Accounting | Bank Reconciliation Clerk | Record Retention Clerk | Cash Disbursement Clerk | Payroll Clerk |
|---|---|---|---|---|---|---|---|---|---|---|
| 1. Issue cash receipt forms and log numbers issued | | | | | | | | 2 | | |
| 2. Issue cash and obtain cashier's signature for amount issued | 2 | | | | 5 | | | | | |
| 3. Receive and process cash receipt transactions: | | | | | | | | | | |
| (a) gifts received | | 5 | | | 2 | | | | | |
| (b) student payments | | | | 5 | 2 | | | | | |
| (c) auxiliary enterprise cash receipts | | | 5 | | 2 | | | | | |
| (d) restricted grant and contract payment and miscellaneous receipts | 5 | | | | | | | | | |
| 4. Batch-total cash receipts and reconcile with cash on hand | | | | | 2 | | | | | |
| 5. Audit receipts and reconciliation, deposit cash, and update daily bank balance report | 1 | | | | 5 | 2 | | | | |
| 6. Receive working capital cash returned by cashier | 2 | | | | 5 | | | | | |
| 7. Receive and log unused cash receipts returned by cashier | | | | | 5 | | | 2 | | |
| 8. Receive authorization to process cash disbursements and transfers | 1 | | | | | | | | | |
| 9. Issue blank checks and log numbers issued | | | | | | | | | 2 | |

|  |  | | | | | | | |
|---|---|---|---|---|---|---|---|---|
| 10. | Cut and issue checks | | | | | | 2 | |
| 11. | Batch-total checks issued and transmit check copies and bank transfer checks to accounting | | | | | | 2 | 5 |
| 12. | Receive and log unused checks | | | 2 | | | | |
| 13. | Audit cash disbursements, enter transactions into accounting records, deposit bank transfer checks, and update daily bank balance report | | | | | 2 | | |
| 14. | Enter payroll disbursement and distribution data into the accounting records and update daily bank balance report | | | | | 2 | | 5 |
| 15. | Receive and review daily bank balance report | 2 | | | | 5 | | |
| 16. | Receive and store cash receipts and check copies | | | 2 | | 5 | | |
| 17. | Receive bank statements and log date of receipt | | | | 2 | 5 | | |
| 18. | Reconcile bank statements and log date of completion | | | | 2 | | | |
| 19. | Enter bank reconciliation adjustments into accounting records and update daily bank balance report | | 5 | 2 | | | | |
| 20. | Receive and store reconciled bank statements and canceled checks | | | 2 | | 5 | | |

*Explanation of Decision Matrix 78.*

| Step | Action Responsibility | Action |
|------|----------------------|--------|
| 1. | Record Retention Clerk | Issues, at the beginning of the day, the next sequential series of cash receipt forms to the cashier and logs the numbers (first and last) issued. |
| 2. | Chief Fiscal Officer | Issues working capital cash to the cashier and obtains his signature acknowledging its receipt. |
| 3. | Cashier | Processes cash received from the chief development officer for gifts and grants received, from students for payments to be applied to their accounts, from the director of auxiliary enterprise units for cash collections, and from the chief fiscal officer for payments received to cover restricted grant and contract expenditures and other miscellaneous payments. Endorses checks received with a restricted endorsement, places cash in cash drawer, issues a validated cash receipt for monies received, and files the retained copy of the receipt. |
| 4. | Cashier | At the end of the day, puts retained copies of receipts issued and originals and copies of voided receipts in numerical sequence, batch-totals them, and reconciles the cash count with the batch total. |

*Explanation of Decision Matrix 78, Cont'd.*

| Step | Action Responsibility | Action |
|------|----------------------|--------|
| 5. | Accounting | Receives cash receipts, cash, and cash reconciliation report from the cashier. Verifies cash count and cashier's reconciliation. Audits cash receipts to be sure that all receipts are included in the batch, that the batch total is correct, that the receipts have been properly coded, and that each receipt clearly identifies the purpose for which payment was received or that supporting documentation identifying the purpose is attached. Prepares bank deposit form in duplicate, deposits cash, and obtains validation that deposit has been made on the duplicate deposit form from the bank. Enters cash transaction data into the general ledger accounts and appropriate subsidiary ledger accounts in the accounting system, obtaining authorization from the chief fiscal officer to open any new accounts required to do so, and updates the daily bank balance report to reflect the amounts deposited in each bank account. |
| 6. | Chief Fiscal Officer | Receives working capital cash from cashier, signs acknowledgment of receipt, and places cash in safe. |

*Explanation of Decision Matrix 78, Cont'd.*

| Step | Action Responsibility | Action |
|------|----------------------|--------|
| 7. | Record Retention Clerk | Receives unused receipts from the cashier, logs numbers (first and last) returned, and returns them to storage. |
| 5. | Cash Disbursement Clerk | Receives authorization from the chief fiscal officer to cut cash disbursement and transfer checks. |
| 9. | Record Retention Clerk | Issues the next series of checks to the cash disbursement clerk and logs the numbers (first and last) issued for each bank account from which disbursements or transfers are to be made. |
| 10. | Cash Disbursement Clerk | Cuts and issues checks. |
| 11. | Cash Disbursement Clerk | Places voucher copies of checks issued and originals and voucher copies of voided checks in numerical sequence and batch-totals checks drawn on each account. |
| 12. | Record Retention Clerk | Receives unused checks returned by the cash disbursement clerk, logs numbers (first and last) returned, and returns unused checks to storage. |
| 13. | Accounting | Receives and audits check vouchers submitted by cash |

*Explanation of Decision Matrix 78, Cont'd.*

*Step   Action Responsibility   Action*

disbursement to verify that the batch total is correct, the proper amount has been disbursed, required supporting documentation is attached, and the charges have been properly coded. Deposits transfer checks following the procedures set forth in step 5. Enters cash disbursement transaction data into the appropriate general ledger and subsidiary ledger accounting records and updates the daily bank balance report to reflect transfers and disbursements.

14.   Accounting

Receives payroll disbursement data and enters distribution of payroll, withholdings, and required institutional fringe benefit matching or contributed cost into the general ledger accounting records. Updates the daily bank balance report to reflect disbursement of payroll.

15.   Chief Fiscal Officer

Receives and reviews the daily bank balance report.

16.   Record Retention Clerk

Receives cash receipts and the daily reconciliation report covering the receipts, voucher copies of cash disbursement checks, and a copy of the daily bank balance report. Verifies that all copies of cash receipts and checks issued

| *Step* | *Action Responsibility* | *Action* |
|---|---|---|
| | | have been accounted for and places documents received in storage. |
| 17. | Bank Reconciliation Clerk | Receives bank statements and canceled checks from banks. Logs date of receipt and follows up with banks if statements are not received when due. |
| 18. | Bank Reconciliation Clerk | Sorts canceled checks into numerical sequence and reconciles bank statements to their general ledger control account, identifying any adjustments necessary. |
| 19. | Accounting | Enters adjustments required to reconcile bank accounts into the appropriate general ledger accounts and updates the daily bank balance report to reflect such adjustments. |
| 20. | Record Retention Clerk | Receives and stores reconciled bank statements and canceled checks. |

*Explanation of Decision Matrix 79.*

| Step | Action Responsibility | Action |
|------|----------------------|--------|
| 1. | Payroll Clerk | Formulates recommended payroll procedures and calendar with input from the director of personnel. |
| | Chief Fiscal Officer | Reviews and approves recommended procedures and calendar developed by payroll. |
| 2. | Advisory Committee | Reviews recommended payroll procedures and calendar submitted by the chief fiscal officer and recommends presidential approval. |
| | President | Approves payroll procedures and calendar. |
| 3. | Chief Fiscal Officer | Publishes payroll calendar when authorized to do so by the president. |
| 4. | Payroll Clerk | Enters employment data into the payroll system. |
| 5. | Payroll Clerk | Issues, to each department, attendance records and time cards for each employee assigned to the department. |
| 6 & 7. | Payroll Clerk | Receives completed attendance records and time cards submitted by each |

## Decision Matrix 79. Payroll Disbursement—Regular Employees.

Legend of decision-making roles
1 – Authorizes action
2 – Action responsibility
3 – Approves recommendation
4 – Recommends action
5 – Provides input

*Participants in Decision-Making Processes*

| Procedural Steps | President | Advisory Committee | Chief Academic Officer | Department Heads | Chief Fiscal Officer | Payroll Distribution Clerk | Personnel Director | Payroll Clerk | Data-Processing Director | Cash Disbursement Clerk | Record Retention Clerk | Accounting |
|---|---|---|---|---|---|---|---|---|---|---|---|---|
| 1. Formulate payroll procedures and calendar | 2 | 4 | | | 2 | | 5 | 4 | | | | |
| 2. Review and approve procedures and calendar | | | | | 5 | | | | | | | |
| 3. Publish payroll calendar | 1 | | | | 2 | | | | | | | |
| 4. Enter data into payroll system | | | 5 | | | | 5 | 2 | | | | |
| 5. Issue attendance or time cards | | | | | | | | 2 | | | | |
| 6. Receive completed attendance or time cards | | | | 5 | | | | | | | | |
| 7. Audit attendance and time cards and enter data required for payroll computation into payroll system | | | | | | | | 2 | | | | |
| 8. Receive payroll register | | | | | | | | 2 | | | | |
| 9. Audit payroll register and enter required adjustments into payroll system | | | | | | | | 2 | 5 | | | |
| 10. Authorize disbursement of payroll | | | | | 2 | | | 4 | | | | |

| | | | | | | |
|---|---|---|---|---|---|---|
| 11. Obtain payroll checks | 5 | | | | | 5 |
| 12. Obtain signature plates | 5 | | | 2 | 5 | |
| 13. Cut and sign payroll checks | | | 2 | 2 | 2 | 2 |
| 14. Receive unused payroll checks | | | | 5 | 5 | |
| 15. Receive and audit payroll checks and void any incorrect checks | | 2 | 5 | 5 | | |
| 16. Obtain corrected checks to replace voided checks and enter corrected data into the payroll system | | 2 | | | 5 | |
| 17. Distribute payroll checks | | 5 | 2 | 2 | | |
| 18. Transfer funds to the payroll bank account | 2 | 4 | | 5 | | |
| 19. Enter payroll distribution into accounting records | | 5 | | 5 | | 2 |
| 20. Authorize disbursement of amounts withheld from employee payroll checks and any required matching payments | 1 | | | | 2 | |
| 21. Obtain data required for federal and state reports | | 2 | 5 | 2 | | |
| 22. Issue required federal and state reports | 2 | 5 | 5 | 5 | | |

*Explanation of Decision Matrix 79, Cont'd.*

| Step | Action Responsibility | Action |
|------|----------------------|--------|
| | | department and audits them to verify that cards have been returned for all employees. Follows up with department heads who have not submitted cards for their employees. Verifies, for wage earners, that the daily hours and total hours agree and adjusts the total number of hours if they do not. Verifies, for monthly payroll employees, that they are entitled to payment for absent days for vacation, sick leave, emergency leave, and the like. Logs receipt of cards and enters data required for payroll computation into the payroll system. |
| 8 & 9. | Payroll Clerk | Obtains payroll register run from data processing and audits run against individual attendance records and time cards. Enters correction data into the payroll system when errors are discovered. |
| 10. | Chief Fiscal Officer | Reviews payroll register with payroll clerk and authorizes cutting of payroll checks. |

*Explanation of Decision Matrix 79, Cont'd.*

| Step | Action Responsibility | Action |
|------|----------------------|--------|
| 11, 12, 13, & 14. | Director of Data Processing and Accounting | Obtain payroll checks from the record retention clerk, obtain check signatures plates from the chief fiscal officer and the president, cut payroll checks and apply signatures in the presence of accounting, and return unused payroll checks to the record retention clerk. |
| 15 & 16. | Payroll Clerk | Audits payroll checks against corrected payroll register and voids incorrect checks. Obtains corrected replacement checks from the cash disbursement clerk and enters voided check and replacement check data into the payroll system. |
| 17. | Payroll Clerk | Gives checks to an employee other than the department head in each department for distribution to the employees of that department. Receives and turns over to the chief fiscal officer for safekeeping returned payroll checks that could not be distributed to employees. |

*Explanation of Decision Matrix 79, Cont'd.*

| Step | Action Responsibility | Action |
|------|----------------------|--------|
| 18. | Chief Fiscal Officer | Arranges for the transfer of funds required to cover payroll to the payroll bank account. |
| 19. | Accounting | Receives payroll disbursement data from payroll, determines how payroll charges should be distributed, and enters payroll distribution, withholding, and institutional matching or contributed cost data into the general ledger accounting records. |
| 20. | Chief Fiscal Officer | Obtains, from accounting, the identification of disbursements required to cover amounts withheld from employees' paychecks and any matching or contribution payments required by federal and state regulations or the institution's fringe benefit plans. Authorizes cash disbursements to make these required payments. |
| 21. | Payroll Clerk | Obtains, from data processing, the data required to meet payroll reporting |

*Explanation of Decision Matrix 79, Cont'd.*

| Step | Action Responsibility | Action |
|------|----------------------|--------|
| | | requirements and prepares the required forms for such reporting. |
| 22. | Chief Fiscal Officer | Reviews payroll reporting forms prepared by payroll; signs and issues them. |

# Glossary of
# Position Titles and
# Management Functions

| Title or Function | Definition |
| --- | --- |
| Academic Requirements Committee | A committee composed of appointed or elected representatives of the faculty at large who advise the administration about the criteria that should be applied in the selection of students to be admitted and about requirements for the completion of the institution's academic programs. |
| Accounting | The staff members in the fiscal office who are responsible for entering data into the accounting system and generating budget status and financial reports from those data. |
| Accounts Payable Clerk | The staff member in the fiscal office responsible for |

|                            | maintaining the accounts payable subsidiary records and records of payment to vendors. |
|----------------------------|---|
| Advisory Committee         | A committee composed of senior administrators and other members that the president deems appropriate that advises the president in administering institutional operations and provides him with the assurance that the effect of a decision on all areas is considered in arriving at that decision. |
| Alumni Association         | The organized association representing the graduates and former students of the institution. |
| Analytical Studies Team    | A group of faculty members and administrators, appointed by the president, that evaluates the multi-year plan. |
| Athletic Committee         | A committee composed of athletic staff and coaches, alumni, faculty, and a student representative appointed by the president to formulate policy recommendations for the operation of the intercollegiate athletic program. |

| | |
|---|---|
| Auxiliary Enterprise Managers | The managers of student housing, food services, the bookstore or student store, the student union, and faculty and staff housing, who share certain functions and responsibilities. |
| Board of Trustees | The governing board of the institution, including all of its standing and ad hoc committees. |
| Bookstore or Student Store | The facilities used to provide students, faculty, and staff with textbooks required for coursework, as well as stationery and other items. |
| Budget Control | The function, carried out by a staff member in the fiscal office, of ensuring that budgetary funds are available to cover a planned expenditure before a commitment is made to incur the expenditure. |
| Cashier | Fiscal office staff members involved in receiving, receipting, and accounting for all cash receipts received by the institution. |
| Chief Academic Officer | The senior administrator responsible for directing all academic and academic |

support functions, including career development and counseling services. Usually titled the vice president or academic dean.

Chief Development Officer

The senior administrator responsible for all fund raising (excluding federal and state student financial aid programs), public relations, alumni relations, and publications. Usually titled the director of development.

Chief Fiscal Officer

The senior administrator responsible for directing the business service, financial management, auxiliary enterprises, central services, and plant operations and maintenance activities. Usually titled the vice president for business affairs or business manager.

Chief Student Affairs Officer

The senior administrator responsible for directing all student services and nonacademic counseling activities. Usually titled the dean of students.

Contract Physicians

Doctors, hospitals, or clinics engaged in contractual relations with the institution to provide health care services

|  | beyond the capability of campus-based health care staff. |
|---|---|
| Counselors | All professional personnel and faculty who are involved in providing academic or nonacademic counseling services to students. |
| Curriculum Committee | A committee composed of appointed or elected representatives of the faculty at large that advises the administration on all matters related to the subject and content of courses of instruction offered by the institution. |
| Department Heads | The administrators of academic or nonacademic organizational units reporting to one of the senior administrators, possibly through another administrator who has been assigned the responsibility of directing their activities. |
| Director of Alumni Relations | The person who administers the development office, which maintains cordial relations between alumni and the institution so as to enhance alumni's continuing interest in and support of institutional programs. |

Director of Athletics

The person responsible for administering the institution's intercollegiate athletic program.

Director of Career Development

The person who administers the office involved in providing career selection and development guidance to students.

Director of Central Stores

The person responsible for inventory control, receipt, and issuance of common-use supplies from a central service facility.

Director of Church Relations

The person in the development office who maintains cordial relations with supporting church constituencies so as to enhance their continued interest in and support of institutional programs.

Director of Financial Aid

The person who administers the office that is responsible for making decisions about student financial assistance awards and maintaining all related records.

Director of Food Service

The administrator responsible for supervising the staff involved in the operation of facilities used in the preparation and serving of food

|  | to students, faculty, staff, and third parties. |
|---|---|
| Director of Grant and Contract Administration | The administrator responsible for ensuring that the requirements of all restricted grants and contracts are adhered to from the date of award receipt to the date of termination of award. |
| Director of Health Services | The administrator responsible for supervising the staff involved in providing campus-based health care services to students and in arranging for such additional health care as they may require if the staff does not include physicians. |
| Director of Personnel | The administrator responsible for handling all personnel processes for nonacademic employees and maintaining compensation and benefit records for faculty. |
| Director of Planning | The administrator responsible for assisting the president in coordinating all activities involved in the annual formulation of the institution's multi-year plan. |
| Director of Public Relations | The administrator responsible for projecting the most |

favorable and realistic image of the institution to its constituencies through all media and forums and for interpreting public attitudes to the institution.

| | |
|---|---|
| Director of Recruiting and Admissions | The administrator in charge of the office responsible for recruiting and admitting students to the institution. |
| Director of Student Housing | The administrator responsible for supervising the staff involved in managing the operation of campus-owned facilities used for the housing of students. |
| Director of the Student Union | The administrator responsible for managing the operation of campus facilities used for student activities and social events and institutionally hosted events. |
| Discipline Committee | A committee composed of appointed or elected representatives of the faculty at large that renders judgment in cases of student or faculty violations of institutional rules and regulations that are submitted to it. |
| Faculty | The members assigned to an academic organizational unit. The term does not |

|                              | encompass the faculty at large acting as a body. |
|------------------------------|--------------------------------------------------|
| Faculty Welfare Committee    | A committee composed of appointed or elected representatives of the faculty at large that advises the administration regarding all matters, except promotion and tenure, that involve the rights and responsibilities of faculty members. |
| Grant and Contract Accountant | The person responsible for maintaining special records required to control, account for, and report on expenditures that are reimbursable from restricted grants and contracts. |
| Legal Counsel                | Any external lawyer or legal firm retained to advise the governing board or institutional administrators on legal matters. |
| NDSL Clerk                   | The staff member in the fiscal office responsible for administering all activities related to the disbursement and collection of National Direct Student Loans and the maintenance of all related records. |
| Payroll Clerk                | The staff member responsible for computing and |

disbursing compensation
due to all employees and for
maintaining records of gross
compensation and each de-
duction therefrom for each
employee.

Planning Committee

A committee composed
of the senior administrators
and other members that the
president deems appropriate
that advises the president
regarding all matters related
to the formulation of the
institution's multi-year plan.

President

The chief executive and
operating officer.

Promotion and Tenure
Committee

A committee composed
of appointed or elected
representatives of the faculty
at large that advises the
administration on matters
related to promotion and
tenure policies, procedures,
and implementation.

Purchasing Clerk

The person responsible for
the centralized procurement
of all goods and services
other than bookstore, student store, food, and library
acquisition purchases.

Records Retention Clerk

The staff member in the
business office responsible
for the storage, retrieval,

and issuance of all records,
cash receipts, and checks
other than those records that
are required to carry out the
office's current activities.

Registrar | The person responsible
for maintaining all records
related to students' academic
achievement and credits
earned, as well as for analyzing enrollment data to
determine the results of
academic operations and
reporting the results of those
analyses.

Security Force | The staff employed by the
institution to protect the
safety of campus property,
employees, students, and
visitors.

Senior Administrators | The heads of the four
functional areas of opera-
tion: academic affairs,
student affairs, development,
and fiscal affairs. Each
administrator carries out the
same responsibilities for the
suborganizational units
under his or her respective
control.

Staff | Nonacademic personnel,
whether assigned to an
academic or nonacademic
organizational unit.

Student Accounts Receivable Clerk

The staff member in the fiscal office responsible for maintaining the subsidiary accounting records related to charges assessed to each student and the student's payment of such charges.

Student Organizations

All organized, self-administered student groups, including student government, societies, and clubs, recognized by the institution as having been established to carry out activities funded in part or entirely by fees assessed by the institution.

Students

Individual students acting for themselves, as well as individual students or groups of students acting on behalf of the entire student body, but not as a student organization.

# Index

planning representative of, 54; president on, 26–27; and presidential assessment, 10, 29, 39–41; and presidential search and selection, 30–33; and promotion and tenure, 138, 140; and recruitment and admissions, 275; and registration, 173, 179; responsibilities of, 23, 26; and restricted grants, 347, 351; search committee of, 30–33; secretary of, 42, 44; and security and safety, 459–460; selection of, 10, 34–38; self-study of, 10, 28, 42–45; and staff discipline, 429–431; standards for, 23–29; standing committees of, 25, 29; and student activities and government, 259–260; and student housing, 503–504; and student union, 513–514; and wages and salaries, 435, 438. *See also* Chairperson of trustees

Truth in Lending Statement, 378, 403

Tuskegee Institute, ISATIM at, 6

**U**

Uniform expense categories, in annual operating budget, 85–86

United Negro College Fund (UNCF), 3–4

U.S. Department of Education, 234, 241

U.S. Office of Education, 170

U.S. Supreme Court, and draft registration, 289

Utilities, layout drawings of, 448–449

**V**

Vehicles: access to campus by, 482; maintaining and scheduling use of, 450

Vendor: and central stores, 386; and purchasing and accounts payable, 383

Veterans Cost of Instruction Payment Program (VCIPP), 285

Vice-president for business and fiscal affairs. *See* Chief fiscal officer

**W**

Wages. *See* Compensation

Welfare. *See* Faculty welfare committee

Work orders, for maintenance, 449, 452–458

Work standards, for maintenance, 449, 465–470

Workload assignments, and grant and contract administration, 205–206

Wynn, C., 5–6

73492